Date Due			
DEC 1	MAR 8		
DEC 15	APR 30		
JAN 5	JAN 24		
JAN 18	SEP 26		
AUG 3	MAR 11		
OCT 12 '62	DEC 1		
DEC 14			
APR 5			
MAY 24			
OCT 18			
OCT 30			
JAN 8			

ary

McGRAW-HILL SERIES IN
SOCIOLOGY AND ANTHROPOLOGY

RICHARD T. LaPIERE, *Consulting Editor*

SOCIAL DYNAMICS

McGRAW-HILL SERIES IN
SOCIOLOGY AND ANTHROPOLOGY

RICHARD T. LaPIERE, *Consulting Editor*

Baber   MARRIAGE AND THE FAMILY

Barnett   INNOVATION: THE BASIS OF CULTURAL CHANGE

Bergel   URBAN SOCIOLOGY

Bowman   MARRIAGE FOR MODERNS

Davie   NEGROES IN AMERICAN SOCIETY

Dornbusch and Schmid   A PRIMER OF SOCIAL STATISTICS

Gittler   SOCIAL DYNAMICS

Goode and Hatt   METHODS IN SOCIAL RESEARCH

Hoebel   MAN IN THE PRIMITIVE WORLD

Hoebel, Jennings, and Smith   READINGS IN ANTHROPOLOGY

House   THE DEVELOPMENT OF SOCIOLOGY

Landis   RURAL LIFE IN PROCESS

LaPiere   A THEORY OF SOCIAL CONTROL

LaPiere   COLLECTIVE BEHAVIOR

LaPiere   SOCIOLOGY

Lemert   SOCIAL PATHOLOGY

McCormick   ELEMENTARY SOCIAL STATISTICS

Queen and Carpenter   THE AMERICAN CITY

Tappan   CONTEMPORARY CORRECTION

Tappan   JUVENILE DELINQUENCY

Thompson   POPULATION PROBLEMS

Walter   RACE AND CULTURE RELATIONS

Young   SOCIAL TREATMENT IN PROBATION AND DELINQUENCY

SOCIAL DYNAMICS

Principles and Cases
in Introductory Sociology

JOSEPH B. GITTLER

PROFESSOR AND CHAIRMAN, DEPARTMENT OF SOCIOLOGY,
UNIVERSITY OF ROCHESTER

McGRAW-HILL BOOK COMPANY, INC.

NEW YORK   TORONTO   LONDON

1952

v

23295

SOCIAL DYNAMICS

TO *Josy*
AND HER GRANDPARENTS

Preface

Two and a half decades ago Charles Horton Cooley, in a presidential address before the Michigan Academy of Science, Arts, and Letters, distinguished between two sorts of knowledge. "One, the development of sense contacts into knowledge of things," he called spatial and material knowledge. "The second is developed from contact with the minds of other men, through communication, which sets going a process of thought and sentiment similar to theirs and enables us to understand them by sharing their states of mind." This he designated as social knowledge. "It might also be described as sympathetic, or in its more active forms, as dramatic, since it is apt to consist of a visualization of behavior accompanied by imagination of corresponding mental processes." * In recent years, sociologists and anthropologists, notably Robert E. Park, Robert Redfield, Herbert Blumer, and Robert MacIver, have reemphasized this distinctive nature of social knowledge.

Detailed case studies, because of their vivid and dramatic accounts of human experiences and social relationships, tend to transmit that type of knowledge which Cooley defines as social. Case materials, adequately recorded, reveal those aspects of human behavior which the reader can comprehend with sympathetic interpretation. Knowledge of human nature demands that one assume the role of the other and experience, with emotion and empathy, the other's covert nature—his attitudes, values, feelings—as well as his manifest overt character. Two persons may perform an identical task or behave in exactly the same way, but each action may have a different meaning, a diverse value. And it is the *meanings* to which humans attribute their actions that constitute the real essence of their social natures. The sciences of social man must, therefore, take into account the less obvious aspects of human behavior. Human-cultural phenomena are dynamic; society is alive and changing. It must be felt as well as seen; it must be experienced, at least vicariously,

* "The Roots of Social Knowledge," *American Journal of Sociology*, Vol. XXXII (1926–1927), p. 60; also Charles Horton Cooley, *Sociological Theory and Social Research* (New York: Henry Holt and Company, Inc., 1930), p. 290.

as well as observed. For this kind of comprehension the case method has special significance.

The collection of case studies for this volume was begun several years ago in order to supplement the reading usually prescribed for students in introductory sociology. An ever-increasing number of cases were found which were appropriate to the various fields covered in the course. As they accumulated and were used in many classes, it became clear that students were attracted by this kind of material. Concepts and principles which they frequently found difficult to comprehend in their texts became clarified and their pertinence recognized.

It must be clearly understood that the cases are presented, not as proof of sociological principles, but as examples of them. Proof is obtained by other techniques. No instructor will fail to supply students with demonstrable proof whenever it is available.

This book, then, should be regarded as an adventure, in which teacher and student consider the principles that the sociologist has by slow, laborious, and painstaking effort formulated about men in their group life as they are portrayed in the fabric of social living. It is a challenge to the student to understand himself and his society. It is hoped that some students will find sufficient incentive to go further and add new knowledge and insights to the field of sociology.

The author wishes to acknowledge the contributions of the following persons to this volume: To Lami Gittler, whose tremendous contribution cannot be accurately measured since it is so indissolubly a part of the author's entire endeavor; to Dean Harold V. Gaskill and William G. Murray of the Industrial Science Research Institute of Iowa State College, whose generous support, interest, and encouragement made this book a reality; to Rachel Lowrie, for the tedious job of editing the manuscript; to my friends and colleagues Edna Douglas, David M. Fulcomer, Ernest Manheim, Richard T. LaPiere, Meyer F. Nimkoff, and Stuart A. Queen for the hours they spent reading the manuscript and for their many valuable suggestions as to additions and changes; to Katherine Collier, through whose diligence and indefatigability the many bibliographical details were compiled; to my students George A. Freeman, Charles Robbins, and Delbert Smith for their assistance in the preparation of the manuscript; to Charliene Baird, for the excellent typing job on the manuscript; and to all the publishers and authors who have kindly granted permission to use their materials.

JOSEPH B. GITTLER

Ames, Iowa
March, 1952

Contents

Introduction: *The Nature of the Social and the Meaning of Sociology*

A. THE MEANING OF SOCIAL RELATIONS: SOCIAL RELATIONS AS SYMBOLIC-MEANINGFUL RELATIONS

Man, who is a *homo sapiens,* is not born a social being, nor does he possess culture at birth. He is, at birth, a plastic, pliable, biological entity which is constantly molded and shaped into a *person,* with meanings, values, interests, wishes, and attitudes, by association with other persons. The patterns of these associations are group patterns. Various groups in society furnish different aspects of man's social nature. The primary group, such as the family and the child's play group, shares his basic *human-social nature;* secondary groups and institutions give him his *human-cultural nature.* In other words, man is born a biological individual who acquires a social nature and becomes a person.

These persons are not isolated phenomena, nor are they static and inert. They are ever active and interactive. All social relations are to be thought of as a special type of interhuman activity, as a type of interaction. The term *relations* implies a reciprocal influence, a mutual connection among the elements. The concept of interaction has become one of the fundamental and most nearly universal ideas to designate this process of mutual, ongoing relationship in each of the fields of knowledge— physical, biological, and social. However, while interaction may be conceived of as a nearly universal process, it should not be inferred that interaction as it takes place in the inorganic or organic order is the same in all respects as is interaction in the superorganic (human-social) realm.

Social interaction consists of that behavior by which an individual influences the overt actions or the state of mind of another. It is inconceivable that in the absence of interaction we could have a social group, a social system, or a society. "A million completely isolated human beings do not represent a social phenomenon or a society, since they do not influence one another." *[1] In the same way, separate and disparate planets do not make a solar system. Life cannot be understood merely through inert, noninteracting, isolated aggregates of cells. For both physical and biological realities to be, they must be represented as becoming. Process is essential to being; interaction is a necessary part of reality.

Social interaction differs from other types of interaction, such as the impact of billiard balls (physical interaction) or the contact of food with the stomach cells (biological interaction), in that social interaction involves *meaning, value, purpose,* and *symbols.* A person responds not to what another individual says or does, but to the *meaning* he imputes to that which the individual has said or done. In the physical and biological worlds there are no meanings. The billiard balls do not *understand* that it is the purpose of the impact to cause motion, nor does the stomach *comprehend* the purpose of food. In these situations the interaction is automatic, inevitable, and mechanical. It is not *because of* the rules of the game that the billiard balls decide to move. Nor is it because of the nutritional value of the food intake that the stomach "decides" to proceed with its digestive processes.

Human-social beings, unlike purely physical and biological entities, give meanings to things before they react to them. What they make of the stimuli, whether these are material things or other persons, constitutes the basis of human interaction. "What humans make of humans and things" is what is meant by meaningful interaction.

The following experimental case study reveals the connection between the meanings and values (symbols) which man attaches to given situations and his responses to them. The experiments were conducted at the Hawthorne Works of the Western Electric Company, in Chicago, between 1924 and 1927.[2]

In one of the departments of the company, the workers wound small induction coils on wooden spools. The workers were divided into two groups, each group's members had about the same amount of experience in the work and also had about the same average output. Group A was considered the test group and was to work under variable illumination intensities, while Group B was called the control group and worked under illumination intensity which was kept constant. The groups worked in two different buildings. The test group worked under three different intensities of light, 24, 46 and 70 foot-candles, while the control group worked on a more or less constant level of 16 to 28 foot-candles. The purpose of this experi-

* Footnotes will be found at the end of each part.

ment was to measure the differences in production efficiency as it was related to differences in illumination. Mr. C. E. Snow of the National Research Council of the National Academy of Sciences who was in charge of the experiment at the Western Electric Company sums up his results: "This test resulted in very appreciable production increases in both groups and of almost identical magnitude. The difference in efficiency of the two groups was so small as to be less than the probble error of the values. Consequently, we were again unable to determine what definite part of the improvement in performance should be ascribed to improved illumination." [3]

A second test was then performed using a test group and a control group as previously mentioned. This time the control group worked under a constant degree of artificial illumination of 10 foot-candles, while the test group illumination was decreased from 10 to 3 foot-candles by 1 foot-candle at a time. Mr. Snow sums up the findings of this experiment:

"After the level of illumination in the test group enclosure changed to a lower value, the efficiencies of both the test and control groups increased slowly but steadily. When the level of the illumination for the test group finally reached 3 foot-candles, the operatives protested, saying that they were hardly able to see what they were doing, and the production rate decreased. The operatives could and did maintain their efficiency to this point in spite of the discomfort and handicap of insufficient illumination." [4]

Additional tests and experiments were performed with the girls in the coil winding department. In this instance, the light was increased each day and the girls were questioned each day in regard to their reaction to these changes. As the amount of light was increased the response was very favorable. Then for a day or two electricians came in ostensibly to change the bulbs for further increase of illumination but in reality simply changed the light bulbs of a given size for others of the *same* size. The girls under the impression that the light was being increased continued to comment favorably on the change. After this the intensity of the light was decreased and the girls were so informed. After a period of this decrease the experimenter again had the electrician change bulbs which had no effect on the intensity of the illumination. The girls reacted as was expected by saying they did not like working in the dimmer illumination. However, their production rate did not change materially during any stage of the experiment.

In a further experiment in the same plant, the illumination at the bench was reduced from the original amount of light to which the girls had been accustomed to 0.06 of a foot-candle, which is approximately equal to the intensity of illumination coming from ordinary moonlight on a clear night. Not until this point was reached was there any appreciable decline in the production output rate. The girls seemed able to maintain their efficiency even with the very low intensity of light. They claimed that they suffered no eyestrain and that they were less tired than when they worked under bright lights.

It is clear from these experiments that the workers did not respond purely as organic entities to the variations in light intensities but rather to the meanings they injected into the given situation. In fact, the girls commented favorably on the "increased" light intensity when the electrician took out bulbs of a given size and inserted bulbs of the same size. This is an illustration of social interaction being carried on by meanings. As this occurs between objects and humans, so it occurs between humans and humans. A acts; B perceives this action and seeks to ascertain A's intention. B then responds to the meaning or interpretation he has attached to A's act.

Just as illumination fails to explain what makes the worker work, appropriate investigations would in all probability show that other physical factors also fail to reveal the direct cause-and-effect relationships that we are able to obtain in physical experimentation. The worker's efficiency did not vary only in accordance with the changing physical conditions in the workrooms. Heat, cold, the purely spatial arrangement of machines, atmospheric pressure, and moisture in the plant are inadequate in explaining what are essentially human-social events. It cannot be denied that physical factors contribute substantially to the process of work relations and work production. All social events have a physical dimension. However, while physical conditions are *necessarily* involved in social situations, the physical does not *sufficiently* account for the social. If man were but a physical entity (or merely a biological entity) he would respond to fluctuations in intensity of illumination or other physical stimuli just as any other physical object responds to stimuli. For example, if man were like tungsten filament, he would react to the fluctuations in light intensity in an inevitable, determinate manner. If an increase in illumination makes for an increase in work production, a decrease in illumination cannot produce a similar result unless man is constituted of more than merely physical components.

It should be clear then that human-social interaction is meaningful and symbolic. Meaningful-symbolic behavior is a human attribute because humans *create* their symbols. Man alone is capable of this act. Lower animals are similar to persons who have the receiving apparatus for wireless messages but are unable to send messages. Men without symbols would be much like apes. Instances of children growing up without symbols because of deafness and blindness, like Laura Bridgman and Helen Keller, are most instructive. It took them a long time to understand the nature of symbolic communication, and until they were able to master this they were *in* human society but not a part *of* it.

B. LANGUAGE AS A SYMBOLIC INSTRUMENT: THE CASE OF HELEN KELLER

In the following story* Helen Keller describes the changes which the acquisition of language brought to her life.[5] Language is obviously man's most significant symbolic medium for the communication of meanings. Without language there would be persons without symbols; without symbols the world around man would have little meaning. Helen Keller, it should be noted, began to learn language at the age of seven. Her memory of the years prior to that age, she claims, were vague. She even questions whether she had any "ideas" or "thoughts" during that period. The meanings of things through word symbols are one of the most potent factors in man's socialization process.

The most important day I remember in all my life is the one on which my teacher, Anne Mansfield Sullivan, came to me. I am filled with wonder when I consider the immeasurable contrast between the two lives which it connects. It was the third of March, 1887, three months before I was seven years old.

The morning after my teacher came she led me into her room and gave me a doll. The little blind children at the Perkins Institution had sent it and Laura Bridgman had dressed it; but I did not know this until afterward. When I had played with it a little while, Miss Sullivan slowly spelled into my hand the word "d-o-l-l." I was at once interested in this finger play and tried to imitate it. When I finally succeeded in making the letters correctly I was flushed with childish pleasure and pride. Running downstairs to my mother I held up my hand and made the letters for doll. I did not know that I was spelling a word or even that words existed; I was simply making my fingers go in monkey-like imitation. In the days that followed I learned to spell in this uncomprehending way a great many words, among them *pin, hat, cup* and a few verbs like *sit, stand,* and *walk*. But my teacher had been with me several weeks before I understood that everything has a name.

One day, while I was playing with my new doll, Miss Sullivan put my rag doll into my lap also, spelled "d-o-l-l" and tried to make me understand that "d-o-l-l" applied to both. Earlier in the day we had had a tussle over the words "m-u-g" and "w-a-t-e-r." Miss Sullivan had tried to impress it upon me that "m-u-g" is *mug* and that "w-a-t-e-r" is *water,* but I persisted in confounding the two. In despair she had dropped the subject for the time, only to renew it at the first opportunity. I became impatient at her repeated attempts and, seizing the new doll, I dashed it upon the floor. I was keenly delighted when I felt the fragments of the broken doll at my feet. Neither sorrow nor regret followed my passionate outburst. I

* From *The Story of My Life* by Helen Keller. Copyright 1903 by Helen Keller, reprinted by permission of Doubleday & Company, Inc.

had not loved the doll. In the still, dark world in which I lived there was no strong sentiment or tenderness. I felt my teacher sweep the fragments to one side of the hearth, and I had a sense of satisfaction that the cause of my discomfort was removed. She brought me my hat, and I knew I was going out into the warm sunshine. This thought, if a wordless sensation may be called a thought, made me hop and skip with pleasure.

We walked down the path to the well-house, attracted by the fragrance of the honeysuckle with which it was covered. Some one was drawing water and my teacher placed my hand under the spout. As the cool stream gushed over one hand she spelled into the other the word *water,* first slowly, then rapidly. I stood still, my whole attention fixed upon the motions of her fingers. Suddenly I felt a misty consciousness as of something forgotten—a thrill of returning thought; and somehow the mystery of language was revealed to me. I knew then that "w-a-t-e-r" meant the wonderful cool something that was flowing over my hand. That living word awakened my soul, gave it light and hope, joy, set it free! There were barriers still, it is true, but barriers that could in time be swept away.

I left the well-house eager to learn. Everything had a name, and each name gave birth to a new thought. As we returned to the house every object which I touched seemed to quiver with life. That was because I saw everything with the strange new sight that had come to me. On entering the door I remembered the doll I had broken. I felt my way to the hearth and picked up the pieces. I tried vainly to put them together. Then my eyes filled with tears; for I realized what I had done, and for the first time I felt repentance and sorrow.

I learned a great many new words that day. I do not remember what they all were; but I do know that mother, father, sister, teacher, were among them— words that were to make the world blossom for me, "like Aaron's rod, with flowers." It would have been difficult to find a happier child than I was as I lay in my crib at the close of that eventful day and lived over the joys it had brought me, and for the first time longed for a new day to come.

The emotional experiences of Helen Keller have been aptly explained in conceptual terms by Cassirer, one of our foremost philosophers. He has this to say about the symbolic nature of man: [6]

Man lives in a symbolic universe. Language, myth, art, and religion are parts of this universe. They are the varied trends which weave the symbolic net, the tangled web of human experience. All human progress in thought and experience refines upon and strengthens this net. No longer can man confront reality immediately; he cannot see it, as it were, face to face. Physical reality seems to recede in proportion as man's symbolic activity advances. Instead of dealing with the things themselves man is in a sense constantly conversing with himself. He has so enveloped himself in linguistic forms, in artistic images, in mythical symbols or religious rites that he cannot see or know anything except by the interposition of this artificial medium. His situation is the same in the theoretical as in the practical sphere. Even here man does not live in a world of hard facts, or according to his immediate needs and desires.

C. THE SYMBOLIC PROCESS EMERGING IN ROLE
TAKING AND IN THE DEFINITION OF THE SITUATION

Some interesting questions may now arise. Whence does a given individual obtain the particular values and symbolic meanings that he attaches to a given situation? Does he invent original meanings for every stimulus that impinges upon him? Is he that much of a creative being? Or does he take over the definitions and meanings of the situation from others? If he does the latter, we have another interesting attribute of social relations and social interaction. It appears safe to say that most of the meanings that an individual attaches to an experience come from others. From birth, man finds his behavior prescribed and restrained by other people. Parents frequently set the initial patterns of early childhood behavior. Through disapproval, disgust, punishment, and other forms of prohibition, they seek to avoid deviation from the socially "correct" patterns. An individual tends to act differently and at the same time "properly" as a member of a family, as a member of a Rotary club, and as a member of a baseball team. Different roles are assumed in different group situations. In each case the situation confronted by the individual is *defined* by those around him. It is through this definition of a situation that one obtains the attitudes and views of the group and is, thereby, able to take over the expectations and understandings of his group. This gives him a set of symbols and meanings which serve to direct his behavior relative to given stimuli and situations in socially approved ways.

This is not to deny that while situations are defined by others for the individual most of the time, the individual may still lend his own personal interpretation and meaning to a given situation. W. I. Thomas and F. Znaniecki, who, in their monumental work on the Polish peasant, introduced into sociology the concept of the *definition of the situation,* distinguish between those definitions of the situation which are laid down for the individual by his culture and his group and those which represent the individual's own conception and interpretation of a given situation. The former they call *public* definitions; the latter, *personal*.

As they have stated, "the human personality is both a constantly producing factor and a continually produced result of social evolution, and
this double relation expresses itself in every elementary social fact. . . ." [7]
Both phases are essential to the concept of the definition of a situation.
In the following case, the child in school for the first time meets situations for which his previous experience furnishes him no adequate
definition.[8] He then either works out a definition in collaboration with
his classmates or he accepts the definition of the situation furnished
by the teacher.

Cousin Frances sits with the circle of kindergarten students. It is her first day
of school. Thus far all has gone well, and Miss Lamb, the teacher, has made the
little girl feel quite at ease. From the first moment that Frances entered Miss
Lamb's room the whole new situation which she found herself a part of—the
whole of her new surroundings—and the whole of her past experience carried
within her own little personage—have been conditioning or modifying her behavior. Of this fact Frances is partly conscious and partly unconscious. As Frances
looks about the circle, she spies Dale, the boy who lives next door. Dale sitting
nearby is the situation or object presented. She defines the situation as she has
defined it many times before. Here is Dale whom she often plays with and talks
to. The situation defined, the attitude that she will play with him and talk to him
now arises. . . . She goes toward him and begins a conversation. But her progress
is hesitating and her speech subdued due to her new environment. At this point
the teacher intervenes. Evidently Frances has defined the situation wrongly. A
crisis—a minor one—is at hand.

"What shall I do?" says Frances to herself. "No one has ever stopped me from
playing and talking with Dale before. How shall I act toward this intruder, called
the teacher, who thus interferes with the way I am used to doing things? Shall
I cry, or shall I smile, or shall I be angry?"

. . . Thinking that perhaps this is the way things usually happen in school, she
decides to return to her little red chair. This she does without unnecessary ado.

Miss Lamb then proceeds to talk to Frances. She says school is a place where
everyone has work to do, and that each must stay in his place and keep quiet so
that he and everyone else can get their work done. And Miss Lamb is glad too
that Frances decided not to bother anyone and returned to her own seat. Thus
the teacher tried to re-define the situation for Frances and set up a counter-
attitude which will change the habit of action or behavior.

A few days later the same thing confronts Frances. But now she finds herself
possessed of her own definition and its attitude and Miss Lamb's definition and
its attitude. She compromises, and instead of going to Dale and talking, she merely
talks to him in a low voice, without leaving her place. This time the teacher—
and the pupils—decide that if Frances is going to keep them from their work,

she will have to sit apart from the group. Here is another minor crisis with a similar re-definition of the situation calling up the same counter-attitude.

Frances now passes to the stage where she whispers to Dale, and more crises interjected by Miss Lamb are necessary to fix the new definition and the new attitude. Finally a major crisis comes when as a result of Frances' whispering the whole class must do its work over. The unsocialness of her conduct drives home the school definition and fixes her concurrent attitude. Then after a time when Frances has several times refused herself the luxury of whispering and the attitude of prohibition has become integrated with the habit of prohibition, the process passes from the realm of consciousness to that of unconsciousness—the school conduct of Frances is good and she knows it as such and keeps it thus. In her own eyes and the eyes of others, she is a "good girl" at school.

George Herbert Mead was among the early social psychologists to note the importance of role taking by an individual in assuming for himself the meanings and values that others attach to a given situation.

The physiological mechanism of the human individual's central nervous system makes it possible for him to take the attitudes of other individuals, and of the organized social group of which he and they are members, toward himself, in terms of his integrated social relations to them and to the group as a whole; so that the general social process of experience and behavior which the group is carrying on is directly presented to him in his own experience, and so that he is thereby able to govern and direct his conduct consciously and critically, with reference to his relations both to the social group as a whole and to its other individual members, in terms of this social process. Thus he becomes not only self-conscious but self-critical; and thus, through self-criticism, social control over individual behavior or conduct operates by virtue of the social origin and basis of such criticism. That is to say, self-criticism is essentially social criticism, and behavior controlled by self-criticism is essentially behavior controlled socially. Hence, social control, so far from tending to crush out the human individual or to obliterate his self-conscious individuality, is, on the contrary, actually constitutive of and inextricably associated with that individuality; for the individual is what he is, as a conscious individual personality, first in so far as he is a member of society, involved in the social process of experience and activity, and thereby socially controlled in his conduct.[9]

It should be noted that Mead does not conceive of human personality, with all of its attitudes, interests and meanings, and behavior forms, merely as a passive, inert, automatic recipient of the ways and expectations of his immediate group or the larger society. He does not merely respond to the "commands" of society; he corresponds. Values are not imposed on humans; they are composed by them. "Expectations stamped with group approval do not impinge upon group members as alien and imposed, but as socially desirable personal standards. These standards of conduct have arisen in experience through intercommunication in reaction to common life situations. Consequently, the expectations to which a person responds are patterns of behavior he expects from others and which he may expect from himself. Once a person incorporates these group expectations in himself he uses them in weighing and criticizing his potential future behavior as well as the behavior of others." Man creatively, and with understanding and purpose, *accepts* and *adopts* the ways of his group; the animal merely *receives* the impositions of his trainer.

In a homogeneous culture and society where the members possess the same background of experiences from their earliest years, social equilibrium and social stability are achieved through human conformity. Most primitive societies and most peasant societies are of this kind. Nonconformity is relatively difficult since the background is so unvaried. What one does, he expects others to do, and what others are, he tends to be. To rephrase Emerson: "Whoso would be a man" in these societies, "needs be a conformist."

In a heterogeneous society, the picture is quite different. A heterogeneous society is mostly a stratified society. It consists of groups of people with different backgrounds and frequently with conflicting or at least competitive interests and diverse values. These diverse interests and values are often subordinated, submerged, or even suppressed for the sake of a more dominant and commonly shared interest. When this happens, social relations give rise to social systems, social groups, and clearly defined societies.

Social relations may therefore involve common understandings, shared values, and cooperative behavior leading to group life; or they may involve opposing values and uncooperative behavior, resulting in interhuman strife, social tensions, disorganization, and disunity; or they may be as short lived as a passing human experience, disappearing with the occasion responsible for the experience. The essence of the first, or of group living, consists of an ethos—that is, shared values, shared objectives, shared preferences, and a feeling of being alike and belonging together. There cannot be a unit (group or society) of interacting persons until its members have developed a semblance of cultural and psychological unity. A community of ideas and values takes care of the first; an emotional solidarity and an *esprit de corps,* the second. Discordant relations may typify social relations, but they do not signify group relations. When complete discord gives rise to some accord we are seeing the formation of the social entity, the group.

One further point should perhaps be mentioned about social groups. In all *organized* social groups and societies, the members not only share common values and have an *esprit de corps* but each interacting individual defines for himself, at the same time that it is being defined for him, his relative *position* in the group.[10] We say that he gets to know and accept his *role* in the group. This role defines his minimum set of obligations to the group. Without defined roles and accompanying obligations, social organization is almost impossible. Industry as a functioning entity of interrelated parts is inconceivable without the worker understanding and accepting *his* job and a member of management *his* position and what is expected of him. To the extent that roles are undefined and uncertain, an industrial relationship lacks organization and integration. Thus it has been observed repeatedly that a newly hired worker frequently experiences all sorts of uncertainties, bewilderment, frustrations, and inadequacies until he understands clearly what is expected of him.

This, then, is what is meant by social relations. It means *symbolic interaction*; it means *defined situation;* and if it leads to social entities —groups, organizations, societies—it means *shared understandings and conventions* and clarified roles in order to carry out the shared objectives and values. In the industrial plant, for example, meaningful processes of interaction constantly manifest themselves between worker and worker, worker and foreman, worker and manager, with each participant tending to assume the role that the culture of the plant has defined as appropriate to his position and job. It is only when a worker, a foreman, or a manager deviates from his expected role, or when one's role is diversely defined, that disagreement and plant disorganization set in.

D. SOCIAL RELATIONS, THE SOCIAL SCIENCES,
SOCIOLOGY

It has perhaps been obvious to the reader that several fields—psychology, political science, economics, jurisprudence, sociology—have been concerned with the general areas of social relations and social groups. The social sciences, by definition, are primarily involved in knowing the social world. We might ask, however, if there is a logical division of labor among the social disciplines which would enable us to understand the role and precise framework of each in its approach to the social?

Indeed there is. Each social science has a set of assumptions, a set of concepts, and a set of compendent propositions and principles that sets it off logically from the other social sciences. Each of the social sciences makes certain assumptions about the nature of man. Each takes for granted that man in his symbolic-meaningful behavior is motivated by a specific set of normative and value-filled impulsions and ends that tend to account for that behavior. The field of economics has as its primary focus the study of man motivated by his desire to obtain material goods and services. To this end he has found it necessary to act (and interact) with others in order to obtain for himself a maximum of economic goods by making rational choices among alternative wants. During the course of his years on earth he has therefore built up systems and patterns of acting together in order to obtain these material objects. He has worked in agriculture, in industry; he has invented banks; he has devised stock markets; he has established mercantile firms. Each seeks to satisfy *primarily* basic economic wants, and only *incidentally* other human wants. Furthermore, each of these systems implies that men have gotten together on the basis of a set of common values and shared ends to satisfy these needs. In other words, he has found or joined groups whose primary functions consist of the satisfaction of economic wants.

We might ask, however, if man is solely an economic being. Are his motivations purely economic? Does he form economic groups only? Obviously this is not the case. Man in his relations to man has formed states, families, Rotary clubs, bridge clubs, music groups, schools— even associations to terminate associations. While all of these may perhaps be said to have some economic function, none of them can be said to be *primarily* economic in purpose.

Let us raise some further questions. Is there anything common to all these groups? Are there any principles or concepts that may universally explain the functioning of all human groups? Are there features common to all group life? Can we classify specific groups into general categories of group types? What accounts for the formation of all groups? For classified types of groups? What are the essential differences among these group types? What roles do they perform in the general structure of human society? What goes on within and among groups? What patterns of interaction characterize certain groups? And what results from group interacting with group? In raising these questions, it becomes clear that we are not solely concerned with the structure and functioning of a specific group—the economic, political, familial—but rather our focus is on the analysis of the group per se.

It is this concern about the *generic* aspects of group life that constitutes one of the major orientations of sociology.[11] Sociology is the study of the forms and processes of human togetherness. It attempts to get at the elemental, underlying, all-pervading aspects of human association. In this respect it is different from the frames of reference of the other social sciences. Sociology is not only interested in man as a member of an economic group, political group, or religious group; it is interested in the generic nature of human groups.

Sociology is also concerned with social processes—with competition, for example. However, there are many forms of competition—competition in business, in the family, in the classroom, on the ball field, in the church, and in voluntary clubs. Competition characterizes man in his group associations; it is involved in man's togetherness with man—not only in his economic or political togetherness, but in his *human* togetherness. The system of concepts and principles governing these basic forms and dynamics of human association constitutes the field of sociology.

Let us illustrate how one such sociological concept and principle might be applied to all human-group living. There is a principle in sociology which states that people tend to consider their own groups superior to other groups; they possess feelings of superiority toward their own way of life. This is called *ethnocentrism*. Interestingly enough, it appears that ethnocentrism is a rather universal characteristic of group life. Members of "primitive" tribes manifest a strong predilection for their own members and hostility toward "outsiders," or those who are not members of their own tribe. The ethnocentric feeling is characteristic of contemporary racial, nationality, and religious groups. Political parties, fraternal organizations, and many other types of social groups give rise to these exclusive and superiority feelings among their members.

Frequently ethnocentrism is found in industrial relations. In a large electrical-parts plant (let us call it plant A) in a city in New England, there was much dissatisfaction and tension between workers and management and among workers themselves. The plant suffered from a rather long history of internal disorganization as evidenced by a high labor turnover, absenteeism, and interworker quarreling on the job.

At the end of each shift, the majority of workers from plant A who did not travel home in private cars took buses which had already picked up workers of another large electrical plant about two miles away. It happened rather frequently that workers from both plants, traveling home in the same bus, would become involved in discussions of their respective plants. Even though the workers of plant A were dissatisfied with their own jobs and the operations in the plant, if a worker from plant B made a disparaging remark about plant A they were quick to spring to its defense. Such assertions of pride in plant A were heard as: "We have the best engineers in the country." "Plant A was the first to come out with television." Even the lamest defense possessed elements of local group vanity and esteem.

These illustrations should suffice to point out how ethnocentrism, a sociological concept, reflects the feelings of members not only of a particular group—a factory group, a religious group, or a nationality group —but of groups as such. It is an *elemental,* all-pervading characteristic of group life.

E. SOCIOLOGY, COMMON SENSE, AND THE SCIENTIFIC METHOD

The social sciences seek to approach the social world scientifically, not in a common-sense way, nor with artistic insight, nor by purely philosophical methods. Common-sense judgment, for example, is often the most fallacious. Common sense constitutes those untested beliefs that are handed down from generation to generation and are accepted fullblown by large masses of people. Common sense is the equivalent of folk wisdom, usually finding its expression in folk sayings, aphorisms, and proverbs.

It is the all-too-great faith in common-sense knowledge that often obscures its latent contradictoriness. Note the contradiction in the two sets of expressions of pure common sense, each on the same theme. "Look before you leap," and "He who hesitates is lost." "Absence makes the heart grow fonder," and "Out of sight, out of mind." Many other varieties of common-sense contradictions may be garnered. Nevertheless, one frequently notices an aura of self-approbation and self-certainty in social judgments, especially when the judgments are accompanied by pronounced appeals that "it's just plain common sense." To the real scientific mind, this appeal should point to signs of intellectual danger. Science does not permit contradictions. In science a thing either is or is not. Scientific method, whether in the physical or the social realm, is *logical, objective, empirical,* and *verifiable.*

We have said that *objectivity* constitutes one of the fundamental characteristics of the scientific approach. Objectivity implies verifiability; scientific knowledge is verifiable knowledge. Scientist A must be able to discover the same facts as scientist B, given the same conditions. If he is unable to do so, then what B knows is not scientific or objective. It is subjective. His knowledge is too dependent on his own subjective, personal whim and imagination. Objective knowledge is knowledge that is independent of the knower.

The following case dramatizes one aspect of the scientific attitude— an objective detachment on the part of the scientist himself even when he is under great stress.

F. A CASE OF SCIENTIFIC OBJECTIVITY IN TIME OF GREAT CRISIS [12]

In 1940–41, certain physicians in Warsaw had an unprecedented opportunity to observe the pathological effects of starvation.

This is what happened.

On October 16, 1940, the German occupation forces in Warsaw established an official ghetto. All "Aryans" were evacuated from the area. Eight-foot-high brick walls, topped with broken glass, closed the exits. Only one gate was left open for closely watched contact with the outside: the "Transferplatz," where once a week food was delivered—bread made from wormy flour mixed with plaster and sawdust, and rotten potatoes. Otherwise, there was complete isolation for approximately 500,000 men, women, and children. (Before the war there were 330,000 Jews in Warsaw, but their number increased after the German invasion.)

As soon as the Ghetto was established, the Jews began to organize their existence. A Society for the Promotion of Health was formed to give medical aid. Soup kitchens (for bread-and-water and potato-and-water gruel) were set up. Twenty thousand house committees collected supplies for children. Schools were started, textbooks being copied by hand by the boys and girls. Newspapers— illegal—appeared, in Hebrew, Yiddish and Polish. All this in the midst of a tremendous struggle simply to exist. Living quarters were unbearably crowded —there was scarcely a square yard of empty space in the whole walled-in section. And there was no soap, no fuel, no gas or electricity, and often no water.

At the end of a year, all reserves of food were gone: the last bag of rice from the shelf, the last bit of sugar, the last piece of dried fruit, the last little tin of fish.

All the horses had been eaten. A day's ration, by then, consisted of 800 calories. (In this country, the usual quantity is 3,000 calories or more.) The mortality rate, of course, rose very high, about 500 for each twenty-four hours. When a man died, or a woman or child, his clothes were removed—after all, there was no way to buy cloth; every rag must be saved—and the naked body was then placed in the street. This was to escape the Germans' exorbitant burial tax. Later, the bodies would be collected on carts and dragged by starving fellow-citizens to anonymous mass graves.

On July 21, 1941, came the first order for deportations from the Ghetto. By four o'clock each day, so many Jews must be ready—ready for death. First went the sick and the aged, to be poisoned, gassed, burned; then the intellectuals, who were systematically hunted down and killed. Next went the unemployed, followed by those who did not work for the war effort. Even in the Ghetto, the Germans had set up war plants; and for a time some 10,000 young workers were exempt from the general order, segregated in a so-called "small ghetto" of their own. But all along, their parents and children were taken from them, snatched out of their arms, and dragged away to be killed.

After six months of deportations the Ghetto population had gone down from 500,000 to 40,000 and the Mayor of the community, Adam Czerniakow, had committed suicide in despair; but during this period the Jews had secretly mobilized. Guns, revolvers, hand grenades had been smuggled into the district. Underground arsenals had been built, elaborate plans for street combat worked out, and a system of medical stations set up for expected casualties.

The first armed resistance began on January 19, 1942. S.S. and Latvian groups had entered the Ghetto in the morning for an attack on the remaining 40,000 Jews. They found barricades manned with fighters, fighters who fired on them and killed them—killed Germans! A call was sent out for tanks, and a thousand or more Jews were killed; then the troops withdrew, apparently stunned by the unexpected resistance. For a while, even the daily deportations ceased; but during this period (several months) a force of approximately 9,000 German soldiers was collected and equipped with artillery, armored trucks, tanks, flame-throwers and airplanes. Finally, on April 19, 1942, the final assault began: the proud German Army against the wretched Ghetto Jews. During the first days 3,000 Jews were killed. On April 21, snatches of a radio broadcast were heard in New York, although quickly cut off: "The last 35,000 Jews in the Ghetto of Warsaw have been condemned. The people are being murdered. Women and children are defending themselves with their naked arms. Save us!"

The battle lasted forty-two days. Nazi arsenals were seized and blown up. Five hundred Jews slipped out of the district to break open the Pawiak jail, and all prisoners (including German deserters) went over to the Ghetto fighters. Suicide squads of Jews crawled under German trucks with high explosives. Single individuals attacked tanks with hand grenades. Finally the Germans decided the whole district must be destroyed with incendiary bombs.

It is almost impossible to imagine those last nightmare days, with entire families rushing from flaming houses into the face of machine guns, with streams of city's inhabitants cornered in narrow streets and run down by tanks. Hospitals were invaded, and the patients killed in their beds. Thousands were burned alive. There was nowhere to step but on corpses—and this day after day, with no escape, and no expectation of help from any side, or kindness or mercy or pity or hope. Every building was a fortress until it lay in ashes. At last, on the forty-second day, only one was left, with the Jews' blue-and-white flag still waving above it. The battle went from floor to floor, until, at the end, on the roof, the last Ghetto fighter wrapped himself in his flag and threw himself down onto the burning ruins.

In the face of the systematic degradation and destruction of the Jews, their physical resistance is surprising. Still more remarkable is their moral courage. Perhaps the most dramatic evidence of this is the story of a group of Ghetto physicians who launched a cooperative research project to study the effects of starvation on the human body—their own bodies included. Dr. Milejkowsky, health commissioner of the district, organized a committee which established special wards for adults and children, and rebuilt the laboratories (completely destroyed by the 1939 Nazi invasion) as well as possible. Many essential instruments were, of course, lacking; these had to be brought from outside the Ghetto and smuggled in at the risk of death. Practical work began in February, 1942, and monthly sessions were held to discuss the observations of the physicians. Two age groups—one of six to twelve, and the other of twenty to forty—were decided upon, in order to exclude from the investigation the biochemical disbalances of infancy, adolescence and advancing age. Everyone knew that his work could be interrupted suddenly by individual death—his own, or his patients'—or by mass catastrophe. Everyone knew that the work was likely, anyway, to conclude only in death. But the doctors worked feverishly, without a day's interruption, and in the months at their disposal accumulated a quantity of experiments and observations which would have taken many years to collect under normal conditions. At last, as the approaching crisis grew desperate, it became clear that the manuscript must be removed from the Ghetto while there was yet time. It was delivered to Dr. Witold Orlowski, Professor of internal medicine at the University of Warsaw.

None of the twenty-two collaborating physicians survived. The only one still alive after the battle of the Ghetto, Dr. Emil Apfelbaum, died in January, 1946, as a result of his experiences.

I saw a copy of the document for the first time two or three years ago, and was deeply moved by it—a treatise which must surely be unique in scientific history. The manuscript was carefully written in longhand on official German Army stationery, in Yiddish. A friend translated parts of it to me at the time. There were six studies: "The Pathology of Starvation," "Clinical and Biochemical Observations About Starvation," "The Clinic of Hunger in Children," "Clinical Studies of the Circulatory System in Extreme Hunger," "Blood and Hunger," and "Eye Disturbances in Hunger." The papers have recently been translated into

French under the title, *Maladie de famine,* and published in Warsaw by the American Joint Distribution Committee. The book was sent to me a few weeks ago.

There is no mention of Hitler in the 262 pages of this work. The word "Nazi" does not appear. There is no discussion of politics, and no note of self-pity. The only reference to anything not strictly scientific is at the head of Dr. Apfelbaum's contribution: "I dedicate this work to the memory of my daughter Irene who died the death of a martyr." There is also a short editorial footnote on page eighty-four to the effect that the dermatologist of the project, Dr. Raszkies, was sent to Treblinka (an extermination center) where he died in the "cyclon chamber" in 1942. His paper apparently was lost.

The complete scientific detachment of the authors of these studies from their own fate, and from the infernal background and surroundings of their studies, is almost incredible. The content of their findings is amazingly copious in view of the great lack of research facilities. There are a few pictures of patients in the final stages of starvation, which give a clear impression of the miserable poverty of the hospitals. (And the accusing, hopeless, insane stare of the pitiful children will haunt all readers of the book.)

From the Actual Papers

Dr. A. Braude-Heller: "The mental changes and attitudes of the children are among the earliest symptoms of hunger: their apathy, which increases with the progress of starvation. The child loses his alertness, does not play, his movements grow slow. At the same time one observes changes of characters: the children become disagreeable and quarrelsome. They seem extremely sad. Their intellectual development seems to stop, sometimes they appear about insane. In the most advanced stage of the disease the children lie on their sides, bent, their legs folded. Such a sickroom full of children covered up to their necks, even in summer (because of their constant chilliness), is quite characteristic. They don't move, act very quiet, but they do not sleep, they suffer from insomnia. In advanced cases they can neither walk nor sit."

Dr. J. Stein: "The hunger in the Ghetto surpassed everything we have seen or heard on the subject." The official diet of 800 calories daily contained virtually no fat, very small amount of vegetable protein, and almost no vitamins. It was little but carbohydrate. The average weight of the adult patients who had lived on this diet was between 30 and 40 kilograms (from 70 to 90 pounds), 20 percent to 50 percent less than normal. The lowest weight observed was that of a thirty-year-old woman, 152 centimeters tall (about five feet) weighing 24 kilograms (about 64 pounds).

Dr. Apfelbaum: "The organism which is destroyed by prolonged hunger is like a candle which burns out: life disappears gradually without a visible shock to the naked eye. The hungry sufferer grows lazy. He is a miser who avariciously guards what is left to him—that is, his last physical reserves. His motions are calculated, his slowness, sometimes even the complete lack of motion for several days, are very characteristic; his tendency to remain in a lying position, the somnolence, the silence, the sluggishness of the reflexes, and the mental drowsiness: this is the customary picture of cachexia due to hunger.

"Our study has aimed at an understanding of the mechanism which regulates this economizing of energy. The results should throw some light on the pathology of hunger. The material that was at our disposal cannot be compared with any thus far known, because of its magnitude and duration, and the advanced degree of starvation."

The orderly scientific experiment of the Ghetto physicians, which proceeded through the first period—of starvation—was interrupted by the second period—of extermination. Their laboratories were smashed; their hospitals were burned; and, most important, the object of their study, man, was destroyed wholesale. Nonetheless, the work went on, as best it could. Up to the end there was a little group of physicians, gathered in a basement by the Ghetto cemetery, discussing, writing, editing, correlating their facts and their conclusions, until they themselves died of the symptoms they so accurately described, or were led away to slaughter, or perished in the fighting. They have given scientists a book which will be a rewarding source of information. Even more: they have left the world an abiding testament to human self-respect and dignity.

FOOTNOTES TO PART ONE

Asterisks indicate footnotes quoted from original source of case material.

1. Pitirim A. Sorokin, *Society, Culture and Personality* (New York: Harper & Brothers, 1947), p. 40.

2. C. E. Snow, "A Discussion of the Relation of Illumination Intensity to Productive Efficiency," *The Tech Engineering News,* November, 1927. Cited in F. J. Roethlisberger and William J. Dickson, *Management and the Worker* (Cambridge, Mass.: Harvard University Press, 1941), pp. 16–17.

*3. Roethlisberger and Dickson, *op. cit.,* p. 16.

*4. *Ibid.*

5. Adapted from Helen Keller, *The Story of My Life* (New York: Doubleday & Company, Inc., 1903), pp. 21, 22–24.

6. Ernst Cassirer, *An Essay on Man: An Introduction to a Philosophy of Culture* (New Haven, Conn.: Yale University Press, 1944), p. 25.

7. W. I. Thomas and Florian Znaniecki, *The Polish Peasant in Europe and America* (New York: Alfred A. Knopf, Inc., 1927), Vol. II, p. 1831.

8. From Kenneth McGill, "The Social Aspect of Classroom Teachers' Problems," unpublished manuscript. Cited in Willard Waller, *The Sociology of Teaching* (New York: John Wiley & Sons, Inc., 1932), pp. 300–301. Reprinted by permission of the publishers.

9. George H. Mead, *Mind, Self and Society* (Chicago: University of Chicago Press, 1934), p. 255.

10. In Part Three, additional attributes of group behavior will be discussed. We shall there indicate more explicitly the factors that make for a group as well as the various classifications of social groupings.

11. We wish to mention here that while sociology may be distinguished from social psychology and cultural anthropology, the three fields are so closely related that in this volume on sociology will include also

the basic principles in social psychology and social anthropology. All three fields may be said to be interested in the generic aspects of social relations. If their basic foci and axes of orientation are different, it may be said that sociology is primarily concerned with the social group, social anthropology with the products of human-social interaction—or culture—and social psychology with the influences of the group, culture, and other persons in shaping the personality of the individual, *i.e.,* in the socialization of the individual.

If social reality is conceived as a triangle, each corner of this triangle consisting of a basic aspect of this reality—the individual, the group, and culture—it should become clear that the study of any of these aspects, *ipso facto,* involves the other two. It is the

ing and serving as necessary elements in the analysis and understanding of the group.

As with the individual and the group, so with culture. Culture results from persons acting together (group) on a symbolic-meaningful plane. Culture also may be completely understood only in so far as it constitutes one corner of the triangular figure of social reality. Just as any part of a triangle depends for its existence on the other two, so it is that the *basic* nature of social reality is triborn and includes the individual, the group, and culture.

By *basic nature* we mean the elements (individual, group, and culture) that are always involved in social action and social relations. The basic elements may, of course, take on specific forms and characteristics.

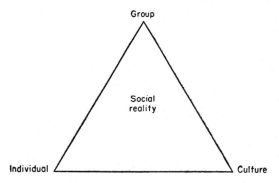

combined impact of culture and the group through which culture manifests itself that the individual develops into a symbolic being. His potential symbolic nature takes on values, attitudes, habits, interests, sentiments, ideas—in short, he becomes a person, a socialized individual; he possesses a personality. The study of personality formation and personality content are the primary frames of reference of social psychology.

In the same manner, fully to understand the nature of the group, it is necessary to understand the confluence of the vectors of individual and culture constantly coexist-

Different people with different personality traits, various group types, and diverse culture traits and patterns constitute the particular manifestations of social life and social reality. But as the eyeglass lens, by its very nature, involves both a convex and a concave lens, as coexistent phases, so with social reality. Social reality presupposes the concomitance of a threefold perspective.

12. Martin Gumpert, "The Physicians of Warsaw," *The American Scholar,* Vol. 18, No. 3 (1949), pp. 285-290. Permission granted by the United Chapters of Phi Beta Kappa.

PART TWO

Sociology of Personality

A. MAN IS NOT BORN A SOCIAL BEING: THE CASES OF ANNA AND ISABELLE

In order to become a social being, man must acquire those supraorganic characteristics of habits, beliefs, knowledge, attitudes, and sentiments which develop as a result of his associations with other persons who possess these attributes. Man is born a biological entity *capable* of developing a social-cultural nature. Unlike lower animals, he is born with the necessary biological base—large brain, complex nervous system, organic apparatus for language developments, high level of sense coordination—that potentially enables him to become socialized or culturalized. However, man's biological characteristics are no guarantee of his social and cultural attributes. They are necessary conditions, but they are not sufficient. Most of man's behavior which we regard as social comes from learning, from communication with other socialized beings, from contact with the social. It follows, therefore, that we can expect normal biological *homo sapiens* to lack humanness and sociality if peculiar circumstances in his environment cut him off from persons with human-social characteristics. The two cases that follow reveal how utterly limited and undeveloped are the personalities of the two girls due to their extreme isolation from social influences since birth. Their natures, other than their organic features, are almost nonhuman at the time of their discovery. Social natures call for social molding. Anna's case serves to show that isolation up to the age of six offered adequate reason for her unsocialized behavior. Even though she may have been feeble-minded at the start, her subsequent progress after she was removed by the authorities and placed in a more social environment would not have been possible if she had remained in isolation. In Isabelle's case, the failure to acquire any form of speech until the age of six was mainly responsible for her failure to acquire the cultural meanings of things. Language which is learned is, obviously, the chief medium for social experiences and the primary instrument in the acquisition of a cultural nature.

THE CASE OF ANNA [1]

According to the *New York Times* for February 6, 1938, a girl of more than five years had been found "tied to an old chair in a storage room on the second floor" of a farm home seventeen miles from a small Pennsylvania city. The child, said the report,

> was wedged into the chair, which was tilted backwards to rest on a coal bucket, her spindly arms tied above her head. She was unable to talk or move. . . . "The child was dressed in a dirty shirt and napkin," the officer said. "Her hands, arms, and legs were just bones, with skin drawn over them, so frail she couldn't use them. She never had enough nourishment. She never grew normally, and the chair on which she lay, half reclining and half sitting, was so small the child had to double her legs partly under her."

The reason for this situation was that the child, Anna,[2] was illegitimate. She was the second illegitimate child the mother had borne, and since the mother resided with her father and other relatives in the paternal household, she found her father so angry that he was averse even to seeing this second child. Hence she kept it in an out-of-the-way room.

Upon reading this report the writer and a student assistant, Richard G. Davis, went to see the child. Later, subsequent trips were made, and between visits reports from various persons connected with the child were received by mail. Our records seem reasonably complete and confirm the salient facts in the *Times* account.[3]

By the time we arrived on the scene, February 7, Anna had been in her new abode, the county home,[4] for only three days. But she was already beginning to change. When first brought to the county home she had been completely apathetic—had lain in a limp, supine position, immobile, expressionless, indifferent to everything. Her flaccid feet had fallen forward, making almost a straight line with the skeleton-like legs, indicating that the child had long lain on her back to the point of exhaustion and atrophy of her foot muscles. She was believed to be deaf and possibly blind. Her urine, according to the nurse, had been extremely concentrated and her stomach exceedingly bloated. It was thought that she had suffered at one time from rickets, though later medical opinion changed the diagnosis to simple malnutrition. Her blood count had been very low in haemoglobin. No sign of disease had been discovered.

Upon our arrival, three days after she was brought to the county home, most of these conditions still prevailed. But her stomach had retracted a little and she had become fairly active, being able to sit up (if placed in a sitting position) and to move her hands, arms, head, eyes, and mouth quite freely. These changes had resulted from a high vitamin diet, massage, and attention. In spite of her physical condition she had an attractive facial appearance, with no discernible stigmata. Her complexion, features, large blue eyes, and even teeth (in good shape though not quite normal in size) gave her a favorable appearance.

Since Anna turned her head slowly toward a loud-ticking clock held near her, we concluded that she could hear. Other attempts to make her notice sounds, such as clapping hands or speaking to her, elicited no response; yet when the door was opened suddenly she tended to look in that direction. Her feet were sensitive to touch. She exhibited the plantar, patellar, and pupillary reflexes. When sitting up she jounced rhythmically up and down on the bed—a recent habit of which she was very fond. Though her eyes surveyed the room, especially the ceiling, it was difficult to tell if she was looking at anything in particular. She neither smiled nor cried in our presence, and the only sound she made—a slight sucking intake of breath with the lips—occurred rarely. She did frown or scowl occasionally in response to no observable stimulus; otherwise she remained expressionless.

Next morning the child seemed more alert. She liked food and lay on her back to take it. She could not chew or drink from a cup but had to be fed from a bottle or spoon—this in spite of the fact that she could grasp and manipulate objects with her hands. Toward numerous toys given her by well-wishers all over the country she showed no reaction. They were simply objects to be handled in a distracted manner; there was no element of play. She liked having her hair combed. When physically restrained she exhibited considerable temper. She did not smile except when coaxed and did not cry.

She has thus made some progress during her three days in the county home. Subsequently her progress in the home was slower. But before dealing with her later history, let us first review more completely the background facts in the case.

Anna was born March 6, 1932, in a private nurse's home. Shortly thereafter she was taken to a children's home. For a time she was boarded with a practical nurse. To those who saw and cared for her, she seemed an entirely normal baby— indeed, a beautiful child, as more than one witness has asserted. At the age of six to ten months she was taken back to her mother's home because no outside agency wished the financial responsibility of caring for her. In her mother's home she was perpetually confined to one room, and here she soon began to suffer from malnutrition, living solely on a diet of milk and getting no sunshine. She developed impetigo. The doctor, according to the mother, prescribed some external medicine which made the child "look like a nigger" and which the mother ceased to use for that reason. The mother,[5] a large woman of twenty-seven, alleges that she tried to get the child welfare agency to take Anna, but that she was refused for financial reasons. The mother, resenting the trouble which Anna's presence caused her and wanting to get rid of the girl, paid little attention to her. She apparently did nothing but feed the child, not taking the trouble to bathe, train, supervise, or caress her. Though she denies tying the child at any time, it is perhaps true that the child was restrained in some way (by tying, confining in a crib, or other-wise) and gradually, as her physical condition became worse, due to confinement and poor diet, became so apathetic that she could be safely left unrestrained without danger of moving from her chair. Anna's brother, the first illegitimate child, seems to have ignored her except to mistreat her occasionally.

The bedroom in which Anna was confined was reported to have been extraordinarily dirty and contained a double bed on which the mother and son slept while Anna reclined in a broken chair. The mother carried up and fed to Anna huge quantities of milk. Toward Anna's fifth birthday the mother, apparently on advice, began feeding her thin oatmeal with a spoon, but Anna never learned to eat solid food.

Anna's social contacts with others were then at a minimum. What few she did have were of a perfunctory or openly antagonistic kind, allowing no opportunity for *Gemeinschaft* to develop. She affords therefore an excellent subject for studying the effects of extreme social isolation.

Ten days after our first visit Anna showed some improvement. She was more alert, had more ability to fix her attention, had more expression, handled herself better, looked healthier. Moreover, she had found her tongue—in a physical sense. Whereas it had formerly lain inactive back in her mouth, she now stuck it out frequently and with enjoyment. She showed taste discrimination, for she now resisted taking cod-liver oil, which she had previously not distinguished from milk. She was beginning, in fact, to dislike any new type of food. Visual discrimination was attested by the fact that she apparently preferred a green pencil to a yellow one. She smiled more often, regularly followed with her eye the movements of the two other small children temporarily quartered in her room, and handled her toys in a more definite fashion. She could sit up better and, while lying down, could raise her head from the pillow. She liked now to sit on the edge of the bed and dangle her feet. The doctor claimed that she had a new trick every day.

She had not, however, learned any way to seek attention, to manifest wants, to chew, or to control her elimination. Only one sociable stunt had she begun to learn—rubbing foreheads with the nurse, a sport of which she later became very fond. On the other hand, her ritualistic hand play, a noticeable trait at this time, was entirely asocial.[6]

On this second visit we took along a clinical psychologist, Edward Carr. He began by checking the reflexes, finding none that were defective. He then gave Anna a three-figure form board test used in the Form L Revision of the Stanford-Binet. Anna was unable to place the blocks in the appropriately shaped holes, though apparently by chance she did once place the round piece satisfactorily. She more readily removed the blocks from the board and played with them idly for a time. When Mr. Carr first attempted by pantomime to get her to place the blocks, she seemed to concentrate, but only momentarily; and this concentration, so limited in results, apparently tired her too greatly for further efforts.[7]

The next visit, on March 22, revealed little change, except for slight physical improvement. She could lift her hips from the bed; the nurse had induced her to laugh outright by tickling her and laughing uproariously herself; and the nurse believed that Anna recognized her. The doctor had changed his early optimistic opinion; he now believed the child was congenitally deficient.

After another month Anna was five pounds heavier, more energetic, given to laughing a good deal, and credited with having made a sound like "da." But that was all.

On June 9, another month later, she had scarcely improved in any respect. When tested by the writer according to the items of the Gesell schedule, she seemed to rank with a one-year-old or better in motor activities involving hands and eyes. But with regard to linguistic and purposive behavior, she lagged behind. If any estimate were made, it could be said that she definitely ranked below the one-year-old child.

By August 12 she was still improving physically. Her legs had calves in them, and she liked to exhibit her strength in roughhousing. She would laugh heartily, often make a "tsha-tsha-tsha" sound with her lips, once or twice making a verbal type of sound, though meaningless. When held by someone, she could "walk" by putting one foot in front of the other in ostentatious steps. Her interest in other persons had become more obvious, her responses more definite and discriminating.[8]

Until removed from the county home on November 11, there were few additional changes. By this time she could barely stand while holding to something. When put on a carpet she could scoot but not crawl. She visibly liked people, as manifested by smiling, roughhousing, and hair-pulling. But she was still an unsocialized individual, for she had learned practically nothing.

If we ask why she had learned so little—not even to chew or drink from a glass—in nine months, the answer probably lies in the long previous isolation and in the conditions at the county home. At the latter institution she was early deprived of her two little inmates and was left alone. In the entire establishment there was only one nurse, who had three hundred and twenty-four other inmates to look after. Most of Anna's care was turned over to adult inmates, many of whom were mentally deficient and scarcely able to speak themselves. Part of the time Anna's door was shut. In addition to this continued isolation, Anna was given no stimulus to learning. She was fed, clothed, and cleaned without having to turn a hand in her own behalf. She was never disciplined or rewarded, because nobody had the time for the tedious task. All benefits were for her in the nature of things and therefore not rewards. Thus she remained in much the same animal-like stage, except that she did not have the animal's inherently organized structure, and hence remained in a more passive, inadequate state.

On our visit of December 6 a surprise awaited us, for Anna had undergone what was for her a remarkable transformation—she had begun to learn. Not that she could speak, but she could do several things formerly considered impossible. She could descend the stairs (by sitting successively on each one), could hold a doughnut in her hand and eat it (munching like a normal child), could grasp a glass of tomato juice and drink it by herself, could take a step or two while holding to something, and could feed herself with a spoon. These accomplishments, small indeed for a child of seven, represented a transformation explainable, no doubt, by her transference from the county home to a private family where she was the sole object of one woman's assiduous care.

Anna had been in the foster-home less than a month, but the results were plain to see. Her new guardian was using the same common-sense methods by which mothers from time immemorial have socialized their infants—unremitting attention, repetitive correction, and countless small rewards and punishments, mixed always with sympathetic interest and hovering physical presence. These Anna was getting for the first time in her life.

One thing seemed noticeable. Anna was more like a one-year-old baby than she had been before. She was responsive in the untutored, random, energetic way of a baby. When one beckoned and called her, she would make an effort to come, smiling and going through excited extra motions.

A month later more improvement along the same lines was noted. Though grave limitations remained, Anna was definitely becoming more of a human being.

Still later, on March 19, 1939, her accomplishments were the following: she was able to walk alone for a few steps without falling; she was responsive to the verbal commands of her foster-mother, seeming to understand in a vague sort of way what the latter wanted her to do; she definitely recognized the social worker who took her weekly to the doctor and who therefore symbolized to her the pleasure of an automobile ride; she expressed by anxious bodily movements her desire to go out for a ride; she seemed unmistakably to seek and to like attention, though she did not sulk when left alone; she was able to push a doll carriage in front of her and to show some skill in manipulating it. She was, furthermore, much improved physically, being almost fat, with chubby arms and legs and having more energy and alertness. On the visit prior to this one she had shown that she could quickly find and eat candy which she saw placed behind a pillow, could perform a knee-bending exercise, could use ordinary utensils in eating (e.g., could convey liquid to her mouth in a spoon), could manifest a sense of neatness (by putting bread back on a plate after taking a bite from it). Limitations still remaining, however, were as follows: she said nothing—could not even be taught to say "bye-bye"; she had to be watched to tell when elimination was imminent; she hardly played when alone; she had little curiosity, little initiative; it seemed still impossible to establish any communicative contact with her.

On August 30, 1939, Anna was taken from the foster-home and moved to a small school for defective children. Observations made at this time showed her to have become a fat girl twenty pounds overweight for her age. Yet she could walk better and could almost run. Her toilet habits showed that she understood the whole procedure. She manifested an obvious comprehension of many verbal instructions, though she could not speak.

In a report of an examination made November 6 of the same year, the head of the institution pictured the child as follows:

Anna walks about aimlessly, makes periodic rhythmic motions of her hands, and, at intervals, makes guttural and sucking sounds. She regards her hands, as if she had seen them for the first time. It was impossible to hold her attention for more than a few seconds at a time—not because of distraction due to external stimuli but because of her inability to concentrate. She ignored the task in hand to gaze vacantly about the room. Speech is entirely lacking. Numerous unsuccessful attempts have been made with her in the hope of developing initial sounds. I do not believe that this failure is due to negativism or deafness but that she is not sufficiently developed to accept speech at this time. . . . The prognosis is not favorable. . . .

More than five months later, on April 25, 1940, a clinical psychologist, the late Professor Francis N. Maxfield, examined Anna and reported the following: large for her age; hearing entirely normal; vision apparently normal; able to climb stairs; speech in the "babbling stage" and "promise for developing intelligible speech later seems to be good." He said further that "on the Merrill-Palmer scale she made a mental score of 19 months. On the Vineland social maturity scale she made a score of 23 months." [9]

Professor Maxfield very sensibly pointed out that prognosis is difficult in such cases of isolation. "It is very difficult to take scores on tests standardized under average condition of environment and experience," he wrote, "and interpret them in a case where environment and experience have been so unusual." With this warning he gave it as his opinion at that time that Anna would eventually "attain an adult mental level of six or seven years." [10]

The school for retarded children, on July 1, 1941, reported that Anna had reached 46 inches in height and weighed 60 pounds. She could bounce and catch a ball and was said to conform to group socialization, though as a follower rather than a leader. Toilet habits were firmly established. Food habits were normal, except that she still used a spoon as her sole implement. She could dress herself except for fastening her clothes. Most remarkable of all, she had finally begun to develop speech. She was characterized as being at about the two-year level in this regard. She could call attendants by name and bring in one when she was asked to. She had a few complete sentences to express her wants. The report concluded that there was nothing peculiar about her, except that she was feeble-minded—"probably congenital in type." [11]

A final report from the school, made on June 22, 1942, and evidently the last report before the girl's death, pictured only a slight advance over that given above. It said that Anna could follow directions, string beads, identify a few colors, build with blocks, and differentiate between attractive and unattractive pictures. She had a good sense of rhythm and loved a doll. She talked mainly in phrases but would repeat words and try to carry on a conversation. She was clean about clothing. She habitually washed her hands and brushed her teeth. She would try to help other children. She walked well and could run fairly well, though clumsily. Although easily excited, she had a pleasant disposition.

THE CASE OF ISABELLE [12]

Born apparently one month later than Anna, the girl in question, who has been given the pseudonym Isabelle, was discovered in November, 1938, nine months after the discovery of Anna. At the time she was found she was approximately six and a half years of age. Like Anna, she was an illegitimate child and had been kept in seclusion for that reason. Her mother was a deaf-mute, having become so at the age of two, and it appears that she and Isabelle had spent most of their time together in a dark room shut off from the rest of the mother's family. As a result Isabelle had no chance to develop speech; when she communicated with her mother, it was by means of gestures. Lack of sunshine and inadequacy of diet had caused Isabelle to become rachitic. Her legs in particular were affected; they "were so bowed that as she stood erect, the soles of her shoes came nearly flat together, and she got about with a skittering gait." Her behavior toward strangers, especially men, was almost that of a wild animal, manifesting much fear and hostility. In lieu of speech she made only a strange croaking sound. In many ways she acted like an infant. "She was apparently utterly unaware of relationships of any kind. When presented with a ball for the first time, she held it in the palm of her hand, then reached out and stroked my face with it. Such behavior is comparable to that of a child of six months." [13] At first it was even hard to tell whether or not she could hear, so unused were her senses. Many of her actions resembled those of deaf children.

It is small wonder that, once it was established that she could hear, specialists working with her believed her to be feebleminded. Even on nonverbal tests her performance was so low as to promise little for the future. Her first score on the Stanford-Binet was 19 months, practically at the zero point of the scale. On the Vineland social maturity scale her first score was 39, representing the age level of two and a half years! [14] "The general impression was that she was wholly uneducatable and that any attempt to teach her to speak, after so long a period of silence, would meet with failure." [15]

In spite of this interpretation, the individuals in charge of Isabelle launched a systematic and skillful program of training. It seemed hopeless at first. The approach had to be through pantomime and dramatization, suitable to an infant. It required one week of intensive effort before she even made her first attempt at vocalization. Gradually she began to respond, however, and, after the first hurdles had at last been overcome, a curious thing happened. She went through the usual stages of learning characteristics of the years from one to six not only in proper succession but far more rapidly than normal. In a little over two months after her first vocalization she was putting sentences together. Nine months after that she could identify words and sentences on the printed page, could write well, could add to ten, and could retell a story after hearing it. Seven months beyond this point she had a vocabulary of 1,500–2,000 words and was asking complicated questions. Starting from an educational level of between one and three years (depending on what aspect one considers), she had reached a normal level by the time she was eight and a half years old. In short, she covered in two years the stages of learning that ordinarily require six.[16] Or, to put it another way, her I.Q. trebled in a year and a half.[17] The speed with which she reached the normal level of mental development seems analogous to the recovery of body weight in a growing child after an illness, the recovery being achieved by an extra fast rate of growth for a period after the illness until normal weight for the given age is again attained.

When the writer saw Isabelle a year and a half after her discovery, she gave him the impression of being a very bright, cheerful, energetic little girl. She spoke well, walked and ran without trouble, and sang with gusto and accuracy. Today she is over fourteen years old and has passed the sixth grade in a public school. Her teachers say that she participates in all school activities as normally as other children. Though older than her classmates, she has fortunately not physically matured too far beyond their level.[18]

B. THE FAMILY AS PRIMARY IN SHAPING BASIC PERSONALITY TRAITS: THE CASE OF FIVE GENERATIONS OF BEGGARS

We have said in the beginning of this section that man is born with the biological apparatus which potentially enables him to acquire a social-cultural nature or personality. Through his contacts with socialized individuals the child acquires numerous interests, wishes, attitudes, habits, beliefs, and feelings about people, objects, and ideas. While it is true that no two personalities are identical and that each individual has a unique organization of traits, many aspects of personality are shared with others and are similar to those of others in the same social environment. In both instances, uniqueness or similarity, the process of personality formation involves association with social influences.[19]

No influence is initially as great, however, as the primary group on the individual. By the primary group is meant that system of association which is intimate and face to face. The primary-group concept was introduced by Charles Cooley. For him this group was primary in shaping the basic personality traits of individuals. He conceived of the primary group as the simplest, the first, the most universal of all forms of association. He saw it as the core of all social organization, remaining in some form even in the most complex systems. It is this group, especially in the form of the family, which passes on the traditions of a society, and it is in this group—in its comrade and playmate aspects— that the first movements of social impulse are felt. Cooley elaborates this idea further when he says: [20]

> By primary groups, I mean those characterized by intimate, face-to-face association and cooperation. They are primary in several senses, but chiefly in that they are fundamental in forming the social nature and ideals of the individual. . . . The most important spheres of this intimate association and cooperation—though by no means the only ones—are the family, the play-group, and the neighborhood or community group of elders. These are practically universal, belonging to all times and all stages of development; and are accordingly a chief basis of what is universal in human nature and human ideals.

Sociologists have reached a rather wide consensus on the influence and role of the primary group in personality formation. We will mention two of these influences here:

1. The primary group is responsible for the universals of personality. That is, the sentiments of love and of hero worship and the feelings of social right and wrong and of sympathy find their expressions among urban Americans, American Indians, Australian Arunta, and the Siberian Chuckchee. Anthropologists in their studies of many societies are often struck by the similarities in feelings of people in isolated areas with those of our own societies. These are the personality universals found among all races, all classes, and all societies. It is human nature in contradistinction to cultural nature—or that which varies with race, class, and a particular society. To repeat, it is this universal nature that is ascribed to the influence of the primary group—the family, the neighborhood, the child's play group. Deep sympathies spring from deep involvements; human understanding from human sentiments.

2. The primary group, especially the family, is responsible for the formation of the child's basic personality traits derived from the standards and values peculiar to the family. By this is meant those traits that are handed down through family tradition and family customs within the home, from generation to generation. For the most part, family traditions are similar among most families in a given culture or subculture. But each family has its own memories, ceremonies, or parent-child relations that are unique. Family tradition frequently operates in

the development of continuity between the occupations of the father and his sons. If a child grows up as a member of a poor Negro family or an urban beggar family, there is considerable cultural pressure brought to bear on him to play the *same role* in society as his father's. Many of the similarities between children and their parents may be due to this carrying forward of specific roles in society. The following is a case study of five generations of a begging family living in a Southern city of about 160,000. After the begging practice initially brought on by dire economic circumstances was engaged in by the first generation, subsequent generations found it rather easy to adopt the begging practice themselves. This was possible because they were reared within the family pattern of beggar status. Begging became feasible and justifiable in their own eyes, while in the eyes of the community begging was expected of those in their particular "social position" or "status." [21]

Some sixty years ago a young man, Thomas Jed, in his early twenties took up residence in a small southern town of three or four thousand population. The fragmentary information available indicates that he came from an adjoining state, though little is actually known of his past. He was at that time a heavy drinker. So far as we are able to learn, he had no communication with any of his relatives, excepting one brother, after he reached this town. This brother lived in one of the prairie states to the southwest, and apparently was comfortably situated. He, in later years, sent Thomas considerable money, and at one time offered to remove Thomas and his family to the prairie section and help him get established, but this offer was rejected.

Shortly after Thomas took up residence in this town he married into a family, with a large kinship connection in the locality, who were, and still are, of low economic and social status in the community. The men worked at menial occupations and had small incomes. However, these families have always had an exceptional reputation for thrift and for economic responsibility. Their credit even today is accepted without question by the merchants of the town, and it is an unheard of thing for any member to have been dependent on a public agency. A strong familism seems to have prevailed which made of it a sort of self-aid group. All unfortunate members seem to have been provided for out of the family coffers, and loans of one member to another for small economic enterprises have been rather common. In this respect the family seems to have fulfilled almost ideally the family responsibilities imposed by the mores of the Old South.

The family created by Thomas' marriage became a problem almost immediately. Births occurred in rapid succession. In all, eight children were born, two of whom died in childhood. From almost the beginning the family was dependent. Thomas, because of his drinking, was never able to provide the income necessary to care for the needs of his family. But Mrs. Jed's relatives rose to the occasion and supplied the deficit, so that the family was not dependent on public agencies. Thomas was not able to hold paying jobs and soon confined his productive activities to running a small fish market. As a matter of fact his place of business hardly could be designated by the term "market" for it consisted only of a few barrels set out by the sidewalk, and his patronage was principally among the Negroes.

His drinking habit seems to have been chronic, and as a result the economic condition of his family grew worse rather than better. Each additional child brought greater expense without any additional income. This increased burden fell on Mrs. Jed's relatives, and it is to their credit that they practically supported the family for more than twenty years.

In the home Thomas seems to have had the patriarchal ideal of being lord of all he surveyed, but he seemed much more interested in protecting his rights than he did in exercising them. He resented the interference of his wife and his wife's relatives in the way he reared his children, but he exerted no great effort to rear them himself. Consequently they grew up with a minimum of training. They attended school only in so far as the law required, and none of them completed the elementary grades. Likewise in the matter of occupational training, the children were never forced to work and never had to contribute to the family income. In the words of Mrs. Jed's nephew, "In spite of the protests of Mrs. Jed and the relatives, Thomas never taught the boys to work."

All of the children married in their early adult years. One of the girls married a local man and seems to have succeeded very well for a few years. The two boys and one of the girls moved soon after their marriage to a city of about 100,000 located some fifty miles from the town in which they were reared and were followed shortly by Thomas and Mrs. Jed. The remaining two girls moved with their husbands to other sections of the South. Within a few years, however, all of the girls had acquired children, had lost their husbands through death or through desertion, and finally, finding themselves widows with children to care for, joined their parents and brothers in the city.

Thus, the course of a few years finds the whole immediate kinship group transferred from a small town to a city. It consisted at this time of an aged couple who had always been economically incompetent, of four widows with a total of thirteen children, and of two younger men with families. One of these men had a large and increasing family, and the other had acquired his father's drinking habit, so that he was scarcely able to support himself and his wife even when he tried.

The whole kinship group, of course, almost immediately fell into dependency, but they no longer received aid from Mrs. Jed's relatives. They now became charges of the public. The old family pattern, however, carried over, and the family solidarity held fast, so that in the new situation the members comprised a compact social group. As Mrs. Jed's family had comprised a co-operating group in maintaining independence, the new group carried on co-operating activities in dependency. Any aid received by one family was readily shared with others who might not have been so "fortunate." This, of course, brought them into ill repute with social agencies. Case workers found that they could not treat any family in the connection as a unit, and to reconstruct the whole group was a task of such magnitude as to stagger the most optimistic worker. As a result, the family became a "bug-a-boo" for family agencies. It became known as "A bunch of worthless beggars that nothing could remedy."

Membership in the family became as definitely a stigma among social agencies as certain racial marks are among some social groups. The members, thus, soon found it impossible to secure aid from social agencies and were forced to resort to other means. They applied to churches and to other social organizations and received considerable aid. Some members tried going back to the town of their birth, but found that they were welcomed no longer by their more distant relatives and that their lot was no better than in the city. At various times members tried moving to other cities, but, since they seem never to have used aliases, their identity was quickly disclosed. Sooner or later, therefore, all have returned.

All of this conflict with social agencies tended only to increase the social distance between the family and society which to the family the agencies represented. Accompanied by the familism which already existed, the opposition developed very strong in-group feelings between the members and strong out-group feelings toward society, especially social agencies.

Blocked from securing help from social agencies, the members showed considerable aptitude for securing aid from other sources. Begging was resorted to by many of the members. Thomas Jed became an ordinary street beggar and Mrs. Jed became a house-to-house beggar. One of the widows developed into probably the most successful residence beggar in the city. Another member became an habitual church beggar. Other members have secured aid from agencies when they could, received help from churches frequently, and have begged when necessary.

In their begging activities, the adult members of the family have made liberal use of the children. Children have been taken by their parents or have been sent alone to solicit aid from agencies and from churches. They have been sent out occasionally on the street to beg alone. And almost invariably the adult doing residence begging has carried one or more children along as a sample of the "half dozen sick children at home." One of the widows, who does residence begging, carried her youngest daughter, an anemic-looking child, along on these begging expeditions until this daughter was married at the age of nineteen. Since then she has been making use of her grand-children.

As the children have reached adulthood and have gotten married their families have become constant or occasional public charges. The living members of the kinship group consist of the second, third, fourth, and fifth generations, the original Thomas and Mrs. Jed having died several years ago. A number of the third generation have families, and a few of the fourth generation have married in their teens and have young children. And for every marriage, with the exception of two, there is a case record on file in some relief agency in the city in which they live. The two marriages to which exception is made are those of two women of the third generation who were taken from their mother when they were very young and were reared in an institution. In so far as the author has been able to learn, the families of these two women have a clear record both as regards to delinquency and dependency. From the standpoint of relief agencies, the descendants of Thomas and Mrs. Jed represent at the present time an annual case load of approximately fifty individuals. The records of these agencies, however, only represent a small part of the total aid secured by this family. Individuals, churches, and civic organizations have been importuned as persistently as have the relief agencies, and perhaps with greater success.

C. CULTURE PATTERN AND BASIC PERSONALITY STRUCTURE: THE CASE OF THE KASKA INDIANS

In the last section we mentioned two influences of the primary group on personality formation: personality universals and basic personality traits lodged for relatively lengthy periods among previous family members. In recent decades, anthropologists have devoted considerable attention to the relationships existing between culture and personality. Edward Sapir, Margaret Mead (*From the South Seas*), and Ruth Benedict (*Patterns of Culture*) gave recognition to the fact that personality and cultural institutions were always found in some persistent relationship. Abram Kardiner, following Sapir, Mead, and Benedict, sought to establish the fact that there were different basic personality types in different societies. By analyzing intensively three primitive cultures— the Tanala, the Comanche, and the Marquesan—he came to the conclusion that primary institutions surrounding food, sex, and early training disciplines were responsible for furnishing the child, through the primary group, with his basic personality structure. This basic personality structure, in turn, becomes the progenitor of the secondary institutions governing religious, recreational, and aesthetic behavior.[22] For example, Kardiner writes that the Comanche were a people with great individual initiative.

> Enterprise, courage, and initiative were attributes needed in the individual to perpetuate the society. It was a society in which the young and able-bodied male bore all the burdens. . . . Perforce, the society was a democracy in which status must be constantly validated. The discipline to which the individual must conform in childhood could not therefore be of a kind that would impede development and growth, especially along those lines most valuable to the society. Accordingly we find that no impediments were placed in

the path of development; the self-esteem, courage and enterprise of the individual were fostered by every possible device, and the qualifications he had to meet in later life were consistent with constellations created in childhood. It is therefore not surprising to find that in their religion the Comanche had no concept of sin and no complicated ritual for reinstatement in the good graces of the deity. A Comanche who wanted "power" simply asked for it, or demonstrated his fortitude. In other words, the practical religion was merely a replica of those conventions which guaranteed the fullest cooperation between the males and their common enterprise.[23]

Another anthropologist, Cora DuBois,[24] tested Kardiner's basic personality hypothesis in studying the Melanesian Alorese in great detail, employing all the newest techniques in anthropological survey and psychological projective testing. Among the Alorese, women bore the brunt of the vegetable-food economy. This meant that children had maternal care only for the brief period in the morning before the mother left for the fields and for a short time after her return. Children were left, therefore, to the care of older siblings, relatives, or other persons and had little help in building feelings of security. Feelings of tension and anxiety were persistent and parents were not looked upon as a support in times of trial and trouble. Interestingly enough, the God concept among these people was of a rather amorphous being; religious rites appeared to be performed perfunctorily and only in time of acute crises. Interpersonal relations in this society were filled with quarrels, distrust, and anxiety. These two situations should serve to illustrate the relationship between economic techniques and parental attitudes toward children which have a marked effect on the child's basic personality structure. This, in turn, shapes the nature of secondary institutions such as religion, recreation, and so on. Obviously the relationship is much more easily established in simple societies than it is in Western, urban, complex ones. Western society is not made up of a simple homogeneous culture. It is a conglomeration of cultures, and thus it is much more difficult to discern the relationship.

In the following case study [25] of a simple society—Kaska Indians—an attempt is made to account for the shaping of basic personality structure through the parent-child relationship, that is, through the primary group and its institutions. Here the parents, particularly the mother, withdraw themselves from emotional interaction with the two- and three-year-olds. The parental attitude seems to be affectionate but passive, with no strong emotional tie. This seems to create a child who also holds himself aloof and ultimately becomes uncommunicative and introverted.

There is another strong cultural trend which affects the personality growth of the individual. There is little discipline in this society, and hence strong feelings of individualism.

The Kaska Indians today inhabit the northern area of British Columbia and South Yukon Territory from the Continental Divide on the west to the Rocky Mountains on the east. Climatically this area is in the polar continental zone of extremely cold winters and warm, even hot, summer days. Biotically it is in the forest belt of spruce, jackpine and poplar, a region hospitable to moose, bear, caribou and a number of smaller, fur-bearing animals.

Lower Post, the trading post for this region, is located at the confluence of the Dease and Liard Rivers, about 150 miles below the headwaters of the Liard. The settlement extends from the Liard River to the Alaska Highway, a distance of about a quarter of a mile, and is about a mile long. Three stores are the nucleus of the town, the merchant personnel, the policeman and the game warden constituting the permanent residents of the community. During the summer months, when the Indian families and white trappers return from the bush, the population swells to about 200 persons. Most of the Indians are Kaska. From about May to September the Indians remain in Lower Post. They trade their furs and then relax after the strain of the rigorous winter life. Before they leave they also stock up for the new trapping season, which begins in November after the first heavy snowfalls.

The data presented below were collected during a three months' stay in Lower Post, from June to September, 1944, and a six months' stay in 1945. June to August was spent in Lower Post, September to December at a winter settlement of Kaska Indians on the Upper Liard River. Rapport was such that at the trading post I exchanged visits with eight Indian women who had children, and in addition could observe the activities of other children and parents as they loitered around the trading stores. The presence of my own two children undoubtedly aided in establishing rapport. In the bush we were completely accepted as participant members of the small community and were fitted into the matrilocal set-up by being assigned appropriate native kinship terms. In spite of these advantages, however, it was not easy to obtain specific information by verbal communication. For one thing most of the culture patterns are highly unformalized, so that a mother could not say what general procedures people followed with relation to children. Also, although most of the Indians speak a simple English, they are extremely introverted and taciturn so that spontaneous discussions were limited. The most frequent Indian contribution to a conversation was "Yes" or "No." Most of my information, therefore, was gained through participant observation.

The hunting-trapping-trading economy of the Kaska Indians necessitates a long winter stay in the busy season. Late in July families begin to pull out of Lower Post for their trapping areas. By the middle of September the last stragglers have rolled up their tents and are busy transporting their winter outfit to their trap lines. Trap lines are owned by individuals, usually the man, but occasionally by an unattached woman. Until spring a single family or a matrilocal group of three or four families lives in isolation in its winter cabins with only a rare visitor. Winters are long, dark, and intensely cold. By October the rivers begin to freeze, not to run again until March. Winter temperatures average about 35 degrees below zero, Fahrenheit, occasionally dropping to 60 or 70 below. Daylight is at a premium during winter; in December there are days of almost 20 hours of darkness. This is balanced in June and early July when it is light about 24 hours a day. On the trap line a woman may frequently remain home alone for days with her young children and daughters while her husband, sons and sons-in-law are visiting and setting traps. All Indian women interviewed said they liked the winter life with its work and isolation. The cabin there in the bush is referred to as "home." But by winter's end the people are again eagerly looking forward to their summer's visit to the post, with its opportunities for sociability.

The atomic nature of the Indian community in Lower Post is quickly perceived. No attempt is made to set up a planned community. Each family pitches its tent where it pleases, usually at a spot near the river bank having sufficient trees and brush around to insure privacy from other dwellings. Occasionally, related families will set up adjacent tents.

Sociability takes the form of groups of men, women and children loitering in front of trading posts, exchanging visits, drinking and dancing together, participating in gambling games. Dances, gambling, and drinking parties are eagerly anticipated and almost every night during midsummer one or another of these activities will take place. Nevertheless, unless stimulated by alcohol, social interaction is rarely intense. At a dance it may take an hour or even two before the ten or fifteen participants are sufficiently at ease with one another to venture onto the dance floor. There is somewhat more spontaneous interaction between adolescents, particularly of the same sex. Intra-sexual chasing, tickling, hugging, wrestling is readily provoked and greatly enjoyed. Similar intersexual "horsing around" is more inhibited and usually initiated after dark, or after the ice between the sexes has already been broken by a dance or a few drinks.

The individualistic manner in which the Kaska participate in group activities can be illustrated in the following situations: Arrangements for a dance are made without prior planning and in a completely informal manner. On the spur of the moment someone will say, "Ask Pete to play fiddle tonight?" Word will get around that Pete is being asked "to make dance." At about midnight folks begin to drift toward an empty cabin usually used for dancing. Should Pete not feel like playing that night, the group disperses. Pete is under no compulsion to cooperate, although he usually does. In the same way anyone may leave the dance on impulse without any apparent thought as to how his absence will affect the party. Alcoholic beverages are prepared by individuals, on rare occasions by two individuals, who then invite a few friends to share them. This is in sharp contrast to the practice of the whites at Lower Post who cooperate in making brews, five or six individuals contributing supplies, money and services toward making liquor which may later be shared among ten persons.

Sanctions in this loosely knit Indian community are rarely severe. Although there is a nominal chief appointed by the Canadian government he exercises no authority whatsoever. Criticism is the strongest sanction. No matter how much a man's behavior may be disapproved of, barring actual endangering of the life of others, he will be accepted, respected and supported by his kin and friends, although they may tell him he is doing a bad thing, scold him and urge him to mend his ways in the case of severe misconduct, or simply gossip about his faults. This was graphically illustrated with relation to sexual misbehavior. Promiscuity of the girls with visiting soldiers was severely disapproved of by the older people. Nevertheless the girls were not ostracized nor were they disrespected as individuals. They were lectured by one of the old men, criticized and gossiped about, but no one denied them friendship or hospitality. In general people prefer to avoid the resentment of others by minding their own business.

Rorschach tests interpreted for 28 Indians confirm the picture of introversion and emotional aloofness observable in much of Kaska behavior.[26]

Children are wanted and welcomed by their parents. The actual birth is dealt with casually, no ceremonies marking the occasion. Some mothers are up and active in a week, some take it easy for about a month. The baby is wrapped in a velvet, embroidered "moss bag," now frequently modernized with the substitution of flannel for moss. The infant's legs are firmly bound, but its hands are usually free. I observed no restriction on thumb sucking. The baby is comforted whenever it cries, fed whenever it appears hungry. Babies are breast fed although some take a supplementary bottle. (It is not at all unusual to see a discarded whiskey bottle or a cologne bottle used for this purpose.) The mother takes the baby with her wherever she goes, packing it in its moss bag. Around the camp the child is held in arms; on the trail it is packed on its mother's back, its face toward the mother. A baby rests contentedly on its mother's back and can sleep comfortably with its head nestled on her neck. An older baby has its legs free, but continues to be packed around by its mother or father until it can walk. It appears that the child's initial experiences in life are such as to foster a sense of security. Since the people are undemonstrative and emotionally aloof, however, there is not much open demonstration of affection.

Weaning usually occurs between one and three years of age and is a gradual process. The child is urged to stop suckling by being talked to and scolded. A persistent child, however, will be allowed to the breast till he stops the habit of his own accord. An older child goes to his mother's breast, undoes her dress and helps himself whenever he wants to.

Training for elimination control occurs at about two years and is not severe.

The mother takes the child with her into the bush to indicate to him the expected behavior. Conformity is expected to come from the child. As one mother put it, "I never say anything. He learn himself." Young boys from about a year and a half to about two years have a large hole slit in their pants for ease in self-training. Others wear no pants at all during this period. By three years most children go alone into the bush around the camp to eliminate in privacy. A child who persistently soils beyond this age is criticized and scolded.

A more severe attitude is taken with regard to masturbation. Such activity is discouraged with threats of insanity. It is important to note, however, that parents sincerely believe insanity to be a possible consequence of masturbation.

A child walks and talks when he is developmentally motivated to do so. He receives no pressure from others. The taciturnity of the parents offers little stimulation for a child to express himself verbally. My own young son was always a source of amusement to the little Indian children because of his constant stream of chatter.

When a child can walk he is left more and more to himself, a process of emotional weaning taking place. He fulfills his activities with little parental supervision. If he hurts himself he must go to his mother or father for comfort. Only in situations of immediate danger—if a child walks too close to the cut-bank above the river, or approaches too near the fire—will a parent interrupt the child's activity. The laissez faire attitudes of parents in many cases is not an active rejection of the child; "passive acceptance" would probably better describe the relationship. This is particularly so for the child living with both his true parents. The child living with but one true parent and a step-parent is more isolated emotionally since a step-parent usually considers his spouse's child by a former marriage to be out of his jurisdiction. One seven-year-old orphaned child presented a picture of very severe isolation. The boy exhibited attachment to no one, not even to his grandfather with whom he lived. He roamed around alone, usually failed to respond to his grandfather's requests, and frequently prepared his own meals from cans. When his grandfather nagged him to go to the summer missionary school he simply "disappeared," sleeping on a white trapper's porch and eating whatever left-over food he could find at our camp. Food was one of the few things this boy responded to with enthusiasm. About 10 percent of the children live with at least one step-parent. Often a two-year-old can be seen walking alone, playing or crying out of sight and hearing of his parents. For example, I twice had to remove two-year-olds from the road to permit trucks to pass, the parents of the children being nowhere in sight. One two-year-old was sitting in the road howling while his parents were shopping in the trading store. Finally someone picked him up and brought him to his mother who then held him and patted him while she continued making her purchases. It is generally the case that if the crying child is brought to his mother, or if he goes to her, he will be picked up and quieted. A petulant child, hanging around his mother's skirts, is absently indulged so long as he hangs around.

Rather than directly refuse a child anything, the parent will use sly tricks to distract a child from an object. For example, a two-year-old wanted some of his mother's chewing gum. In her pocket the mother slipped the gum out of its wrapper and showed the child the empty wrapper, saying she had no gum left. Later when she wanted the gum for herself she pointed out an airplane to the boy and, as he looked up, popped the gum into her mouth. Being caught in a lie by the child did not appear to disturb this parent. Such experiences reenforced the child's loss of faith in his parents.

The only temper tantrums that were observed occurred in children eighteen to twenty-four months of age. The child was either ignored or picked up and removed from the frustrating situation. That these temper tantrums may be an expression of resentment against the early emotional weaning is suggested by the fact that the ages of the two phenomena coincide.

It seems likely that being thrown on his own at so early an age involves a serious threat to the child's sense of security. Psychologists have pointed out for children in our own society that a very frequent reaction to lack and loss of love is a withdrawal from affectional relationships.[27] The early emotional weaning experienced by the Kaska child may well be an etiological factor in the emotional isolation and introversion exhibited by these Indians. The childhood situation appears to offer some compensations to the child. Warm sibling ties develop; for sisters particularly, this warm tie is retained all through life. The child is also given ample opportunity to develop self-sufficiency and to acquire a sense of independence. These are qualities which permit at least conscious adjustment to a sense of aloneness.[28]

A low energy level prevails among children, manifested in little gross motor activity. This is undoubtedly related to poor nutrition. A good deal of the time young children sit quietly close to their parents, who discourage too great boisterousness. Children who run about constantly, shout and are more aggressive toward their playmates are thought of as too wild.

Playgroups are small, consisting of close-aged siblings or relatives. The structure of these groups is atomic. There is little cooperative play and even this is at a low level of organization. For example, a child may throw a toy boat to which a rope is attached into the river and another child will pull it in, entirely spontaneously and with no pre-discussion of roles. When the second boy tires of pulling it in, the first does his own pulling without comment. Cooperation is accepted but not expected. There is no formalized or organized group play. Predominantly there is parallel play. As an example take two or three boys, each sailing his own boat in the river with little reference to each other, outside of occasional comments or exclamations. A new child joining the group adds his presence and activity but leaves the structure of the group undisturbed. A child motivated to leave simply walks off without disturbing the activities of the others. Nevertheless children usually play in groups of twos and threes, apparently finding gratification and stimulation in the mere presence and exclamation of fellow mates.

From the foregoing it can be seen that the qualities of emotional aloofness and individualism also manifest themselves in the play relationships among children. Group interaction in play is weak and the *child maintains his identity* in group activity.

Sibling relationships are good. As stated above, close-aged siblings invariably play together. Indeed, being isolated in the bush for nine long winter months they are likely to see few children other than siblings and maternal parallel cousins until they return to the post. Physical aggression among children is infrequent. Culture values are strongly oriented against aggression. An older child being beaten by his younger sibling smiles as he disengages himself from the onslaught. Should he fight back his parent will scold, "That's your brother. Don't hit your brother." Children may tease one another, for example by taking away another's pet toy.

Without strong positive pressure from adults and without formal education the young child readily learns cultural activities. A little two-year-old can occasionally be seen fetching water from the river in a small pot. The child's voluntary contributions to camp chores are accepted. Children are permitted to use sharp knives, scissors, and axes as soon as their activities demand the need of these tools. A five-year-old was seen making a rolling toy for himself. He nailed the round top of a coffee tin to a thin pole, using the flat side of a sharp axe to pound the nail through. This same boy was playing with a fly hook at the river front. No one paid any attention to him till the hook caught in my daughter's overalls. Then the boy was scolded for his carelessness.

Older children are expected to help around the camp. A girl of six or seven is asked to pack small wood into the house and attend to other routines commensurate with her abilities. A ten or eleven-year-old girl is assisting in the bulk of the housework. In addition she sets and visits rabbit snares, assists in sawing and splitting wood. In winter she may set a few traps, the fur from which will become her own to sell. A boy's education for his economic role in the family begins at about ten years of age when he starts to accompany his father or brothers fishing, hunting and trapping, and watching them prepare the various manufactures needed by the family. He is also expected to haul, saw and split wood. Educational methods are extremely flexible and indirect. A child learns primarily by observing how a thing is done. So long as he can fairly well approximate the finished product, the steps whereby he managed to achieve it are not rigorously prescribed. For example a six-year-old child was asked to build a fire in the stove. No further instruction was offered. The child put the kindling on top of the heavy wood and consequently the fire failed to catch. Her guardian did nothing but rebuilt the fire and set it herself.

No one in this society is bogged down with work. A girl contributing heavily to household chores still has a great deal of free time. During her leisure she is her own boss, although she is expected to return quickly to camp whenever her assistance is needed. A boy enjoys even more free time.

It appears to be not so much the pressure of other people that brings about

socialization but more importantly the values inherent in the cultural patterns as
answers to the problems that the individual will face growing up in his milieu. For
example, a boy eagerly accompanies his father on the trap line. To subsist in the
adult culture the boy needs trapping experience and knowledge. A good hunter
and trapper is respected, has a definite prestige with girls and can reassure himself as to his self-sufficiency. Therefore, although trapping is an extremely rigorous
business, the task has a strong enough positive valence to make the boy eager to
begin it. On the other hand the boy who fails to become a good trapper and who,
upon marriage, cannot support his wife and family does not face severe depriva-
tion, for he will be assisted in supporting his family by his wife's family.

From the above it can be seen that socialization for the Kaska is a consistent
process which steadily re-enforces the personality qualities which were initiated
at the break between infancy and childhood.

D. RACE, CLASS, AND PERSONAL BEHAVIOR PATTERNS:
A STUDY IN SOCIAL CLASS AND COLOR
DIFFERENCES IN CHILD REARING

In more complex cultures, basic personality structure does not depend
on the over-all culture pattern of the total society characteristic of primitive tribes. A society such as we have in the United States is far too
heterogeneous to have a direct effect on personality. Rather subcultures
and their group proprietors within the larger social complex exert their
major influences on personality formation. W. Lloyd Warner, an anthropologist and sociologist, in many of his studies tends to indicate that
ethnic and class affiliation in the United States are the most potent forces
in shaping personal-behavior patterns. In a study done by two of Warner's students, Allison Davis and Robert J. Havighurst, the differences
in early child training among white and Negro children of lower and
middle classes in Chicago were investigated. Since there is so much
general agreement among psychologists that the early years of childhood are the most formative in shaping traits and habits which, in turn,
persist into adult life, the study sought to discover how similar or dissimilar were the early years of children divided into the categories mentioned above. Two hundred mothers were interviewed, fifty in each of
the four groups—white middle class, white lower class, Negro middle
class, Negro lower class. A detailed summary of the findings in table
form is included below to indicate the differences in class and color
patterns in early child training in Chicago. It should be noted that
significant class differences exist in child-training practices. The differences between the classes, however, are greater than the differences

between Negroes and whites of the same social class. This will serve to illustrate the segmental aspects of our culture and the different influences exerted upon personality formation in a complex heterogeneous culture.

The authors generalize from their findings by drawing the following conclusion: [29]

1. There are significant differences in child-rearing practices between the middle and lower social classes in a large city. The same type of differences exist between middle and lower-class Negroes as between middle and lower-class whites.

2. Middle-class parents are more rigorous than lower-class parents in their training of children for feeding and cleanliness habits. They also expect their children to take responsibility for themselves earlier than lower-class parents do. Middle-class parents place their children under a stricter regime, with more frustration of their impulses, than do lower-class parents.

3. In addition to these social-class differences, there are some differences between Negroes and whites in their child-rearing practices. Negroes are more permissive than white in the feeding and weaning of their children, but they are much more rigorous than whites in toilet-training.

4. Thus there are *cultural differences* in the personality formation of middle-class compared with lower-class people, *regardless of color,* due to their early training. And for the same reason there should be further but less marked cultural differences between Negroes and whites of the same social class.

5. In addition to the cultural differences between individuals due to early training experience, there are individual personality differences between children in the same family. These are probably due to physiological differences and to differences in emotional relationships with other members of the family.

CLASS DIFFERENCES IN CHILD REARING

Feeding and Weaning

More lower-class children are breast fed only.

More lower-class children breast fed longer than 3 months (Negro only).

More lower-class children are fed at will.

Weaning takes place earlier (on the average) among middle-class children (white only).

More lower-class children suck longer than 12 months (white only).

More lower-class children have pacifiers (white only).

(c) More middle-class children are held for feeding.

(c) More lower-class are weaned sharply (Negro only).

Toilet Training

Bowel training is begun earlier (on the average) with middle-class children.

Bladder training is begun earlier (on the average) with middle-class children.

Bowel training is completed earlier by middle-class children (Negro only).

More middle-class parents begin bowel training at 6 months or earlier.

More middle-class parents complete bowel training at 12 months or earlier (Negro only).

More middle-class parents begin bladder training at 6 months or earlier (Negro only).

More middle-class parents complete bladder training at 18 months or earlier (Negro only).

(c) More lower-class parents complete bladder training at 18 months or earlier (white only).

Father-Child Relations

Middle-class fathers spend more time with children.

Middle-class fathers spend more time in educational activities with children (teaching, reading, and taking for walks).

Lower-class fathers discipline children more (Negro only).

Educational Expectation (Length of Education)

Middle-class expect higher education, expected to go to college.

Occupational Expectations for Children

Middle-class expect higher occupational status for children.

Age of Assuming Responsibility

Middle-class expect child to help at home earlier.

Middle-class girls cross street earlier (whites only).

(c) Lower-class boys and girls cross street earlier (Negro only).

Middle-class boys and girls expected to go downtown alone earlier.

Middle-class girls expected to begin to cook earlier (white only).

Middle-class girls expected to help with young children earlier.

Middle-class girls expected to begin to sew earlier (white only).

Middle-class girls expected to do dishes earlier (Negro only).

(c) Lower-class children expected to get job after school earlier.

(c) Lower-class children expected to quit school and go to work earlier.

Strictness of Regime

Middle-class children take naps in daytime more frequently.

Lower-class boys and girls allowed at movies alone earlier.

Middle-class boys and girls in house at night earlier.

Color Differences in Child Rearing

Feeding and Weaning

More Negro children are breast fed only.

More Negro children are breast fed for three months or more.

More Negro children are fed at will (lower class only).

More Negro children have pacifiers (middle class only).

More white children are weaned sharply (middle class only).

Weaning takes place earlier (on the average) among white children (middle class only).

(c) More white children suck longer than 12 months (lower class only).

Toilet Training

Bowel training is begun earlier with Negro children.

Bladder training is begun earlier with Negro children.

Bowel training is completed earlier with Negro children (middle class only).

Bladder training is completed earlier with Negro children.

More Negro parents begin bowel training at 6 months or earlier (middle class only).

More Negro parents begin bladder training at 6 months or earlier (middle class only).

More Negro parents complete bowel training at 12 months or earlier (middle class only).

More Negro parents complete bladder training at 18 months or earlier (middle class only).

Father-Child Relations

White fathers spend more time with children (lower class only).

White fathers teach and play more with children (lower class only).

Negro fathers discipline children more (lower class only).

Educational Expectation (Length of Education)

More Negro children expected to go to college (lower class only).

Age of Assuming Responsibility

Negro boys and girls cross street earlier (lower class only).

(c) White girls cross street earlier (middle class only).

Negro boys go downtown alone earlier (lower class only).

Negro girls expected to dress selves earlier.

Negro girls expected to go to store earlier.

Negro girls expected to begin to cook earlier (lower class only).

(c) Negro children expected to quit school and go to work later.

Strictness of Regime

Negro boys allowed to go to movies alone earlier.
(c) White girls allowed to go to movies alone earlier.
White boys and girls in house at night earlier.

E. STAGES IN THE SOCIAL GENESIS OF THE SELF: THE DEVELOPMENT OF THE SELF THROUGH THE ACQUISITION OF SELF WORDS

Personality, as regarded by social psychologists and sociologists, is formed to a considerable degree concomitantly with the development of social conduct. It includes one's overt behavioral pattern, one's set of emotional responses, one's intelligence, and one's configuration of attitudes. The last—attitudes—has in recent years become the focus in personality analysis. In fact, the core of personality has frequently been defined by social psychologists as one's cluster of attitudes. Personality has come to stand for the organization of tendencies to act that are developed by an individual in the course of his interaction with others. The tendencies to act toward given stimuli are what is meant by attitudes. They are a person's predispositions to respond, in a positive, negative, or neutral manner, to his environment. Attitudes are vital components of personality structure. Persons constantly form attitudes toward objects, people, and institutions surrounding them. But in addition to these attitudes toward external objects, man also forms attitudes toward his own being, his own self. He takes over the meanings that others have attached to him, and tends to act toward himself as others act toward him.

The self is a subject which is its own object. What this means is that a human being may become the object of his own actions. He may want to "kick himself," he talks to himself, or he may feel good about himself. And how does an individual become an object to himself? By assuming the roles of others—his mother, father, teacher, friends—to himself. These roles he obtains, obviously, in social interaction. Hence, the self, as well as self-consciousness, arises only in social experience.

One other aspect of the self should be mentioned—the *integrated* or *unified self*. We said that self attitudes develop through role taking— the child "plays the role of a mother," a fireman, or a teacher. In doing so he assumes the mannerisms, speech, and locutions of the person he symbolically adopts. However, role taking among children, especially in their play stage, may be and usually is fickle, diverse, varied, and inconsistent. Many different selves manifest themselves over a short period of time. In the course of a few minutes the child may be diving into a pool from a living-room couch, attentively participating in an adult conversation, and "playing house," with dolls as the child's daughters. Children, especially while playing, have poorly integrated selves. The unified self still has to develop and emerge. This is achieved by an additional process involved in role taking. It has been called taking the "role of the generalized other."

We owe the concept of the "role of the generalized other" to George Herbert Mead. He explains that the development of the unified self—a self that remains more or less constant from one situation to another—comes from taking the role of a number of people simultaneously and then defining one's own role in relationship to these other roles. Let us illustrate this by the baseball game. A player who would run to the outfield when the ball is hit by the batter, and then to first base to catch the runner, and then to home plate to snare another runner is not a well-integrated player on the team. Nor, by analogy, would a person who tried to play too many roles in a given situation be well-integrated in the group. However, a first baseman who fits into the team will adjust his first-baseman role to what each player is apt to do in a given play. He expects others to play their positions while he plays his own. He fits his role of first baseman into the total general pattern of baseball playing. He therefore acts toward himself through the image he has of the "generalized other," the total configuration of the team. As in the game, Mead holds, so in group life. An individual develops in time a generalized and integrated pattern of the total role of himself. He may, for example, consistently act as a "playboy," or a "tough guy," or a "meek housewife." In short, a dominant self emerges from many selves. The many have fused and merged to a more or less unified self.

In the following case history the child can be observed to develop a self through his acquisition and use of self words—I, me, my, and so on.[30] Read Bain, a sociologist, kept a record of the development of these self words by his child, referred to as S. F and R are the parents of S. S was born May 24, 1930, and the recordings of her speech and vocalizations begin with the twenty-first day after birth and continue until the self and other words were mastered. Only such data as refer to the self and those words that refer to others were recorded.

The findings in this study tend to confirm other research, in that [31] (1) infants learn the names of others before they learn their own; (2)

indications of self feelings appear in inarticulate form before the acquisition and use of self words; (3) the self words such as "I" subsequently affirm in articulate form the self feelings and self will of the child; (4) the first uses of self words such as "I" appear to be purely imitative, apparently without a sense of the subjective reference; (5) self words arise and obtain their meanings for the infant only in social interaction. (The use of "I" is inconceivable in pure solitude; it is always addressed to an audience, which may of course be an imaginary one.) [32]

Third month, twenty-third day. S distinguishes between F and R and others. Cried loudly when left with strange girl. Stopped at once when F took her up.

6–26. Dawdles at food, although perfectly healthy, (attention-getting?) Seems to respond to her name by turning toward the speaker more quickly than for other sounds. It may be the tone of F and R rather than the name.

7–9. Definite bids for attention; waves "bye-bye." S is much interested by her mirror image and her baby pictures.

8–1. Waves "bye-bye" to herself in the mirror and to R; formerly did it to everyone. (A vague distinction between herself and others?) Pays more attention to S in mirror than to F. When F says "Hello, Mother!" S looks at F in the mirror and then at F out of the mirror and grins.

9–16. F says S reaches for her shoe, doll, etc., when F says "Where's Sheila's shoe?" etc.

9–21. S makes definite responses to about fifteen verbal stimuli. When one says "Where's Mamma's shoe, foot?" etc., S reaches for the object. Some of these responses are self-references. In response to "Where's the baby, where's Sheila?" S covers her face with paper or shawl and then uncovers it with laughter and grinning. In response to "Where's the baby?" (when shown her own or other baby picture) S runs her hand over it and laughs. In response to "Where's your foot, hand, dress?" etc., S reaches for her foot, holds up hand, reaches for her dress, etc. Protests at being left alone and bids for attention.

Was greatly excited by a baby of her own age and seems to interact with it more actively than with adults (cf. 7–9, 8–1, above).

10–0. Winks both eyes in response to "Wink your eyes." F is sure S knows "Read" and "Da-Da" for R. When F says "Where's Read?" or "Where's Daddy?" S turns directly toward R, smiles, and says "Da-Da." F says S says "She-e! She-e!" when she sees her mirror image or her picture.

10–6. When R returned after five days' absence, S recognized him at once. There is no doubt but that S "knows" words. She makes differential, specific responses to "Where's S, F, R, Mamma, Daddy?" and also for objects and parts of her body. Her response to person-words seem to give her greater emotional satisfaction than her responses to thing-words do. She stimulates (imitates?) herself much more than others stimulate her.

10–20. S invariably turns toward F and R and smiles when "Where's F, where's

R?" To "Where's Sheila?" she responds "She-e! She-e!" and looks toward her picture on the mantel. It has been clear for some time that S "understands" sentences long before she can say even single words. It is out of this rudimentary prespeech "memory" that consciousness of self and others arises.

11–0. Much repetitive babbling and imitating, both of herself and of others. F said "ouch!" and S repeated it, explosively, several times. Two of her favorite "words" are "she-she" and "la-la." A combination would form her name. She makes practically all the phonetic sounds.

11–3. "Ow-itch!" and "la!" are still doing constant, explosive duty. When asked "Where's your hair? Let's see your hand?" etc., S frequently refuses to respond, although she knows all these things well. The "your" plainly has no self-reference, but is just part of the total verbal stimulus. She quite consistently takes her hand out of her mouth in response to the verbal command. She "understands" a number of simple sentences.

12–0. No evidence of any self-words (nor any other kind) except "Mamma," "Da-Da," and "Bye"—which are definitely associated with persons and acts. She teases, i.e., does things she knows are forbidden and enjoys it. Has begun to "talk" in a new way—sharp, staccato, explosive, "Bla! Blop! Bla!" Points at things and looks at things we point to; increasing interest in parts of her body. Responds to "sing, Sheila!" by "singing."

13–0. During the last two or three days S has learned the names and faces of twelve relatives whom she has never seen before. When one says "Where's ——? Go to ——," she points or goes to the right person. This may be a response to the speaker's gestures rather than to his words.

13–13. Language habits greatly improved in accuracy and number, but no clear consciousness of self except marked self-assertion and "teasing."

14–0. Discovered her saying words to herself: "Howdy-do, Mamma, Da-Da, Bobo (the little dog), Biddy," etc. F says this has been going on for some time. Her single-word speaking vocabulary consists of about 21 words: 10 names of persons; 6 actions, viz., "bye-bye," "how-do," "peek," "beautiful," "all gone," "da"; 5 objects. In addition, she "recognizes" by appropriate actions 29 objects and 31 acts. Her working vocabulary is probably close to 100 words.

14–8. S distinguishes "daddy's ear" from "your ear," but the "your" probably does not mean any definite S-sense-of-self. Make-believe play is common now—drinking from empty cup, giving herself a bath, etc. All successful action is accompanied by an explosive "da!"

14–15. Makes blundering attempts at word combinations, with great vocal stress: "How-de-do, Bill!"; "Bye-bye, Dadda!" Shy of stranger, although she hides for fun from F and R.

15–0. Last night in the car S suddenly began to say "see-lah!" and repeated it all the way home. Today she is saying "See-lah! says Mam, Bobo, Dadda," etc.; pats F and R and says, "See's Mamma"; "See's Dadda." This seems to be the first true self-word.

15–8. S shouted the names of all the family who saw us off on the train. All the way across, whenever the train stopped, she would go to the window and shout "bye-bye!" to the whole family, each by name.

15–19. Has almost stopped saying "See says . . . ," except "Sees says doon!"—which she shouts until put down; resents having her hand held while walking. Said "Isee" the other day—imitatively, I judge. The "I" has not been heard since. She does not seem confused by her explosive "See" (look) and "See" (her name). Uses "baby" a great deal but never applies it to herself. She knows her own toys, but allows other children to snatch them with no protest.

16–0. When told to say "Sheila Bain" she says "Baby!" This is another true self-word. In response to "Where's Sheila?" she pats her chest and points to herself.

16–12. S says "baby" when told to say her own name and also whenever she sees another baby, doll, child, or picture of any of them. So this "baby" is both a self-and-other-word, or it is neither.

17–0. Many three and four-word sentences containing everybody's name except her own. "Baby" still used as in 16–12. When S "pats" R she insists on patting F, and vice versa.

17–18. Possessives are quite well established: "See's dadda, See's mamma, Dadd's ba (bath)," etc. Said "I do" several times after hearing an explosive "I do!" from R to F—mere sound imitation, I think. Still refers to herself as "baby" but also uses a rough approximation of her name.

18–0. Rough approximation of R's name, but when told to say "F——," she says "Mamma!" Seldom tries her own name.

19–14. S says "I eat, I sit, I peek," etc., and performs the proper actions. There appears to be no definite bodily-self reference in her use of "I." When told to say Sheila Bain she says "Baby Baim."

19–20. Coming home from a drive, F said "Sheila's house." S said "My house!" and repeated it several times. "I" is much in use with no confusion.

20–0. S says "Seebee Baim, Baby Seebee Baim, Seebee's buch," etc., a great deal. Also, "I do, Seebee eat, my buch, my hair, my eyes," etc., are very common and so far no single case of pronoun-shifting has been noted.

20–4. Great increase of words. "My" and "I" in constant use with no confusion.

20–7. Likes to "argue," e.g., shouts "Mon" when you say a picture is a baby, and vice versa. Strongly insists that F and R be treated equally, e.g., when R takes a cigarette, S says "Dadda, get Mamma Cig-a-match!" All her a's are broad or Italian although both F and R use the western A.

20–14. "Seebee" has become "Sheebee." "I see you" appears to be repetitive but is used properly. No confusion in self and other words noted so far.

20–17. Used "my" for "I"—"My see you."

20–20. F says S used "me"—"Bye-bye, Dadda, Mamma, me!"

20–21. First clear case of a preposition—"Go back to Mamma!" Noticed another "my" for "I."

21–0. "My" for "your" or "the" is apparently a fixed confusion, although it occurs infrequently: "Dadda, take my baby"; "My baby go bye-bye."

21–12. "I," "my," "you," "your," and possibly "me" are used correctly.

21–14. In response to "What's your name?" S sings "My name, my name is Sheebee Baim!" Goes around singing "My name, my Dadda, my Mamma" with a definite, explosive sense of possession.

21–18. S whispers to herself and to F and R.

21–22. F reports S said "Baby bumps herself."

21–25. S has invented a telephone game with the curtain pull. She speaks only her own part, making proper pauses for the other person.

21–28. Said "Dadda bumps me."

22–0. Said "I bump myself." (F's report.)

22–3. Calls her toy cabinet "my office"—"I go work in my office." Shows everybody her six months' baby picture—"See Sheebee? See that baby?"

22–8. After a child of her own age had snatched several toys from her, S suddenly objected. She said nothing, although she knows the words. This is the first instance of possessiveness for her things. She does a great deal of helping: "I help Dadda, I help Mamma!!"

22–13. She takes her fingers out of her mouth when told, but usually says, "I bite my wrist, elbow, or arm," and does it.

22–15. "What's your name?" "Sheebee." "What else?" "Baim." "What's Daddy's name?" "Eed." "What else?" "Baim." All the people she knows are "Baim."

22–18. "I," "my," "me," "mine," "you," "your," are correctly used with occasional confusion between "I" and "my." Have not noticed "myself" or "herself" since the two doubtful cases mentioned. Never says "I tickle you," but "I giggle your nose, or Dadda's nose"; not "I bump myself," but "I bump my hand, foot," etc.

22–26. Says "I love Mamma's Sheebee" for "Sheebee's Mamma." This inverted possessive is common, but the correct form is also used.

22–28. "Mamma, see! Baby's hair is yellow, like mine!" (pointing to a picture).

23–8. When S is upstairs and hears someone come in, she calls "Is it Do? Is it Ray?"—through eight or ten names, when she knows all the time it is Jean.

24–0. Started vocabulary count today: 406 words. Most of these can be readily understood by strangers; all are stereotyped sounds referring to specific things or actions. Some are mere verbalisms, of course, as "Oxford is my town," "Ohio is my state." Plurals and forms of the same verb are not counted as specific separate words.

24–4. Much doll-play. S does and says to dolls what F does and says to S.

24–7. R to S, "Careful, or you will hurt yourself." S says "Careful, I hurt myself—Sheila." For some time S has changed "you" and "your" to the first person with no confusion. Uses second person pronouns some but third person very little. Has said "we" repetitively but with no clear we-reference.

24–9. Vocabulary count completed. The list is probably not complete but a considerable number has been acquired since May 24, so this is approximately correct for S's two-year-old vocabulary. The "recognition" vocabulary is considerably greater.

CLASSIFICATION

1. Common nouns	336
2. Proper nouns (places, Oxford, etc.)	9
3. Proper nouns (persons)	71
4. Pronouns (I, me, my, mine, myself, we, us, your, something, it, both, any, none)	14
5. Conjunctions (and)	1
6. Prepositions (in, on, down, to, up, of, like, around, over, from, after, before, under	13
7. Adjectives and adverbs	76
8. Verbs and actions	125
Total	645

24–16. S says "I bring Mamma my shoes," meaning F's shoes. Seldom uses "your" although "you" is common.

24–24. Said "I's" for "I'm." Only time I've noted this.

24–30. Said "We go uptown; we go upstairs." First use of "we" showing clear intent to include self with another.

25–6. Says "my" for "your" quite regularly although she uses "my" correctly for her own things.

25–9. When R says "I'll take you upstairs," S protests loudly, "No! No! I go upstairs by myself!" This myself insistence applies to everything. Cats, dogs, dolls, etc., are all called "Bain" with deep emotion. (She learned the n-sound a couple of months ago.)

25–13. "Mine" and "my" are used frequently and with great self-feeling. "Mine" is often used for "my"—"I want mine own cup!"

25–19. R scolds S for wetting on the floor. S says "No! Not Sheebee—Dadda!" and spanks R's cheek: "No do it any more, Dadda!" S calls others by their last names; heretofore all persons have been "Bain."

25–21. S says "Janet goes to see my Mamma, no, her Mamma." First use of third personal pronoun and also first verbal self-criticism. At a friend's house S says "This is mine house," but her laugh shows she knows it is not.

25–26. "Alan goes to see his Mamma!" S is also using "your" correctly.

26–6. Out driving, everything S saw elicited "That's my house, pig," etc. When F said "No, that's not your house," S laughed and said "No, it's a game!"

26–11. S said "That's ouah cah!" R said "What do you mean by 'our'?" S said "Daddy's and Mamma's and mine."

26–14. "Daddy, get your coat, we're going uptown."

26–18. Tonight S said "I want to. I want to!" R said "Who is I?" S said "I is me!"

26–24. Great sympathy for F, who bumped herself.

26–27. "We," "us," "our," "you," "your," "his," "her," commonly and correctly used.

26–30. Calls up the "groceryman" and orders ten or twelve different articles (toy-telephone), says "goodbye," and reports with great satisfaction: "There! I told the groceryman to bring all the groceries!"

27–7. S said "See those people? They are my friends. All the people are my friends." "These" and "Them" are also used occasionally.

FOOTNOTES TO PART TWO

Asterisks indicate footnotes quoted from original source of case material.

1. Kingsley Davis, "Extreme Social Isolation of a Child," *American Journal of Sociology,* Vol. XLV, pp. 554–562; Kingsley Davis, "Final Note on a Case of Extreme Isolation," *ibid.,* Vol. LII, pp. 433–437. Permission granted by the University of Chicago Press.

*2. Out of regard for the parties concerned, correct names of persons and places are not given.

*3. It is doubtful that the child's hands at the time of discovery were tied. It is more likely that she was confined to her crib in the first period of life and at all times kept locked in her room to keep her from falling down the steep stairs leading immediately from the door and to keep the grandfather from seeing her. It is doubtful if the child was ever kept in the attic, as the report also stated.

*4. She remained in the home more than nine months, being removed on November 11 to a foster-home. The institution is primarily for the aged and infirm in the county where Anna lived, but contains cases of nearly all types.

*5. The mother was reported to have the mentality of a child of ten. We did interview the persons who gave the intelligence test but did not interview the mother herself. She seems probably subnormal, and this is the opinion of most people who know her. But it is doubtful if her status is any lower than that of a high-grade moron,

and she may be merely a dull normal. Anna's father, according to one story, is a wealthy farmer living in the same rural section as the mother, distantly kin to her. Another story has it, however, that a syphilitic married man in the near-by town is the father.

*6. She would hold one hand in front of her with the little finger pressed against the palm, the other three fingers close together and straight out, and would then manipulate the hand shaped in this way close to her eyes. Often when doing this she would hold a finger of her other hand in her ear. These actions gave her an idiotic appearance. She showed more skill in bending the fingers than any of us could exhibit.

*7. Mr. Carr, who represented the Psycho-educational Clinic at Pennsylvania State College, found that Anna showed accommodation for both light and distance, that she winked when a pencil was suddenly shoved toward her eyes and when a tumbler was struck with a spoon just behind her ear, and that the patellar and planter reflexes were present. It being impossible to administer any standardized tests involving language, he examined her with references to the motor-behavior items in Gesell's developmental scale. The items passed included the following: resisting head pressure (appears normally at four months), lifting head while in prone position (six months), sitting up (nine months), clasping cubes (six months), picking up cube (six months), scribbling (eighteen months—but this "scribbling" appeared to us to be an accident).

*8. Anna had for weeks been without any playmates in her room. As a test a little boy (aged five) was brought in. We all left the room and peered back. Anna took a definite interest in him. She tried her trick of looking hard into his eyes and moved her head near his to rub foreheads. She clapped her hands, manifesting more interest in him than he in her. The nurse said that Anna had played with kittens a few days previously by swinging them by their tails. We secured two kittens and put them on her bed. This time she became paralyzed with fright. She made little noise, except a stifled yell once or twice, and she made no effort to get away or push the kittens off. This paralyzed type of reaction was characteristic. Initiative seemed virtually impossible for her. A temper tantrum previously exhibited had this character. She waved her head from side to side and flipped her hands up and down—a nervous, futile sort of tantrum behavior. It was as if she had no channels of expression or action, no mode of dealing with the environment. As soon as the kittens were out of sight she forgot about them, but the fright returned whenever they were placed in her presence. During her fright she broke into the first crying spell the writer had witnessed. It was a real child's cry.

*9. Letter to one of the state officials in charge of the case.

*10. *Ibid.*

*11. Progress report of the school.

*12. Francis N. Maxfield, "What Happens When the Social Environment of a Child Approaches Zero," unpublished manuscript.

*13. Marie K. Mason, "Learning to Speak after Six and One-half Years of Silence," *Journal of Speech Disorders,* Vol. 7 (1942), p. 299.

*14. Maxfield, *op. cit.*

*15. Mason, *op. cit.,* p. 299.

*16. *Ibid.,* pp. 300–304.

*17. Maxfield, *op. cit.*

*18. Based on a personal letter from Dr. Mason to the writer, May 13, 1946.

19. In recent years, social anthropologists, social psychologists, and sociologists have arrived at commonly held principles governing personality formation. Personality is regarded as the result of three interacting systems: (*a*) the genetic; (*b*) the cultural or the group, which is responsible for the socially common characteristics of an individual; and (*c*) the private, which gives rise to those unique social personality characteristics resulting from an individual's personal creative abilities and the peculiar combination of social circumstances converging on the individual.

20. C. H. Cooley, *Social Organization* (New York: Charles Scribner's Sons, 1915), pp. 23–24.

21. From Harlan W. Gilmore, "Five Generations of a Begging Family," *American Journal of Sociology,* Vol. XXXVII (1931–1932), pp. 768–774. Permission granted by the University of Chicago Press.

22. It should be noted that serious criticism of Kardiner's viewpoint does exist. Kardiner's basic concept and theory are summarized in Ralph Linton, *The Science of Man in the World Crisis* (New York: Columbia University Press, 1945), pp. 107–122. For critical evaluation, see Kingsley Davis, *Human Society* (New York: The Macmillan Company, 1949), p. 275; Don Martindale and Elio D. Monachesi, *Elements of Sociology* (New York: Harper & Brothers, 1951), p. 321.

23. Abram Kardiner, "The Concept of Basic Personality Structure as an Operational Tool in the Social Sciences," in Linton, *op. cit.,* pp. 113–114.

24. Cora DuBois, *The People of Alor* (Minneapolis: University of Minnesota Press, 1944).

25. From Frances W. Underwood and Irma Honigmann, "A Comparison of Socialization and Personality in Two Simple Societies," *American Anthropologist,* Vol. 49, pp. 557–565.

*26. John J. Honigmann, "Kaska Culture and Ethos," unpublished manuscript.

*27. D. H. Levy, "Primary Affect Hunger," *American Journal of Psychiatry*, Vol. 94 (1937), pp. 643–652.

*28. Horney finds for the detached-personality type "a need for *self-sufficiency*. Its most positive expression is resourcefulness. . . . It is the only way he can compensate for his isolation," Karen Horney, *Our Inner Conflicts* (New York: 1945).

29. Allison Davis and Robert J. Havighurst, "Social Class and Color Differences in Child-rearing," *American Sociological Review*, Vol. 11, No. 6 (December, 1946), pp. 703–704, 710. The class and color differences are statistically reliable at the 5-per-cent level. "It will be seen that the differences tend to go together; a letter (c) indicates that the finding contradicts the general tendency of the results. For example, the general tendency is for lower-class children to be treated more permissively than middle-class children with respect to feeding and weaning. Contradictory to this tendency, however, more middle-class children are held for feeding."

30. Read Bain, "The Self-and-other Words of a Child," *American Journal of Sociology*, Vol. XLI, pp. 770–775.

31. *Cf.* Charles Horton Cooley, "A Study of the Early Use of the Self-words by a Child," *Psychological Review*, Vol. XV (1908), pp. 339–357, reprinted in Charles Horton Cooley, *Sociological Theory and Social Research* (New York: Henry Holt and Company, Inc., 1930), pp. 229–247. M. W. Shinn, *The Biography of a Baby* (Boston: Houghton Mifflin Company, 1900).

32. Cooley, *Sociological Theory and Social Research*, p. 232: " 'I' is a differentiation in a vague body of personal ideas which is either self-consciousness or social consciousness, as you please to look at it. In the use of 'I' and of names for other people, the *ego* and *alter* phases of this consciousness become explicit."

PART THREE

The Social Group
and Collective Behavior

A. INTRODUCTION: THE NATURE OF THE GROUP
AND TYPES OF GROUP CLASSIFICATION

A wide variety of definitions of the term *group* exists. For the sociologist, the human-social group has a special meaning. The group, for him, constitutes an entity of two or more persons in mental-symbolic interaction. This entity or unit of interacting personalities is formed when a common interest (or interests) arises among a number of persons who identify themselves with this interest and are thus held together by a sense of belonging with one another because of it. Thus, a member of a Rotary club believes in the Rotary Code and therefore manifests an *esprit de corps,* a consciousness of kind, and a feeling of unity with others in the Rotary club who also believe in the code. A human-social group therefore involves a number of persons with a common interest and value, interacting with one another overtly and covertly, and giving rise to a sense of oneness and unity among themselves. Thus the group involves several attributes:

1. Two or more persons
2. Common and agreed-upon interests and values
3. A *persistent* and *organized* pattern of interaction [1]
   a. On an overt and definable plane, through an actual and observable process of affiliating, participating, and acting together to fulfill these values (joining, paying dues, attending meetings, physical residence in a particular place)
   b. On a covert plane (through personal identification, feeling of belonging, and attachment to a common value or number of values, and to each other)

The human-social group is different from a physical aggregate in that the latter consists merely of a collection of physical units in a given area. The animal herd is also distinguishable from the human-social group in that animal interaction is primarily synaptic and sensory; human interaction is symbolic.

The human-social group is also to be distinguished from the *social category*. This term refers to a number of persons with a common characteristic of social (symbolic) significance including such classifications as youth, old people, children, women, Negroes, and so on. These categories are significant because membership in them serves to influence one's behavior and attitudes. There are specific values attached to these categories both by society and by their own members. We frequently tend to act toward a Negro, for example, in accordance with society's (and our personal) evaluation of Negroes. We assign status to him; we define his position in society. Members of a social category therefore possess a set of values. They may also interact with one another. A social category is different from a social group, however, because it does *not* possess organization or a pattern of persistent, recurrent, and *definitive* interaction.

Many attempts have been made to classify human-social groups. The possible types are perhaps infinite. The classifications depend on the index or axis one employs as a basis for classification, just as the classification of chemical elements in Mendeleef's periodic table depends on the indices of atomic number and atomic weight. It may be "place," giving rise to such types as neighborhood groups, communities, and nations. Classification of groups may be based on ego involvement, giving rise to primary and secondary groups. Groups may be divided on the basis of number, age, sex, duration (transitory groups as against permanent groups), or a multitude of other feasible classifications.

In recent years great weight and interest have been focused upon the degree of formality or informality in organization of the group as the basis for group classification.

We have said that group organization consists of a system of interrelated functions, activities, and roles among the group's members. When this system is embodied in a set of official and explicit rules set down in constitutions, established precedents, charters of incorporation, and directives, the group is *formally* organized. The instruments governing the interpersonal relationships of members are impersonal, formal, deliberate, rational, and planned. Examples of such groups are governments, business corporations, civic clubs, and labor unions. Members of these groups are attached to the impersonal norms and values of the group. A political party attracts persons primarily because of what the party stands for ideologically rather than because of any appeal the members may have for one another personally, as in the case of the intimate friendship circle, the clique, the buddy group in the army, or the juvenile gang.

These latter groups are illustrations of the *informal* group. They lack not only a formal and prescribed structure of prearranged positions and functions, but also deliberate, planned procedures for governing the relations of their members. Their relations tend to be informal, personal, and face to face. In the informal group, there is characteristically greater loyalty to other members than to the norms of the group. In the formal group, quite the reverse is true.

No group, especially no informal, face-to-face one, exists in isolation, independent and unrelated to other groups, except in small primitive societies where the total society tends to be synonymous with the informal group. Every informal group either overlaps and touches other groups, like two neighboring families, or is part of a larger formal group or social system, as the family in the community, the neighborhood in the city, a clique of workers in a department of an industrial plant, friendship circles on a college campus. *All large, formal social groupings tend to contain as part of their internal structure these informal clusters of human-social groups.*

It should be borne in mind that while the group is real, it is not a thing or a substance; it is a relationship, a system. It is because of this that the group as such cannot act; only the individual acts. The individual does not think, act, or feel in exactly the same way in each of the groups to which he belongs. His behavior varies as his relationships to others change. At a given time he may be just a member of one particular group, such as a child in the family (Fig 1a). It is also true that

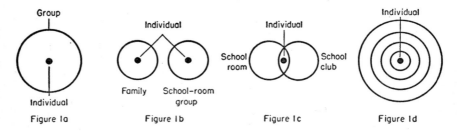

Figure 1a   Figure 1b   Figure 1c   Figure 1d

the child may, at the same time that he is a member of his familial group, be a member of his schoolroom group (Fig 1b). Or a child's group membership may overlap between schoolroom group and school club (Fig. 1c). Finally, a child's group membership may be divided into a pattern of group concentricity (Fig 1*d*): he is part of his family, he and his family are part of the community, the community in turn is part of the state, and the state is part of the nation.

B. EXPERIMENTAL CASES ON THE ROLE OF THE
INFORMAL GROUP IN WORKER PRODUCTIVITY

In the following case study of a group of workers in an industrial organization, we can readily see the influence of the informal group on worker productivity. It should be noted that the informal groups in the plant organization meet all the requirements of our definition of the group: (1) persistent and recurrent patterns of interaction; (2) a definable and observable system of overt interaction among its members; (3) evidence of interpersonal identification in the form of group loyalties; (4) a set of common values and norms in setting their own production quotas; and (5) a system of organized roles (note worker-leaders arising with special functions—one to deal with "outsiders," another to enforce the norms of the informal group among its members).

In addition, the following principles, hypotheses, and definitions tend to emerge from the worker group situation that may have application to other informal group situations:

1. The norms and standards of the larger formal industrial organization tend to influence the behavior of the small informal groups.

2. When opposition arises to some of the norms of the larger organization, the informal, face-to-face group devises its own norms, such as their own standards for production quotas.

3. If the informal group is not based on opposition to the norms of the larger organization, the informal group within the more formal one strengthens the motivations to reach the more formal goals.

4. Members of the informal group develop a harmonious *sharing* of interests; individual self-interest tends to be subordinated.

5. Informal groups in the plant give rise to informal leaders.

6. These informal leaders act as instruments for crystallizing and enforcing the standards for the group's activities.

7. Nonconformity to the informal group's norms is punished.

8. Members of the informal group are ready to help each other in fulfilling the group's norms.

9. The leader acts as the major defensive instrument for his group to the outside environment of the larger organization.

10. A hierarchy of informal leadership emerges in the group. The higher the rank of a person within the group, the more nearly his activities conform to the norms of the group.[2]

In April, 1927, six girls were selected from a large shop department of the Hawthorne Works.[3] They were chosen as average workers neither inexperienced nor expert, and their work consisted of the assembling of telephone relays. A coil, armature, contact springs, and insulators were put together on a fixture and secured in position by means of four machine screws. The operation at that time was being completed at the rate of about five relays in six minutes. This particular operation was chosen for the experiment because the relays were being assembled often enough so that even slight changes in output rate would show themselves at once in the output record. Five of the girls were to do the actual assemble work; the duty of the sixth was to keep the others supplied with parts.

The test room itself was an area divided from the main department by a wooden partition eight feet high. The girls sat in a row on one side of a long workbench. The bench and assembly equipment were identical with those used in the regular department, except in one respect. At the right of each girl's place was a hole in the bench, and into this hole she dropped completed relays. It was the entrance to a chute, in which there was a flapper gate opened by the relay in its passage downward. The opening of the gate closed an electrical circuit which controlled a perforating device, and this in turn recorded the completion of the relay by punching a hole in a tape. The tape moved at the rate of one-quarter of an inch a minute and had space for a separate row of holes for each operator. When punched, it thus constituted a complete output record for each girl for each instant of the day. Such records were kept for five years.

In this experiment, great emphasis was laid on the rate of output. Output is easily measured, i.e., it yields precise quantitative data, and experience suggested that it was sensitive to at least some of the conditions under which the employees worked. Output was treated as an index.

Arrangements were made that a number of records should be kept. Unsuitable parts supplied by the firm were noted down, as were assemblies rejected for any reason upon inspection. In this way the type of defect could be known and related to the time of day at which it occurred. Records were kept of weather conditions in general and of temperature and humidity in the test room. Every six weeks each operator was given a medical examination by the company doctor. Every day she was asked to tell how many hours she had spent in bed the night before and, during a part of the experiment, what food she had eaten. Besides all these records, which concerned the physical condition of the operators, a log was kept in which were recorded the principal events in the test room hour by hour, including among the entries snatches of conversation between the workers. At first these entries related largely to the physical condition of the operators: how they felt as they worked. Later the ground they covered somewhat widened, and the log ultimately became one of the most important of the test room records. Finally, each of the operators was interviewed several times by an experienced interviewer.

The girls had no supervisor in the ordinary sense, such as they would have had in a regular shop department, but a "test room observer" was placed in the room, whose duty it was to maintain the records, arrange the work, and secure a cooperative spirit on the part of the girls. Later, when the complexity of his work increased, several assistants were assigned to help him.

When the arrangements had been made for the test room, the operators who had been chosen to take part were called in for an interview in the office of the superintendent of the Inspection Branch, who was in general charge of the experiment and of the researches which grew out of it. The superintendent described this interview as follows: "The nature of the test was carefully explained to these girls and they readily consented to take part in it, although they were very shy at the first conference. An invitation to six shop girls to come up to a superintendent's office was naturally rather startling. They were assured that the object of the test was to determine the effect of certain changes in working conditions, such as rest periods, midmorning lunches, and shorter working hours. They were expressly cautioned to work at a comfortable pace, and under no circumstances to try and make a race out of the test." This conference was only the first of many. Whenever any experimental change was planned the girls were called in, the purpose of the change was explained to them, and their comments were requested. Certain suggested changes which did not meet with their approval were abandoned. They were repeatedly asked, as they were asked in the first interview, not to strain but to work "as they felt."

The experiment was now ready to begin. Put in its simplest terms, the idea of those directing the experiment was that if an output curve was studied for a long enough time under various changes in working conditions, it would be possible to determine which conditions were most satisfactory. Accordingly, a number of so-called "experimental periods" were arranged. For two weeks before the operators were placed in the test room, a record was kept of the production of each one without her knowledge. In this way the investigators secured a measure of her productive ability while working in the regular department under the usual conditions. This constituted the first experimental period. And for five weeks after the girls entered the test room no change was made in working conditions. Hours remained what they had been before. The investigators felt that this period would be long enough to reveal any changes in output incidental merely to the transfer. This constituted the second experimental period.

The third period involved a change in the method of payment. In the regular department, the girls had been paid according to a scheme of group piecework, the group consisting of a hundred or more employees. Under these circumstances, variations in an individual's total output would not be immediately reflected in her pay, since such variations tended to cancel one another in such a large group. In the test room, the six operators were made a group by themselves. In this way each girl received an amount more nearly in proportion to her individual effort, and her interests became more closely centered on the experiment. Eight weeks later, the directly experimental changes began. An outline will reveal their general character: Period IV: two rest pauses, each five minutes in length, were established, one occurring in midmorning and the other in the early afternoon. Period V: these rest pauses were lengthened to ten minutes each. Period VI: six five-minute rests were established. Period VII: the company provided each member of the group with a light lunch in the midmorning and another in the midafternoon, accompanied by rest pauses. This arrangement became standard for subsequent Periods VIII through XI. Period VIII: work stopped a half-hour earlier every day—at 4:30 p.m. Period IX: work stopped at 4 p.m. Period X: conditions returned to what they were in Period VII. Period XI: a five-day work week was established. Each of these experimental periods lasted several weeks.

Period XI ran through the summer of 1928, a year after the beginning of the experiment. Already the results were not what had been expected. The output curve, which had risen on the whole slowly and steadily throughout the year, was obviously reflecting something other than the responses of the group to the imposed experimental conditions. Even when the total weekly output had fallen off, as it could hardly fail to do in such a period as Period XI, when the group was working only five days a week, daily output continued to rise. Therefore, in accordance with a sound experimental procedure, as a control on what had been done, it was agreed with the consent of the operators that in experimental Period XII a return should be made to the original conditions of work, with no rest pauses, no special lunches, and a full-length working week. This period lasted for twelve weeks. Both daily and weekly output rose to a higher point than ever before: the working day and the working week were both longer. The hourly output rate declined somewhat but it did not approach the level of Period III, when similar conditions were in effect.

The conclusions reached after Period XII may be expressed in terms of another observation. Identical conditions of work were repeated in three different experimental periods: Periods VII, X, and XIII. If the assumptions on which the study was based had been correct, that is to say, if the output rate were directly related to the physical conditions of work, the expectation would be that in these three experimental periods there would be some similarity in output. Such was not the case. The only apparent uniformity was that in each experimental period output was higher than in the preceding one. In the Relay Assembly Test Room something was happening which could not be explained by the experimentally controlled conditions of work.

The question remains:

With what facts, if any, can the changes in the output rate of the operators in the test room be correlated? Here the statements of the girls themselves are of the first importance. Each girl knew that she was producing more in the test room than she ever had in the regular department, and each said that the increase had come about without any conscious effort on her part. It seemed easier to produce at the faster rate in the test room than at the slower rate in the regular department. When questioned further, each girl stated her reasons in slightly different words, but there was a uniformity in the answers in two respects. First, the girls like to work in the test room; "it was fun." Secondly, the new supervisory relation or, as they put it, the absence of the old supervisory control, made it possible for them to work freely without anxiety.

For instance, there was the matter of conversation. In the regular department, conversation was in principle not allowed, in practice it was tolerated if it was carried on in a low tone and did not interfere with work. In the test room an effort was made in the beginning to discourage conversation, though it was soon abandoned. The observer in charge of the experiment was afraid of losing the cooperation of the girls if he insisted too strongly on this point. Talk became common and was often loud and general. Indeed, the conversation of the operators came to occupy an important place in the log. T. N. Whitehead has pointed out that the girls in the test room were far more thoroughly supervised than they ever had been in the regular department. They were watched by an observer of their own, an interested management, and outside experts. The point is that the character and purpose of the supervision were different and were felt to be so.

The operators knew that they were taking part in what was considered an important and interesting experiment. They knew that their work was expected to produce results—they were not sure what results—which would lead to the improvement of the working conditions of their fellow employees. They knew that the eyes of the company were upon them. Whitehead has further pointed out that although the experimental changes might turn out to have no physical significance, their social significance was always favorable. They showed that the management of the company was still interested, that the girls were still part of a valuable piece of research. In the regular department, the girls, like the other employees, were in the position of responding to changes the source and purpose of which were beyond their knowledge. In the test room, they had frequent interviews with the superintendent, a high officer of the company. The reasons for the contemplated experimental changes were explained to them. Their views were consulted and in some instances they were allowed to veto what had been proposed. Professor Mayo has argued that it is idle to speak of an experimental period like Period XII as being in any sense what it purported to be—a return to the original conditions of work. In the meantime, the entire industrial situation of the girls had been reconstructed.

Another factor in what occurred can only be spoken of as the social development of the group itself. When the girls went for the first time to be given a physical examination by the company doctor, someone suggested as a joke that ice cream and cake ought to be served. The company provided them at the next examination, and the custom was kept up for the duration of the experiment. When one of the girls had a birthday, each of the others would bring her a present, and she would respond by offering the group a box of chocolates. Often one of the girls would have some good reason for feeling tired. Then the others would "carry" her. That is, they would agree to work especially fast to make up for the low output expected from her. It is doubtful whether this "carrying" did have any effect, but the important point is the existence of the practice, not its effectiveness. The girls made friends in the test room and went together socially after hours. One of the interesting facts which has appeared from Whitehead's analysis of the output records is that there were times when variations in the output rates of two friends were correlated to a high degree. Their rates varied simultaneously and in the same direction—something, of course, which the girls were not aware of and could not have planned. Also, these correlations were destroyed by such apparently trivial events as a change in the order in which the girls sat at the workbench.

Finally, the group developed leadership and a common purpose. The leader, self-appointed, was an ambitious young Italian girl who entered the test room as a replacement after two of the original members had left. She saw in the experiment a chance for personal distinction and advancement. The common purpose was an increase in the output rate. The girls had been told in the beginning and repeatedly thereafter that they were to work without straining, without trying to make a race of the test, and all the evidence shows that they kept this rule. In fact, they felt that they were working under less pressure than in the regular department. Nevertheless, they knew that the output record was considered the most important of the records of the experiment and always closely scrutinized. Before long they had committed themselves to a continuous increase in production. In the long run, of course, this ideal was an impossible one, and when the girls found out that it was, the realization was an important element of the change of tone which was noticeable in the second half of the experiment. But for a time they felt that they could achieve the impossible. In brief, the increase in the output rate of the girls in the Relay Assembly Test Room could not be related to any changes in their physical conditions of work, whether experimentally induced or not. It could, however, be related to what can only be spoken of as the development of an organized social group in a peculiar and effective relation with its supervisors. . . .

At this point the attention of the investigators turned sharply from the test room to the regular shop department from which the girls had come. Why was the mental attitude of the girls different in the test room from what it had been in the department? In their conversation with one another and in their comments to the observers, the girls were full of comparisons between the test room and the department, very much to the disadvantage of the latter. They felt relief from some form of constraint, particularly the constraint of supervision. They were exceedingly disparaging about the supervisors in the department, although management felt that the department had particularly good supervisory personnel. These facts suggested that the management of the company really knew very little about the attitudes which employees took toward conditions in the plant and very little also about what constituted good supervisory methods. . . .

The interviewing was then extended to include a much larger group of employees than any hitherto studies, with the object of learning more about their feelings and attitudes. A beginning was to be made in the Inspection Branch, representing about 1,600 skilled and unskilled employees in both shop and office work. In the report of January 1931, the investigators stated that their purposes had been the following: "First, we wanted to know how employees felt about their work and the way they were treated; second, we desired to learn the manner in which the company policies were being applied and employees' reactions to them; third, we were hopeful that something would come out of these employee expressions which could be used to develop and improve the training of supervisors."

The supervisors in the Inspection organization were called together, and the project was described to them. Their criticism was invited, and various points in the plan were discussed at this meeting. Five interviewers were chosen from among the supervisors to conduct the interviews. Women were selected to interview women, and men to interview men. The interviewers were not to interview employees whom they knew, since their acquaintanceship might influence what was said. In particular, it was obvious that no one should interview any worker over whom he had administrative authority. Records of the interviews were to be kept, and comments on the working situation were to be set down as nearly verbatim as possible, but all records were to be confidential. The names of the persons interviewed were not to be associated with the records, and any identifying statements were to be omitted. This rule was kept so well that it limited the usefulness of the records. It meant that the details of particular interviews could not be put together to give a picture of an entire working group or department.

In accordance with these plans, the interviewing of employees in the Inspection organization was begun in September, 1928, a year and a half after the beginning of the Relay Assembly Test Room experiment. It was completed early in 1929. So favorable were the results that the decision was made to extend the program to the Operating Branch. For this purpose, the Division of Industrial Research was organized on February 1, 1929, with functions which were stated as follows:

"1. To interview annually all employees to find out their likes and dislikes relative to their working status.

"2. To study the favorable and unfavorable comments of employees.

    a. To initiate correction or adjustment of causes of unfavorable comments.

    b. To determine upon benefits to be derived from favorable comments and to instigate ways and means of acquiring these benefits.

"3. To conduct supervisory training conferences for all supervisors using employee interviews as a basis.

"4. To conduct test studies relative to employee relations, fatigue and efficiency."

The investigators discovered, in the course of the regular interviews, evidence here and there in the plant of a type of behavior which strongly suggested that the workers were banding together informally in order to protect themselves against practices which they interpreted as a menace to their welfare. This type of behavior manifested itself in (a) "straight-line" output, that is, the operators had adopted a standard of what they felt to be a proper day's work and none of them exceeded it by very much; (b) a resentment of the wage incentive system under which they worked—in most cases, some form of group piecework; (c) expressions which implied that group piecework as a wage incentive plan was not working satisfactorily; (d) informal practices by which persons who exceeded the accepted standard, that is, "rate killers," could be punished and "brought into line"; (e) informal leadership on the part of individuals who undertook to keep the working group together and enforce its rules; (f) feelings of futility with regard to promotions; and (g) extreme likes and dislikes toward immediate superiors, according to their attitude toward the behavior of the operators. The investigators felt that this complex of behavior deserved further study.

In view of these considerations, the decision was taken in May, 1931, to assign selected interviewers to particular groups of employees and allow them to interview the employees as often as they felt was necessary. The story of one of these groups is characteristic of the findings reached by this new form of interviewing. The work of the employees was the adjustment of small parts which went into the construction of telephone equipment. The management thought that the adjustment was a complicated piece of work. The interviewer found that it was really quite simple. He felt that anyone could learn it, but that the operators had conspired to put a fence around the job. They took pride in telling how apparatus which no one could make work properly was sent in from the field for adjustment. Then telephone engineers would come in to find out from the operators how the repairs were made. The latter would fool around, doing all sorts of wrong things and taking about two hours to adjust the apparatus, and in this way prevented people on the outside from finding out what they really did. They delighted in telling the interviewer how they were pulling the wool over everybody's eyes. It followed that they were keeping the management in ignorance as to the amount of work they could do. The output of the group, when plotted, was practically a straight line.

Obviously this result could not have been gained without some informal organization, and such organization in fact there was. The group had developed leadership. Whenever an outsider—engineer, inspector, or supervisor—came into the room, one man always dealt with him. Whenever any technical question was raised about the work, this employee answered it. For other purposes, the group had developed a second leader. Whenever a new man came into the group, or a member of the group boosted output beyond what was considered the proper level, this second leader took charge of the situation. The group had, so to speak, one leader for dealing with foreign and one for dealing with domestic affairs.

The different supervisors were largely aware of the situation which had developed, but they did not try to do anything about it because in fact they were powerless. Whenever necessary, they themselves dealt with the recognized leaders of the group.

Finally, the investigator found that the group was by no means happy about what it was doing. Its members felt a vague dissatisfaction or unrest, which showed itself in a demand for advancements and transfers or in complaints about their hard luck in being kept on the job. This experience of personal futility could be explained as the result of divided loyalties—divided between group and the company.

In order to study this kind of problem further, to make a more detailed investigation of social relations in a working group, and to supplement interview material with direct observation of the behavior of employees, the Division of Industrial Research decided to set up a new test room. They chose a group of men—nine wiremen, three soldermen, and two inspectors—engaged in the assembly of terminal banks for use in telephone exchanges, took them out of their regular department, and placed them in a special room. Otherwise no change was made in their conditions of work, except that an investigator was installed in the room, whose duty was simply to observe the behavior of the men. In the Relay Assembly Test Room a log had been kept of the principal events of the test. At the beginning it consisted largely of comments made by the workers in answer to questions about their physical condition. Later it came to include a much wider range of entries, which were found to be extremely useful in interpreting the changes in the output rate of the different workers. The work of the observer in the new test room was in effect an expansion of the work of keeping the log in the old one. Finally, an interviewer was assigned to the test room; he was not, however, one of the population of the room but remained outside and interviewed the employees from time to time in the usual manner. No effort was made to get output records other than the ones ordinarily kept in the department from which the group came, since the investigators felt that such a procedure would introduce too large a change from a regular shop situation. In this way the experiment was set up which is referred to as the Bank Wiring Observation Room. It was in existence seven months, from November 1931 to May 1932.

The method of payment is the first aspect of this group which must be described. It was a complicated form of group piecework. The department of which the workers in the observation room were a part was credited with a fixed sum for every unit of equipment it assembled. The amount thus earned on paper by the department every week made up the sum out of which the wages of all the men in the department were paid. Each individual was then assigned an hourly rate of pay, and he was guaranteed this amount in case he did not make at least as much on a piecework basis. The rate was based on a number of factors, including the nature of the job a worker was doing, his efficiency, and his length of service with the company. Records of the output of every worker were kept, and every six months there was a rate revision, the purpose of which was to make the hourly rates of the different workers correspond to their relative efficiency.

The hourly rate of a given employee, multiplied by the number of hours worked by him during the week, was spoken of as the daywork value of the work done by the employee. The daywork values of the work done by all the employees in the department were then added together, and the total thus obtained was subtracted from the total earnings credited to the department for the number of units of equipment assembled. The surplus, divided by the total daywork value, was expressed as a percentage. Each individual's hourly rate was then increased by this percentage, and the resulting hourly earnings figure, multiplied by the number of hours worked, constituted that person's weekly earnings.

Another feature of the system should be mentioned here. Sometimes a stoppage which was beyond the control of the workers took place in the work. For such stoppages the workers were entitled to claim time out, being paid at their regular hourly rates for this time. This was called the "daywork allowance claim." The reason why the employees were paid their hourly rate for such time and not their average hourly wages was a simple one. The system was supposed to prevent stalling. The employees could earn more by working than they could by taking time out. As a matter of fact, there was no good definition of what constituted a stoppage which was beyond the control of the workers. All stoppages were more or less within their control. But this circumstance was supposed to make no difference in the working of the system, since the assumption was that in any case the workers, pursuing their economic interests, would be anxious to keep stoppages at a minimum.

This system of payment was a complicated one, but it is obvious that there was a good logical reason for every one of its features. An individual's earnings would be affected by changes in his rate or in his output and by changes in the output of the group as a whole. The only way in which the group as a whole could increase its earnings was by increasing the total output. It is obvious also that the experts who designed the system made certain implicit assumptions about the behavior of human beings, or at least the behavior of workers in a large American factory. They assumed that every employee would pursue his economic interest by trying to increase not only his own output but the output of every other person in the group. The group as a whole would act to prevent slacking by any of its members. One possibility, for instance, was that by a few weeks' hard work an employee could establish a high rate for himself. Then he could slack up and be paid out of all proportion with the amount he actually contributed to the wages of the group. Under these circumstances, the other employees were expected to bring pressure to bear to make him work harder.

Such was the way in which the wage incentive scheme ought to have worked. The next question is how it actually did work. At first the workers were naturally suspicious of the observer, but when they got used to him and found that nothing out of the ordinary happened as a result of his presence in the room, they came to take him for granted. The best evidence that the employees were not distrustful of the observer is that they were willing to talk freely to him about what they were doing, even when what they were doing was not strictly in accord with what the company expected. Conversation would die down when the group chief entered the room, and when the foreman or the assistant foreman entered everyone became serious. But no embarrassment was felt at the presence of the observer. To avoid misunderstanding, it is important to point out that the observer was in no sense a spy. The employees were deliberately and obviously separated from their regular department. The observer did not, and could not, pass himself off as one of them. And if only from the fact that a special interviewer was assigned to them the members of the group knew they were under investigation.

The findings reached by the observer were more detailed but in general character the same as those which had emerged from the early interviews of other groups. Among the employees in the observation room there was a notion of a proper day's work. They felt that if they had wired two equipments a day they had done about the right amount. Most of the work was done in the morning. As soon as the employees felt sure of being able to finish what they considered enough for the day, they slacked off. This slacking off was naturally more marked among the faster than among the slower workmen.

As a result, the output graph from week to week tended to be a straight line. The employees resorted to two further practices in order to make sure that it should remain so. They reported more or less output than they performed and they claimed more daywork allowances than they were entitled to. At the end of the day, the observer would make an actual count of the number of connections wired—something which was not done by the supervisors—and he found that the men would report to the group chief sometimes more and sometimes less work than they actually had accomplished. At the end of the period of observation, two men had completed more than they ever had reported, but on the whole the error was in the opposite direction. The theory of the employees was that excess work produced on one day should be saved and applied to a deficiency on another day. The other way of keeping the output steady was to claim excessive daywork allowance. The employees saw that the more daywork they were allowed, the less output they would have to maintain in order to keep the average hourly output rate steady. The claims for daywork allowance were reported by the men to their group chief, and he, as will be seen, was in no position to make any check. These practices had two results. In the first place, the departmental efficiency records did not represent true efficiency, and therefore decisions as to grading were subject to errors of considerable importance. In the second place, the group chief was placed in a distinctly awkward position.

The findings of the observer were confirmed by tests which were made as a part of the investigation. Tests of intelligence, finger dexterity, and other skills were given to the workers in the room, and the results of the tests were studied in order to discover whether there was any correlation between output on the one hand and earnings, intelligence, or finger dexterity on the other. The studies showed that there was not. The output was apparently not reflecting the native intelligence or dexterity of the members of the group.

Obviously the wage incentive scheme was not working in the way it was expected to work. The next question is why it was not working. In this connection, the observer reported that the group had developed an informal social organization, such as had been revealed by earlier investigations. The foreman who selected the employees taking part in the Bank Wiring Observation Room was cooperative and had worked with the investigators before. They asked him to produce a normal group. The men he chose all came out of the same regular shop department, but they had not been closely associated in their work there. Nevertheless, as soon as they were thrown together in the observation room, friendships sprang up and soon two well-defined cliques were formed. The division into cliques showed itself in a number of ways: in mutual exclusiveness, in differences in the games played during off-hours, and so forth.

What is important here is not what divided the men in the observation room but what they had in common. They shared a common body of sentiments. A person should not turn out too much work. If he did, he was a "rate-buster." The theory was that if an excessive amount of work was turned out, the management would lower the piecework rate so that the employees would be in the position of doing more work for approximately the same pay. On the other hand, a person should not turn out too little work. If he did, he was a "chiseler"; that is, he was getting paid for work he did not do. A person should say nothing which would injure a fellow member of the group. If he did, he was a "squealer." Finally, no member of the group should act officiously.

The working group had also developed methods of enforcing respect for its attitudes. The experts who devised the wage incentive scheme assumed that the group would bring pressure to bear upon the slower workers to make them work faster and so increase the earnings of the group. In point of fact, something like the opposite occurred. The employees brought pressure to bear not upon the slower workers but upon the faster ones, the very ones who contributed most to the earnings of the group. The pressure was brought to bear in various ways. One of them was "binging." If one of the employees did something which was not considered quite proper, one of his fellow workers had the right to "bing" him. Binging consisted of hitting him a stiff blow on the upper arm. The person who was struck usually took the blow without protest and did not strike back. Obviously the virtue of binging as punishment did not lie in the physical hurt given to the worker but in the mental hurt that came from knowing that the group disapproved of what he had done. Other practices which naturally served the same end were sarcasm and the use of invectives. If a person turned out too much work, he was called names, such as "Speed King" or "The Slave."

It is worth while pointing out that the output of the group was not considered low. If it had been some action might have been taken, but in point of fact it was perfectly satisfactory to the management. It was simply not so high as it would have been if fatigue and skill had been the only limiting factors.

In the matter of wage incentives, the actual situation was quite different from the assumptions made by the experts. Other activities were out of line in the same way. The wireman and the soldermen did not stick to their jobs; they frequently traded them. This was forbidden, on the theory that each employee ought to do his own work because he was more skilled in that work. There was also much informal helping of one man by others. In fact, the observation of this practice was one means of determining the cliques into which the group was divided. A great many things, in short, were going on in the observation room which ought not to have been going on. For this reason it was important that no one should "squeal" on the men.

A group chief was in immediate charge of the employees. He had to see that they were supplied with parts and that they conformed to the rules and standards of the work. He could reprimand them for misbehavior or poor performance. He transmitted orders to the men and brought their requests before the proper authorities. He was also responsible for reporting to the foreman all facts which ought to come to his attention. The behavior of the employees put him in an awkward position. He was perfectly well aware of the devices by which they maintained their production at a constant level. But he was able to do very little to bring about a change. For instance, there was the matter of claims for daywork allowances. Such claims were supposed to be based on stoppage beyond the control of the workers, but there was no good definition of what constituted such stoppages. The men had a number of possible excuses for claiming daywork allowance: defective materials, poor and slow work on the part of other employees, and so forth. If the group chief checked up on one type of claim, the workers could shift to another. In order to decide whether or not a particular claim was justified, he would have to stand over the group all day with a stop watch. He did not have time to do that, and in any case refusal to honor the employees' claims would imply doubt of their integrity and would arouse their hostility. The group chief was a representative of management and was supposed to look after its interests. He ought to have put a stop to these practices and reported them to the foreman. But if he did so, he would, to use the words of a short account of the observation room by Roethlisberger and Dickson, "lose sympathetic control of his men, and his duties as supervisor would become much more difficult." [4] He had to associate with the employees from day to day and from hour to hour. His task would become impossible if he had to fight a running fight with them. Placed in this situation, he chose to side with the men and report unchanged their claims for daywork. In fact, there was very little else he could do, even if he wished. Moreover, he was in a position to protect himself in case of trouble. The employees always had to give him a reason for any daywork claims they might make, and he entered the claims in a private record book. If anyone ever asked why so much daywork was being claimed, he could throw the blame wherever he wished. He could assert that materials had been defective or he could blame the inspectors, who were members of an outside organization. In still another respect, then, the Bank Wiring Observation Room group was not behaving as the logic of management assumed that it would behave. . . .

The workers in the room were obsessed with the idea that they ought to hold their production level "even" from week to week, but they were vague as to what would happen if they did not. They said that "someone" would "get them." If they turned out an unusually high output one week, that record would be taken thereafter as an example of what they could do if they tried, and they would be "bawled out" if they did not keep up to it. As a matter of fact, none of the men in the room had ever experienced a reduction of wage rates. What is more, as Roethlisberger and Dickson point out, "changes in piece rates occur most frequently where there is a change in manufacturing process, and changes in manufacturing process are made by engineers whose chief function is to reduce unit cost wherever the saving will justify the change. In some instances, changes occur irrespective of direct labor cost. Moreover, where labor is a substantial element, reduction of output tends to increase unit costs and instead of warding off a change in the piece rate may actually induce one."

What happened in the observation room could not be described as a logical reaction of the employees to the experience of rate reduction. They had in fact had no such experience. On the other hand, the investigators found that it could be described as a conflict between the technical organization of the plant and its social organization. By technical organization the investigators meant the plan, written or unwritten, according to which the Hawthorne plant was supposed to operate, and the agencies which gave effect to that plan. The plan included explicit rules as to how the men were to be paid, how they were to do their work, what their relations with their supervisors ought to be. It included also implicit assumptions on which the rules were based, one of the assumptions being that men working in the plant would on the whole act so as to further their economic interests. It is worth while pointing out that this assumption was in fact implicit, that the experts who devised the technical organization acted upon the assumption without ever stating it in so many words.

There existed also an actual social situation within the plant: groups of men, who were associated with one another, held common sentiments and had certain relations with other groups and other men. To some extent this social organization was identical with the technical plan and to some extent it was not. For instance, the employees were paid according to group payment plans, but the groups concerned did not behave as the planners expected them to behave.

The investigators considered the relations between the technical organization and the social. A certain type of behavior is expected of the higher levels of management. Their success is dependent on their being able to devise and institute rapid changes. Roethlisberger and Dickson describe what happens in the following terms: "Management is constantly seeking new ways and new combinations for increasing efficiency, whether in designing a new machine, instituting a new method of control, or logically organizing itself in a new way." The assumption has often been made that these changes are designed to force the employee to do more work for less money. As a matter of fact, many of them have just the opposite purpose: to improve the conditions of work and enable the employee to earn higher wages. The important point here, however, is not the purpose of the changes but the way in which they are carried out and accepted.

Once the responsible officer has decided that a certain change ought to be made, he gives an order, and this order is transmitted "down the line," appropriate action being taken at every level. The question in which the investigators were interested was this: What happens when the order reaches the men who are actually doing the manual work? Roethlisberger and Dickson made the following observations: "The worker occupies a unique position in the social organization. He is at the bottom of a highly stratified organization. He is always in the position of having to accommodate himself to changes which he does not originate. Although he participates least in the technical organization, he bears the brunt of most of its activities." It is he, more than anyone, who is affected by the decisions of management, yet in the nature of things he is unable to share management's preoccupations, and management does little to convince him that what he considers important is being treated as important at the top—a fact which is not surprising, since there is no adequate way of transmitting to management an understanding of the considerations which seem important at the work level. There is something like a failure of communication in both directions—upward and downward.

The worker is not only "asked to accommodate himself to changes which he does not initiate, but also many of the changes deprive him of these very things which give meaning and significance to his work." The modern industrial worker is not the handicraftsman of the medieval guild. Nevertheless, the two have much in common. The industrial worker develops his own ways of doing his job, his own traditions of skill, his own satisfactions in living up to his standards. The spirit in which he adopts his own innovations is quite different from that in which he adopts those of management. Furthermore, he does not do his work as an isolated human being, but always as a member of a group, united either through actual cooperation on the job or through association in friendship. One of the most important general findings of the Western Electric researches is the fact that such groups are continually being formed among industrial workers, and that the groups develop codes and loyalties which govern the relations of the members to one another. Though these codes can be quickly destroyed, they are not formed in a moment. They are the product of continued, routine interaction between men. "Constant interference with such codes is bound to lead to feelings of frustration, to an irrational exasperation with technical change in any form, and ultimately to the formation of a type of employee organization such as we have described—a system of practices and beliefs in opposition to the technical organization."

The Bank Wiring Observation Room seemed to show that action taken in accordance with the technical organization tended to break up, through continual change, the routines and human associations which gave work its value. The behavior of the employees could be described as an effort to protect themselves against such changes, to give management the least possible opportunity of interfering with them. When they said that if they increased their output, "something" was likely to happen, a process of this sort was going on in their minds. But the process was not a conscious one. It is important to point out that the protective function of informal organization was not a product of deliberate planning. It was more in the nature of an automatic response. . . .

It is curious how, at all points, the Relay Assembly Test Room and the Bank Wiring Observation Room form a contrast. In the former, the girls said that they felt free from the pressure of supervision, although as a matter of fact they were far more thoroughly supervised than they ever had been in their regular department. In the latter, the men were afraid of supervision and acted so as to nullify it. . . . Both groups developed an informal social organization, but while the Bank Wiremen were organized in opposition to management, the Relay Assemblers were organized in co-operation with management in the pursuit of a common purpose. Finally, the responses of the two groups to their industrial situation were, on the one hand, restriction of output, on the other, steady and welcome increase of output.

C. TYPES OF GROUP INTEGRATION AND GROUP COHESION
AS ILLUSTRATED IN THE FAMILY PATTERN

In recent years, especially during the last decade, sociologists have concerned themselves with the problem of group cohesion. Early attempts at analysis of social solidarity, as it was then referred to, were reflected in the writings of Émile Durkheim and Ferdinand Tönnies.[5] Since World War II, interest in group cohesion has expressed itself in terms of "group morale." [6]

Many definitions have been suggested for group cohesion and group morale. What should the concepts be from a scientific, objective, operational standpoint? In the preceding section, we said that for a group to be a group it must possess a minimum of the following attributes: (1) multiple personnel, (2) a set of values, (3) a recurrent and organized pattern of overt affiliation and interaction among the personnel leading to the fulfillment of these values, and (4) subjective identification of the personnel with the values and with each other. These are the factors that are present in every human-social group. Factors 3 and 4 are those which uniquely differentiate the human-social group from other social aggregates. These factors exist in varying degrees in different groups.

The degree of presence or absence of each of these factors (factors 3 and 4) will determine the extent to which a group is integrated and the extent of group cohesiveness and group morale. Club A, which has an active member participation by perfect attendance at meetings, and whose members possess a high *esprit de corps,* feeling of belongingness, or profound sense of loyalty to the club (to the club's values and to each other), is to be distinguished from Club B, whose attendance at meetings is as good as Club A's but whose members lack the feeling of loyalty or personal identification. Club A may be said to manifest a higher degree of group integration or group cohesion. Furthermore, an individual may not *overtly* affiliate himself with a group (register, matriculate, pay dues), but nevertheless *feel* himself a part of a group. There are thus varying degrees and kinds of group integration.

The diagram below illustrates a highly integrated group, type A, with a high degree (+) of *overt affiliation* and *covert identification;* type D, most poorly integrated; and types B and C of medium integration. B possesses large overt affiliation (+) and poor sense of belonging among its members (—), while C shows a high (+) sense of identification with a small (—) number of affiliates.

GROUP COHESIVENESS

	Overt Affiliation	Covert Identification
A	+	+
B	+	—
C	—	+
D	—	—

Three family case studies are cited to illustrate three different degrees of family group integration—highly integrated, moderately integrated, and unintegrated.*[7]

1. *Highly Integrated Family*

There were four members of the Baxter family—father, mother, and a pair of twins, a boy and a girl. The parents were 44 and 43, and the children 19. They lived in half of a 50-year-old double house in the better residential district of a

* Reprinted from *The Family Encounters the Depression* by Robert Cooley Angell. Copyright, 1936, by Charles Scribner's Sons; used by permission of the publishers.

Michigan town known for its wealth and cultivated traditions. Their neighbors were a banker, a newspaper editor, a lawyer, two salesmen, a shoestore proprietor, the owner of a farm-implement store, a judge, and a carpenter. Less than three blocks away were the main street, the library, a grade school, three churches, a lumber yard, and a park. The house itself was one of the Victorian era, with high ceilings and a generous yard. Fine old elms shaded the yard and the street in front. Only the lower floor was wired for electricity and Welsbach burners were still used in the bedrooms.

The furnishings of the house were in keeping with Mr. Baxter's income of $5000 a year and with his position in the community as an insurance agent and a county highway commissioner. There were several antique pieces of furniture and a tapestry or two. Other possessions included a radio, sporting equipment of various kinds, and an inexpensive automobile. The family also owned a cottage at a nearby lake and held a membership in a country club there.

Mr. Baxter was in good health, inclining a little toward stoutness, but energetic and interested in sports. He was cheerful and frank, a man who tried hard to win, but a good loser too. He neither took life lightly nor did he take it so seriously as to rob it of its joy. He read a good deal, considering how little time he had free from his two jobs. In magazines his taste ran to light fiction; and although many of the 100 or more books he read in a year were of the same sort, he occasionally perused a biography, an historical work, or a novel of the better types such as one of Galsworthy's. Though not a college man, his tastes were not dissimilar from those of the college men of the community.

His social and community activities were many. He was an officer in both the Chamber of Commerce and the Rotary Club and belonged to two lodges. He was very fond of bridge and was a member of two bridge clubs, one made up of married couples, the other a stag organization. His associates and friends were the leading citizens of the town. He was a vestryman of the Episcopal Church and faithful in attendance.

Mr. Baxter had not saved a great deal, partly because of the many calls on his pocketbook and partly because he was by nature generous. This was particularly true where the members of his own family were concerned, for he wanted them to have the best opportunities possible. He was a model husband and father and never showed any favoritism or antagonisms within the family circle. Inclined to feel that his wife and his son were a little too idealistic in their conceptions, he charged this to lack of contact with the rude world of realities and was tolerant of their views.

Mrs. Baxter was also very energetic. In fact she tended to overdo. She was a member of the D.A.R., an officer of a women's club and of the Board of Education, was in the guild of the Episcopal Church and active in the Michigan Federation of Women's Clubs. This was all in addition to her housework, which she did by herself, and very thoroughly. She had had a college education, specializing in music, and before her marriage had taught the piano. She did not read quite so

much as her husband, for she found little time, but she took two women's magazines and a few club and political publications. Her other amusements were golf,
bridge, and going to the movies.

It was due to her unceasing efforts that the home was so pleasant. She saw to it
that the house and yard were kept in fine order, and she frequently rearranged
rooms in order to vary the home and make it attractive. The Baxter household had
a reputation for hospitality for which she should receive the chief credit.

Her position on the Board of Education brought a small salary which she saved,
as far as possible, for the education of the children.

Her friends, like her husband's, were drawn from the most highly educated
circles in the community and she was considered more or less a leader among
them. Her attitude toward the rest of the family was one of sincere affection and
helpfulness. She shared both triumphs and disappointments. Her one weakness
was an extreme sensitivity to what others said, especially family members, so that
she was frequently hurt by trivial remarks which really had no significance.

Marjorie was a slight girl of medium height, whose healthy freshness and pretty
features made her extremely attractive. She had, however, suffered at one time
from infantile paralysis, and, though this had left no external mark, she was not
as strong as she appeared to be. She had learned to swim, dance, and otherwise
enjoy the recreations of her friends. Her nature was a sunny, cheerful one and she
was known for her "pep."

At this time she was in a small college, a happy member of a sorority and doing
excellently in her studies. Her particular interests were music and dramatics. She
loved to read, principally novels and plays. Her best friend was winning state
honors in public speaking and debating.

She too made family life pleasant for the rest. She was frank, sincere, and
thoughtful. Though capable of penetrating observation and criticism, she never
offered her opinions in a malicious spirit. Like her mother she was somewhat sensitive of others' criticism of her.

Harlow was larger than his sister, very tall and rather slim. Like the rest he was
energetic, but perhaps a little more nervous than the others. He had engaged all
through high school in many branches of sports and kept himself in constant
training.

His personality was an odd mixture of sincerity and cynicism. He was loyal and
devoted to his family and friends but at the same time somewhat contemptuous of
the "great unwashed" public. He was serious and conscientious to a fault. Reading
took a great deal of his time. Beside the usual youthful taste for fiction and adventure stories, he had a real fondness for substantial works dealing with economic
and political problems. He was the type to enjoy chess and studious bridge as well
as outdoor sports.

He was at this time attending the same college as his twin sister. There he was
a fraternity member, class officer, advertising manager of the college paper and a
member of the tennis and basketball teams. His only earnings were $2.50 a week

from his newspaper work. His friends were the active and more intelligent students on the campus.

The Baxters are interesting from an historical viewpoint. Mrs. Baxter's lineage was distinguished, and there were artists, judges, writers, and editors among her living relatives. The family, however, took on no airs and had worked hard to earn itself a position in the community, especially since the time of a bankruptcy just after the War. That they had succeeded in this endeavor is attested by the high opinion in which they were held by the people of the community.

The social organization of the family was a closely woven texture with the mother at the center. She, more than any one else, had a definite ideal and definite plans for reaching it. It was she to whom all turned for consultation and advice. Mrs. Baxter and Marjorie were closer to one another than any other pair, but there was no exclusiveness in their relation. The twins were conscious of the pride their parents had in them and the ambitions for their future, so that it was their chief care not to disappoint these high expectations.

Family life was not always harmonious, but the little frictions were such as soon disappear in the wider stream of family interests and hopes. Temporary annoyance was often due to the frank criticism given, but in the long run this was not a disrupting but an integration factor, for it emphasized the interdependence of the members.

The Baxters did a good deal together. They frequently played golf, or bridge, went driving, or attended church or a movie as a group. Every Sunday night they held open house and their friends dropped in to pop corn, play simple games, and otherwise enjoy a sociable evening.

The "we" feeling in this family was very strong. One never thought of his own welfare alone. Though the objectives of the family were never consciously enunciated and discussed, there was a felt unity of purpose which was very powerful.

2. Moderately Integrated Family

There were three generations in the Haskins household—the maternal grandmother, aged 75, the parents, both 49, and three children, boys of 20 and 17, and a girl of 15. They lived in a fashionable suburb of Detroit where they were surrounded by well-to-do neighbors whose houses cost from $20,000 to $30,000. Their house was of moderate size, well furnished, and equipped with electric refrigerator, electric range, and other modern devices. The family income of about $16,000 enabled them to keep a Packard car, to have a maid who came in by the day, and in addition a laundress and scrubwoman who came two days a week.

Mr. Haskins was in the real-estate and insurance business. He had risen to the presidency of a brokerage which was a very successful firm. He was a steady worker, not nervous, rarely angry. His health had always been excellent and he possessed a fine physique—6 feet 2 inches tall and weighed 170. He had been a physical instructor in the army during the War.

His sense of humor was notable and he was constantly joking at the dinner table. This trait led to his keen enjoyment of Robert Benchley, Donald Ogden Stewart, and other writers of this sort. His reading was not confined to this type of book, however, for he read much serious literature. His other forms of recreation were golf, touring, fishing and hunting in Canada, and, above all, bridge. He was an expert at the latter game and enjoyed some prestige in the neighborhood on that basis. His friends were business men of his own type who were members of his clubs.

Though he liked to spend money on cars and on vacation trips to Canada or Florida, he was cautious in money matters and never played the stock market. He paid all bills promptly and wished the other members of the family to be methodical with the allowances which he gave them.

He was a trifle reserved, even within the family circle. Though always just in dealing with the children, he was usually firm. The only exception had been his leniency toward the younger boy, William, who had been expelled from school for misdemeanors.

Mrs. Haskins had not been very well for some time. She had had several operations. Her desire to entertain and go out socially made her do too much and left her nervous and irritable. She was vivacious outside the family circle, but within it was inclined to be short tempered and cross. Occasionally, however, she was very amusing. Her "society" interests led to an emphasis on etiquette, which sometimes annoyed the children. She was fond of playing bridge and also enjoyed going with her husband on trips. Her friends were of the "bridge club" type.

Mrs. Haskins had complete control of the household budget, but was not particularly economical or efficient in this capacity. She bought new furnishings more often than seemed necessary to the rest, and spent excessive amounts entertaining. To the children she was generous, but favored first one and then another, thus causing jealousies.

Her angry outbursts toward other members of the family were discounted as resulting from her poor health. She never quarrelled with her husband, but found it very difficult to get along with her mother, who held notions about raising the children which Mrs. Haskins considered old-fashioned.

Mrs. Williams, the grandmother, was in fair health for her age. She also tried to do more than her health made wise. Her recreations were reading and automobile riding. She tried to aid with housework, but her efforts hindered rather than helped. She was very economical, and spent her $40 a month pension from the government frugally. (Her husband had been a captain in the Civil War.) Her one extravagance was gifts to the children. She played no favorites in this, but she was more fond of Franklin, the older boy, than of the rest, probably because she had taken care of him for some time when he was a baby.

Franklin was a tall, healthy university student, bright, but rather superficial in his academic work. He carefully avoided introspection and was inclined to live a pleasurable sort of existence. He worked in the summer time and bought his clothes out of his earnings. Like his father, he was punctual in payment of bills.

His principal recreations were horseback riding, canoeing, tennis, shooting, bridge, and reading. His friends were fraternity men and sorority girls of good character. In the family, he felt sorry for his grandmother and tried to make things pleasant for her. He was critical of his younger brother for his high-school misbehavior and his general thoughtlessness. For his father he had the highest respect.

William was a lad of a good deal of capacity, but lazy and easygoing. Bland and self-assured, he was a brilliant writer for his age and had worked spasmodically for the high-school paper. He had never worked during vacations and even neglected his chores around the house. Golf, cards, and reading were his amusements, and he mingled with a questionable set of youngsters of an irresponsible type. He was constantly borrowing money from other members of the family and had no notion of saving. He had even resorted to poker playing and selling old clothes to raise funds. He was not at all companionable with the rest of the family. He disregarded his parents' wishes frequently and would not associate with his brother.

Marie was in junior high school at this time. She was more like Franklin than like William. A good student, but a little lazy, she was energetic in her play and enjoyed swimming and horseback riding. She was beginning to go out with boys and liked to buy clothes. However, she was in general frugal and saved her allowance. She idolized her father and mother, was somewhat resentful toward her grandmother who constantly criticized her notions, and sided with Franklin against William, who teased her.

The Haskins were very proud of their lineage, which extended back beyond the Revolution in this country to aristocratic English ancestors. On the living-room wall was the family coat of arms. William was the only one who did not take his lineage seriously.

The household seemed to be organized on a rather individualistic basis. Whatever leadership there was was exercised by Mr. Haskins. There were some family "affairs" such as Sunday afternoon rides with the grandmother, but the children usually participated half-heartedly and unwillingly. During Christmas and birthday celebrations there was a more genuine sense of solidarity. There was very little sharing of troubles or ambitions. Each one kept his affairs very much to himself. Thus, although there was considerable family pride in an abstract sort of way, there was a minimum of cooperative activity and experience.

3. *Unintegrated Family*

The Clarks lived in Pontiac, Michigan, where Mr. Clark had been for many years a foreman over the watchmen and elevator men in an automobile factory. He was 48, his wife was 44, there was a married daughter living in the same city, a boy in college who did not return even in the summer, except for a brief visit, and a little girl, aged nine. Thus there were really only three in the household group at this time. Their six-room house was one of a large number of those that the automobile company had built and sold to its employees. The families in the neighborhood were those of better-paid workers, and their yards and houses were well kept up. The Clarks' furniture was adequate and kept in good condition. They owned an inexpensive car, and they were in the habit of getting a new one every two years. Mrs. Clark had a fur coat, Mr. Clark belonged to a lodge, the home contained a radio and a telephone, and they entertained occasionally, all of which showed a high standard of living for a worker's family.

Mr. Clark was short and stocky, a little inclined to stoutness. He was very strong, both because of constant work and because of an emphasis throughout his life on physical recreation. He had had some college training and was fond of reading, but his eyes were rapidly giving out. Though a very sincere person, he was inclined to be dogmatic, and was very short-tempered when crossed. He had a few friends but indulged little in social activities. However, he belonged to a patriotic organization. He was distant, even to the members of his own family. Quiet and detached, he never seemed to "warm up" to any one. He had no ideal of a united, cooperative family life. He seemed to be quite willing that the members of the family should live together under one roof without any close ties of affection. The two older children had had to earn all their money from an early age. Because of this lack of any feeling that he should help them get started in the world, these children had become bitter toward their father.

His wife had a mild, easy-going, compromising temperament, but she was somewhat weary of the drudgery of continuous hard work. She none the less managed to maintain a certain optimism. Her principal job was the running of the household. Her hobbies were music and raising flowers. She, like her husband, belonged to a patriotic society. Her relatives and the neighbors with whom she was friendly were very fond of her. Her usual cheerfulness made her a pleasant companion. She was quite close to her children, but seemed to have little depth of affection for her husband.

Arthur, the boy away at college, was hard-working, serious and intelligent. He had supported himself entirely since leaving high school. His sense of the unfairness of his father's treatment of himself and his older sister had led him to stay away from home except for Christmas and occasional week-ends.

Alice, the nine-year-old daughter, had been indulged much more than either of the other children, and was consequently a little spoiled.

Although Mr. and Mrs. Clark cherished a secret ambition to have their children succeed, both intellectually and economically, Mr. Clark's theory seemed to be that this would come to pass only if they were left to fight their own battles. The married daughter and Arthur, brought up in this way, had little "home" feeling. Despite this, they felt affection for their parents.

The family had always been dominated by the father. His word was law, and no project of which he disapproved received any backing from him. The answer of the children had been revolt. Mrs. Clark had tried to be the go-between and diplomat of the family, but with slight success. Solidarity was almost entirely of the bread-and-butter or symbiotic variety. There were no common activities except the meals. Christmas and Thanksgiving celebrations were the only family occasions.

D. HIGHLY COHESIVE INFORMAL GROUPS AND THEIR RELATION TO OUTSIDERS

In the last few years, several research studies and analytical monographs have appeared dealing with the relations of members in established informal groups with outsiders and with the relations of these members to newcomers and their assimilation into the group.[8] From these investigations it was discovered that: (1) the cohesive, informal, primary group manifests in each of its members a deep feeling of responsibility to others of the group; (2) each member is highly sensitive to the opinion of the others in the group; (3) in times of stress—as in war combat or in antisocial acts among juvenile gang members—the feelings of responsibility and sensitivity serve to reduce the sense of fear among the individual members in carrying out their tasks even if they involve threatened injury; (4) strong group cohesiveness tends to lead to exclusiveness in the group membership and the members are usually distrustful and suspicious of outsiders; and (5) newcomers have to prove themselves before they are fully accepted into the group.

In the two situations presented below, we see some of these propositions illustrated. The first is a description of a combat outfit in Italy during World War II. It was written by Bill Mauldin, who lived the life of a soldier in the front line and emerged during the war as a great artist able to reveal in text and cartoons the true soldier. The second case describes the interpersonal relations of boys in a street-corner gang.

1. *Men in an Army Combat Team* [9]

While men in combat outfits kid each other around, they have a sort of family complex about it. No outsiders may join. Anybody who does a dangerous job in this war has his own particular kind of kidding among his own friends, and sometimes it doesn't even sound like kidding. Bomber crews and paratroopers and infantry squads are about the same in that respect. If a stranger comes up to a group of them when they are bulling, they ignore him. If he takes it upon himself to laugh at something funny they have said, they freeze their expressions, turn slowly around, stare at him until his stature has shrunk to about four inches and he slinks away, and then they go back to their kidding again.

It's like a group of prosperous business men telling a risqué joke and then glaring at the waiter who joins in the guffaws. Combat people are an exclusive set, and if they want it to be that way, it is their privilege. They certainly earn it. New men in outfits have to work their way in slowly, but they are eventually accepted. Sometimes they have to change some of their ways of living. An introvert or a recluse is not going to last long in combat without friends, so he learns to come out of his shell. Once he has "arrived" he is pretty proud of his clique, and he in turn is chilly toward outsiders.

That's why, during some of the worst periods in Italy, many guys who had a chance to hang around a town for a few days after being discharged from a hospital where they had recovered from wounds, with nobody the wiser, didn't take advantage of it. They weren't eager to get back up and get in the war, by any means, and many of them did hang around a few days. But those who did hang around didn't feel exactly right about it, and those who went right back did it for a very simple reason—not because they felt their presence was going to make a lot of difference in the big scheme of the war, and not to uphold the traditions of the umpteenth regiment. A lot of guys don't know the name of their regimental commander. They went back because they knew their companies were very short-handed, and they were sure that if somebody else in their own squad or section were in their own shoes, and the situation were reversed, those friends would come back to make the load lighter on them.

2. *Boys in a Street-corner Gang* [10]

When I started to play in the alleys around my home I first heard about a bunch of older boys called the "Pirates." My oldest brother was in this gang and so I went around with them. There were about ten boys in this gang and the youngest one was eleven and the oldest one was about fifteen. . . .

Tony, Sollie, and my brother John were the big guys in the gang. Tony was fifteen and was short and heavy. He was a good fighter and the young guys were afraid of him because he hit them and beat them up. Sollie was a little guy about twelve years of age. He couldn't fight, but he was a smart guy and told stories and made plans for the gang. He was the brains of the gang. My brother was fifteen and was bigger than Tony and was a good fighter. He could beat any guy in the gang by fighting, so he was a good leader and everybody looked up to him as a big guy. I looked up to him as a big guy and was proud to be his brother. . . .

When I started to hang out with the Pirates I first learned about robbing. The guys would talk about robbing and stealing and went out on "jobs" every night. When I was eight I started to go out robbing with my brother's gang. We first robbed junk from a junk yard and sometimes from the peddler. Sometimes we robbed stores. We would go to a store, and while one guy asked to buy something the other guys would rob anything like candy and cigarettes and then run. We did this every day. Sollie always made the plans and Tony and John would carry out the plans.

The gang had a hangout in an alley and we would meet there every night and smoke and tell stories and plan for robbing. I was little and so I only listened. The big guys talked about going robbing and told stories about girls and sex things. The guys always thought about robbing and bumming from school and sometimes from home. . . .

Besides robbing, the gang went bumming downtown and to ball parks and swimming. On these trips we always robbed everything we could get. . . .

When I was ten the gang started to rob stores and homes. We would jimmy the door or window and rob the place. I always stayed outside and gave jiggers. The big guys went in and raided the place. They showed me how to pick locks, jimmy doors, cut glass, and use skeleton keys and everything to get into stores and houses. Every guy had to keep everything a secret and not tell anybody or he would be beat up and razzed. The police were enemies and not to be trusted. When we would get caught by the police we had to keep mum and not tell a word even in the third degree.

I looked up to my brother and the other big guys because of their courage and nerve and the way they could rob. They would tell me never to say a word to anybody about our robbing. My mother didn't even know it. Some kids couldn't be in the gang because they would tell everything and some didn't have the nerve to go robbing. The guys with a record were looked up to and admired by the other guys. A stool-pigeon was looked down on and razzed and could not stay in the gang. . . .

The guys stuck together and helped each other out of trouble. They were real good pals and would stick up for each other. They were always planning new crimes and new ways to get by without being caught. Everyone hated the police and looked upon them as enemies. Anybody who was friendly to the police were not trusted. The plans for stealing were always secret and anybody who talked about them to fellows outside of the gang or to the police was not trusted and became an enemy of the Pirates. . . .

E. THE CROWD AS A FORM OF COLLECTIVE BEHAVIOR

In sociology, the term *collective behavior* is used in a special sense. It refers to the forms of collective action that are *not* governed by a set of organized roles, sustained system of rules and regulations, or feeling of unity among the participants. Rather, collective behavior is the study of spontaneous, unorganized forms of collective activity. It includes such concepts as crowds, mobs, publics, panics, manias, fads, revivals, and other unplanned, unchannelized, collective expressions. The crowd simply represents a special type of this kind of collective action.

Sociologists have classified crowds into several types, including the *casual* crowd (a momentary collection of people seeking similar ends, such as boarding a bus); the *spectator* or *conventional* crowd (a gathering of people with a central focus and similar ends, passive in character, and less ephemeral than the casual crowd, such as sports audiences);

the *expressive* crowd (a gathering of people with little central focus on any objective, where activity is engaged in as an end in itself and for personal release from tension, such as dancing crowds and religious orgies); and the *acting* aggressive crowd (a collection of individuals with a central objective toward which activity is directed, such as a lynching mob).

All of these crowd types, while different from each other in one or two attributes, possess characteristics which are common and general to all of them. This sets the crowd off from other forms of human collectivities such as the human-social group. A crowd may be characterized: (1) by the physical presence of its members; (2) by lack of organization among its members; (3) by its short-livedness; (4) by the anonymity and emotional involvement of its participants; (5) by the suggestibility among its members which makes for a circular interstimulation; and (6) by the presence of cultural-background factors conducive to the formation of crowds.

In the first case, we have an illustration of an expressive crowd in action. It is clear that the initial excitation of the minister followed by the cumulative, circular interstimulation among the members of the congregation works the gathering up to a high frenzy of wild cries, physical, uncontrolled shakes, and shrieks of hysteria—all serving as release to pent-up urges and internalized personal compulsions. The crowd in this case acts as a means for expression of previous religious attitudes and feelings; the crowd does not generate or create the attitude. These attitudes have been built up over a long period of time; the funeral crowd permits their expression into overt action.

The same may be said about the second case, which describes the behavior of a mob in a lynching situation. The active crowd forms when an unusual event (or even a rumor of an unusual event) occurs which violates community mores. It is for this reason that there must always be a cultural background for the creation of this kind of crowd or mob. Anger, excitement, and frequently hysterical assertions mount, and the members interact with one another on an exceedingly emotional plane. Leaders emerge who tend to channelize the crowd's activities in the direction in which they are already moving. The focus of the participants becomes strongly centered on their purpose, and when the high level of emotional tension is reached the crowd fulfills its intentions. It dissolves after a period of action, when emotions begin to level off and individuals return to a semblance of individual awareness.

1. *A Case of an Expressive Crowd: The Funeral of "Sister President"* [11]

A short time ago, while I was principal of a little backwoods high school and a participant-observer in a small town on the Mississippi Delta, I was caught up in one of the greatest social events ever to befall our little community.

Lo and behold! "Sister President," mother of the church, had died when "she was just getting ready for the annual convention of the missionary society at Jackson." Word-of-mouth reported that she had died one year, one month, and one day later than her husband, "Reverend President," the greatest preacher ever to have circulated in those parts. Rumor had it that a good neighbor upon being informed of Sister President's death immediately fell dead herself.

The staunch church members quickly proceeded with the arrangements for the funeral. Circulars in the form of handbills were printed and distributed throughout the communities of the county, announcing the time of the funeral and the prominent personages to appear on the program. Reverend H—— was to officiate, and a prominent singer was to come all the way from Rosedale, a distance of ninety miles, to sing "over" Sister President one of her favorite songs—"Life Is Uncertain, but Death Is Sure."

The day of the funeral finally came. Very few of the persons (if any) went to work that morning and some had driven scores of miles to be present. St. Andrew's Church could not accommodate everyone interested, so as a consequence hundreds of persons were milling around the sides and front of the building.

At about eleven o'clock, shortly after services had begun, the frame walls of the church started to crack under the immense strain of the large numbers within, so someone had the idea of finishing the services at the school.

Shortly I saw great numbers of persons "swarming" over to my institution. Fowls and pigs that heretofore had been walking complacently in the roadway now fluttered, cackled and bolted in various directions, adding to the confusion. I rushed out to contact the minister or whomever I could to ascertain what was happening, but I was immediately pushed aside. Pretty soon I saw a dozen or more persons running with a casket in the direction of the building. Someone finally told me in a wild-eyed fashion that—"the church is fallin' down—dey gonna finish havin' it at the school."

I rushed back indoors to attempt to dismiss the children, but saw them already scampering in all directions. One of my teachers (a refined, quiet, modest little lady, if ever there was one) jumped out of the window. Children were trampled upon and "shooed" out. Some were crying, others were laughing and had gone into the auditorium along with the crowd.

After approximately one half hour, the seats were arranged. Additional benches had been brought over from the church and one had been placed around the walls. One of the ministers was complaining miserably about his pocketbook containing one hundred dollars that had been stolen as the crowd rushed from the church to the school.

The services got under way again. Eight or ten ministers were seated on the platform together with the combined church choirs. Seated down front were the members of the various mystic burial orders to which Sister President had belonged. Two groups that I recall were the Knights and Daughters of Tabor, and the members of the Order of the Beautiful Star. The Knights carried in their hands cardboard swords, and the members of the Beautiful Star were dressed in white robes having on their heads paper crowns on which were pasted silver stars. They had all filed in ceremoniously and had been allowed to be seated—the crowd being held back. When they had taken their seats the people rushed in and sat on whatever was available. Some of the persons were sitting two and three to a seat, on one another's laps. Others sat on the window ledges and still others reclined against the walls.

The "rattling" of feet began, and as the ministers delivered their sermons various members of the audience would give shrill screams and fall prostrated. Responsive ushers would place these persons out on the lawn and a relative or friend would burn chicken feathers, placing the fumes to the noses of the victims to revive them. (The feathers had been brought along especially for this purpose.)

The eminent singer from Rosedale, an elderly gentleman, was late in arriving and was unable to force his way through the crowd to the platform. News of his presence finally got to the stage and one of the preachers stated that—"if the good brother from Rosedale will go 'round to the side, we might kin git him in through the window." This he did. He was able to sing Sister President's selection.

Occasionally a choir member would get so enraptured through the rendering of a song that she too would be overcome and would have to be carried outside. The pianist cried sadly throughout the services and from time to time she would look mournfully out to the audience, resting her chin downwards on one shoulder. Some of the persons were not quite "out" when they yelled and resisted attempts to remove them. With wild swinging of the arms and with cries of "unloose me," "unloose me," they struggled against anyone attempting to take hold of them. In instances like these the more muscular ushers would "grapple" with the victims and would secure "arm locks" on them, holding them taut until they were subdued.

Finally, the great Reverend H——, who had reserved last place on the program for himself, gave his sermon. He started off very piously and soberly, talking of Sister President's wonderful spirit, her achievements, and her general love of humanity. With consistent "egging" from the ministers on the platform and with cries of "come on," "come on," Reverend H—— too entered into the spirit of the occasion. He snarled, gnashed his teeth (displaying a set of bright yellow gold), gurgled, growled, and gasped, apparently losing control of himself at intervals. Dramatically and with appropriate gestures he likened Sister President to a "great soldier":

"An' standin' therfo' havin' her loins girt with truth—and havin' on the breas' plate of righteousness. And her feet shod wid the preparation of the gospel of peace—and above all—'bove all—takin' the shield of faith, and the helmet of salvation and the sword of the spirit, which is the word of God."

This last part of the sermon was repeated over and over again for increased emphasis. One lady sang out from the back of the audience in a high shrill voice—"It's early in the evenin'—and my soul is getting tired." Others remarked "Well" and "Lord" at heightened intervals. (Words can scarcely express the tension that pervaded the room.)

The audience "rattled" their feet, clapped their hands and cried out "Amen! Amen!" With much mopping of his brow, Reverend H—— (with his coat now hanging partly off) was pulled back to his chair by some of the other ministers, some of whom shook his hands and others of whom patted him on the back. At this time the choir started up a chant of the "Old Ship of Zion." With the first verses being sung, at least a score of persons screamed and cast their arms into the air—"Have mercy, Lord." With each successive verse an increasing number joined in. When they proceeded to the words, "it has landed my dear mother," bedlam broke loose. Some of the people danced if they could find any space, patting themselves on the legs while slipping sidewise, some caressed their neighbors, others slapped someone, and still others were content to just "give out" with piercing yells. This continued for at least twenty minutes, finally coming to an end with grunts and a dwindling of the "rattling" of feet.

The announcement was given that the audience could now "view the remains." As the persons passed the coffin some said "Goodbye, Sister President—I'll be seeing you soon." Others just wept, drying their eyes with one hand, while finishing up a sandwich with the other, as food had been brought along. It was well after three o'clock when the "viewing" was over.

When they attempted to inter the remains of Sister President, several persons had to be withheld from jumping into the grave. One person succeeded and had to be helped out of the excavation.

After the tires that had gone flat were fixed, the mules hitched to the wagons, and the drunken persons "gathered" up, they all made the long trek home to talk for months about the "time" they had had, and to await with patience the next great occasion.

2. *A Case of a Lynching Mob* [12]

Shortly after nine o'clock on Monday, September 8, 1930, George Grant, Negro, alleged slayer of the Brunswick Chief of Police, was shot to death in a second floor cell of the McIntosh County jail at Darien, Georgia. He had been placed there only a few minutes before by National Guardsmen and the county sheriff. A member of the Guard was in the jailhouse yard and the commanding officer of the Guard was within hearing distance of the fatal shots; the county sheriff was in a downstairs room of his house which opens upon the narrow corridor leading to the second floor cells.

During the last summer of 1930, there were repeated burglaries of the bank and stores of Darien. There were indications that the guilty persons were amateurs. All of the burglaries had occurred on Thursday and Sunday nights after midnight.

Unknown to anyone except the town night watchman, the mayor deputized Ora Anderson, fifty-five years old, to aid in apprehending the burglars.

About midnight on Sunday, September 7, seeing some men on the street, Special Officer Anderson hid near the bank. These men went on up the street. After a time, however, a Negro man came along on the outer edge of the sidewalk, going in the direction of the bank. There was no evidence that he was planning to rob the bank other than that it was late Sunday night, that the bank had been entered before on Sunday night, and that he was going along the sidewalk in its direction. A few feet behind him came a second Negro, who passed close beside Anderson's hiding place. Anderson stated that the Negro saw him and, pulling a gun, said "You son of a b——, I've got you where I want you," and began firing. One bullet went through his shoulder, another struck his trigger finger, a third went into his leg, a fourth pierced his gun barrel, and the fifth went wild. Though dazed and wounded, Anderson fired at the Negroes as they turned and ran down the slope toward the river's edge and disappeared in the thicket.

Anderson called to the night watchman who was nearby; and presently the fire bell was rung, and many of the townspeople turned out. Upon learning the cause of the alarm, the Negroes who had responded returned quietly to their homes. The sheriff, who was not well, sent his daughter for his only deputy. He also telephoned Glynn County officers and requested bloodhounds. Citizen guards were stationed at the Altamaha River bridge and along the edge of the marsh.

After a while Chief Freeman and a deputy from Brunswick came, and they with the local deputy entered the marsh with a flashlight. After two hours' searching, they cornered a Negro, later believed to have been George Grant, upon a narrowing point of land between the river and a wide ditch. The Negro fired upon them repeatedly. All three officers were wounded; Chief Freeman died instantly. The pursued Negro escaped further into the marsh.

When the sheriff learned of Freeman's death and the wounding of the two deputies, he called to Statesboro and Blackshear for bloodhounds, and notified the sheriffs of many other counties that a "race riot" was threatening at Darien. During the early morning hours, excited officers and men rushed into Darien from a dozen counties.

Seeing that the situation was fast getting past the control of the local sheriff and his one wounded deputy, the chairman of the county commissioners called upon state officials to send the National Guard. Shortly after daylight eighteen National Guardsmen arrived from Savannah.

By good daylight bloodhounds were baying in the marshes, and at nine o'clock George Grant called out "Prisoner surrenders," and came out of the marsh with hands high in the air. The National Guardsmen, several sheriffs and deputies, and hundreds of excited people were along the edge of the old rice field, not far away. Grant surrendered to the sheriff, saying that he had done no shooting, but that he was with "Nigger Freddy Bryan," who had wounded Anderson and killed Freeman. A .32 pistol with three empty chambers was in Grant's possession. Freeman had been killed with a .38. Had Grant thrown one pistol away, or had somebody else killed Freeman? Grant answered Anderson's description of height, weight, and stocking cap of the Negro who walked past his hiding place near the bank shortly after midnight, but not of the Negro who had fired upon him.

When Grant voluntarily surrendered, he was on the opposite side of a deep ditch from the sheriff; in crossing it the Negro fell into the water over his head. As he scrambled out, more than a score of people had guns drawn, and threatened to kill him. Others came, and by the time the Guardsmen arrived to escort Grant to the jail, approximately a hundred armed men were begging the sheriff to let them kill him.

Surrounded immediately by Guardsmen, and then by a couple of hundred hangers-on, Grant was marched through the town to the jail, less than a mile away.

On the way to the jail, while the prisoner was in the custody of the Guardsmen, special officer Anderson and at least one other man hit Grant over the head with the butts of heavy pistols. Along the line of march a big man carrying a rifle, reported to have been a guard at a nearby county camp, threatened three Negro boys innocently standing in a store door; cursing in boisterous fashion, this man persistently urged the crowd to lynch Grant. Others were yelling, "Lynch the damn son of a b——!" "Let us have him!" and the like. The mayor stated that a county commissioner, trying to keep the mob from its purpose, was summarily told by one of the upcountry man hunters: "Shut your mouth and keep it shut, and that right quick!" Excitement was at a high pitch.

Upon arriving at the jail, members of the Guard placed Grant in the "bull pen" on the second floor. The sheriff locked the grated door on the cell corridor, leaving Grant free to go through the inter-connecting corridor from one cell to another. The sheriff's only key to the solid steel door at the head of the stairs was gone. He told the investigator that he was not disturbed about the missing key, for he knew "some of the folks wanted it, and had taken it." Hence the solid steel door was left open. The Guardsmen who placed Grant in the second floor cells entered by the outside west door, and left the jail by the same doorway, posting a uniformed man there to guard it. However, there were two other entrances which were left unguarded.

The crowd which had followed Grant to the jail went in and out of the sheriff's yard, porch, and rooms at will. A Brunswick lawyer, the local state senator, and several other people from Darien called attention to this fact, but nothing was done about it.

While people were coming and going through the sheriff's rooms, he was on a cot by the window with a "fainty spell" (his own words). One of his teen-age daughters was on the porch screaming hysterically that the sheriff's only deputy, wounded in the marsh, had just died (which was not a fact; the deputy recovered), and calling for somebody to go kill the "nigger." Her condition was so hysterical that it was brought to the attention of a local physician who was in the crowd. An older woman from Brunswick also loudly demanded the lynching of the Negro.

While the women continued to scream, and the crowd within and about the jailhouse kept coming and going, with the sheriff still lying in a stupor, three shots, with a slight interval between, were heard on the second floor. After a few moments, a fourth shot rang out. George Grant had been killed in the McIntosh County jail. His blood dripped through into a white woman's cell below.

When the body was brought down for a coroner's inquest, the Brunswick woman was loath to see it go away—she wanted it burned then. It was taken to Brunswick in a truck, and is reported to have been placed before a white undertaker's establishment so the public could "come and see" who killed Chief Freeman.

F. AN EXPERIMENTAL CASE IN PANIC BEHAVIOR [13]

At eight P.M. eastern standard time on the evening of October 30, 1938, Orson Welles with an innocent little group of actors took his place before the microphone in a New York studio of the Columbia Broadcasting System. He carried with him Howard Koch's freely adapted version of H. G. Wells's imaginative novel, *War of the Worlds*. He also brought to the scene his unusual dramatic talent. With script and talent the actors hoped to entertain their listeners for an hour with an incredible, old-fashioned story appropriate for Hallowe'en.

Much to their surprise the actors learned that the series of news bulletins they had issued describing an invasion from Mars had been believed by thousands of people throughout the country. For a few horrible hours people from Maine to California thought that hideous monsters armed with death rays were destroying all armed resistance sent against them; that there was simply no escape from disaster; that the end of the world was near. Newspapers the following morning spoke of the "tidal wave of terror that swept the nation." It was clear that a panic of national proportions had occurred.

Unfortunately it would be impracticable to present here the 135 case studies available from the interviews. Each gives a fascinating story in itself; if each were studied a fuller appreciation of the intricacy of the panic would result. We shall content ourselves with a few examples.

WELL EDUCATED—FRIGHTENED

Mr. Robbins is twenty years old, single, a junior in a New Jersey college. His father is an executive in a large business concern. The family is very well to do. Mr. Robbins, Jr. has his own car and his own stocks. He is a Protestant and occasionally attends church.

Young Robbins was driving in his car with a friend. They were returning to college after visiting the friend's girl. They were just ready to cross the New Jersey border when they tuned in to station WABC. There was dance music and then a news flash telling of the meteor. Robbins was admiring the Columbia news broadcasting reports, for they seemed to have people on the spot for all emergencies. When Professor Pierson from Princeton began to talk, Robbins thought he had heard of him and soon began to get worried. He and his friend were very upset when they learned that the route to Trenton was closed. Since his family lived in New Jersey, he stopped at a drugstore to phone and see if they were all right. There were four people in the drugstore and he excitedly told them the news. In the phone booth he was told that the lines were jammed and he couldn't get the call through. By the time he got out of the phone booth, the people in the drugstore were hysterically listening to the radio. He became convinced that "something was wrong" and decided to drive back to rescue his friend's girl. While driving top speed they kept the radio tuned and heard the Secretary of the Interior which meant to them that "control was out of our hands." He turned the radio off because he "could not bear to hear the worst." He prayed "if there is a God to help us now." "I was waiting for doom to strike. I could practically smell the gas." They tuned back to other stations shortly to get other reports. Then they turned back to WABC to hear the announcer say his was the last station on earth. Then they knew it was a play. But they were drenched in perspiration. Robbins could not digest his food properly for the next few days and said he lost five pounds during the evening.

Robbins's answers in the interview indicate that in spite of a good deal of formal training, he is a man of conventional tastes and average intelligence. When asked what magazines he read he indicated *Esquire, Reader's Digest, Collier's*. He said he read no books other than those assigned to him. In the newspapers he is chiefly interested in sports, society, and foreign news. When asked about his interests he mentioned tennis and the advertising business. This conformity to the social group seems due not merely to Robbins's age. In answer to the question concerning the things he was most proud of he said, "My background, my family tree, and my advanced knowledge."

This man probably knows more than the average person but he lacks the ability to think independently. Hence he is particularly susceptible to prestige suggestion. He was inclined to believe the broadcast because it came over CBS which had a "good reputation for news." The Princeton professor and the government official greatly impressed him. His knowledge and education are for him a matter of social standing rather than sources upon which he can draw for understanding. He prays to "God if there is one" rather than trust his knowledge. All his knowledge did for him was to make him realize that "every phenomenon is possible." This means that for a person as conventional as he is, every danger will be regarded as real if it is presented with authority.

Very important in accounting for Robbins's reaction is the fear he had that something will happen to make him financially insecure. He pictures as the major catastrophe that could occur in the United States "a great class struggle in the not distant future. Unless the quality of the people running the country improves the country will degenerate." "Things are very insecure at present. The President is meddling into everything and as long as he is in power things cannot improve." In the war crisis during the fall of 1938 he was not concerned about the people involved but about "business and my own stocks." Here was a crisis that was affecting him drastically, together with his friends and his family. These were precisely the people he had always feared were scheduled for trouble and his deep worry for his class gave him a standard of judgment which made him believe that "the end of our civilization" (but not the end of the world) had come.

WELL EDUCATED—NOT FRIGHTENED

Dr. Hamilton is a physician, twenty-nine years old, married with one small child. At present he is just building up his own private practice in a New Jersey industrial town. He has saved enough money during his last two years' work as doctor in a CCC camp to pull him through the uncertain year ahead of him. He is a Protestant but never goes to church. He lives in a rented house with his office downstairs and living quarters upstairs. He has his own car and telephone.

Dr. Hamilton was listening to the radio in his office around 7:50. Then he was interrupted and came back when the *War of the Worlds* broadcast was on "when they got the artillery out." He had missed the first part and did not know the program was a play. For a moment he believed the reports but quickly doubted the reality of the stories because of the rapidity with which things moved. He tuned to a couple of other stations and then turned back to Welles and enjoyed the play. He thinks the idea of Martians "is fun to play with but there is not much to back it up."

For Dr. Hamilton life is interesting and satisfactory. When asked what things in his life he would want to have different, he answered, "Not a thing at the moment. Of course, I would like to have a better established practice." There is no doubt in his mind, however, that he will soon be able to achieve the latter. He says that he worries less than other people and thinks he has "always had things pretty lucky."

The doctor's wishes are free of any desire for self-aggrandizement. No items of social standing are checked. They are devoid of any hint of a feeling of personal insufficiency or incompleteness. He feels neither threatened from within nor from without. This is not because he is ignorant of possible misfortunes for he reads a great many books on economics, science, politics, philosophy and biography. He seldom reads magazines. The only worry he has is that we might be involved in a war in which he would be drafted. This might mean the destruction of his work and he himself might be crippled. The only thing he is afraid of is that he "would lose the use of his hands." He is not afraid of anything except physical impacts which he cannot control. And war, with all its destructiveness, he regards contemptuously as the result of other peoples' foolishness.

Dr. Hamilton is a person of more than average analytical ability. He is free of sentimentality and impatient with people who live "humdrum existences." He says he is not proud of anything—only content. He does "not play around with ideas" unless there is some data to base them on.

It is clear from these two case studies that "education" alone is no sure insulation from panic. The personalities of Robbins and Dr. Hamilton are very different.

Each has used formal training for different purposes. For Robbins, knowledge produces a passive concern with events; for Hamilton, it is a tool which he uses to obtain the adjustment he wants. For Robbins, life is a matter of carrying on a tradition which he believes is now seriously threatened; for Hamilton, it is something he feels he has mastered and to which he looks forward with confidence.

ECONOMICALLY INSECURE—FRIGHTENED

Mr. Lewis is a young man, twenty-four years of age, employed testing calibrators. He is single and lives with his ailing mother who is completely dependent on him. They own a home in a working-class neighborhood in a New Jersey city, have no phone but a '36 model car. He has a Catholic background but never goes to church. Having finished high school he is now studying to become a fashion designer.

He was visiting at a friend's home when the friend suddenly called him into the room where he was listening to the radio telling him that "we are being invaded." He first thought it was all "baloney," but upon hearing the gunfire at familiar places and when his friend was so utterly convinced that the whole broadcast was true he, too, accepted it as such. They both got in the car to warn his family and the neighbors. On the ride he smelled the gas the announcer had been talking about and also saw red in the sky. His only concern was "to flee the city." They listened to the radio only for a short while. Everybody in his friend's house was rushing away. He thought the announcer was talking about a gas that would destroy the eastern part of the country. For him it was a temporary catastrophe. The army would rush to the people's aid. When home he turned the radio on— the announcer was just telling that the "gases had passed over." Incidentally he looked at the radio page and saw the announcement of a play. So he went up to the newspaper office to discover that "other people had made fools of themselves too."

His main objection to the broadcast is "not the dramatic content but the use of actual names." He admits himself that the thing that made him inclined to believe in the broadcast was "the proximity to the place where I live." The general "hysteria" of the people he was with also affected him. He felt "we were caught right on the porch." His main concern was: "Now I will not be able to finish school. Next I thought about my family—my mother, sitting unaware of the catastrophe."

Mr. Lewis's reaction is not founded on a lack of intellectual ability to approach the situation described in the broadcast. Although without a great amount of education he is intelligent and interested in understanding things clearly. He reads four newspapers daily, two of them, *The New York Post* and *The Daily Worker,* very carefully. He mentions as his most absorbing interests, literature and economics. He reads *The Nation* and *The New Masses* regularly as a subscriber. He finds no time now to read books because he is working very hard. But he excuses it by saying "he used to before." His favorite radio programs are "symphonic broadcasts, F.D.R. speeches." He has followed the Czechoslovakian crisis closely, "always waiting to hear the worst." As the most useful developments in the last twenty years he considers "machinery"; most dangerous he considers "Fascism." Rocket ships and interplanetary communication he considers "slightly possible in future times." He feels that "man controls events on this earth." When asked if life is possible on Mars he answered "Why not? Of course I have read that life there is possible only under very difficult conditions but still there might be other forms of life than our own." He is not a scholar but he is an alert sort of person trying to educate himself on the track of things. The best indication of his intellectual clear mindedness is the fact that despite his fear of Fascism, and his belief in some sort of life on Mars, he did not interpret the broadcast as either an invasion of the Nazis or the Martians. He believed it to be a "temporary catastrophe" which involved personal danger and an individual end of him, his friends and neighbors. It meant to him "not being able to finish school," that is, not being able to get to a stage where he could do the kind of work he wanted. It also meant to him "having my mother sit there unaware of the catastrophe," that is, not being able to take care of her. In brief, the broadcast meant to him the failure of his personal life. He accepted it as the interruption of his life rather than as a catastrophe related to some meaningful concept. The broadcast was accepted as true not because the "invasion from Mars" made any sense to him, not because the "end of the world" was a familiar frame of reference, but because he knew no reason why anything bad should not happen to him.

All the answers given to questions concerning his personal life point to great insecurity. This insecurity is partly economic, inasmuch as his mother is dependent on him. But, on a deeper level it is an insecurity concerning himself and his ability to do the kind of work he would like to do. His present job consists of routine, but not secure, work which he hates but must keep to make a living. He wants to become a fashion designer. Aside from the insecurity of his present job he is questioning his abilities to be a good designer. When asked what were the things in his life which he would like to have different he answered: "A different job." When asked what he would most like to have he said: "Old-age security, job security, interesting type of work." All answers point to dissatisfaction with his present situation and his insecurity concerning the future. But when asked what were the three things he was most proud of, he did not mention his artistic talents. Instead he said: "My sincerity, and I am proud of America." In other words, there was not only no actual achievement he could point to but also no ability which might eventually provide for the desired achievement.

We cannot say whether or not Mr. Lewis is talented or whether he will ever be able to make any commercial use of latent talents. Hence it is impossible to estimate the real basis of his feeling of insecurity. But most important here is the fact that he is working against time. When asked what were the three things he was most afraid of, he said, "fear that I won't become a good fashion designer, fear that I won't live long enough to do what I want to." Since he has to work for a living, since he has not accomplished anything to date as an artist, he is chiefly concerned with what he can do with the time he has left. After all, he is only twenty-four years old and has life ahead of him. But the catastrophe told by the broadcast would have cut out precisely all his expectations. The broadcast seemed plausible to him because of its local character, and because of the fact that it was just the piece of bad luck he has been fearing would happen to him. He can fight economic troubles and cope with spiritual demons. But he needs to be alive to do it.

His acceptance of the broadcast as true might also be due partially to a sense of relief. He has his doubts about his ability. He has set himself a task he is sincerely determined to carry out. But his aspiration is proving a burden. He admits that "life often seems futile." This "temporary catastrophe" would free him from his present responsibilities to himself and to others.

Economically Insecure—Not Frightened

Mr. Chandler is thirty-six years old, married with no children. He is a painter but has been out of work most of the time ever since the depression. He lives in an apartment in a poor semi-business section of a New York suburb. He has no car or telephone. He finished grammar school and then went to business school. He is a Protestant and goes to church occasionally.

Mr. Chandler turned to the Orson Welles broadcast incidentally. His wife and her sister's family were with him. He started to listen "when a meteor had fallen." "When I heard that I was very much interested. I have always been interested in things of that kind. I thought maybe my brother-in-law could drive me to the place where the meteor had fallen. I listened further. But when the reporter said he and a professor had travelled eleven miles in ten minutes it seemed impossible. As a result of the news flashes the streets would be crowded. They could not possibly have gotten there so fast. So I took up a newspaper and saw it was a play. From then on it was so fantastic I would not have believed it anyway."

Mr. Chandler accepted the story first as true because of the topic and the technique used. But despite the fright of his co-listeners, he was doubtful almost immediately. He made adequate checks by consulting the paper and noticing the regular air-mail plane which he felt would not be flying if there were something really wrong. His doubt began because of the discrepancy between the expected crowding of the streets and the reported speed of the announcer.

Chandler accepted the account of a fallen meteor as a physical phenomenon in which he was interested. He did not expect any further developments of this phenomenon. His natural reaction was that he would like to go and see the meteor. He imagined that this would be the reaction of most people and hence suspected that the streets would be crowded with cars. Since he has no car, he had to wait and get more reports from the radio. These he expected. But instead, an announcer and professor were on the spot almost at once. And in place of hearing more about a meteor he heard about something no one could identify or describe. Rather than wait for the announcer to find an adequate terminology for the event, Mr. Chandler consulted his newspaper so that he could "place" this adventure in its proper frame of reference. He had "read a lot of adventure stories like that," and from then on enjoyed the drama.

Mr. Chandler is a man who has his own opinions about things and is not easily dissuaded. When asked how he behaved when in conversation with an older person who disagreed with him, he said he maintained his views rather than seeming to give in. Mr. Chandler furthermore is not afraid of the "unbelievable" or the "unknown," but considers them things to be physically mastered. Although not well educated in the formal sense, he reads two daily papers, listens to radio news, and reads the *National Geographic*. The interview revealed no religious interpretations. The major catastrophe he can picture happening to the American people is a natural catastrophe of some kind. When asked what he would most like to have he said: "No war, no depression and an interesting type of work," adding that everything else would be taken care of if he had these three.

Mr. Chandler takes all things at their face value apparently because of his personal courage, his own feeling of personal security, and his shrewd reasoning. When asked what were the three things he was most afraid of, he said, "Nothing." This he said, in spite of the fact that he has been out of work most of the time in the last ten years and has no money at all. The lack of money worries him but does not give him any feeling of insufficiency or inferiority for he does not believe it is in any way his fault. He spends his spare time "painting works of art" and thinks he has painted "some pretty good ones." When asked what he would like to have changed, he said, "I would like to have a job that would give me enough money and leisure to afford painting on the side."

The cases of Mr. Lewis and Mr. Chandler are in striking contrast. Both would like to be doing something else than they are doing at the moment, both would like "an interesting type of work," both would like to become artists. But for Mr. Lewis a failure as an artist would mean economic failure and a confession of inability, whereas for Mr. Chandler art is merely a hobby which he would like to indulge if he had money to study it.

Chandler feels self-sufficient and psychologically secure—given a job, no depression, and no war he thinks he could adjust himself satisfactorily. Lewis, on the other hand, wants old-age and job security—a guarantee that there will be no impacts from the outside. This difference is the more interesting since it is Lewis who now has a job. Because Lewis is psychologically insecure he is terrified by the broadcast which means that he can never be a success; because Chandler is at ease with himself and his conditions, he takes the broadcast realistically.

RELIGIOUS PERSON—FRIGHTENED

Miss Jane Dean is an unmarried woman, fifty-seven years old. She lives with her sister in a house she owns. Her home is in a small New Jersey town. She has a modest but secure income. Miss Dean only went to grammar school. She is a Protestant who attends services frequently.

She had tuned in the radio accidentally in company with her sister, at the time when "beings came out of the meteor." She says, "Of course I did not make any attempt to check up on the broadcast. When I hear something like that I take it for granted it is true." At 8:30, when the station identification was made, she turned her radio off, assuming that "it was the end of everything." Then she sat and prayed with her sister until a friend called her on an unrelated matter, and, during the discussion, told her it was a play. She confirmed this by calling a newspaper office. At this point she reports, "I got plenty mad. I had been asking God for forgiveness of my sins so that I would not be committed to eternal purgatory. I was glad I asked forgiveness anyhow even if I did not have to."

In Miss Dean's case there was a frame of reference quite adequate to account for her fright. She "knew that the forces of God were overpowering us," and was sure "we were given punishment at last for all our evil ways." She did not doubt the broadcast for a second because her religious beliefs had made her expect a catastrophe. As she states herself, "I knew we would be punished sooner or later."

Apparently she did not listen to the end because: "I wanted to have a chance to atone for my sins. I prayed and hoped it would do me some good. It eased our hearts so we were resigned." She did not mind death but wanted to die forgiven because "it is the life after life which is important." It is "not worthwhile" to try to save this life.

Miss Dean's mental world is a narrow one whose boundaries seem largely determined by religious dogmas and from which external events in the real world are deliberately excluded. She prides herself on not reading much in the local newspaper except the church news. She does not read any magazines because she does not want to "waste her time reading trash." On the radio she listens mainly to hymns. When asked what developments in any field she considered most useful she refused the whole idea of progress by saying "none will really help us." She is completely ignorant of scientific or other achievements and furthermore refuses even to believe they are possible. For her, people live chiefly to commit sins and to be punished for doing so. The most dangerous development in the last twenty years is the "way young people behave." Her religious background made her state that the most realistic part of the broadcast was "the sheet of flame that swept over the entire country. That is just the way I pictured the end." (There was no mention of any sheet of flame in the broadcast.)

One may assume that Miss Dean is a deeply frustrated woman who has turned fanatic since her religion is the only explanation she can find for a life bare of joys. She has made a virtue of frustration. Just what personal experiences in the past have led her to this condition we do not know. She mentioned "conflicts in her life," but refused to elaborate on them.

For her it is a sin to live a full life. When asked what were the things she was most proud of she answered, "Don't you know that pride cometh before a fall?" The life after this life will compensate for her troubles. She checks as the only desirable thing, "no war in the next fifty years," leaving out all items providing for the development of personality or the enrichment of social life.

Thus for Miss Dean an end of the world is not only a plausible proposition but one that she may almost want to happen. It is an event that vindicates her beliefs and gives meaning to the kind of life she has led. She and her sister are resigned and prepared for the event while other people who have freely indulged in sin must face a horrible reckoning.

FOOTNOTES TO PART THREE

Footnote 4 is directly quoted from original source.

1. By a persistent pattern of interaction is meant a pattern that is not fleeting, amorphous, or fortuitous, such as a street-corner crowd, but relatively enduring and recurrent. By an organized pattern of interaction we mean a *system* of interrelated functions and a coordination of member activities. Organization arises when individuals assume their roles in relation to others —roles of leaders, followers, presidents, secretaries, subleaders, foremen, and so on.

2. George C. Homans, *The Human Group* (New York: Harcourt, Brace and Company, Inc., 1950), p. 141. Also, F. Merei, "Group Leadership and Institutionalization," *Human Relations,* Vol. II (1949), p. 28: "The leader is stronger than any one member. He is weaker than *group traditions,* and is forced to accept them. He is stronger than the individual member, weaker than the 'plus' which a group is over and above the sum of the individuals in it. He is stronger than the members, weaker than the formation."

3. From George C. Homans, "The Western Electric Researches," in *Fatigue of Workers: Its Relation to Industrial Production,* by the Committee on Work in Industry of the National Research Council (New York: Reinhold Publishing Corporation, 1941), pp. 58–62, 63–67, 75–86.

*4. F. J. Roethlisberger and W. J. Dickson, *Management and the Worker,* Business Research Studies, No. 9 (Cambridge, Mass.: Harvard Business School, Division of Research, 1939). All quotations relating to the Western Electric researches are from this study as well as from the book of the same title by the same authors.

5. *Cf.* Émile Durkheim, *The Division of Labor in Society,* translated by George Simpson (New York: The Macmillan Company, 1933); Ferdinand Tönnies, *Gemeinschaft und Gesellschaft,* translated by Charles P. Loomis and published under the title of *Fundamental Concepts of Sociology* (New York: American Book Company, 1940).

6. See special issue of *The American Journal of Sociology,* Vol. XLVII (November, 1951); G. B. Watson (ed.), *Civilian Morale* (Boston: Houghton Mifflin Company, 1942); W. F. Ogburn (ed.), *American Society in Wartime* (Chicago: University of Chicago Press, 1943); S. A. Stouffer and others, *Studies in Social Psychology in World War II* (Princeton, N.J.: Princeton University Press, 1949), Vols. I and II.

7. Reprinted from *The Family Encounters the Depression* by Robert Cooley Angell, pp. 18–25, 31–36, 39–42. Copyright, 1936, by Charles Scribner's Sons; used by permission of the publishers.

8. Ronald Lippitt, "An Experimental Study of the Effect of Democratic and Authoritarian Group Atmospheres," in "Studies in Topological and Vector Psychology," by K. Lewin, R. Lippitt, and S. Escalona, *Studies in Child Welfare,* Vol. XVI, No. 3 (1940); E. Mayo and G. F. F. Lombard, *Teamwork and Labor Turnover in the Aircraft Industry of Southern California* (1944); Stouffer and others, *op. cit.,* Vol. II; Edward A. Shils, "Primary Groups in the American Army," in Robert K. Merton and Paul F. Lazarsfeld (eds.), *Continuities in Social Research* (Glencoe, Ill.: The Free Press, 1950), pp. 16–39.

9. From *Up Front* by Bill Mauldin.

Copyright, 1945, by Henry Holt and Company, Inc. Used by permission of the publishers.

10. Clifford R. Shaw, *The Jack-Roller* (Chicago: University of Chicago Press, 1929), pp. 10–11.

11. From Joseph H. Douglass, "The Funeral of 'Sister President,'" *Journal of Abnormal and Social Psychology,* Vol. 39 (1944), pp. 217–220. Used by permission of the American Psychological Association.

12. From Arthur F. Raper, *The Tragedy of Lynching* (Chapel Hill, N.C.: The University of North Carolina Press, 1933), pp. 203–207.

13. Hadley Cantril, *The Invasion from Mars* (Princeton, N.J.: Princeton University Press, 1940), pp. 3, 167, 168–182.

PART FOUR

The Community and Social Class

A. THE MEANING OF COMMUNITY AND COMMUNITY TYPES

For a community to be recognized as a community, or for a collection of individuals to be designated as a community, it must possess all the attributes previously mentioned as characteristic of the human-social group together with one additional attribute. The people are territorially oriented: they reside in a given locale or area in which they trade; their children go to school there; and they participate in the social institutions of the circumscribed area. These are the external, overt manifestations of group life in a given locale. In addition, the members of a community not only act together but we find that they share a consciousness of spatial unity; they possess a sense of belonging to a place. Thus there are persons who not only live in New York, or Iowa, or Georgia but who also *feel* like New Yorkers, Iowans, or Georgians.

It might be well to make a further distinction here between a community and a neighborhood, which is also territorially anchored. The difference consists in the community's being a larger and less intimate unit of organization than the neighborhood. The members of a neighborhood are in face-to-face contact; in the community both primary and secondary contacts prevail. The community, in fact, is composed of neighborhoods as interdependent units.

In addition to this difference in size and type of interpersonal relations, the community supplies the basic needs of the local inhabitants through the presence, in the locality, of the necessary human institutional organizations providing the essential economic, religious, educational, and professional services. The neighborhood, on the other hand, sometimes grows up around one institution, a church or a school, and furnishes at most only two or three essential services.

This should not be interpreted as meaning that a community is self-sufficient. No community, even the largest city, is self-sufficient. A community should rather be thought of as being self-subsistent; a neighborhood is not.

As with other human-social groups, communities may be contiguous to each other; they may overlap; or they may exist within other communities. Classification of communities depends also on the index we employ as the basis of classification: degree of primary relations, size, duration, special interests and functions (resort towns, industrial towns, farming villages), or any other scientifically workable instrument. In recent years, however, sociologists have increasingly employed the concept of polar types in delineating communities.

Before we indicate the types of human communities sociologists have consistently referred to, we should perhaps say a few words about the method and logic involved in determining community types. In contemporary scientific methodological theory, the notion that truth and knowledge can be obtained through pure observation—pure empiricism, as it is called—has been abandoned. Observation depends on conceptualization; the percept on the concept. Without some guiding idea or concept, or frame of reference, we do not even know what facts to gather.

How do we go about knowing a tree, for example? We try to study the tree chemically, or botanically, or geologically, or perhaps sociologically (perhaps it is conducive to group activities such as picnicking, children's playing, or young peoples' courting). We employ the frame of reference of chemistry, or the concepts of botany, or the assumptions of sociology. This means that there is no science without concepts, things without ideas, facts without abstractions. This is what Alfred North Whitehead, one of the world's great philosophers, meant when he wrote that the "paradox has been well established that our utmost abstractions constitute the most potent weapons in the control of concrete facts."

It is for this reason that science has had to invent abstract tools, ideal entities, pure types in order to understand the actual reality. Thus the perfect Euclidean circle with a circumference of $2\pi r$ and an area of πr^2 cannot actually be duplicated in the external physical world. Similarly, the entire field of thermodynamics is based on what would happen in a frictionless engine even though such an engine is an actual impossibility. In the same sense, the scientist has mentally constructed the perfect vacuum, perpetual motion, the pure Nordic, as tools for understanding the given. Such constructs or ideal types become important tools for the analysis and comprehension of existing data.

The same devices have been employed in the social sciences and in sociology. We speak of primary groups, economic man, capitalism, democratic government, the upper class—each constitutes an abstract notion, a pure image, an ideal type. Democracy, in essence, implies complete political self-rule of a people. Only by keeping in mind the perfect notion, the pure image of democracy, are we able to understand the extent to which democracy is in actual operation. By conceptualizing the perfect primary group we can understand the degree of primariness in a particular group. The ideal type acts as a pivot around which we orient our knowledge of the actual and the given.

Now, as governments vary among themselves in degrees of democracy, they deviate from the ideal construct of democracy. The same is true with groups and their attribute of primariness. If a government has very little democracy it must have something more of another type; we say it approaches dictatorship—a contrary ideal type. As a group recedes from its pole of primariness it approaches the pole of secondary, or formal, relationships. In short, ideal types are useful in sociological analysis if they are paired into polar types, each of the pair constituting the exact contrary construct of the other, as north and south poles, rural and urban communities, zero and infinity, sacred and secular.

This principle of polarity is a maxim of intellectual search, like the principle of causality, against the abuse of which it may serve as a help. . . . In physical science the principle of polarity would thus be represented by the principle of action and reaction, and the principle that wherever there are forces there must be resistance. In biology it has been expressed by Huxley, in the aphorism that protoplasm manages to live only by continually dying. Philosophically it may be generalized as the principle, not of the identity, but of the necessary copresence and mutual dependence of opposite determinations. . . . Professor Marshall, in his *Principles of Economics,* has used the same figure to denote the mutual dependence of the economic factors of supply and demand.[1]

In community analysis sociology has employed such polar types as *Gemeinschaft* and *Gesellschaft,* rural and urban, primary and secondary, folk and civilization, sacred and secular, familistic and contractual, communal and associational.[2] For our purposes, we shall consider these pairs synonymous in their connotations. They imply the terminal extremes of a continuum between which existent communities may be allocated. If the three communities described below were so placed along a continuum with the poles "idealizing" the internal system of social relationships in these communities in terms of primitive folk and modern urban, the pattern would appear to be approximately as follows:

This brings up the question as to what we mean by these polar types. If we take the terms *folk* and *urban* as synonymous with all of the other paired polar types, they signify opposite systems of social relations that can be summed up as follows: [3]

Primitive Folk	*Modern Urban*
1. Personal ties and relationships only important ends	1. Interpersonal ties as means to ends; more impersonal relations
2. Traditionalistic (long-established social habits govern action)	2. Rationalistic (ends and means are consciously weighed in social action)
3. Sacred	3. Secular
4. Small in size	4. Large in size
5. Folk wisdom	5. Science and mechanics
6. Familism	6. Individualism
7. Moral relations	7. Instrumental relations
8. Static society	8. Rapidly changing society
9. Little division of labor	9. Extensive division of labor
10. Homogeneous	10. Heterogeneous and complex
11. Self-sufficient	11. Interdependent
12. Nonliterate	12. Literate
13. Isolation	13. Extensive contact
14. Provincialism	14. Cosmopolitanism
15. Production for use	15. Production for the market
16. Ritualistic	16. Temporal
17. Governed by custom	17. Governed by law

In the cases that follow, we have selected a highly primitive, simple community among the Andaman Islanders; a rural community whose traits are still of folk-sacred nature, the Amish; and a large, modern, urban American city, New York.

B. THREE TYPES OF HUMAN COMMUNITIES

1. *The Andaman Islanders* [4]

The Andaman Islands are part of a group of islands which lie in an area from Cape Negrain in Burma to Achin Head in Sumatra and are sub-divided into the Great and Little Andaman with outlying islets, which cover about two-hundred and ten miles from north to south.

The Andaman Islanders are all of one race but they can be differentiated into several groups in accordance with their language and customs. They fall into two main categories—the Great Andaman group which includes all the inhabitants of the Great Andaman except for the natives in the interior of the South Andaman who are called Jarawa. The Little Andaman Group consists of the natives of the Little Andaman plus those of the North Sentinel Island and the Jarawa of South Andaman.

The inhabitants of the Great Andaman live in small communities all over the islands, primarily on the coast but some in the forest area in the interior. Each of these local groups or communities lead their own lives independent of the other groups. There is a limited amount of contact and communication among the various groups for such occasions as feasting and dancing or visiting. There is, however, quarreling between groups which create feuds that might last for many months. Between groups who are separated by any distance there is no contact at all. The members of a local group keep to their own group for the most part, only leaving to visit friends in areas close by their own community.

A tribe is made up of several local groups who speak the same language and have a specific name. The tribe itself is unimportant in the conduct of social life, the independent groups regulating their own affairs. The local groups are sub-divided by the inhabitants in accordance with their place of residence—coast or interior. Some of the tribes consist of those who live on the coast while some include both natives of the interior and the coast.

The local groups themselves have only one division and that is into families. This is the only division that the Andamanese have unlike many other primitive societies which frequently have "clans."

The coast dwellers are designated as *Ar-yoto*, and the forest dwellers as *Erem-taga*. The sole difference between them is in the way they obtain food. The *Ar-yoto* are expert in fishing and turtle-hunting, getting much of their food from the sea. They make canoes to be used both for hunting and for travelling from one camp to another. A portion of their food they obtain from the forest such as fruits, roots, and wild pig. The *Erem-taga* obtain their food from the forest and the small inland creeks. They are completely ignorant of turtle hunting but are much more skillful in hunting pigs than the *Ar-yoto*.

Although there are tribes, the local independent group is the land-owning group, rather than the tribe. Each holds certain hunting rights in a given area.

In the more favorable locations smaller areas are held by the local groups; in the coastal areas the amount of space held is much smaller in size than that occupied by local groups in the interior part of the forest area. The average size of the local group is about 40 or 50 people and the average tribe is made up of about ten local groups.

The group into which a man or woman is born is regarded as the group to which he belongs, but there does not appear to be any restriction about changing one's group if the adopted group is willing to take him in. This happens when young people of two different groups marry and might then choose to reside in either of the groups.

Since the local group is the land owning group a man can hunt all over the land of his own group but cannot hunt over other lands unless he obtains permission from the group which holds the land. Within the group's own land there are a number of camping places in which the group lives for various parts of the year.

The groups are semi-nomadic in their own territory. The coastal-dwellers shift from one camp to another every few months for a variety of reasons. When a death occurs in a camp it is deserted for several months. Camp is frequently changed at the beginning of a new season since some spots are more favored than others at a particular time of the year. Camps are frequently changed after a few months because all refuse is thrown away close to the camp and after a few months the camp becomes uninhabitable.

Those who live in the forest do not shift much or nearly so often, since it is much more difficult for them to move their belongings. For the greater part of the year, during the rainy season they reside in the chief camp. During the cool and hot seasons they move to temporary camps and visit other groups. With the start of the rainy season they move back to the chief camp.

The Great Andaman natives all have permanent encampments which are the headquarters of the group. Here either a large communal hut or a carefully planned village is erected. The communal hut is built by the men and the women make the mats for it from palm leaves. Such a hut lasts a number of years and can be patched when necessary.

The coast-dwellers usually erect a semi-permanent village which is carefully arranged about a clearing near the coastal forest. It is close to a spring so that the natives have water and are well sheltered although near to hunting and fishing grounds. The village usually consists of eight huts carefully placed around the central clearing and facing inward. Each hut is occupied by a man, his wife, children and dependents. A widower or bachelor occupies a hut of his own. . . .

This arrangement typifies the village make up. In the married people's hut reside the man, his wife, children and occasionally dependents who are unmarried girls or widows or widowers with children. Unmarried men or widowers without children live in huts of their own. Each family has its own fireplace where most of the cooking is done and in which a fire is kept going. Sometimes two families will build their huts together with each family retaining its own section. Brothers will often have this kind of living arrangement.

The communal hut is really much like the arrangement of the village with the hut's walls adjoining and a central roof for all the huts. A dancing ground is to be found in the center similar to the ones in the villages.

The way in which the camps are arranged clearly illustrates the constitution of the Andamanese local groups. There are of course, the temporary camps which were mentioned previously. These are of two kinds—the camps which are put up for about two or three months and are always built along the village plan and not as a communal hut, and the hunting camp in which the natives spend only a few days at a time and are simply shelters made into a lean-to of leaves.

Shortly after sunrise the camp awakes and a meal is made of food that was saved from the previous day. The men then start off on their day's hunting or fishing. The women of the community supply the vegetable foods as well as the firewood and water for the camp. While the men are hunting, the women and children collect firewood and gather fruits and seeds in the forest. Only a few old men and women and some children remain in the camp. By afternoon the men return to camp with the day's hunt and the preparation for the chief meal of the day is begun. When a pig is brought in it is cooked in the public cooking place and then cut up and distributed among the families who in turn cook their own meals in their own huts. They eat with their own immediate family members. Bachelors and unmarried women eat by themselves.

When the meal is completed and darkness falls the men frequently dance accompanied by a song sung either by one of the men or by a chorus of women. After the dance they eat again. Another pastime is the telling of stories primarily about hunting and the same man may go on telling numerous tales until it is time to sleep and then the camp settles down with each family in its own hut.

The coast dwellers are not so greatly affected by the seasons as the tribes in the interior. Fishing and collecting molluscs can be done all through the year. During the rainy season they fish and hunt pigs in the forest. In both the hot season and the cool one they pay visits to one another but it is particularly during the fine weather that two or more local groups meet and enjoy social life.

The groups need little besides their food and their weapons and implements. Each person makes his own tools and the wives make their own baskets and nets. Although the economic life of the group approaches a sort of communism there is a notion of private property. Land and hunting areas are owned by the local group and each individual has an equal right to it. There is a private ownership of certain trees. If a man finds a tree in the forest which he feels is suitable for a canoe he tells the others about it describing the location and henceforth it is regarded as his property. Even if he makes no use of it for several years no one else will cut it down without asking permission of its owner.

Similarly a pig belongs to the man whose arrow strikes it first; a honeycomb belongs to the man who cuts it down; the roots dug up by a woman belong to her; the fish and prawns that she gets in her net are hers. Any weapon that a man makes he owns and he cannot dispose of his wife's belongings without her permission.

Each family builds its own hut and takes care of its repairs. Even in the communal hut each family is responsible for the upkeep of their particular section. When a canoe is built a number of men join in its making but it belongs to the man who selected the tree and it is he who supervises the cutting and shaping. The owner can do anything with the canoe he pleases and those who helped in the building have no rights in it.

The Andamanese constantly exchange presents with one another, both among those who have not seen one another for some time as well as in the daily life of the camp. Between equals the exchange of gifts must balance in value while younger people may give gifts to older people without receiving anything in turn. When two neighboring local groups meet an important part of the gathering is this exchange of gifts. The visitors bring with them and distribute gifts and in turn receive gifts from their hosts when they depart.

Good manners require the Andamanese to grant any request made of them. When a man is asked for any of his belongings he will immediately fulfill the request. If the two men are equals a gift having the same value will be given. Among an older married man and a young married one or bachelor, the younger does not make requests, and if the older man makes requests, the younger does not always expect a return. Thus it is that possessions are constantly being exchanged.

There is no division of labor within the local groups except those between the sexes. Each man is expected to be able to hunt and fish; to make canoes and tools. The work between men and women is sharply differentiated. The men hunt, fish, and make the tools they need for these occupations. The women collect fruits and roots; catch prawns and crabs; provide the family water and firewood; and do the family cooking. The common cooking is done entirely by the men.

The Andamanese villages have no organized government. The affairs of the village are conducted by the older men and women. The younger members respect their elders and submit to their authority. Another important factor in regulating community life is the deference to certain personal qualities. Those who are skilled in hunting and warfare, are generous and kind, and are good tempered, attain important status in the village and may have more influence than an even older man. Younger men will attach themselves to these men, try to please them with gifts, and help in work such as canoe making. Each group usually has one such man who has a great deal of influence. The wives of such men usually exercise the same sort of influence among the women as their husbands do among the men.

The Andamanese do not appear to have any formal system of punishment for crimes. There are two kinds of acts which are regarded as wrong—those which harm the individual and those which do not harm any individual but are disapproved of by the whole group. Quarrels may break out among the men and a good deal of anger is displayed. If the anger is very violent an individual may be killed and property destroyed and women and children will flee to the jungle. Usually a man of influence in the village can check such outbursts. In the rare instances where this is not done and murder is committed it is left to the victim's family or friends to extract vengeance. If the murderer is formidable he may go unpunished, hiding for several months and then return to the village again.

Other crimes of anti-social nature such as laziness, marital infidelity, lack of proper respect for elders, meanness, bad temper, and miserliness, go unpunished, for the person still is given his necessary food but he soon finds himself held in low esteem and his position in the village becomes very inferior.

Another type of crime is that of breaking ritual prohibitions such as burning beeswax or killing a cicada which is supposed to cause bad weather. There is no punishment for such behavior except that it is believed that breaking these laws will bring supernatural punishment which will affect the individual as well as the whole community. Children are corrected when they behave improperly but they are never punished.

Marriage is arranged by older men and women. Some children are betrothed by their parents while they are still infants. Children are much loved by the Andamanese and are given much affection, attention, and petting by all the villagers. The infant is cared for by the mother but a nursing mother will often suckle children of other women. They are not weaned until they are three or four years old. The infant is constantly carried about by the mother and sometimes by the father. After they can walk they accompany their mothers on their expeditions. At five or six boys are taught the occupation of men, and girls pick up knowledge from their mothers in their tasks. They are treated very kindly, never punished and rarely scolded. At the age of eight to ten they begin to be of real service to their parents or foster parents as adoption of children who have lost their parents is very common. Foster parents will treat their adopted children in exactly the same way as they treat their own children.

Man and woman's duties to his or her relatives are scarcely distinguishable from the duties which he or she owes to others. A young married man owes certain duties to all older married men of his father's age much like those that he owes to his father except that he must be more constant in his attention to his father.

The Andamanese believe that there are spirits who live in the forest and the sea. Generally they remain unseen but sometimes a man or woman will report having seen one. These spirits are supposed to be spirits of dead men and women. The jungle spirits live in villages in the forest, and if one wanders alone in the forest, he may be captured and killed; those who are very brave may be spared and allowed to return home. A man who has had such an experience is supposed to be endowed with a gift for magic. He may return to the forest spirits from time to time.

Except for those who have made friends with them, the spirits are dangerous causing illness and death. It is thought that a person is more vulnerable to attack when he is alone and thus it is always better to be in a group when away from the native village. Many objects are regarded as being helpful in keeping these malignant spirits at bay such as fire, arrows, human bones, beeswax, and red paint. A man or woman will always carry a firebrand at night even to go a few yards since this will protect him from the spirits. They will never whistle at night because this may attract the notice of the spirits but singing is supposed to keep them away.

Many things are supposed to possess magical properties. Red ochre is made by burning yellow ochre and then combined with pig or turtle fat and made into a red paint which is applied to throat, chest and ears for colds, coughs, and earaches. It is also taken internally for other complaints. From a plant from which the Andamanese obtain a valuable fibre for making bow strings, they also derive various curative benefits. A certain type of tree has leaves which are supposed to keep the forest spirits at bay. Black beeswax too has magical attributes and is used extensively in the treatment of pleurisy. Many other substances are thought to have similar curative properties. Another favorite method of cure for ills among the Andamanese is scarification. The place where a pain occurs is scarified—a number of small incisions are made in the skin with quartz or glass. These cuts are deep enough to cause a little oozing of blood but not deep enough to cause a real flow. This process is carried on solely by women and is one of the most commonly used methods among the Andamanese.

2. An Old Order Amish Settlement [5]

"And be not conformed to this world" is one of the cardinal religious principles observed by the Old Order Amish of Lancaster County in Pennsylvania. The community in which these people live may also be said to be nonconforming because it differs rather sharply from other communities. There are about 3,500 of the Old Order Amish in the Lancaster County area and they all belong to one community, stretching eastward from the city of Lancaster for about 25 miles and nearly 15 miles wide at its eastern terminus.

The Old Order Amish constitute what may be called a socio-religious community which is strictly rural.

The Old Order Amish are also referred to as House Amish in contradistinction to two schismatic groups which now worship in church buildings called "meeting houses." The first split occurred in the 1870's and 1880's and the second one shortly after 1900. Both of the groups that split from the Old Order are spoken of as Church Amish or Amish-Mennonites, but they belong to separate conferences. Before these splits, all these people were designated "Amish" and such compound terms as "Old Order Amish," "House Amish," and "Church Amish" were not necessary because all of them worshipped in homes and barns and all of them were extremely conservative and steadfastly maintained the many traditional practices of the group.

The garb and mode of life of the Amish differentiate them sharply from other people. The Amish consider themselves a "peculiar" people who lead a "peculiar" life because the Bible says that God's people are peculiar and are not conformed to the world (see Titus 2:11–14; Romans 12:2). Because of these principles many interesting practices and customs prevail. The Amish men all have long hair, banged across the forehead and at the back of the head. All men part their hair in the middle. Unmarried men shave, but married men must wear a beard though they may not grow a mustache. The outer articles of clothing for men, women, and children are made at home and are cut along the same patterns for each group. The men and boys wear broadfall trousers, secured with plain, home-made suspenders. The dress coats have no lapels and no outer pockets and are secured with hooks and eyes (work coats and jackets may have buttons and even zippers). All male members wear broad, flat, black hats in winter and broad, flat straw hats in summer.

Women of the same age groups wear outer clothing of identical pattern and none of it is made of printed goods. Only solid colors are worn but some variation in color is permitted. Black, blue, purple, and grey are popular. Married women wear aprons which match the color of their dresses, whereas young, unmarried girls wear white aprons. No woman is permitted to cut or curl her hair and all comb their hair exactly alike. Young girls braid their hair but older ones do not. Owning or wearing jewelry is forbidden by the church. Girls and women wear white devotional head covering and identical home made bonnets. Church regulations forbid the wearing of all "store hats."

The ownership of automobiles, telephones, radios, musical instruments, and non-Biblical story books is forbidden by the church. Tractors may be owned and operated for belt power, but they may not be used to operate implements in the field. Buggies and wagons are built alike and painted alike. Young, unmarried men nearly always use an open or topless buggy painted black, while older men and married men use a square, box-like wagon, the body of which is painted grey and the carriage black. Dashboards and whip sockets are prohibited.

It is a remarkable fact that the nonconformity practices of the Old Order Amish, which differentiate them sharply from other people, have been maintained for centuries and are still being maintained in a compact agricultural industrial area. The tenacious way in which the Old Order has been maintained probably comes chiefly from their history of misunderstanding, persecution, and death. A strong sense of martyrdom is seared into the memory of the Amish, and this sense does much to tie them together and to make them look with apprehension and disapproval at "the world."

A keen awareness of a tragic past together with an observance of the several religious principles already pointed out is not the only consideration which conditions the basic characteristics of the socio-religious community of Old Order Amish. The Swiss Brethren, the forebears of the Amish, were determined to break completely with the social order of the day and to readopt the social order of the early Christians as it was described in the Bible, more particularly in the Sermon on the Mount and the New Testament in general. In the 16th century this meant the creation of a new social order. In this order or voluntary association of Christians nothing was to be accepted or approved on the basis of custom or law, but all activities and practices were to be based on "The Bible standard."

The socio-religious program of the Amish and the Mennonites hinges to a remarkable degree on several Bible standards. It represents an attempt to give literal interpretation to Biblical injunctions concerning, for example, nonresistance, adult baptism, humility, nonconformity to the world, the unequal yoke with unbelievers, and discipline and unity.

The community pattern of the Old Order Amish in Lancaster County is amorphous. Churches do not provide focal points for community relations because these people do not have church buildings; schools do not bring about close ties with non-Amish because they are secular institutions and the principle of separation from the world serves to create cleavages in the school districts; villages and towns do not tie trading areas together because of the same principle of separation from the world. Religious, kinship, ethnic, and linguistic ties on the other hand, serve to make one large, sprawling community out of the entire settlement of Old Order Amish which covers an area of about 150 square miles.

The Old Order Amish community is divided into church districts, which in the summer of 1940 numbered 18. Each district ordinarily includes as many families as can be accommodated conveniently in the fortnightly house services. Most of the districts have about 100 church members. As church membership is attained through baptism, which ordinarily takes place early in the adolescent period, the number of people to be accommodated in the services is about twice the church membership.

The districts also serve as church administrative units. In each unit there are several lay ministers (untrained) and a deacon. Ordinarily there is one bishop for every two districts. It is the responsibility of the deacon to administer the poor fund, which is sustained by the district. The church operates on the congregational pattern and technically each district can maintain its own regulations with reference to nonconformity and other cherished principles. Actually, however, uniformity in disciplines and customs is maintained throughout the whole community because departure from the "old order" leads to a feeling of nonfellowship which immediately translates itself into social and religious barriers and problems.

As commercial forms of entertainment are prohibited by the church, social activities and recreation are practically synonymous. In social activities church districts are practically ignored. Friends and kinfolks visit back and forth, regardless of location. Moreover, for the "singings" of the young people every Sunday evening, there are no cellular divisions in the community. The young men from all corners of the community may participate in any singing.

Although there are no fixed focal points in the Old Order Amish community, the community does have a central point of concentration. When church officials from the whole community want to meet they frequently select a home in Leacock Township, which for many years has been considered the heart of the community. Farm places in this general area can be reached most conveniently from all parts of the community. The village of Intercourse in Leacock Township is also a popular meeting place and a "pairing off" place on Sunday evenings for boys and girls who go to the singings.

Cultural patterns are longer preserved in the Old Order Amish community than among most other groups because it is a definite church policy to preserve the old order. It should be understood, however, that the "old order" applies particularly to social and religious practices and does not imply a congealed agricultural pattern. In fact, in agriculture the old order really means the new order, insofar as changes and improvements do not clash with definitely established principles of faith.

The religious program and the social organization of the Old Order Amish have changed less since they came to America than perhaps those of any other group. The distinctive dress serves to illustrate and substantiate this point. The relatively static position of the social patterns results directly from the fact that they are based on definite religious principles.

The principle of separation from the world is still vigorously maintained by the Old Order Amish. Although in Europe the program of compulsory separation was frequently a bilateral arrangement, between the Brethren and "the world," in this country it has been unilateral. Because of this principle and the associated concept of brotherhood within the church, the various Old Order Amish communities in Pennsylvania, Delaware, Virginia, Ohio, Indiana, Illinois, and elsewhere, dissociate themselves sharply from the larger society or community which immediately surrounds them, but all are closely tied together in a religious and social brotherhood. Protracted visits are common between these widely separated communities, sometimes prompted by religious considerations and frequently by the desire of young men and women to extend their circle of acquaintances. Marriage with persons outside the church is forbidden and trips are not infrequently made with the definite purpose of finding a suitable mate.

Franklin's maxim about early to bed and early to rise is well observed by the Amish farmer. All members of the family except the smallest children arise between 4 and 5 o'clock in the morning. Milking and other chores require from 1 to 2 hours, depending on the number of cows that are to be milked and the number of hands available. Between 5:30 and 6 o'clock breakfast is served. If milk is sold, it is hauled to the station just before or after breakfast. Shortly after 6 o'clock the day's operations are begun. Field work receives most attention in spring and summer, and stripping tobacco and hauling manure are the important tasks of the winter.

Work in the barns or fields continues until 11 o'clock, which is dinner time. If the weather is not too disagreeably hot, field work is resumed shortly after 12 o'clock. On hot days, a rest of 30 minutes to an hour may be taken. Supper on the

Amish farm is served between 4 and 5 o'clock, usually about 4:30. Chores come immediately after supper. During the rush season, one or several men may again work in the field after supper until dark. Between 8:30 and 9 o'clock, most of these people go to bed.

Sunday is a day of rest; only essential tasks are done. No milk is hauled to the station for sale. Business transactions of all kinds are prohibited. Nevertheless, the day is filled with activity and the family arises at about the usual time. House services are held fortnightly in each district and they begin at 9 o'clock in the morning. Many of the participating members arrive as early as 8:30. By this hour they have finished the usual chores, have had breakfast, changed their clothes, and driven some distance with horse and buggy.

House services are staggered between adjoining districts so that when not held in the local district, it is possible to attend services in the neighboring district. Usually, however, the free Sunday is spent in visiting which is the one form of social indulgence and pleasure not denied to the Amishman. He visits with a zest and appreciation few other people can appreciate. Relatives are so plentiful that they are lost count of and social rounds are never completed.

Other Christian duties are tended to on Sunday; searching the Scriptures is an obligation. Bishops, preachers, and deacons find it essential to read the Bible so that they may perform their duties properly. As these officers are selected from among the lay members by lot, constant study of the Bible is essential.

The conservative Amish still conduct their services in the German language. German Bibles, prayer books, and hymn books are used. This means that children must be taught to read German and this responsibility rests on the parents. Much time is devoted to this task on Sundays.

Sunday evenings the young people gather for singings—the only social activity in which they can participate in large groups. Formerly there were folk dances and games but these became too rowdy.

The daily routine, as set forth, includes all children of school age. Nearly all youngsters who report in the school at 9 o'clock in the mornings have already helped with the morning chores. In the evening they carry out tasks that have been assigned to them.

Although there is a sharp difference in activities between week days and Sundays, there is no definite cycle of work during the week. The only difference in day-to-day work the informants could think of was that the barn "is well cleaned on Friday and Saturday so that little of this work needs to be done on Sundays." On Mondays it is again necessary to do a little more work to get the barn in good order.

Unlike some other rural sections, Wednesday and Saturday evenings are not shopping nights in the Amish community. Purchases are made on any week day, although rarely after dark. Many go shopping on Friday or Saturday in preparation for Sunday. Usually the head of the household drives to the crossroads store or a nearby village to buy for the family.

Until recently, the Pennsylvania German farmers combined commercial farming with a program of self-sufficiency in an unusually effective way. Commercial farming was not carried on for its own sake, but as a means whereby the farmer sustained himself and his children on the land. Farming was not practiced to make money, but money was made to support the farm. Large scale commercial farming has never become common in Pennsylvania German communities.

Wheat has been an important cash crop for these farmers since colonial days. In Lancaster County, since the Civil War, tobacco has supplemented wheat as a cash crop. More recently, potatoes, tomatoes, and even peas have supplemented the cash income of the farmers of the county.

Cash income is also realized from the sale of animals and animal products. During the colonial period many cattle and hogs were raised and marketed. Since about 1800, the feeding and fattening of cattle has persisted, although dairy cows are now replacing feeder cattle. Hog and sheep raising has declined, but poultry production has increased greatly. All these activities are part of a highly diversified form of commercialized farming.

As commercialization was extended and intensified, self-sufficiency declined. Today the Amish farmers' production and consumption are closely tied up with the market economy. During colonial years, the farmers here produced the clothes they wore from flax, wool, and hides, they were fully self-sufficient in fruits and vegetables, and were more than self-sufficient in the production of flour and meat. Today they buy some ready made clothes; they buy most of the fruit and some of the vegetables they eat. If the housewife still bakes bread, she buys flour, made from western wheat. Local wheat, when sold, is used as pastry flour. Many farmers buy the pigs they later kill for meat as well as the animals they later slaughter for beef. Not infrequently a professional butcher kills these animals for the farmer.

Self-sufficiency is in retreat. In the summer of 1939, five commercial bakers had bread routes running through the Amish community to serve an increasing number of patrons. Grocery trucks and even meat trucks pass through the community to serve numerous customers. During the apple and peach seasons, fruit vendors come up to the Amish houses confident of making sales. The grocer is selling the Amish farmers more and more canned vegetables. Some of these farmers buy the butter for their tables. This practice would be even more common if the Sunday's milk supply could be sold, but as it is, this milk is usually skimmed and the cream is then churned.

It should not be assumed that the Amish farmers have forgotten their vegetable gardens. Most of them still have good gardens which are fairly well maintained by replantings throughout the summer. However, the older generation is more devoted to the garden than the younger generation. Young housewives are beginning to "figure on" all the costs of raising and canning peas, corn, tomatoes, and other items. The next step is simple and may not be long delayed.

Many Amish housewives still can and preserve great quantities as well as a great variety of food. To can from 500 to 700 quarts of fruits and vegetables is not uncommon. In addition, many still prepare many gallons of apple and pear butter, can and preserve much meat, prepare great quantities of jellies, and store away impressive quantities of dried apples, beans and corn. Fruits and berries for canning, however, are nearly all purchased. The fact that these items are bought, centers increasing attention on the cost differential between products canned at home and products bought in cans. Housewives are not overlooking the fact that, for home canning the fruit, glasses, rubber, sugar, and other items may have to be bought, and they are also talking about the value of their time. More and more of them are becoming convinced that the finished product can be bought at a saving—and they act accordingly.

It is doubtful that rural women anywhere in this country do more needlework and sewing than the women and girls of the Amish families. Only underclothes are bought ready made. Because of the principles of nonconformity, these people do not buy ready made dresses, overalls, shirts, men's suits, or even dress over-coats. Men's overcoats and men's suits are frequently made by women in the community who have special competence in this work, but most of these outer clothes are made by the housewives and grown daughters.

The making of outer clothes at home means a considerable saving in the cost of the finished product, particularly if the time spent in making them is not appraised too highly. As there are no style changes, clothes are never discarded until worn out, and this practice, of course, makes for economy.

Commercially made carpets, except rag carpets, are prohibited under the prin-ciple of nonconformity. Congoleum and linoleum of simple design are per-mitted. Rag carpets are not prepared on a loom by a professional carpet maker, but the rags used in their manufacture are saved in the homes and are sewn into strips, preparatory to weaving. The result is a relatively cheap but durable carpet.

Amish women spend much time over embroidery work, quilting, and making carpets and pillow cases. Each daughter begins to fill her dower chest with things of this kind at an early age. She accumulates embroidered pillow cases, several pieced, embroidered and stitched quilts, hooked rugs, and other household items.

Religious taboos play a part in the self-sufficiency of the conservative Amish. No money is spent for jewelry, non-Biblical story books, commercial entertain-ments, musical instruments, men's haircuts, and beauty-parlor work.

Mutual aid and cooperation are cardinal principles in the life of Amishmen, who are expected to translate them into everyday action. Informal associations incidental to exchanging help, however, have been decidedly restricted by in-creased commercialization of many farming activities. Aid programs still survive, but they are limited more and more to occasions of distress.

In former years, the Amish, like their neighbors, had threshing bees, corn-husking and log raising bees, bees for the preparation of cider and schnitz and butchering and quilting bees. The job of moving was also a neighborhood affair. Only a few of these activities survive, and in modified form. Threshing is now done by an almost self-sufficient crew and requires no exchange of labor; corn-husking bees are a distant memory; log raising bees, now changed into barn raising bees, are still popular; cider is no longer prepared on most farms and only a little schnitz is dried, usually from purchased fruit; some cooperation still takes place in regard to meat, but the commercial butcher is more and more used; quilting bees still take place; moving now gives a commercial trucker a chance to earn a few more dollars.

There is a good deal of cooperation in harvesting grain, filling silos, and making hay. These operations require much manpower, and high priced machinery can be used to advantage. To pool both manpower and machinery is mutually ad-vantageous. Neighborhood rings to perform these tasks are common, but they are frequently confined to brothers and near relatives. Among nonrelatives, cash settlements are usually made if participants contribute unequal amounts of work.

A few unusual activities still provide neighborhood bees. One of the Old Order Amish told of a pipe laying bee he had several years ago. He had provided an ex-cellent system of running water on the place by tapping a spring on a ridge about a mile away. To help dig the trench for the pipe, he extended an invitation to friends and neighbors and so many came that the pipe was laid between breakfast and dinner. Such bees are essentially social gatherings at which rather elaborate meals are served. Similar bees may be staged to cut wood or saw lumber for home use.

The barn-raisings which survive in the county seem to be a modernized version of the early log-raising bees. The rapidity with which a barn is erected by this cooperative method is amazing to outsiders. First, several carpenters are hired to prepare the foundation for the barn and to pre-cut all the required pieces of lumber. When these preliminaries are done, word is sent out that the barn-raising is to take place on a certain day. Farmers come from all directions early in the morning, and the work of setting up the barn begins immediately under the direction of a foreman or boss. By evening, a $5,000 to $10,000 barn stands erected, although the shingles may not all be in place. It is not unusual for 200 or 300 farmers including both Amish and non-Amish to take part. Frequently there are complaints that the presence of so many men hinders rather than helps construc-tion. All get a big dinner.

Worldly amusements, particularly in commercialized form, are completely taboo. An Amishman cannot attend shows, dances, worldly parties, fairs, card games, or any pleasurable activity sponsored by "the world." So these people look to each other to satisfy their social propensities, and visiting is carried on with an en-thusiasm that is rarely matched in other groups.

Sunday, a day of rest and worship, provides a splendid opportunity for visiting. The fortnightly services are the important events of their days, and give people a chance to hear what is going on elsewhere and more particularly in the com-munity. It is possible to arrive at the place of worship some time before services begin at 9 o'clock and it is unusual to leave right after the Sunday meal has been served at the end of the services. Men, women, and children find plenty of company at these gatherings for conversation and play.

Between 2 and 4 o'clock when most of the members return home, the young people have learned at whose place "singing" is to take place in the evening; frequently it is to be held in the same house. After the chores are done, preparation to go to the singing begins. The young man grooms himself, his horse, and his open buggy. The horse's tail, mane, and hair are trimmed if they need it. The harness and wagon are cleaned, polished, or washed if that seems necessary. The young man puts on his best attire and so does his sister. Usually they go to a designated place where young people assemble to pair off. The village of Intercourse, centrally located in the large Old Order community, is the place where the young people usually gather from all directions at early hours. By 8 o'clock most of them are again on the road, headed for the singing with their chosen partners. In the house of the host, they gather around a table to sing church hymns, *einstimmig*. Singing is often interspersed with riddles or conundrums. Refreshments are always served. Everyone is expected to leave for home before midnight.

On Sundays when there are no services there is even more time for visiting. All the Amish have a wide *Freundschaft*—many relatives—and it is taken for granted that at least the near kinfolks must be visited as often as possible. Parents and grandparents make it a point to visit all children and grandchildren at least several times a year. As only every second Sunday is really available for family visits and as children and grandchildren are usually numerous, most of these people are behind in what they consider an ideal visiting schedule.

Among the Old Order Amish, however, who still drive with horses, visits that last several days and even several weeks are still common. Staying overnight with a friend is fairly usual in the winter. Houses are usually large, beds are numerous, and food is plentiful. While carrying on field work in the community, the writer was frequently invited to stay overnight.

Long visits to distant Old Order Amish communities are common. There are such communities near Norfolk, Virginia; Dover, Delaware; in central Pennsylvania, chiefly in the Kishacoquillas Valley; in western Pennsylvania; in Ohio, Indiana, Illinois, Iowa, and some other states. There are likely to be relatives in one or several of them and there is much visiting back and forth, principally in the winter, or in August when work is somewhat slack. These visits usually cover several weeks and may include several homes.

Bishops and preachers visit distant communities partly out of a feeling of duty, and there they deliver many sermons. One informant pointed out that St. Paul and other early church leaders also traveled and preached to the scattered Christians.

These protracted visits have several noteworthy byproducts. Young, unmarried persons often find their life mates in this way and the Amish farmers become familiar with farm practices prevailing in other places, some of which they may find useful and profitable.

The Amish family like the Amish community is closely knit, socially and economically. The frequent visits paid to near relatives certainly are an expression of close family ties as is the aid extended by parents to children to start them farming; responsibility of aiding those in need rests, first of all, upon the family. Only when family aid fails to meet the needs of distressed individuals does the community take over the assistance.

It is largely the responsibility of the parents to teach values and to create attitudes in the children which will incline them to follow in the footsteps of their forefathers. This task is not a small one for a peculiar people that practices nonconformity. Children must be told why they cannot have clothes, bicycles, and many toys like those of other children; why the family cannot have electric lights, car, a radio. The total impression of the children must be one of separateness, difference, and one of strong disapproval of the world and all its doings. That the children may understand the religious services and read available religious books, including the Bible, they must be taught to speak and read German.

Amish parents cooperate with the public school to the end that they want their children well-trained in the 3 R's. Adequate competence in the 3 R's is attained in the elementary grades, they feel, and public education beyond the eighth grade or beyond the age of 14 is opposed. Moreover, they believe it is their responsibility to train the children to become competent farmers and housewives with experience as a good assistant teacher.

As all Amish children are required to become farmers or to engage in some closely associated work in rural areas, the question arises whether many of these youngsters are not thwarted in ambitions. That some children experience disillusionment on this score may well be granted but most parents do remarkably well in cultivating a sense of values in their children which centers their interest and plans on farming.

When informants were asked about varied ambitions on the part of their children, they replied that farming offers adequate opportunity to give expression to these differences. Even in a specialized form of farming, variations are possible in approach and execution. The opportunity to exercise special talents in farming was also stressed. Soil, stock, crop, and marketing problems are cited in abundance to demonstrate this point. "Why, a good farmer does not even treat two cows, two horses, or even two pigs alike."

The success of the Amish in training their children to be enterprising and satisfied farmers has arrested the interest of agricultural specialists in the county. This program, one of them pointed out, stands in marked contrast to what is taking place in several non-Amish, non-Pennsylvania-German communities in the southern part of the county, where children do relatively little farm work during their grade-school years and not a great deal when attending high school. In part, this results from the parents' attempt to shelter children from "hard work" and to imitate urban practices. Moreover, during the formative school years, the parents constantly direct their children's attention to opportunities in non-farm activities and "practically tell them that they will be failures if they have to work as hard as their parents on a farm." These communities are gradually disappearing because there are no children to take over the family farms. Pennsylvania-Germans, mainly sectarians, are taking over the land.

The Amish train children differently. All family discussions take it for granted that the children will farm some day. Failure to farm or engage in some closely related activity is spoken of as failure and perhaps even a disgrace to the family and the community. Youngsters are assigned definite tasks at an early age. Boys and girls 8 and 9 years old are already a great help in the house and in doing chores and field work. Nearly all of them milk cows at this age and the boys begin to do field work with horses and implements. Frequently these youngsters are given a calf, pig, sheep, or some chickens to raise and market, or they may be given a small plot of tobacco to tend and sell. Good work is encouraged and commended. In this training there is no time for high school. The Amish boy is a well-trained farmer, who usually wants to farm, by the time most children graduate from high school.

As the training of the young in the Amish home is designed to perpetuate the accustomed way of life, the young people become baptized and join the church shortly after they have finished the elementary grades in school. It is partly the responsibility of the parents to encourage this step but most of the young people join the church without any particular encouragement. However, there are exceptions, and boys tend to be more recalcitrant or hesitant than girls.

Responsibility extends beyond bringing children into the church. The many church regulations and principles must be upheld. Church taboos are numerous and require an unusually well-disciplined life. In a moment of weakness, a member may go to a movie or commit some other indiscretion. Unless proper and immediate amends are made, the violator may be read out of the church and be shunned. When this dreaded punishment is invoked, no member of the family or the church may speak with the shunned individual although every act of kindness is shown him. The shunned member cannot eat with the family, but is served separately at a small table. Shunning is a real burden to the family involved but the purpose is to persuade the sinner to make proper amends and again enter into full fellowship with the church.

The family cycle of the Old Order Amish differs somewhat from that of other people, even in courting and the wedding ceremony. The baptismal ceremony inducts the young fully into the fellowship of the church. From this period (ages 14 to 18 generally) up to the age of about 20, the young people attend singings regularly. This is the courting period. Between the ages of 16 and 18, a boy receives his driving horse, open buggy, harness, and several blankets. With this equipment he is prepared to take his chosen girl home from the singings, and on these trips the serious plans are laid. By the time the girl approaches the age of

20 and the boy is in his early 20's, plans are usually made for marriage. Many preparations have already been made during the preceding years. The girl will have spent much time filling a hope or dower chest. By the time of the marriage the chest is usually more than filled and the accumulation is usually enough for the first housekeeping. The girl will also have earned as much cash as possible. To do this she may have worked as a house servant in the home of a friend or she may have gathered potatoes, or picked fruit in a nearby commercial orchard. She may also have raised a calf or some chickens and turned them into cash.

The prospective bridegroom also accumulates as much cash as possible, by working as a hired hand or by raising tobacco or potatoes on a plot of ground assigned to him. Usually the young people have accumulated a considerable amount of cash and necessities by the time they are ready to marry.

Weddings in the Old Order Amish community always take place after the harvest season, and custom decrees that the wedding day fall on a Tuesday or Thursday. Some time before the wedding a Schteckleimann—a deacon or minister acting in the capacity of solicitor, like Abraham's servant—is selected to learn the attitude of the girl's parents concerning the marriage. In the past, the Schteckleimann also carried the young man's proposal to the girl. The function of this intermediary has become quite nominal in that the young man now is fully aware of the attitude of the girl and her parents toward the contemplated wedding. Custom decrees that the selection of a Schteckleimann and his mission be performed in strict secrecy.

Secrecy shrouds most of the preliminary preparations for the wedding, including the courting. During the courting period, for instance, the young man calls on the girl after she (apparently) and the family (actually) have retired. The young man drives up to the house and with the aid of a flashlight or buggy light makes his presence known. If the girl is interested, she quietly descends the stairs to meet the caller.

Weddings are the most important social events known to the Amish. From 100 to 300 guests may be invited and a king's feast is prepared for them. The newly wedded couple later makes special visits to all families who participated in the wedding and at this time they receive the wedding gifts. Several weeks may be spent in this round of visiting during which time the young couple may spend a night or several nights as honored guests in the homes of numerous hosts. This represents the Amish equivalent of the customary honeymoon trip.

After marriage the young couple no longer attend singings. The man must now grow a beard and he definitely associates himself with the mature members of the community. The bride discards the white apron she wore before her wedding day. As soon as means permit they buy a gray topped buggy and the open buggy may be sold.

Separation and divorce are unknown in the Amish community. Marriage can take place only between members who are in full membership with the church, and the church recognizes separation only on grounds of adultery. Individuals would not be permitted to remarry upon separation. Informants in Lancaster County could not recall that any separation had ever taken place in the Amish community.

Marriage of young couples often brings considerable relief to parents and elders in the community. During the singing period the young frequently cause the older people a great deal of concern by promoting, abetting, or participating in so called questionable activities. Marriage nearly always ends this problem.

After marriage family problems begin. There are usually several children— 6 to 10 in a family are not uncommon. Many of the more liberal Church Amish, who have adopted the automobile and other conveniences, have also adopted the use of some contraceptives; their families are smaller than those of the Old Order Amish and family increases occur at longer intervals.

The aged Amishman and his wife cannot leave the farm in their declining years because of the church regulations. They may move to a crossroads village, but this is uncommon. The Amish farmer is rooted to the soil and that is where he wants to remain. When the time comes to retire from active farming—usually when the youngest son or daughter marries—the aging parents move to a separate part of the house known as "Grossdawdy house." Sometimes this is an addition to the main house and sometimes it is a separate unit. Even if it is merely an addition, it may contain from 1 to 3 rooms downstairs and an equal number upstairs. House services and Grossdawdy additions help to explain why the Old Order Amish cherish large houses.

Grossdawdy does not retire from all work when he retires to his part of the house. He finds as much work outside as he cares to do. Grossmutter sews during the day for children and grandchildren. This work keeps both of them healthily occupied as long as they are active. If they need attention younger members of the family are near. It is doubtful that old people anywhere are more contented than the occupants of the Grossdawdy house who can associate daily with their children and grandchildren and yet can be separate.

Until a generation or two ago, a funeral was an outstanding social event throughout Pennsylvania-German land. With the Old Order Amish it has remained so. Several hundred relatives and friends usually come. Food is prepared for all, and after the funeral, the guests are fed again before they return home. The immediate family, however, is almost completely relieved of responsibility regarding the food. Neighbors run the household and, when necessary, do the chores and other farm tasks.

In general these people are discouraged, and in some instances even prohibited from holding public office. There is a tendency to discourage voting. Formerly these taboos prevented the Amish from voting for school board members as well as from serving on school boards. In recent years, however, more and more Old Order Amish farmers are serving on school boards and more of them vote for school board members. These changes are caused partly by the fact that general school problems have become intensified. Other public offices cannot be accepted nor do many of these people vote for public officials on the county level or above.

The Old Order Amish people form a church body and a church community, but they do not have church buildings. Opposition to church structures has become a matter of nonconformity, although in earlier years, in Europe, services in churches were often either inexpedient or prohibited. The determination to perpetuate the old customs is one reason for maintaining the practice of holding services either in the house or in the barn. Moreover, the early Christians, whom these people try to emulate, apparently did not worship in churches.

The several thousand members in the Old Order Amish community cannot all worship in one house or one barn. The community is divided into districts and the number of districts increases with the size of the community. Older informants remember the time when there were only 9 or 10 districts in the Lancaster County area; now there are 18. In most of the districts there are approximately 100 church members. As membership is confined to baptized individuals, and baptism generally takes place between the ages of 15 and 20, and because whole families attend, the attendance at services is often twice as large as the membership in the district.

Services in a district are held every two weeks. Farmers with larger houses are expected to accommodate the group in winter, whereas those with smaller houses but large barns accommodate the group during the summer. As might be expected, a certain prestige attaches to the ownership or occupancy of a house large enough to provide accommodations for services at any time; some houses have as many as 16 or 18 rooms.

Large houses with ordinary interior arrangements would have difficulty in accommodating 150 to 200 people or more for a religious service but the large homes of the Old Order Amish farmers are especially arranged to take care of huge groups. Toward the center of the house large, double doors are usually installed; when these are opened or removed, a speaker standing in an appropriate place can be seen or at least heard in nearly every part of the house. As many of the Old Order Amish live in houses built by non-Amish people, they have become very ingenious in altering houses to conform to their own standards.

Great preparations are made to entertain the fortnightly meetings. The host and hostess, realizing that their efficiency will be appraised by friends and neighbors on the coming Sunday, overlook no detail in setting the place in order. Most of the work falls on the women although much is done outdoors as well. The house is cleaned and set in order from garret to cellar. All the floors are scrubbed and rag carpets cleaned. Furniture is dusted or washed. Walls may be freshly painted or washed and cellar walls may be whitewashed. Pots, kettles, pans, and tubs are cleaned. The kitchen range and heating stoves are polished. Clean paper is placed on kitchen shelves and all dishes and kitchenware are arranged neatly. The yard may be raked and the fence whitewashed. Everything in the farmyard is put in its place. In the barn the lower story wall may be whitewashed and the cement floor swept. Manure is either hauled into the field or is neatly stacked and covered with straw. The stock is well-bedded with straw.

Religious services usually last from 9 o'clock until about noon. Many gray-top carriages and open buggies begin to come as early as 8 o'clock. They are received by several young hostlers who take charge of the horses and conveyances. The 50 or 60 horses are stabled if the weather is inclement.

In the house, the host seats his guests in the appropriate way. Men and women are seated in separate rooms, and boys and girls are so seated near their elders so that they are under surveillance all the time. In the large central room the men are divided into two groups facing each other. Between these groups stand about four or five chairs which are used by the bishop (if present), the ministers, and the deacon. The men wear their hats until a few minutes before the services begin, even after they are seated. The women and girls wear the required head covering.

During the first hymn, the church leaders retire to a separate room to plan the services and to discuss any cases of discipline that need attention. Not until this consultation is it decided who is to deliver the opening sermon and the long sermon. However, the task of preaching is generally rotated and ministers and bishops can usually tell when they will be called upon to speak. During the second hymn, which is always a song of praise entitled "O Gott Vater, wir loben Dich," the church leaders usually reappear.

Shortly after the church leaders have returned from the "Abroth," (council), singing is discontinued and one of the preachers delivers the opening or "short" sermon usually lasting a half-hour or more. It is against the custom of the church to use notes in a sermon because these interfere with the proper functioning of the spirit. After the opening sermon the congregation kneels in silent prayer. The deacon then reads a chapter from the New Testament. Next comes the sermon of the day which usually lasts an hour, and sermons lasting from 15 to 30 minutes longer are not uncommon. When the long sermon is about half-finished, the speaker usually observes that in view of the fine words already spoken he does not intend to keep the assemblage much longer, but the listeners know that the sermon will last at least another 30 minutes.

After the main discourse a few witnesses are called upon to give testimony concerning the truth of the sermon, because the Bible says, "In the mouth of two or three witnesses every word may be established." The witnesses are usually the bishops, ministers, and deacons who are present, but other members may also be called upon. The witness may limit his testimony to a mere "Yea and Amen" or he may deliver a short sermon in which the words *schone Lehre* (fine teachings) are frequently repeated. In these statements encouragement is usually given to young ministers.

After the benediction the deacon announces where the next meeting is to take place, the names of those who intend to get married, and other information relating to church activity. If disciplinary problems are to be considered the deacon requests all members to remain seated after the singing of the closing hymn. All non-members, including the young people who have not yet been baptized, leave the meeting and the person whose case is to be considered is also asked to leave the group. The violator and his alleged misdeeds are discussed and a course of action is usually agreed upon. For a minor violation an immediate apology is sufficient. "Wild and reckless" youths seem to come in for most attention in these closed meetings. Reports may have reached the elders that some youngster smoked a cigarette or a pipe, or that he patronized a "hotel" (liquor store) or movie; for these acts it is relatively simple to make amends immediately.

After the service, preparations are begun at once to serve the noon meal. The young unmarried women usually help the hostess prepare and serve the food. The host, with the help of the older boys, removes most of the benches from the large rooms and two long tables are set up. One table is used by the men and boys and the other by women and girls. The older people eat first. No plates are provided—only cups, knives, forks, and spoons, which remain unchanged for the various guests who succeed each other at the table. Several bowls or plates of each food are placed on the table so it is unnecessary to pass the dishes. Before beginning to eat, all heads are bowed in silent prayer; no audible grace is ever spoken.

After the dinner comes an hour or two of the much-enjoyed visiting; then the guests start for home. Close friends and relatives may stay and have a full evening meal before they leave.

The Old Order Amish do not practice infant baptism. Those who give evidence of "true conversion" are baptized and received as members. Usually boys and girls become baptized some time after they have finished elementary school. They are always encouraged to become baptized before they reach the age of 20 years.

Young people are not subjected to a long, formal program of indoctrination and training before they join the church. During their grade school years they are taught by their parents to read German and they are required to read the Bible. This reading at home and the regular Sunday services provide most of the training they receive, before they join the church. When they decide to join, a bishop instructs them in the principles of the church in a separate room during the early part of the Sunday services; 6 or 7 meetings of this kind take place before baptism by the bishop.

Leadership is a highly important function in a socio-religious group which practices separation from the world, and nonconformity. It becomes increasingly difficult and complicated in a community that seeks stability in a highly competitive agricultural and industrial environment. Class structure seems to adhere in every community and is discernible in the Old Order Amish community. The basis of this structure, however, has features which differentiate it from most other communities.

Because of the principle of separation from the world, this community is made up of fellow church members only. As an agricultural way of life is one of the tenets of the church, the people are all engaged in farming or very closely associated occupations. Class differentiation can therefore not well be based on religious or vocational differences. Even the church leaders—the bishops, ministers, and deacons—are farmers and are not paid for their religious work. There are no differences resulting from school attendance for no member in the community has had more than an elementary schooling.

The community is completely uniform in ethnic composition, for all the ancestors of these people came from the Rhineland of Europe during colonial times. There are thus no "old families" who occupy or claim to occupy preferred niches in the community. Moreover, there are only about 30 family names in the community and the great majority of the Amish families today have one of only about a dozen family names. During the course of the last two centuries these few families have inter-married constantly, so that the community now is one large *Freundschaft,* a term used loosely to designate kinfolk. If a member of the community is asked how many second-cousins he has, the chances are he will throw up his hands and say "Can't count them" or "Hundreds of them."

There is therefore very little hereditary class-structure in the community. It is true that, for a generation or two, certain families may enjoy the prestige that goes with large farms and buildings, but in the course of several generations family fortunes vary and thus prestige shifts.

Church regulations and disciplines serve to eliminate some differences that might otherwise express themselves in a class structure. The facilities these people may possess and the garb they wear are subject to church approval and help to maintain equality among the members.

Not all forms of inequality are eliminated by church regulations, however, and in the forms of inequality that do exist a kind of class structure expresses itself. As these people have a deep agricultural tradition, their values lie largely in this field. Items in the material culture that enhance prestige and standing in the community are land ownership and good farm improvements, particularly barn and house, good stock, and good farm machinery. A member who owns a good farm is looked up to, particularly if he has a large barn and house. Some farmers are admired because they have large herds of dairy cows, others for their successful feeding operations. A farmer who maintains his farm in a high state of fertility is respected and farmers who put a great deal of manure on the land usually have prestige.

The farmer who "gets ahead" (pays off debts and buys farms) is much admired. Farmers who succeed in expanding their operations and have desirable social qualities generally are leaders in the community. It is they who are generally considered for positions of leadership in the church. This is particularly true of men who, in addition to their successful farming, show certain spiritual qualities and an interest in church matters.

The functions of each office—bishop, minister, and deacons—are carefully prescribed. Only the bishop may administer the rites of the church, such as baptism, marriage, and communion, and only he may ordain new ministers and discipline members; one bishop usually serves two districts. Ministers carry the main burden of preaching; there are usually several preachers in each district. The deacon administers the poor fund, attempts to resolve difficulties between members of the community, initiates the disciplining of members who have violated church regulations, reads the Scripture lesson in the Sunday services, and assists the bishop in baptismal and communion services.

Election to the ministry may be actually feared by potential officials. It means that much time must be spent in studying the Bible and much material must be committed to memory. As some of the men read with difficulty, this study presents a real challenge to these tillers of the soil. But the Amish have a deep faith in the system and they believe that the candidate will have divine aid in fulfilling the functions of his office.

Issues and problems which arise in the district can be settled only in meetings in which all members may and usually do participate. Important decisions require unanimous approval and this makes it difficult to change old customs and practices. Old members whose memories and thoughts are steeped in the past rarely see the need of change. A proposed innovation need only be branded with the stereotype "worldly" to settle the issue.

Church officials nevertheless take a leading part in directing the activities of the community. As the deacon is required to investigate problems when they arise, judgment and predilection come into play. He, in turn, reports to the bishop and this official also uses his judgment in dealing with the problem, and as only the bishop disciplines members, he may well use some discretionary power.

The leadership of church officials in the community naturally follows from the fact that church regulations regiment the lives of these people more completely than regulations in most other churches. Moreover, as most of the church officials are relatively successful farmers, they exert much influence in agricultural matters.

Outside leadership is not excluded entirely. Separation from the world does not prohibit business with outsiders nor discourage consulting doctors and some other specialists. Doctors are patronized regularly and a banker may be consulted concerning money problems. Local feed and fertilizer experts are consulted, but this is a rather recent development which intrudes directly into a realm formerly taken care of completely by in-group folk wisdom. It follows that leadership within the community is no longer as inclusive as it once was.

The man is distinctly the head of the household and in most cases directs the affairs of the family. Neither on the family level nor on the community level does the wife initiate or direct important activities. Parent-children relationships are compounded out of a combination of kindness and sternness. Parents want the children to follow in their footsteps and they realize that this end is gained more easily by cultivating affection and trust than by creating a feeling of fear and distrust. Several of them said they train their children to work diligently by encouraging them wherever possible and by complimenting them on good acts and performances. They pointed out that in training children great patience is essential. In general, parent-children relationships are cordial.

Parent-children relationships remain rather intimate as long as the parents live. As the old folks do not retire from the farm, they are present and ready to give advice to the family there. They realize that some discretion must be used in their relation with grown children so a mature son who has taken over the home farm is encouraged to make his own decisions. A number of elderly retired informants said that although they are willing to make suggestions to their sons, they do not care to render important decisions. "We won't always be here," they say, so the son must develop initiative and self-confidence.

By holding the purse strings Amish parents exercise a rather effective control over the activities of the children up to the time of their marriage. Few parents give their children much spending money. This form of control evidently led to some petty crimes a few years ago and it is interesting to see how the resultant problems were solved.

Several young men, who wanted spending money, secretly took a few chickens from their families' chicken barns and sold them. This was repeated several times until a loss was noted by the parents and was reported to legal authorities. The nature of the theft was discovered, but the findings were given to the parents only. The report is that an understanding was then reached between a local official and the parents concerning corrective procedure. The local official gave the boys a strong lecture and declared that each was fined $50, to be produced immediately. As was expected, the boys had to go to their fathers, explain the situation, and ask for the money. The local official, according to the report, secretly returned the fines to the fathers. This procedure proved very effective for it required the boys to make amends with the township official, the parents, and the church.

Problems growing out of ill-advised relations between the sexes are promptly and effectively settled by the church. Divorces are unknown in the community. Whether moral problems are more frequent or more serious today than formerly is difficult to know. Non-Old Order Amish informants are generally of the opinion that the Plain People find it harder now than formerly to control their young people. Opportunities to engage in unapproved activities, they hold, are now more numerous than in the past.

The basic virtues in the community consist largely in maintaining the old order in social and religious life and exhibiting stability and success in a rural way of life, preferably farming. The old order in the spheres of religious and social life bespeaks adherence to the cardinal principles of the church—nonresistance, separation from the world, nonconformity to the world, avoidance of the unequal yoke, and avoidance of manifestations of pride. For the sake of maintaining uniformity and harmony in carrying these principles into effect, the church has to enforce numerous disciplines (such as proscription of the ownership of many worldly improvements and prescription of the type of clothes to be worn by each sex and all age groups) and those who fully abide by them exemplify the cherished virtues of the community.

As it is recognized that the survival of the social organism depends on maintaining a rural life, the successful farmer enjoys much prestige, gains stability and security for himself, and seeks and at least partly attains stability and security for his children. Those who have few children or who fare exceedingly well in their farming are expected to help immediate relatives and others to gain security in farming or some other closely-allied activity.

Expansion of the Old Order Amish community in Lancaster County would have been impossible without hard work and thrift. Those who do hard work and make it count exemplify a basic virtue in the community. Idlers, loiterers, and those who spend time reading nonreligious books and publications run the danger of losing caste. Visiting at appropriate times is the only approved leisure activity.

A good Amish farmer enhances his standing in the community by demonstrating qualities of church leadership. This means that he must familiarize himself with the Scriptures and show that he is in sympathy with church regulations and practices. An exemplary life which places the individual in line for a church office is highly esteemed.

Compliance with church regulations and the approved methods is attained in various ways. Children learn early that they are a separate, chosen people. They are taught to look askance at the world and all its works. The fact that they are different from other children is impressed on them at an early age by the clothes they wear and the way their hair is cut.

3. *A Large Modern Urban Center: A Segment of New York*

Stuart Chase, in his book *Men and Machines,* describes the patterns of behavior in the urbanized and secularized culture of present-day American life.[6] This is a far cry from the simple, integrated life of the Andaman Islanders, and differs in a marked degree from the life of the Amish.

We have no standard religious code. One may take one's pick among two Catholic churches, more than one hundred Protestant sects, and heaven knows how many cults founded by prophets from the hinterland. If you rush up to a New York policeman and announce that you are an atheist, he will tell you to stop blocking traffic. You can have, in urban centers, one god, a whole pantheon, none at all, and nobody—unless you are running for high public office—particularly cares. . . .

If religious standards are in disorder, sexual standards are even worse. We may—in the more civilized centres—select orthodox marriage, trial marriage, companionate marriage, marriage of convenience, or no marriage at all. We may divorce almost at random. We may practise birth control in all circumstances, in specific circumstances, in no circumstances—with learned authority to sanction each decision. We are urged to have small families, large families, no families, to marry when young and poor, to wait until we are old and rich, to marry within our class, to marry above or below it. . . .

Education is in an equal fix. Children should be disciplined, they should be permitted to run wild, they should be sheltered, they should be exposed; parents are the ruination of them, what is so beautiful as mother love? Public schools are bad for them, private schools are worse, while tutors are the most pernicious of all. They should be taught to work, they should be taught to play, they should not be taught anything. . . .

Our occupational habits may be regimented in detail, but as a total phenomenon they are infinitely various. No good American believes in the doctrine that his place is anywhere except at the top. Nobody stays if he can possibly avoid it, in the place in which it has pleased God to put him. . . . There is the constant migration from farm to city; the massive movement of Negroes from the cotton fields to Harlem; while the variety of possible occupations—from deep-sea diving to flagpole sitting—is literally endless.

In the two following excerpts A. J. Liebling and George Sessions Perry characterize additional aspects of the urban way of life as seen in New York City.

a

The finest thing about New York City, I think, is that it is like one of those complicated Renaissance clocks where on one level an allegorical marionette pops out to mark the day of the week, on another a skeleton death bangs the quarter hour with his scythe, and on a third the twelve Apostles do a cake walk. The variety of the sideshows distracts one's attention from the advance of the hour hand. . . .

I like to think of all the city microcosms as nicely synchonized though unaware of one another: The worlds of the weight-lifters, yodelers, tugboat captains, and sideshow barkers, of the book-dutchers, sparring partners, song pluggers, sporting girls and religious painters, of the dealers in rhesus monkeys and the bishops of churches that establish themselves under the religious corporation law. It strengthens my hold on reality to know when I awake with a brandy headache in my house which is nine blocks due south of the Chrysler building and four blocks due east of the Empire State, that Eddie Arcaro, the jockey, is galloping a horse around the track at Belmont, while Ollie Thomas, a colored clocker of my acquaintance, is holding a watch on them. I can be sure that Kit Coates, at the Aquarium, is worrying over the liverish deportment of a new tropical fish, that presently Whitey will be laying out the gloves and headguards for the fighters he trains at Stillman's gymnasium, while Miss Ira, the Harlem modiste, will be trying to talk a dark-complexioned girl out of buying herself an orange turban, and Hymie the Tummler ruminates a plan for opening a new night club. . . .

There are New Yorkers so completely submerged in one environment, like the Garment Centre or Jack and Charlie's, that they live and die oblivious of the other worlds around them. Others are instinctively aware of the wonders of New York natural history, but think them hardly worthy of mention.[7]

b

New York, to the rest of America, is a stupendously rich, glamorously theatrical, noisy, over-excited, idea-ridden, un-American, brutally expensive, rolling torrent of man-swarm.*[8] That, and, of course, a skyline.

To a New Yorker, it's just home, and his own personal piece of it is a neighborhood of a couple of thousand people. The rest of New York's 7,690,000 people, its hundreds of square miles of vertically extruding real estate, and those thousands of sights and sins and smells and sensations not directly involved in the New Yorker's life, simply do not live in his mind as experience, but except when his attention is directed to them, as echo.

New York might be compared to a broad lake, through a part of which runs a current, a stream of outland Americans, some en route to and from Europe, more coming to market and pausing to have a good, if slightly bewildering, time. Since New York's metropolitan area is the nation's biggest manufacturing center, it naturally has many wares to sell. But when the market place closes for the day, the visitor sees before him an exciting endlessly manifold city and he goes cavorting over it.

For example, when I am in New York, I live in a small midtown apartment. Passing trucks and busses, kids frolicking or fighting in the street, make it noisy, and New York's dirty air makes it a hard place to keep clean. But it is, nevertheless, a residence in a small town. I know the people who run the shops, and they know me. I could live the rest of my life without going more than a block away for such living requirements or services as are sold in stores or performed by dentists, doctors, lawyers, etc.

Many aspects of New York life are reflected in our little neighborhood. The grocery is run by an Italian family, which is part of the city's million people of that particular origin. This family is very lively and its members love to yell back and forth across the store at each other as they sell their preserved egg plants and other rich and wonderful Italian fare. The cop on the corner is, of course, one of the town's 500,000 Irish—although not all New York cops are Irish—and the laundryman is one of its 1,000,000 Russians. Elsewhere in our neighborhood are representatives of New York's 500,000 Germans, 400,000 Poles, 300,000 Austrians. The heart of most New York neighborhoods is the delicatessen, since New Yorkers are often without the time, energy, inclination or facilities for cooking dinner after a day's work. It is here that the person with one room, a hot plate and a coffee pot, may stop in the evening, buy two slices of bacon, one egg, a few slices of bread. Having no refrigerator, he must buy only what he can use for his next meal. Our delicatessen is run by Mr. Morris Schwartz, one of New York's two million Jews. He is an extremely nice man, and I suspect the most popular one in the neighborhood. Our maid is a Negro. She lives with 500,000 other Negroes in Harlem, is penalized for her color by Harlem's landlords, but is like so many of New York's Negroes, considerably above the ability-level of most Southern Negroes.

The biggest immigrant group in the city is the one composed of the fugitives from America's small towns, who, incidentally, find when they get there that the town is interested only in what they can do, that their family tree, so far as New York is concerned, can be an old sweet-potato vine. If they are pretentious, New York will never stop hacking away at those pretensions. Yet it is compassionate to the genuine eccentric—especially on Broadway, Columbus Circle, Union Square and in Greenwich Village.

The strands, design, and pigmentation of the New York myth come from the subjective interweaving in the minds of the beholders of such world-famed sights as the Brooklyn Bridge; the Third Avenue bars and antique shops; Rockefeller Center and the Bowery flophouses; the Metropolitan Opera House and Nedicks orange drink stands; cafe society, which goes, primarily not to eat but be seen; the loping old elevated trains; the packed, thundering subways; the bands; the parades; the ten-dollar-a-ticket "Cause" banquets, for when touched, New York's Runyonesque heart is meltingly generous; the crimson, shrieking fire engines roaring down automatically opening lanes of heavy traffic; that inhabited javelin, the 102-story Empire State Building; the stone lions in front of the Library; and the appalling statistics that veritably poleax the imagination. New York spends $2,000,000 a day keeping the city manicured, governed, a going concern. A passenger train arrives every fifty seconds, twenty-four hours a day. Even before war destruction was visited upon Europe's capitals, New York had more telephones than London, Paris, Berlin, Rome and Brussels put together. Two hundred and fifty or so billions of dollars clear its banks in a year, dollars that go not only to the tax collector and the publican, but to the aspirant hoofer from Keokuk, the confidence man from Tallahassee, indeed to whoever captured the imagination of the depositors of that wealth, sells them a sufficiently promising bill of goods.

To pass from legend to geography, Greater New York is divided into five boroughs, which are synonymous with counties. The Bronx is the home of the cheer discourteous, and that poisonous cocktail. Queens is where the race tracks are. The borough of Richmond is Staten Island. Brooklyn is where baseball becomes more aggressively vocal, and where the Navy Yard and Coney Island are. (Will Rogers said New York's subways were built so Brooklynites could get home without being seen.) Manhattan, of course, is what people usually mean when they say New York. Long Island, Westchester County, parts of Connecticut and New Jersey are where commuters live, where New Yorkers week-end, and where the New York complexion, which in the summer is pasty on Friday, pink on Monday, often gets its ephemeral color.

Politically, New York City is traditionally Democratic. So far as the state is concerned, there is the usual struggle between the metropolitan and non-metropolitan area, for upstate New York is Republican and the fight for its forty-seven electoral votes in presidential elections is always desperate and often crucial.

One of New York's biggest businesses is the clothes you wear. Roughly three-quarters of the nation's clothing, nearly all of the ladies' dresses which are not home sewn are New York designed and New York made. Its dress industry is a one-and-a-quarter-billion dollar concern.

From the standpoint of the nation, the three outstanding products of New York are ideas, finance, and amusement.

Yet if the clangor of traffic and whistle of cops make up the dominant note of Times Square, there are other places of wondrous quiet, such as Sutton Place on the East River; Gramercy Park, which is fenced in and to which only the families of its neighborhood have keys; Washington Square, home of New York University, which fringes on Greenwich Village; and up on Morningside Heights, the Columbia University vicinity. But where the city becomes downright pastoral is in beautiful 840 acre Central Park in the heart of Manhattan.

Should a contest be held to find the average New Yorker, the fellow who won it would probably be a white-collar worker who likes simple things such as walks in the parks, dogs—New York has the most dogs, and the lowest dog mortality rate of any city in the nation—newspapers, movies which he usually sees at his neighborhood movie house, and above all, conversation. The average New Yorker reads more than the average American, is more socially conscious, more articulate, slightly more critical of his surroundings, slightly more irritable. He lacks the simplicity of environment of rural folk, and yet if he disapproves of you, he is far less likely to knock your brains out than a Southerner or a Southwesterner, but he is more likely to take legal action when aggrieved. He responds more audibly to newsreels, is more apt to hiss or cheer, than the ordinary moviegoer.

This average New Yorker pays more for almost everything than the rest of the nation. His rent and the rent of the man who sells to him, would be reason enough for these high prices. And since space and time are the ore from which he smelts his living, he is naturally busy trying to wedge sixty-five seconds into a minute, fourteen inches into a foot. Surely no town on earth is more briskly paced. And for this pressure the New Yorker pays in something besides money, something that is drained out of himself.

If the average New Yorker is a Manhattanite, he's proud of the city, and of being a part of it. In his mind Brooklyn, Queens, Richmond and the Bronx are the semi-finals in the contest to see who is going to live in what to him is the most exciting spot on earth.

C. TWO CASES OF URBAN ECOLOGY

Human ecology, as it is used in sociology, deals with the sociocultural patterns of people distributed along a spatial geographical axis. As in the plant and animal world, the distribution of people results initially from competition and struggle for the resources of the earth. On a primitive level, the struggle is for the direct products of nature. On more advanced levels, the struggle is more indirect. It is found in the form of differential land values and in competition for sites for industrial development and for cheaper rents. These processes of struggle and competition for the scarce commodity and resource frequently result in common forms of adjustment among persons and groups living in a particular habitat or locale. People in given areas frequently portray similar sociocultural characteristics.

The importance of the ecological approach to the study of the community was emphasized about three decades ago by C. J. Galpin and Robert E. Park, the former devoting his research studies and analyses to rural areas, the latter to the city.[9]

Since Park's time, abundant studies on the ecology of the city have appeared purporting to show that the life of any large city falls into a complex network of social-cultural-economic zones and communities. Through a process of segregation resulting from economic competition for land, the city gives rise to a mosaic of little cultural communities including the central business district, the slums and foreign colonies, the area of vice and crime, the residential district, and the wealthy suburbs.

It should not be assumed that these areas distribute themselves purely at random. The segregated areas of the city present, upon analysis, a basic pattern of general zones. Several theories as to the nature of this pattern have emerged. In 1925, E. W. Burgess suggested the hypothesis that the pattern consisted of a series of five concentric circles: (1) the downtown area, (2) an area of transition right off the business district, (3) the workers' zone, (4) residential zone of single-family dwellings and high-class apartments, and (5) the commuters' zone.[10]

Homer Hoyt, in 1939, published his sector theory of urban communities. This consisted of a series of wedge-shaped zones widening out from the center of the city and possessing social characteristics different from the other sectors.[11] In 1947, John W. Teeter, using various economic and social data, found Madison, Wisconsin, falling into a combination of concentric circles and wedges.[12]

Whatever the generalized ecological pattern of the city may be, it should not be inferred that the pattern is static, that it remains permanent and unchanging in any one instance. There are dynamic processes operating in the very formation of the pattern and in the alterations that are constantly taking place in the pattern.

Several concepts have emerged in urban ecology as tools for analysis of these processes: [13] (1) segregation, or the sifting of people with similar social and economic characteristics into specific areas; (2) invasion, or the penetration of a segregated area by persons with different social, cultural, or economic backgrounds; (3) succession, or the complete displacement of one group by another in a given area.

In the following descriptive passage, the author depicts in rather nostalgic terms the different ethnic, racial, and cultural groups living in contiguous territories of New York City. It should be borne in mind that these were characteristic of New York in 1924 when the author's book appeared. These sociocultural areas are still present today, but their location and quality have undergone some changes. Another example of urban ecology follows with a description of New Orleans. The reader will observe that in this instance the processes of ecological patterning have been somewhat inhibited by the historical precedents in the settlement of New Orleans.

1. *Around the World in New York* *[14]

New York, like no other city, offers the best study of the nations of the world, samples of each being centered in different sections within easy reach of one another. You can go into the Spanish quarter and forget easily you are in an Anglo-Saxon country. You will be in vaulted, Alhambresque Spain while you are there; listening to songs with guitar accompaniments and feeding on food flavored with condiments imported from Spain. More than that, you can be in different provinces of Spain; for the people of these different provinces, on coming here, gather and form folds of their own, until the Spanish district forms in itself a copy of Spain. The people of each province live in the same proximity to one another as they do in their own country. And not only do they live in the same neighborhood, but they lead the same lives, sing their own songs, and speak their own tongue, which is jealously guarded by the older ones in fear lest the younger ones might lose it and thereby lose their identity as Spaniards of a certain province.

You can go into the French district, and live in France while you are there, with Parisians clustering by themselves nearer to where there is light and gaiety, and the Normans further away on the side streets, withdrawing within themselves.

The southern Frenchmen from Marseilles and Orleans and Tours gather in their own cafes and restaurants to discuss and talk about their gardens at home across the waters, and to sing their own songs, their own provincial love-songs.

If you go further, into the Italian colonies, you will see the streets of Naples, the sidewalks littered with fruit- and vegetable-stands of all kinds; and the gay Neapolitan call of the fishermen on Mulberry Street is the same gay call of the fishmonger of the Neapolitan Strada. If you walk through Little Italy at night you will hear voices floating through open windows, singing to the accompaniment of guitars the songs of Genoa and Naples, of Rome and Triest, and never for a moment think that you are elsewhere than in a southern Italian city. And there is the same antagonism between the northern Italian and the southern one. There is the big, bellowing Calabrian who detests his smaller-sized brother from Sicily, and the Roman-born who has contempt for both of them.

There is the Russian district, with moody Slavs worrying themselves, torturing themselves about this and that and the other eternal question. Big, heavy-boned, broad-shouldered, sunken-eyed Slavs with a mixture of Tartar blood, colorful in their barbaric emotions, powerful in their inert solidarity, more daring because less flighty, more influential because of their resolute steadiness.

And what is one to say about the Hungarian quarter? Where the children of Attila have kept their own tongue so pure that not a single Anglo-Saxon word has penetrated their speech. You can see them daily. Their homes, in crowded tenement quarters, still retain that individuality which is their own. . . .

Further below them is the Rumanian quarter, a race of men considering themselves superior to all others of the Balkan states because they are the descendants of the old Romans, Trajan's soldiers, who conquered the Dacs of Decebal more than fifteen centuries ago, proud of their tongue because it is still the nearest to Latin of any language; they have their own poets here, their own musicians, uninfluenced by the life and the jazz about them, as if they still lived in Bucharest, which in Europe is known as Little Paris. Their own Gipsies live among them, despised and loved by them; hard-working peasants vainly trying to adapt themselves to a different life, disliking the Hungarians, suspecting the Russians, neighbors here across a dividing sidewalk.

The great German population of the city, divided and subdivided when there is peace on the other side, is united when its integrity is attacked or endangered. Slow, careful artisans; slow, careful merchants, with the same *Gemutlichkeit* as at home, still reading their home papers to their wives and children, still leaning back in their soft comfortable chairs, in their immaculately clean homes.

And there are Danish and Finnish, and Norwegian and Serbians, and Slovak and Swedish quarters, each one with its own life, guarding jealously its national characteristics. There is the Syrian district with one principal street and several side streets, one of the oldest in the city, with the houses built a hundred years ago. . . .

And the Chinese quarters, with the picturesque signs and pagoda-style houses, the red-brick walls of streets pasted with announcements and signs and news-papers, on yellow- and green-tinted paper, in that curiously decorative hieroglyphic script in which the laws of Confucius and Lao-tsze are printed.

A map of Europe superposed upon the map of New York would prove that the different foreign sections of the city live in the same proximity to one another as in Europe; the Spanish near the French, the French near the Germans, the Germans near the Austrians, the Russians and the Rumanians near the Hungarians, and the Greeks behind the Italians. People of western Europe live in the western side of the city. Those who have lived on the other side near the sea or a river have the tendency here to live as near the sea or the river as possible.

A reformation of the same grouping takes place every time the city expands. If the Italians move further up Harlem, the Greeks follow them, the Spaniards join them, with the French always lagging behind and the Germans expanding eastward. . . . Is there another city where one can travel from one country into another in less time than it takes to think of doing so? Is there another city that so holds the imagination of the entire world, toward which every head is stretched, toward which so many things gravitate?

2. *The Old New Orleans and the New* [15]

New Orleans is sufficiently different from the general run of American cities to make it an interesting laboratory for studying ecological principles evolved on the basis of data from other cities. Its topography, on casual observation, appears to be rather similar to that of Chicago or of any number of plains cities. Yet in certain respects its topography is very different, and uniquely, it has been changed fundamentally during the history of the city. In its population history it has shown evidence of the processes of accommodation and assimilation of minority groups characteristic of other cities plus long standing patterns of accommodation of racial groups which assimilated very slowly or not at all. As a result of these complex factors, ecological maps of New Orleans look like a crazy-quilt to sociologists acquainted with the ecology of conventional American cities. Actually, however, the city is not without an ecological pattern and this pattern is not difficult to see once the city's topography and history of ethnic groups are understood.

As was said above, the topography of the city is in some respects typical but in other respects it is unique. The city is located on a strip of land roughly five to seven miles wide between Lake Ponchartrain on the north and the Mississippi River on the south. Though eighty miles from the gulf, this land, like all land in the area, was built up by a long process of sedimentation. Therefore, in contrast to inland areas, the higher land is found along streams or where streams once existed while the lowest land is found farther away from streams. Thus, while the land may appear to be perfectly flat, a contour map shows that the land ranges from fifteen feet above to two feet below mean gulf-level.

The highest land in the city is found along the river and ranges from five to fifteen feet above mean gulf-level. Passing north from the river, the altitude declines to two feet below gulf-level. The low area, however, is transversed by "ridges" where bayous are or have been. Thus there is Metairie Ridge, two feet above sea-level running east and west almost parallel with the river and about half way between the river and the lake. There is also a ridge about two feet above gulf-level, running north-south from the end of Bayou St. John to the river, passing the lower end of the French Quarter. We will call this Esplanade Ridge. This ridge divides the city into what may be conceived as two saucers sitting edge to edge, the other edges being formed by Metairie Ridge and the high land along the river. Each saucer is two feet below sea-level at its center and is from two to fifteen feet above sea-level at its periphery. Until relatively modern times the centers of these saucers were swamps and habitation was feasible only along the rims of the saucers. It is in terms, therefore, of the struggle of the nationality groups for residential space around the edges of the saucers that the ecology of the city is to be understood.

New Orleans, of course, was settled by the French. Presumably the particular site was selected because they wanted an inland water route to the gulf coast of the present state of Mississippi where they already had a settlement at Biloxi. Such a route was available through Bayou St. John, Lake Ponchartrain and a series of lakes and bayous which link this lake to the gulf. A short and easy portage between the river and Bayou St. John was provided by Esplanade Ridge which was already in use for this purpose by the Indians when the French explorations and settlement was made. The settlement originated at the junction of Esplanade Ridge and the River and as it expanded it did so mostly to the west where the land was higher than it was to the east. This is the area that is now known as the French Quarter.

Like the settlers in most colonies, the early French settlers of New Orleans were a rather motley lot. They came from various walks of life and various stations in France and probably are not to be considered as coming primarily from any particular social element of the homeland. After a period of frontier hardship, however, they began to be moulded into a quite distinctive and homogeneous group. The French government followed a very liberal policy of land grants to individuals with the result that most of the early settlers became big land holders. This policy was continued by the Spanish government when this territory passed into the hands of that nation. Thus under both France and Spain, there was a tendency for government officials and military personnel sent out to the colony to acquire sizeable land holdings usually without having to purchase them. On these holdings the French established plantations worked with slave labor and rapidly attained prosperity on this basis. Most of them, however, continued to live in the city particularly during the winter and if they lived on their plantations at all they did so in the summer. Their city life was based almost as much on slave labor and the labor of free Negroes as was their plantation life. Thus at the time of the Louisiana Purchase there were twice as many Negroes as whites in the city. As time went on these French plantation owners came to refer to themselves as Creoles and they will be so referred to in the remainder of this paper. The term itself does not refer to land ownership but merely to unmixed descendants of French or Spanish settlers.

This prosperous, land-endowed group, plentifully supplied with colored labor, and gathering in the city for a winter of leisure, made a very favorable situation for an elegant social life. The city being also the colonial capital made this almost inevitable. Such a development seems to have taken place in a large way from 1743 when the great marquis, Pierre Francois de Riguod, Marquis de Vaudreuil, came as governor of Louisiana. He and his wife were accustomed to life in the royal courts of Europe and apparently sought with considerable success to set up a similarly pretentious society in New Orleans. Once established, this pattern was continued by succeeding governors, French and Spanish, with the exception of a brief period under General ("Bloody") O'Reilly who was sent by Spain to suppress a revolt against Spanish rule.

Spanish rule does not seem to have altered the situation in any significant way. The Spanish made no attempt to colonize New Orleans or Louisiana. They did make a half-hearted attempt to teach Spanish in the colony but it attained very indifferent success. For the most part, Spanish officials and military men seem to have found the Creole social life much to their taste and to have been accepted by the Creoles into that social life. Thus they came nearer being assimilated by the Creoles than the reverse. In reality many of them did marry Creoles and others received land grants, established plantations and became part of the Creole aristocracy.

Thus, prior to the Louisiana Purchase, the city was dominated by this Creole landed aristocracy centered around the colonial capital. It was a typical Estate pattern. The emphasis was on inherited wealth in the form of land. There was a law of primogeniture with the surplus sons placed in professions or the government service and stress was laid on social life or leisure time pursuits instead of occupational attainment.

The following description by a French traveler, C. C. Robin, of a reception given in 1803 may give a glimpse of the life of these Creoles prior to the Louisiana Purchase:

"The Louisiana Ladies appeared there with a magnificence that was astonishing in such a colony, and that magnificence could be compared with what is most brilliant in our principal towns in France. The stature of the ladies, generally tall, and their fair complexion, which was set off to advantage by their light dresses adorned with flowers and rich embroideries, gave a fairy-like appearance to these festivities. The last one, especially, astonished me by its magnificence. After the tea, the concert, the dances, the guests descended at midnight into a hall where, on a table of sixty to eighty covers, rose from the midst of rocks the temple of Good Faith, surrounded with columns and surmounted by a dove; underneath was the statue of the allegorical goddess. But further, outside of that hall, the brilliance of the lights attracted the guests under an immense gallery closed by awnings. Forty to fifty dishes, served in different styles, were offered to the choice of four or five hundred guests who were assembled in little groups." [16]

In addition to the Creoles and the Negroes, there were other nationality groups in the city prior to the nineteenth century. A number of Germans had come to the Louisiana territory during the John Law boom in the 1720's and after unsuccessful attempts at settlement on the Arkansas River had settled in the vicinity of New Orleans. Also French immigrants came from Santo Domingo as a result of slave uprisings and from France as a result of the French Revolution during the latter part of the eighteenth and early part of the nineteenth century. Most of these groups were unable to get large land grants and hence did not become plantation owners. In large part they seem to have become dairymen and truck gardeners though many of them also became artisans. There were also, of course, some representatives of numerous other nationalities but they can be ignored in an ecological study.

With this information before us, let us try to get a picture of the city at the time of the Louisiana Purchase in 1803. It contained only 8,475 population (census of 1805) and covered a correspondingly small area. The heart of the city was what is now known as the French Quarter, bounded by Canal Street, Rampart Street, Esplanade Avenue and the river. In this area were the government buildings, what business there was and the homes of the Creoles. The slaves were housed on the premises of their owners so far as possible. Since most of the Negroes, whether free or slave, were employed in service around the homes of the Creoles, and hours were long and travel was by foot, the Creoles desired them to live close to their homes. Thus those who could not be quartered on the premises formed a residential fringe around the Creole section. Outside this Negro zone was the immigrant truck gardening and dairying zone, the latter using land which was too swampy for residence or cultivation but usable as pasture. On the high land adjacent to the river and east of the city this trucking zone expanded into a considerable area. Outside of this area were plantations wherever the land was high enough to permit cultivation. Thus there were plantations along Bayou St. John and along the river on both sides of the city.

Up to the Louisiana Purchase the infiltration of Americans into New Orleans had been small. They came in and out with the shipping and there were some permanent residents but in some degree immigration of Americans had been held back by unfavorable Spanish laws. With the Louisiana Purchase, however, the dam was breached and the tide began to flow. Thus within the five year period from 1805–1810 there was a 125 per cent increase in the white population of the city, and a large part of this increase undoubtedly was American.

These incoming Americans were a sharp contrast to the polished, wealthy Creoles with their elegant social life. While as a group the Americans who came to New Orleans were perhaps not as crude as the American frontiersmen in the open country, certainly they had among them many who were just that crude. In fact the river men who floated down the Mississippi on barges and were known locally as the Kentucks were just as crude and rough and ready as the frontiersmen in any part of the country. Thus in New Orleans, the spreading American frontier ran into a culture which, on a basis of manners and fine appearance at least, was superior to its own; the only case of its kind in American history.

The difference in degree of cultural refinement, however, was not the only difference between the Creoles and the Americans. The Creoles, it will be remembered, laid stress on family tradition, hereditary wealth, leisure and social position. The American, on the other hand, had as his sun god the self-made man. The individual who had been born free and equal, had through his own initiative, industry and thrift gained wealth or success, was the man to be worshiped whether he was the son of a prince, a millionaire, a beggar, a criminal or a simple frontier woodchopper. Thus the two had basically different social philosophies as well as social systems; neither understood the philosophy of the other and neither was much impressed if he did understand. Also the fact that the Creoles were Catholic whereas most of the Americans were Protestant did little to foster mutual affection. Language differences of course increased these tensions, and furthermore, the question which language would be the official language, was an issue of serious moment.

On the basis of their culture, their wealth and their numbers in a more normal situation, the Americans might have been expected to have assumed the role of a minority group but, as usual, New Orleans was not a normal situation. The Americans were representatives of the nation which had just purchased Louisiana and now controlled the government and they were in no psychological mood to be a minority group. Nor was the government in any mood to insist on their playing a minority role. Thus from the beginning, to the tune of much conflict, overt and covert, with the Creoles, they were forced by the factors of the situation into a position somewhat better than that of a minority group.

The course of events brought a rapid improvement in their situation. The passage of the Louisiana territory into the hands of the United States ended all barriers to commerce on the Mississippi River and brought a rapid commercial development in New Orleans. The Creoles with their philosophy of hereditary wealth and leisurely social life had never had much taste for the make or break drive for efficiency characteristic of the commercial world and they did not take to it now. Since most of the tillable land was already held by the Creoles most of the Americans had little chance of establishing themselves as landlords. In any event, the uncertainties, the big stakes and the competition of the business world, had a natural appeal to the worshipers of the self-made man, and they rapidly took over the competitive area as their special domain.

Thus the port figures for the first six months of 1803 show that the shipping was already largely in American hands even before the Louisiana Purchase. Of the 153 cargo ships entering the Mississippi during that period 93 were American, 58 were Spanish and only 2 were French.[17] Similarly, Vincent Nolte who visited

New Orleans in 1806, three years after the Purchase, informs us that the mercantile system was made up of four or five French establishments founded during the French rule, three Scotch counting-houses, one German concern and eight or ten commission houses lately opened by young American merchants from New York, Philadelphia and Baltimore.[18]

This near-monopoly on the thriving commerce of the port city rapidly brought prosperity to the Americans and along with it brought a rapid increase in their numbers. With their nationality status thus backed by wealth and numbers, the Americans increasingly challenged the Creoles for the leadership role, culture or no culture, and the struggle between the two groups grew in severity and bitterness.

This struggle made inevitable an ecological separation of the two groups. The first Americans did live and have their business in the French Quarter but the crowded conditions plus the Creole-American struggle brought growing pressure for them to go elsewhere. Being so heavily engaged in commerce, it was imperative that they stay on the high land along the river but the fact that they moved west instead of east of the French Quarter was perhaps the result of the Marigny affair.

"About 1822 two Americans, James H. Caldwell and Samuel J. Peters, planning to develop a succession of warehouses and cotton presses and other important enterprises (hotel, gas works and water works, etc.), approached Bernard de Marigny with a proposition to buy the whole of his extensive property along the Elysian Field Section. The Creole was extremely unwilling to deal with the Americans, whom he disliked intensely, but was finally persuaded to do so, for a stipulated sum. When the necessary legal documents had been drawn up to conclude the sale, Mrs. Marigny failed to appear at the notary's office. Her signature was necessary to ratify the sale and Marigny used her absence as an excuse to prevent the sale. Infuriated, Mr. Peters is said to have cried out to the Creole: 'I shall live, by God, to see the day when rank grass shall choke up the streets of your old faubourg.'

". . . Outraged but not discouraged, the two pioneers transferred their interests above Canal Street. They felt that the Americans would be glad to congregate there since they would be separate from those whom they regarded as their oppressors. With the assistance of other local American capitalists a considerable part of the holdings of Jean Gravier was purchased." [19]

Whether or not this event is a full explanation, at any rate from about this time on an American section did grow rapidly to the west of the French Quarter. Into this section moved both American residents and American business. This movement was particularly rapid in the early 30's and a survey made by a local newspaper in 1834 showed that about three fifths of the "merchants," two fifths of the "retailers" and four fifths of the "brokers" were by that time in the American section.[20] Thus the city quickly evolved a pattern with the business section around Canal Street as the center, the Creole section to the east and the American residential section to the west of this. Each of these residential areas had Negro slaves living on the premises and a horseshoe shaped fringe of Negro residences around it with the open side of the horseshoe being towards the business section. Outside of this was the trucking-dairying zone.

The strife which produced this residential segregation was manifest in a severe degree in political circles. The Creoles, considering themselves the settlers of Louisiana, felt the government belonged to them, and the Americans, considering that they had purchased Louisiana, felt the government was theirs. The Creoles had been accustomed to use government positions to support their sons who could not inherit land under primogeniture, and the Americans had no inclination to use tax funds to support Creole families. In contrast the Americans wanted the government to build all sorts of facilities which would be of aid to commerce, and the Creoles were not interested in being taxed to bring prosperity to the Americans. These differences were so great that as the two factions attained near equality numerically and financially one government could no longer contain them. Thus in 1836 New Orleans was divided into three municipalities, having one mayor but for all practical purposes having separate governments. In the center was the Creole city bounded on the east by Esplanade Avenue and on the west by Canal Street. To the east of it was the immigrant truck-gardening city and to the west of the Creole section was the American municipality. In all three cases the river was the southern boundary and the lake was the northern boundary.

This separation of the city into three municipalities practically established Canal Street and Esplanade Avenue as national boundary lines. It became a matter of honor and of loyalty to one's cause to live on the proper side of these streets; those who moved into enemy territory were viewed askance if not actually as deserters. And after more than a century these definitions have by no means disappeared.

With this division the American municipality launched an almost extravagant program of public improvements. Old wharves were improved and new ones were built, streets were paved, public schools were developed and public buildings were constructed. Accompanying this was a growing prosperity and a rapid inflow of white population. Thus the white population in the whole city (three municipalities combined) increased from 21,281 in 1830, to 59,519 in 1840, and 91,431 in 1850. Meanwhile there were no more Negroes in the city at the end of this period than at the beginning.

A significant part of this influx of white population was Irish workmen. The growth in commerce and shipping brought laboring jobs and the public works program of the American municipality meant the need for many workmen. To meet these needs there was virtually no local labor supply. There were not enough free Negroes, slaves were too expensive, and the immigrants were happily employed in their crafts and agricultural pursuits. As a result, outside laborers were brought in and these for the most part were Irish immigrants.

This growth in population with the influx of a new immigrant element brought an expansion and reshuffling of the residential areas in the American section. With their mounting wealth the American elements were in a position to move farther out and build themselves new homes. South was the river, north were the swamps, and to the east were the business section and Creole land. Their logical move, therefore, was toward the strip of higher land adjacent to the river, and this move they made, developing a pretentious residential section with large homes and spacious grounds. This section has since been known as the Garden District. At the time it was built, it equaled or surpassed anything the Creoles possessed either in the city or on their plantations, and doubtless served to give the Americans a psychological compensation for their lack of "culture" and family background as compared with the Creoles.

This move of the Americans meant that the Negro residential fringe and the truck gardening zone had to be invaded and pushed out farther. It was the beginning of a process which continued up to relatively recent times both in the Creole and American sections. While in both cases the invasion did take place, the succession was not completed, particularly with reference to the Negro residences, for in all of the older sections of the city today there are scattered small groups of Negro residences which are remnants of a once solid Negro residential zone. Also in moving out the Americans deserted their old residences. Since the Irish were working for the Americans, they were not welcomed in other sections of the city, and being laborers, they needed no land to cultivate. Thus they were glad enough to get the discarded residences and New Orleans gave birth to what has since been known as the Irish Channel.

As the city grew, the Creole area, being adjacent to the central business section, tended to deteriorate and this, with a natural increase in Creole population, created pressure for that group to move out also. If the Americans had their fate sealed as to where they might move, so also did the Creoles. To move east meant crossing the national boundary lines of Esplanade Avenue and invading the immigrant truck gardening section and this would violate their pride and honor. To the west was Canal Street, the central business section and the unthinkable American section. Their only recourse was to move out Esplanade Ridge to Bayou St. John, and here today New Orleans has lovely old homes which are a product of this period. The migration process in this area was similar to that in the American section with some significant differences. The invasion process was about the same but the tendency of the Creoles to stay in the French Quarter in spite of deterioration was much greater. Thus there resulted an extraordinarily large number of what in other cities would be called marooned families, and there are in that area today many homes which are still owned and occupied by descendants of the families who originally built them.

Due to administrative and financial difficulties, the three municipalities were recombined into one in 1855, but by that time the ecological pattern was firmly fixed. Esplanade Avenue and Canal Street were made and the Creole section limited to Esplanade Ridge while the American section was confined to its ridge west of the city.

The strips of habitable land on these ridges were rather narrow and any tendency of these residential areas to widen was quickly checked by the swamps or the river. Therefore, expansion could only take place by building farther and farther out along these ridges. Such building, however, meant greater and greater distances from the central business section, and greater distance meant serious inconvenience when travel was by walking, bicycle or horse and buggy. In the American section, where the growth had been the greatest, the distances became so great as practically to reach the toleration point. Thus further expansion was made with a minimum of land and a minimum of added distance. This was done by making the yards inconveniently small and building the houses close together. Economically, of course, this was reflected in very high land values.

The immigrant truck-gardening section to the east of the city seems to have had, by comparison, relatively few growing pains. Being engaged in agriculture, the residents were not densely settled and, as the city developed, the population turned more and more to non-agricultural occupations. There was little accretion to this area by migration, and the rate of natural increase was not enough to take up for residential uses the land which was thrown out of cultivation. Thus while other sections were crying for land, this section had land to spare. As a result, land in this section became a quicksand for real estate speculators who knew land but did not know New Orleans. For the same reason there was a plentiful supply of land on that side of town for military uses during the First and Second World Wars.

Thus up to the early part of this century the basic ecological pattern of the city was T-shaped. The T was formed by the intersection of Esplanade Ridge and the ridge running along the river. The French Quarter (original French settlement) was approximately at the intersection of this T. The immigrant truck-gardening area was at the east end of the cross bar and on the west end were the central business section, the Irish Channel and the Garden District (American section), respectively. The newer Creole area was on the leg of the T, Esplanade Ridge, running vertically to the river. All of these were long narrow rectangular shaped areas, strung out along the top of the ridges, flanked on both sides by the swamps or the river. The American section and the Creole area were fringed by horseshoe shaped residential areas for Negroes and outside of these was a truck-gardening and dairying zone. The latter used land which was dry enough to cultivate or pasture but too low for residential use.

During the present century several developments have been taking place which have been materially altering this ecological pattern. About 1910 the city began to attain success in a long effort at artificial drainage of surface water. The city had early used canals and drainage ditches to hasten the flow of water from the ridges to the swamps. Then in the latter part of the last century it tried canals with windmill powered pumps to drain lower sections. These pumps were found inadequate and in 1903 they were replaced by electric-powered centrifugal pumps. These were an improvement but still did not have the capacity necessary for a city with the heavy rainfall which New Orleans has. Finally in 1917 a large screw type of electric pump, something like a ship's propeller installed in a large pipe, was developed and this proved adequate to the task. With these pump developments went a gradual improvement in surface and underground drainage facilities. From small beginnings this system was thus expanded until today it has a pumping capacity of 16½ billion gallons per day (24 hours), enough water to cover eighty square miles of land one foot deep. As a result, the water level was gradually lowered until by the 1930's all of the former swamp areas were as effectively drained as the higher areas.

The development of this drainage system ecologically had the effect of changing the topography of the city. In virtually no place in the city is the change of altitude sudden enough that there is any visible difference between high land and low land. With drainage, therefore, the land, for ecological purposes, is perfectly flat and as far as topography is concerned it is all equally desirable for building purposes. Hence the barrier which the swamps had formerly been to residential expansion was now removed and the residential areas began to respond accordingly. The American section most strikingly turned squarely north away from the river and directly toward the center of a former swamp. Thus during the past two decades, census tracts which are in this former swamp area, show population increases of from 700 to 1400 per cent. The Creole section correspondingly spread out in both directions from the Bayou St. John area, though the population pressure here was not nearly so great as in the American section.

About the time these drainage developments were taking place transportation developments were in process which also had marked effects on the ecological pattern. So far as this city is concerned probably the most important transportation development was the street car. Like other social developments, this one cannot be very specifically dated. Horse-drawn cars and steam "dummies," of course, date well back into the past century. The successful electric car was not developed until about 1885 and its effect on the ecology of the city was not very evident until well into the present century. While the street car aided greatly in relieving pressures in the American and Creole sections, probably its most pronounced effect was on the Negro residential fringe. With the street car available it was no longer necessary for the Negroes to live so close to where they worked. In other words, the electric street car made the Negro residential fringe obsolete. As a result, this fringe began to disappear. In its stead, large Negro residential areas began to develop back towards the central business section in the formerly swampy areas between the white residential sections. This concentration has in turn attracted to these areas schools and other facilities for Negroes which are an incentive for more Negroes to move there.

The automobile which had such profound effects on most American cities had a relatively small effect on New Orleans. It augmented the effect of the street car in a number of ways but since it was not commonly used by Negroes and other poor elements in the population, it created no new trends related to these residential areas. The only part of the city where there was sufficient residential pressure to make a demand for residential suburbs was the American side of the city, and here the outlying areas were so swampy that this was impractical. There did develop on the west end of Metairie Ridge over in an adjoining parish a suburb known as Metairie. However, the 1940 census still showed New Orleans as ranking among the lowest cities in the country in the proportion of its population living in the metropolitan area outside the official city.

In general, the drainage system, the street car and the automobile combined, have created a tendency for New Orleans to shift from its former ecological pattern to a zone system similar to that recognized in other cities. However, this pattern is by no means yet completed and it seems likely it will not soon be completed. Vast areas of the city are still socially taboo to large elements of the population and these do not conform to a symmetrical zone pattern. In addition, on the American side of the city, the drainage did not provide enough land to bring the price of building lots down to what would be considered elsewhere as "reasonable." Therefore, building new homes is still expensive and as a result old ones are not recklessly discarded. Consequently the "nice" old residential areas do not deteriorate except under the greatest of duress. And by the time the natural pressures for deterioration have become sufficiently great these areas have accumulated enough tradition to make them antiques. Thus the French Quarter is now protected by special legislation designed to prevent invasion and deterioration. Under this protection it has actually been undergoing a restoration with middle and upper class Americans moving in. Correspondingly the Garden District has tenaciously remained respectable. The 1940 rent map shows that this district is still one of the high rent areas of the city. Very high order rooming houses are about the only degradation it has yet suffered and to date it has not needed special legislation to protect it. However, should that necessity come, its antiquity is such that it will doubtless be museumized in the legislative halls.

In summary, the ecological pattern of New Orleans up to the present century was primarily the result of its topography. This pattern was set by the ridges and limited by the swamps and the river. In the historical process, sections of these ridges were occupied by the different nationality groups and came to be considered their special domain. Due to the ethnic conflicts and status differences between these nationality groups the social definitions of these areas became very strong and highly emotionalized. As a result of the division of the city into three municipalities in 1836 Canal Street became the accepted boundary line between the American section and the Creole section and Esplanade Avenue became the dividing line between the Creole area and the immigrant area. With the development of the drainage system during the present century the swamps disappeared and this land became as well drained as the ridges. Therefore, with the land being so nearly flat, today there is no visible difference between the low land and the high. Thus for all practical purposes topography as an ecological factor has disappeared except for outer limits set by the Mississippi River, Lake Ponchartrain and outlying swamps. In this situation the ecological pattern is tending to respond to modern transportation facilities and develop in the direction of a symmetrical zone pattern. The social definitions of the different areas carried over from the previous era, however, are proving very strong and resistant to change. This resistance is further increased by the fact that suitable land is not available for developing extensive suburbs which would make inevitable the deterioration of the old areas. Therefore, the old areas tend to be preserved and occupied by the same groups as formerly, and wherever necessary protective legislation is provided to facilitate this preservation.

D. SOCIAL CLASS AND SOCIAL STRATIFICATION

Since ancient Greek times, writers of social thought have persistently recognized the reality of social classes. While the precise term had a later origin, the essence of class in terms of privileged and unprivileged, higher and lower prestige or status, master and servant, authority and servility, superordination and subordination, domination and subjection, as well as a host of other words signifying differential social ranking date back centuries. This is doubtless due to the universality of social stratification; inequality is a characteristic of all cultures, although the extent and kinds of inequality vary from one culture to another, from one group to another.

In our analysis of the human-social group, we mentioned that a set of values denotes one of its major attributes. It follows, therefore, that those members of a group who possess a high degree of the element which the group prizes will obtain high status in the group, while those possessing little will have low status. For example, a good football player will have high status in a football team. Physical prowess determines status on a boxing team, intelligence in an intellectual circle.

When we think of social status cutting across many groups and giving a person a rank in the larger community, we approach what is known as *social class*. Indeed, an individual may receive his class rank because of his membership in certain groups such as family, country club, or social circle. While individual members of a particular group, such as the family, occupy different positions in the family, they may all be members of the same social class in the community. An individual's class position is, therefore, the weighted sum of the groups to which he belongs and the relative ranking of these groups with other groups in the community or larger society such as the region or the nation. In short, *a social class may be defined as a category of persons with a set of common attributes which are appraised as status—values in a particular society or culture*. It follows, therefore, that different cultures will emphasize different values and criteria in determining their social classes. In some, birth or family lines constitute the major determinant in class distinctions. Other cultures may stress possessions, personal qualities, personal achievement, official position, or a weighted combination of some or all of these factors. In the United States, no single factor determines one's social ranking, nor does the same set of factors operate as class determinants in all sections of the company. In several New England and Southern towns of declining economic opportunities, factors of lineage, inherited wealth, and length of residence in the community influence one's social-class position in the community; in expanding urban centers, on the other hand, emphasis is laid on wealth, political office, and individual achievement.[21] Whatever makes for class position in a particular community or society, several principles have emerged governing class structure in the United States in general.

1. Movement from one class to another is possible and actually does occur. This distinguishes a class system from a caste system, in which vertical mobility is confined within the caste.

2. There are no official, legal, or religious symbols to mark off class position, such as are found in a caste system. In the rigid Indian caste system, for example, religious sanctions permit marriage only within the caste; a person may marry outside his class in the United States.

3. In American society, high vertical mobility has prevented the formation of precisely definable social classes.

4. The present-day Negro-white system of social relations in the United States, particularly in the South, has features of class-caste mixture.

5. Income, occupation, and education are three major factors in determining class position in most areas of the United States.

6. The class system varies from one part of the United States to another.

7. Social-class membership is frequently the basis for group interaction. (Persons of like economic or educational circumstances tend to form clubs and informal associations and marry one another.) [22]

8. There is a wide range of status distinctions within a single class. (Not everyone born of "good family" is a leader of the upper class.)

9. Differences in child-rearing practices exist among the social classes.[23]

10. Birth rates vary with social class. (The birth rate in urban areas varies with the occupation of the husband, being lowest in the professional group and highest in the unskilled-labor group.) [24]

11. In the United States, some upward mobility does occur. (Among white males about one-third of the sons achieve higher occupational status than that held by their fathers.) [25]

12. A majority (two-thirds) of white American males have sons whose occupational status is either the same as or no better than their own.

13. In the United States, most Americans marry within their own social class.[26]

14. Social-class membership tends to shape basic personality structure.[27]

15. The American creed and ideals of equality have tended to minimize to some extent class awareness and class consciousness among American people.

16. In so far as there is an awareness of class position, Americans predominantly think of themselves as "middle class." [28]

17. Americans tend to be more conscious of the reality of the very highest and very lowest social strata than of the strata in between.[29]

18. Individuals tend to minimize the social-class differences between themselves and those above. Greater distinctions are made by individuals in a social class between themselves and those below them.[30]

19. Sharp cleavages exist in the sociopolitical attitudes of persons in different occupational strata. Those of the upper classes tend to be more conservative.[31]

Attempts to delineate social classes have given rise to several systems of classification. Many European writers following the framework of Karl Marx have divided society, on the basis of political economic power, into the bourgeoisie, petite bourgeoisie, and proletariat, corresponding to the three strata more familiarly known as upper, middle, and lower classes. Others have employed various socioeconomic indices of income, education, occupation, or a combination of them, to categorize social classes. Still others have employed criteria of subjective affiliation (where people believed they belonged) for social-class division. In recent years the system developed by Lloyd Warner and his associates has been in rather wide use. Membership in certain groups and associations constitute the basis of their stratification system, giving rise to what they consider to be the six major social classes in the United States: upper-upper, lower-upper, upper-middle, lower-middle, upper-lower, and lower-lower.

In the following cases, a dynamic profile of life in an upper stratum of society is presented as well as that of a member in a combined lower- and middle-class environment.

1. *The Proper Bostonian: A Case of the Upper-Upper* *[32]

There is a story in Boston that in the Palmy days of the twenties a Chicago banking house asked the Boston investment firm of Lee, Higginson & Co. for a letter of recommendation about a young Bostonian they were considering employing. Lee, Higginson could not say enough for the young man. His father, they wrote, was a Cabot, his mother a Lowell; further back his background was a happy blend of Saltonstalls, Appletons, Peabodys, and others of Boston's First Families. The recommendation was given without hesitation.

Several days later came a curt acknowledgment from Chicago. Lee, Higginson was thanked for its trouble. Unfortunately, however, the material supplied on the young man was not exactly of the type the Chicago firm was seeking. "We were not," their letter declared, "contemplating using Mr. —— for breeding purposes."

To the country at large the Proper Bostonian is not always easily identifiable. He does not necessarily live in Boston Proper. He may still live in the Beacon Hill area of his city, but he is more likely to be found in such socially circumspect Boston suburbs as Brookline, Chestnut Hill, Milton, Wellesley, Needham, Dedham, or Dover—and way stations from Prides Crossing to Woods Hole. He is not especially individual in appearance. Although outside observers have claimed to be able to tell the Proper Bostonian male by waistcoat, and the Proper Bostonian female by hat, these marks are not foolproof. Neither is his speech an infallible sign.

Once identified, however, the Proper Bostonian is a very well defined type—more so, it would seem, than the Proper Baltimorean, the Proper Philadelphian, or the Proper person of any other city. His basic character traits are almost unmistakable. This is undoubtedly because, as the Lee-Higginson story suggests, Boston Society has always devoted a great deal of attention to his breeding. The Proper Bostonian did not just happen; he was planned. Since he was from the start, in that charming Boston phrase, "well connected," he was planned to fit into a social world so small that he could not help being well-defined. He is a charter member of a Society which more than one historian has called more exclusive than that of any other city in America, and which has charter members only. It used to be said that, socially speaking, Philadelphia asked who a person is, New York, how much is he worth, and Boston what does he know. Nationally it has now become generally recognized that Boston Society has long cared even more than Philadelphia about the first point and has refined the asking of who a person is to the point of demanding to know who he was. Philadelphia asks about a man's parents; Boston wants to know about his grandparents.

According to the Boston Chamber of Commerce, Boston is 2,350,000 people. Boston Society, according to the Boston *Social Register,* is 8,000 people. Yet to the strict Proper Bostonian this volume, which admits only one Jewish man, and in a city now 79 per cent Catholic in population, less than a dozen Catholic families,

* Taken from *The Proper Bostonians,* by Cleveland Amory, copyright, 1947, Cleveland Amory, published by E. P. Dutton & Co., Inc., New York.

is impossibly large. Too much attention to it is regarded as a mark of social insecurity, and several Boston Society leaders have never allowed their names to be
listed at all.

Operating on the basis of those Families which it has come to regard as First
Families—only a few dozen in all—Boston Society is fundamentally far less than
half its 8,000 Social Registerites. Out of the total number of Bostonians, few are
called and fewer still are chosen into this fundamental Boston Society. Not content
with excluding some million Bostonians of Irish background, as well as many
hundreds of thousands of Bostonians of Italian, Jewish, Polish, and other backgrounds, it also cheerfully excludes another several hundred thousand or so whose
backgrounds are as undeniably Anglo-Saxon as its First Families' own and who
yet, because of imperfectly established connections with a First Family, can never
hope to become Proper Bostonians.

This figurative handful, the First Family Society of the Proper Bostonian, would
be interesting enough if it had done nothing more, through all the years of its
existence, than hold its social fort against all comers. But it has done considerably
more than this. Despite its numerical insignificance it has set its stamp on the
country's fifth largest city so indelibly that when an outsider thinks of a Bostonian
he thinks only of the Proper Bostonian. When Thomas Gold Appleton a century
ago used the phrase "Cold Roast Boston," he was a Proper Bostonian speaking only
of other Proper Bostonians. But the phrase lasted, not alone for Appleton and his
friends and their descendants, but for Boston itself. In the same way, one small
poem which had its genesis in the social aspirations of just two Boston Families
has become what is probably the closest to a social folksong any city ever had.
Originally patterned on a toast delivered by an anonymous "Western man" at
a Harvard alumni dinner in 1905, it was refined in 1910 by Dr. John Collins
Bossidy of Holy Cross to be recited, apparently for all time, as follows:

> And this is good old Boston
> The home of the bean and the cod,
> Where the Lowells talk to the Cabots,
> And the Cabots talk only to God.

The stamp of the Proper Bostonian on his city has stood the test of time. The
personality of Boston remains the personality of the Proper Bostonian—not only
to such alien critics as the editors of the *New Yorker* and *Time* magazines, and
to countless authors of fiction from Worcester to Hollywood—but in fact. Boston's Irish population may be in control of the city's government, but not for
nothing are they referred to as "the poor, downtrodden majority." Boston as a city
still moves almost as it did in Emerson's day, when he described it as locomoting
as cautiously as a Yankee gentleman "with his hands in his pockets." In 1945 an
up-and-coming court removed the still-existing ban imposed in 1637 on the
"Boston Jezebel," Miss Anne Hutchinson; but only a year later, in 1946, as Boston
was making elaborate plans to be the City of Tomorrow, the park commissioner,

engaged in planning a modern parking space under Boston Common, noted rather sadly that he would still be powerless to do anything about it if any of the oldtime property owners of Beacon Hill wished to take advantage of the ancient and immutable statute permitting them to graze their cows on top of the Common.

Reverence for a Family crest has become a Boston tradition, and while officers of the New England Committee on Heraldry have from time to time attempted to make clear that coats-of-arms have "nothing to do with social position," Bostonians of varying backgrounds have not hesitated to assume them. Many years ago the merchant William Appleton made a business-like study of the problem and came to the conclusion that only eight Boston Families, Appletons included, were entitled to crests. Dissatisfied with this, since the Lowells were not included, the late poetess Amy Lowell went into the matter on her own and figured out that thirteen Families was the correct figure. Only the present Charles Francis Adams would seem to have shown becoming modesty in the debate. Branding as spurious the Lowell crest at that time being carved in Harvard's Lowell House, he declared that to his knowledge only two Families, not alone in Boston but in all of New England—the Winthrops and the Saltonstalls— were worthy of the honor of arms-bearing.

If he has led others astray on his purple path, the Proper Bostonian is blithely unconcerned with the fact. He remains the Man of Family supreme. He has immense pride in his forebears and he includes all of them. The portraits of past black sheep hang on his walls along with those of his stern-faced ancestors whose ways were more tried and true. In a Boston Bowditch home today may be found the portrait of Habbakuk, town drunk of Salem, side by side with that of his son, Nathaniel, the celebrated navigator and mathematician. The Proper Bostonian feels that if certain of his ancestors were distinguished, so much the better, but they do not have to have been. His Family tree, at least in his own mind, is rooted so firmly it needs no ornaments on its branches. When after a dignified Proper Boston courtship of seven years the poet Henry Wadsworth Longfellow married into the Appleton Family, the Appletons felt very pleased about it— for the Longfellows, of course. The poet wasn't, after all, a Bostonian at all, having been born in Portland, Maine. When one of the Boston Forbeses married the daughter of philosopher Ralph Waldo Emerson, the Forbeses began to feel very kindly toward the strange man from Concord; his daughter soon became, in the Proper Boston manner of speaking, "A Forbes."

Some years ago a New York girl who had married into a Boston First Family and who had, in customary fashion, named her first child after her husband, spoke of naming her second son after her own brother. In great agitation a dowager of the First Family came to see her and said, "I hear you are naming your son Alfred. I have been back on the family tree and I cannot find a single record of anyone of that name." For the young wife to protest that she too had a family was useless. In the Boston sense she had none.

No Boston First Family party is complete without some discussion of genealogy.

One of these parties, traditionally a Thanksgiving or Christmas affair, is apt to be so large that many of the guests, though relatives, will be strangers to each other; if afterward one speaks of not connecting with someone, he means, in the Boston manner of speaking, that though he saw the person and may even have spoken with him he did not place him on the Family Tree. For many years the Lowell Christmas night parties, landmarks of Boston's First Family gatherings, would have tested even the antiquarian who occupied himself for a quarter of a century compiling the official Lowell Family genealogy. The Bowditch Family met the problem squarely as recently as 1936 by supplying every guest present with a ten-generation genealogy, a pamphlet designed in looseleaf form with extra space provided for keeping the work up to date.

Occasionally a crisis occurs at one of these parties, as when Calvin Coolidge was elected President and a Boston Coolidge dinner was thrown into an uproar of discussion to determine what exact relation was this man from far-off Vermont. Fortunately the Family included a distinguished professor of mathematics at Harvard, who is a very precise man. After a moment's thought he came up with his answer. "Calvin is my seventh cousin once removed," he said. He was later proved correct.

The dynastic proportions of Boston's First Families are staggering. One way of measuring these proportions is in the class lists of Harvard, to which most sons of First Families have naturally gravitated. A son of the present Senator from Massachusetts represents the ninth successive generation of Saltonstalls, all descendants in the male line, to attend the college, as follows: Nathaniel 1659, Richard 1695, Richard 1722, Nathaniel 1766, Leverett 1802, Leverett 1844, Richard 1881, Leverett 1914, and Leverett 1939. The Wigglesworths have sent to Harvard no less than eight Edward Wigglesworths alone, while Dr. George Cheever Shattuck and Dr. Richard Warren represent, respectively, the fifth and sixth generations of Boston Shattucks and Warrens who have attended the Harvard Medical School.

The First Families have indeed always been noted not only for the recurrence of the same name but also for the recurrence of the same profession. In the Lowell family there were three generations of Judge Johns. Among the Cabots there have been seven successive generations of Samuels, the last three of whom have been manufacturing-chemists. In the Quincy Family there were four direct-line generations of Josiahs, three of them mayors of Boston. For a hundred years there have been Augustus Lorings and Moorfield Storeys and other imposing names in Boston's legal profession. A present member of the Homans Family declares that when she says Dr. John Homans she may mean her great-grandfather, her grandfather, her father, her brother, her nephew, or her cousin—all of that name and all physicians. Beside this name confusion First Family genealogy is further complicated by the overlapping of generations. On the testimony of one writer, whose mother was a Cabot, it "sometimes happened that a Cabot girl would be a great-aunt before she was born."

First Families in Boston have tended toward marrying each other in a way that would do justice to the planned marriages of European royalty. In one Cabot family, out of seven children who married, four married Higginsons. In a Jackson family of five, three married Cabots. In a Peabody family of four boys and two girls, two of the boys and a girl married Lawrences. In one family of Boston Shaws there were eleven children; nine married members of other Boston First Families, one died at the age of seven months, and the eleventh became a Catholic priest.

Yet even this intimate marriage circle has often proved too large. There is scarcely a First Family in Boston without a record in its background of a marriage of cousins. Charles Bulfinch, Boston's greatest architect; Helen Choate Bell, Boston's best-known Society wit; Lawrence Lowell and Endicott Peabody, Boston's two outstanding educators—all chose cousin spouses. Only in the case of Lowell was the relationship even as far removed as a second cousin. Among Peabodys and Hunnewells the marrying of cousins has become almost a tradition; the Hunnewell genealogy is said to have become so complicated through such alliances that it has never been satisfactorily worked out beyond 1892. One Peabody who married her cousin explained cousinly romance as almost inevitable in a Society as closely knit as Boston's, where "we had so many Family parties and picnics and all that sort of thing." Recently when two young First Family cousins became engaged a Boston matron put her official stamp of approval on the young girl's intentions. "Isn't it nice," she said, "Faith isn't marrying out of the Family."

Boston's First Families have been notably strict in their rules on the adoption of children. There have been cases in which elder members of the Family have dissuaded a childless couple from adding offspring of unknown parentage to the Family Tree. In one case a couple who wished to adopt a son were forced, after considerable urging, to compromise on the selection of two daughters instead. Children of these would not then carry on the sacred name. One man who deserves special mention in any history of the Battle of Boston Eugenics is the long-suffering scion of a First Family who was prevented from marrying the girl of his choice because of her inferior social position. The parents went so far as to declare they would publicly disinherit him if he added such an unworthy strain to their proud line. Resolutely, nonetheless, the young man courted his girl and upon the death of his parents married her—thirty years later.

Along with the Family idea the Proper Bostonian has stamped a provinciality upon his city which has through the years shown few signs of decreasing. So long as Anglo-Saxon gentlemen stuck together, one writer has phrased it, the Bostonian felt that the world in which he lived could not go wholly to the dogs. His world, of course, was Boston. "We all," wrote Dr. Holmes in the last century, "carry the Common in our head as the unit of space, the State House as the standard of architecture, and measure off men in Edward Everetts as with a yardstick." Viewed in this later time, Holmes' choice of Edward Everett could scarcely have been more ironic if he had planned it; a giant among Proper Bostonians of his day, Everett is now nationally remembered almost solely for his part at the ceremonies at Gettysburg on November 19, 1863, in which he delayed Lincoln's two-minute Gettysburg address by an oration lasting exactly two hours. But Holmes also expressed a more durable idea. It was he who gave local newspapermen their beloved short word for Boston when he declared that firmly planted in the minds of all true Bostonians is the idea that Boston is the "hub of the solar system."

The Proper Bostonian is not by nature a traveler. In an earlier day he made his Grand Tour, always with particular emphasis on England—for London alone was enough like Boston to suit him—and of late years he has been pushed by wars and other circumstances to various parts of the globe; but basically he remains adamant in his lack of geographical curiosity outside the suburbs of Boston.

As distinguished a Proper Bostonian as Charles Francis Adams, whose business requires his presence in New York every week or so, makes no bones about the fact that, though a man in his eighties, he prefers to ride a milk train to Boston rather than spend a night in a New York hotel. Of all Boston's First Families, the Forbeses, longtime residents of the select suburb of Milton, have always been particularly well known for their love of home and hearth. In the summer they go to Naushon, their own island off Boston's South Shore where there are, in contrast to other Boston summer resorts, not just all Bostonians but all Forbeses. When Cameron Forbes was appointed governor-general of the Philippines many years ago, his brother Ralph was congratulated. "I don't know," said Ralph, "it's kind of tough on Cam—he won't know what's going on in Milton any more."

Particularly the Proper Bostonian expects both the fellow-inhabitants of his city and his visitors to share his high regard for Harvard University. Since all First Families' sons repair there, he wishes it to be recognized as the only college there is. But this is not easy, since the majority of Bostonians have little or no connection with it, and since Boston has half a dozen other colleges as well—not to mention the fact that Harvard is located not in Boston at all, but in Cambridge. Nonetheless the Proper Bostonian has done his best, and to be elected to membership in Harvard's "Corporation," a self-perpetuating group of Bostonians who run the University— and who in recent years have managed to include one or two New Yorkers in their number—is a Bostonian honor not to be compared with anything else. The late Bishop Lawrence, himself a member of the group, once stated that a Bostonian might speak disparagingly of the House of Bishops or the College of Cardinals but not of the Harvard Corporation. An interesting instance of the local attitude occurred some years ago during the Taft administration in Washington. A visitor to Harvard sought to see the late Lawrence Lowell, then president of the university. Having been called to the nation's capital on a matter of business, Lowell could not be seen. The visitor was stopped by a secretary in the outer office. "The President is in Washington," she said, "seeing Mr. Taft."

But despite the dubious distinction he has won for his city in other parts of the land, the Proper Bostonian is still in his own domain regarded in almost all cases with respect and in some instances with actual affection. His private life is almost inviolate. On the Society pages of his papers his treatment is deferential in the extreme, and gossip columns are non-existent in any Boston paper. It has been said that Walter Winchell would have starved to death if he had lived in Boston.

This seeming abdication of journalistic responsibility cannot entirely be explained by the fact that the Boston newspapers are largely controlled by the Boston banks, which are in turn dominated by Proper Bostonians. There is also a sizable amount of evidence to support the thesis that the ordinary Bostonian rather looks up to the Proper Bostonian and is not inclined to laugh at him. Referring to the least endearing of various First Family traits—such as the bluntness of Cabots, the frostiness of Lowells, the tactlessness of Adamses, the perversity of Forbeses, the irascibility of Higginsons, the frugality of Lawrences, and so on— the late lawyer James Byrne once said that to him there was nothing humorous about it. The son of an Irish contractor, Byrne worked his way through Harvard tutoring sons of First Families and later became the only man of his background and religion ever honored with membership on the Harvard Corporation. "It is strong stock," he said, "that can produce the same traits of character in generation after generation. No, I don't laugh at it."

In Boston the member of a First Family lives in a world of special privilege. For him the minor inconveniences of life are all but bypassed. If he lives on Beacon Hill he will probably have a view of the Common or perhaps a fenced-in park of his own, such as on fashionable Louisburg Square, where the twenty-two so-called proprietors or home owners have practically no responsibility to their city at all, own the entire square outright, and meet annually to tax themselves for the upkeep of their park and the care of their street. Trains have changed schedules, stores have changed hours, and courts have changed statutes—all for the First Families. There are people in Boston today who remember the picture of Judge John Lowell, squire of the suburb of Chestnut Hill, who, often late for the 8:25 commuter's special, never missed the train. While a trainful of commuters complained in vain, it was never 8:25 to the engineer until the Judge was aboard. As for Boston's stores, the more exclusive of them have long catered to the whims of First Families irrespective of the fact that other customers are notoriously freer spenders. In the days before government regulations made such practice illegal, it was not unusual for stores to allow a First Family to run a bill for two full years without attempting collection before or beyond the usual formal statement of account rendered.

Harrison Gray Otis, nineteenth century king of Boston Society, had early set a high standard for this sort of privilege when in 1830, on the day fixed for the organization of Boston's present-day city government, he sent word to the members of the city council that he was ill and wished them to convene at his Beacon Hill residence. A few members protested that a municipal inauguration should not be held in a private home, but an invitation from an Otis was a command performance, and held it was.

To the courts—or rather to one particular court, the Massachusetts Supreme Court—the First Families have always repaired for the most remarkable of their privileges. Through its interpretations of their so-called "spendthrift" trusts, Boston's First Family fortunes have long been tied up beyond the reach of any power save possibly, as one financial writer put it, the Communist International. In these trusts, run solely by trustees, heirs to fortunes have been specifically denied the right to borrow money against the inheritances which were left in their names. Some other states have done this much, but the Massachusetts Court has gone a step further. As far back as 1830 it had guaranteed that not only the trusts themselves but also trusts incomes could be put out of the reach of heirs.

The power of the trustee, as long as he is by court definition a "prudent" man, is close to absolute. He rules not only until an heir becomes of age but in some cases all the heir's life. In times of stress trustees have been known to be able to keep all money away from creditors; then, when such storms have blown over, they have been able to turn on the golden faucet once more. The total power and resources of Boston's Family trusts have never been figured, but some years ago one of the city's trustee offices alone paid three per cent of Boston's total tax levy.

Most of Boston's First Families owe their lives of privilege, at least to some extent, to these trusts. The Lowell and Lawrence trusts, united by a Lawrence marriage on the part of the late Augustus Lowell, are particularly formidable affairs. So, too, is the Sears trust. This was established by Joshua Montgomery Sears, a Boston merchant who was so busy making money in the West Indies trade that he didn't take time out to get married until he was in his sixties. On his death in 1857 he left a son, Joshua Junior, who was then two years old. Only a very small part of young Joshua's inheritance, however, was left fluid, just enough, on a day-by-day estimate by the trustee, for bringing him up and educating him. The rest of the estate was thoroughly tied up and shrewdly manipulated so as to increase and multiply until the boy matured. When this happened, the mature Joshua awoke to find himself a wealthier man than even his father might have imagined. At the age of twenty-one he became Boston's largest taxpayer.

The real significance of Boston's trusts, however, lies not in their size but in the fact that they have enabled Boston's First Families to defy economic laws and the cherished American maxim of shirtsleeves to shirtsleeves in three generations. When the match king Ivar Kruger committed suicide and Lee, Higginson & Co., which had backed him to the hilt, went bankrupt to the extent of some $25,000,000 of his worthless stock, the late Lawrence Lowell lost $194,412. But the bulk of the Lowell Family trust funds, invested in Grade A bonds, was still intact; and neither the late Lawrence nor any Lowell since was ever to feel the necessity of getting out and shouldering a pick and starting all over again. When Leverett Saltonstall was having campaign photographs taken on his Needham farm, the pictures of the Senator doing some off-hours work in his garden was regarded as the first evidence of shirtsleeves in the Saltonstall Family in not three but nine generations.

Visitors to Boston are often impressed by the profound awe in which the leading members of the First Families of the city are held. There may be some question as to how far down the line this respect goes on the part of Boston's total population; but among the socially elect and the socially ambitious, there is nothing quite like a genuine First Family patriarch, a Cabot, or a Lowell, a Higginson or a Peabody, on the face of the Boston earth.

The core of the Boston social system is clubdom, and here the status quo remains awe-inspiring. In the feminine field a girl may become a debutante in Boston simply by applying to the secretary of the Parents League for Debutantes and asking for an admission blank. No questions will be asked beyond those on a simple form to be filled out. The fact that she will be on the social stationers' official debutante list, and will have her name in the newspapers as such, does not, however, mean that she will in her debutante year be favored with an invitation to join the Vincent Club or to become a provisional member of the Junior League. Nor does it mean that she will in later years enjoy the elite feminine fellowship inherent in such quaint organizations as the Mahjong Monday Club or a Sewing Circle. Boston's Sewing Circles are a unique feature among present-day city Societies. In other cities these Circles have all but died out; in Boston such Circles as the "97" and the "99"—both of which are named for their founding dates, 1897 and 1899—still go merrily on their way.

Sewing Circle 97 is particularly swank. Limited to sixty members—with three blackballs sufficient to keep out any proposed candidate—it meets once a week for lunch from November through May and costs just $2.00 a year. Members no longer sew for charity as they did in bygone days but instead are asked to contribute two articles of clothing to some charity each season. They meet on Wednesdays, rotating from dining room to dining room in members' houses. A rule of the Circle states severely the terms of this meal: "Luncheon shall be served promptly at 1 p.m. and shall consist of two solids, a sweet, bread, cake, tea, coffee, or chocolate."

In the male field one way of measuring the status quo of the Proper Bostonians' clubs lies in the service records of their chief employees. The Somerset had a James for a full fifty years and now has a Joseph who recently celebrated his twenty-fifth year of stewardship. The Union had Max for twenty-five years and still has two Pats who have divided desk duty for over forty years. The Tennis and Racquet has had Touhey in its locker room since the club was founded in 1904, and the Tavern's Bernard died after thirty years on the job. The City Club Corporation has a Joseph of thirty-five years' standing, and even the Club of Odd Volumes, an organization devoted to some genteel camaraderie as well as to the sampling of rare books, has its John of equal vintage. At the Brookline Country Club Mr. Sleeper served so faithfully and long that he was finally rewarded with membership in the club, and at the Somerset not only the late James, but also the present James and Joseph, have made permanent places for themselves in Boston Society.

Joseph won unusual recognition on January 4, 1945. On that date, at 7:30 in the evening, when the monthly dinner of the Somerset Club was in progress, a fire broke out in the flue of the charcoal broiler in the kitchen. It was four hours before the blaze, which extended to other parts of the club, was totally extinguished, but Joseph's behavior throughout the crisis was exemplary. When the firemen arrived at the club's front door at 42 Beacon Street, Joseph promptly barred the way and ordered them to the service entrance. This action caused some delay in the fire-fighting operations, but members were spared the pain of seeing strangers enter by the front door. Dinner for thirty-one members was already in progress when Joseph first received word of the fire, and he saw to it that all thirty-one were allowed to consume the major part of their meal without being disturbed. Finally, after all main courses had been served, Joseph went from table to table with the advice, still remembered by all present: "There will be no dessert this evening, gentlemen. The kitchen is on fire."

So severe are Boston's leading clubs that even blue-bloods have had to watch their step to gain admission. The late Rodman Weld made a habit of entering his nephews in the Somerset at birth so that they would be ready for election immediately upon their graduation from Harvard. One nephew, Rodman Peabody, has recalled in his diary protesting that he would rather wait a few years after graduation until he could better afford the dues. Upon which he was told by the shrewd Mr. Weld: "Young man, someday you may do something. Whatever you do some member of the Somerset Club will disapprove of it. I will pay your dues until the time when you tell me you would like to." At the City Club Corporation, First Family sons have been known to stand in line as long as fifteen years to get under the wire of its steady 180 limit, and to become a Family member of the Myopia Hunt Club, which has long had a 100 maximum rule, is still a feat of such magnitude that it was accomplished by the president of the State Street Trust Company only after he had spent the better part of two years writing the early history of Myopia. That the majesty of these organizations does not end with a man's election is evidenced by such haughty house rules as the City Club Corporation's ban against smoking during lunch, the Union Club's reading room sign "Only Low Talk Permitted," and the curious note over the only basement floor toilet in the Somerset: "This lavatory is to be used only in the case of emergency."

2. A Case of a Family Whose Members Reside in the Lower and Middle Classes [33]

When Paul Stanley was in high school he played football well enough to gain a reputation which brought him several offers of scholarships. He chose Eastern College because there he would have less competition and would be sure of being subsidized for his four college years. After finishing he sought to enter Harvard Law School but his college record was not sufficiently good to be passed by the board of admissions. He chose a less difficult, professional law school in Boston and in time received his law degree. Meanwhile, he had supported himself by working in the law office of John Bates.

Mr. Bates was a loyal alumnus of the local high school. He once said to Mr. John Breckenridge that "Paul Stanley's a good sound boy. Hard worker and knows people. He's a fellow to watch."

Paul's father and mother had come over from Poland with their respective parents when they were still children. After they had met and married they settled in the Downtown region of Yankee City where Paul, their first child, grew up. They both had worked in the shoe factory and gone to an "Americanization school" to improve their English.

The Stanleys were proud of their home. They owned it outright, and the husband and wife had planted the flower garden. Mr. Stanley had painted the house and fences with two coats of white paint. He placed cast-off tires in appropriate places in the front yard and had given them a coating of white paint. After Mr. Stanley had spaded the ground inside the tires, his wife had planted the petunias. Rows of hollyhocks grew beside the white fences. The smaller sons had collected flat stones and made a walk from the sidewalk to the door. Mr. Stanley dug a trench on each side of the stone walk. Here he half-buried empty beer bottles in neat rows so that they formed a glistening border to the path that his boys had fashioned.

The family was proud of its flower garden and pleased at the returns from the vegetable garden in the backyard. They kept chickens and ducks penned in a small coop in one corner, next to the garage where Mr. Stanley housed his second-hand car. (He had purchased the car from a fellow who had also bought it second-hand.)

Mr. Stanley watered and weeded the lawn and kept it well fertilized with manure from the stables owned by a teamster friend. He also considered himself something of a wag. "You know," he said, while he scattered manure about the garden, "I think those people in the Garden Club should see my garden. I bet they would elect me president. My wife says I'm a better manure spreader than any of them. Maybe they'll give me a prize for that."

Mr. Stanley always appreciated this little joke, but once when Paul heard him telling it he informed him that only peasants talked like that.

He looked down on his neighbors. Not one of them on his street cared for his house and yard as he did. They weren't clean and neat. He had learned all of the current folklore about the Riverbrookers and believed it all. He retold all of the sexual jokes he had heard about them, and at the same time warned his children to keep away from the children of Riverbrookers. He liked the derogatory jokes about Riverbrookers because they put into words what he felt about "some of these Americans."

"Not all of these Americans are so hot. Some of the Yankees are no better than the greenhorn Poles, and you can't blame those greenhorns for acting like pigs because that's the way they were forced to live in the old country."

On his son, Paul, he lavished the greatest affection. When Mr. Stanley wanted to expand and demonstrate how he had gone up in the world since coming from Poland, he first talked of his son's college education and then spoke of "my beautiful white house." He then made comments about "all these Yankees who have lived here forever and never got any place." But now it was different because his own Paul wanted to marry one of those Riverbrookers.

When his wife first started "yelling about that Tyler girl" Mr. Stanley had thought little of it, because the boy, Paul, was doing what everybody else did— having a little fun with a Riverbrook girl. He had an Irish friend who ran a small store up the street who always bragged about how he had screwed lots of them; it was fun because you didn't have to marry any of them. That had amused Mr. Stanley before, but now Paul wanted to marry one of them.

When he tried to talk to his son about it he found it very difficult. It was always difficult to talk to Paul. It shouldn't be that way, but he couldn't help feeling that Paul was somehow or other above him. The first time the subject was mentioned, the boy had told his father that it was none of his business. He had said that Annie was a fine girl. She had gone to high school, and she was no Riverbrooker because she had left her family—to get away from them—and had earned her way while she went through high school. She had been a nurse girl for the Joneses and had learned how to act.

She didn't dress like the others in her family; she didn't act like them; everybody who knew said she had "class"; she was good-looking; and she talked refined and used correct English. Paul had overwhelmed his father with these arguments, reducing him to impotent silence.

Annie Tyler had belonged to the same high school girls' club as Paul's sister. All of her friends said she ought to have credit for what she had done for herself. After a long pause, the father could only say:

"Well, they tell me, 'once a Riverbrooker, always a Riverbrooker.'"

Paul's mother also had quarreled with him about marrying the daughter of a clammer.

"Those Riverbrookers are no good. Now, you have a fine education," she said, "and you can marry a good Catholic girl. Those Riverbrookers are low. Their women will sleep with anybody. They live like pigs."

After a long talk with Mr. Breckenridge, Paul got in his small car and drove down among the small houses on River Street and stopped at the home of Frank Tyler. He knew that Annie, whom he wanted to see, was visiting her parents. She had come down from Hill Street to see her mother on her day off. He started to knock, when he heard the mother and girl quarreling inside. The daughter had asked her mother why she didn't keep the house clean and make her little brothers wash. She said she was very embarrassed when the truant officer had stopped her on the way down and asked her if she would see to it that the boys stayed in school.

The mother had said that the boys were helping their father, and it was none of that nosy truant officer's business if they weren't in school. They were getting old enough to help their father.

"Your brother, Joe, is just as smart as the next one. I want to tell you, young lady, there ain't nothing the matter with him. He ain't aiming to set the world on fire, and he will be as good a shoe worker as the next one. He will be just as good as those kids who go all the way through high school. If things keep on getting bad we'll move across the river 'til they let us alone. We make a pretty good living making shoes and doing a little clamming. The Joneses and Tylers always have and always will. That boy can figure as good as anybody now and he can read whenever he wants to.

"None of the Tylers or Joneses have ever gone beyond grade school exceptin' you and now you act like you was too good for your own folks.

"Why, I went as far as the fourth grade, and your pa went to the fifth. We can read and figure and write all that's needed, and that's enough for anybody. If that officer keeps on botherin' us, we'll move over to the other side of town. We don't have to take nothin' from nobody."

Paul waited for Annie Tyler to come out and then she and Paul walked up to where Annie worked. After he had told her about getting Mr. Breckenridge's approval, they discussed the date of their marriage. When they arrived at the Smith office where Annie was employed they announced the good news to Mr. Smith and arranged for Annie to have the week-end off.

They "ran away and got married." It was so much easier. They both thought it was too difficult to have the relatives there. The wedding caused an open split in Annie's family. They said she had married a "damn foreigner" and "a fellow who was a Catholic." The new Mrs. Paul Stanley found it expedient to widen the break first made by her parents because it meant she wasn't embarrassed by her relatives' visiting her new home. They might have come at times when friends were there, or neighbors might see them; and she didn't have to face going down to visit the dirty homes of her relatives. She wanted children and she didn't want them to be like her own brothers and sisters.

They seldom saw Paul's father and mother, but his sister was a frequent visitor. She usually met her beaux at their house, and Paul and Annie were pleased that his sister had a chance to meet a better class of people in their own home.

When younger, Paul had been proud of the home of his parents. It was the nicest house in their neighborhood. But now he saw it not as the nicest house in the neighborhood but in the larger context of the whole town, and this made it appear just a little ridiculous. He became a little ashamed of the white tires and the rows of glistening beer bottles. The house he bought was over in Newton. He wanted to raise his family away from everything which would make them think of what he had gone through. He wanted a nice new house—"one of those cute little bungalows with a big lawn in front and a concrete sidewalk on the street with new curves and a high-class name."

He had been flattered after graduating from law school when some members of the Caribous had invited him to join their organization. There were only a few Poles in the Caribous and most of the members were Yankees. They were all good fellows.

Before he had left the bank after negotiating with some of the officials for his money, he had been congratulated by several of the bank employees on acquiring the new house. They had kidded him about his coming marriage. A few evenings later one of the bank clerks told a clique mate of his, the manager of a hardware store, that Mr. Breckenridge thought very highly of Paul Stanley. At the moment he was talking, they were enjoying a glass of prohibition beer at the hall of the American Order of Antlers. The Antlers, they felt, had "everyone who counted in Yankee City" as members.

"Paul Stanley's come a long way," he said, "and he's come the hard way. And what's more, he's going a lot further. Nobody who's got what it takes and who's got the backing of Mr. Breckenridge can help but succeed. You know, I think Paul would make a swell member of the Antlers."

"That's a swell idea," his companion replied.

Within the year, Paul was a member in good standing of the Antlers, and he played bridge there several nights a week. He still belonged to the Caribous, but some of the members of the latter organization were beginning to complain that he didn't come around any more.

The Stanleys were now in a clique with Mr. and Mrs. Tim Pinkham, Mr. and Mrs. Dick Jones, and Mr. and Mrs. Jerry Thomas, but people like the Camps, the Frenches, and the Flahertys, whom Paul knew at the Antlers, never invited them to dinner, nor did any of the "nice ladies from Hill Street" ever call on Annie. It is possible that this occasionally worried them, but there is more evidence that their past success was still a pleasant reward and that the present filled them with hope for the future.

"And anyway," they said, "we're going to see to it that our children have every advantage."

Paul's wife never went to the meetings of the Auxiliary. She had made new friends in her neighborhood and had attended one or two meetings of the Art Club. She was not yet a member of this organization, but she was pleased, she told her husband, to be "introduced to several of the nicest ladies in Yankee City."

FOOTNOTES TO PART FOUR

Asterisks indicate footnotes quoted from original source of case material.

1. Morris R. Cohen, *A Preface to Logic* (New York: Henry Holt and Company, Inc., 1944), pp. 74-75.

2. The following sources may be consulted on the use of polar types in sociological literature: Ferdinand Tönnies, *Fundamental Concepts of Sociology,* translated by C. P. Loomis (New York: American Book Company, 1940); C. H. Cooley, *Social Organization* (New York: Charles Scribner's Sons, 1909); Robert Redfield, "The Folk Society," *American Journal of Sociology,* Vol. LII (January, 1947), pp. 293-309; Robert Redfield, *The Folk Culture of Yucatán* (Chicago: University of Chicago Press, 1941); Howard Becker and R. C. Meyers, "Sacred and Secular Aspects of Human Sociation," *Sociometry,* Vol. V, pp. 207-229, 355-370; Émile Durkheim, *The Division of Labor in Society,* translated by George Simpson (Glencoe, Ill.: The Free Press, 1947); Charles P. Loomis and J. Allan Beegle, *Rural Social Systems* (New York: Prentice-Hall, Inc., 1950), pp. 9-30; Oscar Waldemar Junek, *Isolated Communities* (New York: American Book Company, 1937).

3. It should be mentioned that these polar types can be used as a schematic framework for comparing not only community types but social groups or systems of social relations in general.

4. Adapted from A. R. Radcliffe-Brown, *The Andaman Islanders* (Cambridge, Mass.: Harvard University Press, 1933).

5. Condensed from Walter Kollmorgen, *Culture of a Contemporary Rural Community, The Older Order Amish of Lancaster County, Pennsylvania,* Rural Life Studies, No. 4, Bureau of Agricultural Economics, U.S. Department of Agriculture, September, 1942.

6. Excerpts from Stuart Chase, *Men and Machines* (New York: The Macmillan Company, 1929), pp. 278, 279, 280, 281.

7. Excerpts from A. J. Liebling, *Back Where I Came From* (New York: Sheridan House, 1938), pp. 13, 14, 15.

8. Condensed from George Sessions Perry, *Cities of America* (New York: McGraw-Hill Book Company, Inc., 1937), pp. 15-26.

9. C. J. Galpin, *The Social Anatomy of an Agricultural Village,* Agricultural Experiment Station of the University of Wisconsin, Research Bulletin 34 (Madison, Wis.: May, 1915). While Galpin's study was ecological he did not use the term *ecology.* The term *human ecology* made its appearance in 1921 in Robert E. Park and Ernest W. Burgess, *An Introduction to the Science of Sociology* (Chicago: University of Chicago Press, 1921), pp. 161-216. See also Robert E. Park and others, *The City* (Chicago: University of Chicago Press, 1925); Robert E. Park, "Human Ecology," *American Journal of Sociology,* Vol. XLII (1937), pp. 1-15; Louis Wirth, "Human Ecology," *American Journal of Sociology,* Vol. L (May, 1945), pp. 483-488.

10. Ernest W. Burgess, "The Growth of the City," in Park, Burgess, and McKenzie, *The City,* p. 50.

11. Homer Hoyt, *The Structure and Growth of Residential Neighborhoods in American Cities* (Federal Housing Administration, 1939), pp. 75-76.

12. John W. Teeter, "The Ecology of Residential Areas in the Madison Community," Ph.D. thesis, University of Wisconsin, 1947, p. 97.

13. *Cf.* A. B. Hollingshead, "Ecological Organization," in Alfred M. Lee (ed.), *New Outline of the Principles of Sociology* (New York: Barnes & Noble, Inc., 1946), pp. 88-89. Hollingshead notes additional ecological processes: *concentration,* or "the integration of human beings and human utilities in areas where nature or man has made conditions favorable to the satisfaction of subsistence needs"; *centralization,* or "the integration of human beings and

facilities around pivotal points at which social and economic, and cultural interaction occurs most frequently"; *decentralization,* or "the tendency for human beings and institutional agencies to move away from the center of the city"; *routization,* or "the recurrent daily movement back and forth from place of work to place of residence, or the shift into and out of the retail business, amusement, and wholesale districts by the city's population and those who use its services." See also R. D. McKenzie, "The Scope of Human Ecology," in E. W. Burgess, *The Urban Community* (Chicago: University of Chicago Press, 1926), pp. 172–177.

14. Condensed from Konrad Bercovici, *Around the World in New York* (New York: Appleton-Century-Crofts, Inc., 1924), pp. 14–21.

15. H. W. Gilmore, "The Old New Orleans and the New: A Case for Ecology," *American Sociological Review,* Vol. 9 (1944), pp. 385–394.

*16. Alcie Fortier, *History of Louisiana* (New York: 1904), Vol. II, pp. 240–241; Nellie Warner Price, "Le Spectacle de la Rue St. Pierre," *Louisiana Historical Quarterly,* Vol. I, p. 218.

*17. *Annals of Congress. Seventh Congress, Second Session,* 1801, p. 1525.

*18. *Biographical and Historical Memories of Louisiana* (Chicago: 1892), Vol. I, p. 30.

*19. Selma L. Klein, "Social Interaction of the Creoles and Anglo-Americans in New Orleans, 1803–1860," M.A. thesis, Department of Sociology, Tulane University, 1940, pp. 35–36.

*20. *The Bee,* May 29, 1935.

21. Florence R. Kluckhohn, "Dominant and Substitute Profiles of Cultural Orientations: Their Significance for the Analysis of Social Stratifications," *Social Forces,* Vol. XXVIII (May, 1950), pp. 376–393. See also Robert S. Lynd and Helen M. Lynd, *Middletown in Transition* (New York: Harcourt, Brace and Company, Inc.; 1937); Allison Davis, Burleigh B. Gardner, and Mary R. Gardner, *Deep South* (Chicago: University of Chicago Press, 1941); W. Lloyd Warner and Paul S. Lunt, *The*

Social Life of a Modern Community (New Haven, Conn.: Yale University Press, 1941); W. Lloyd Warner and Paul S. Lunt, *The Status System of a Modern Community* (New Haven, Conn.: Yale University Press, 1942); E. L. Anderson, *We Americans: A Study of Cleavage in an American City* (Cambridge, Mass.: Harvard University Press, 1937); Everett C. Hughes, *French Canada in Transition* (Chicago: University of Chicago Press, 1940); K. MacLeish and K. Young, *The Culture of a Contemporary Rural Community: Landoff, N.H.,* Rural Life Studies, No. 3, U.S. Department of Agriculture, Bureau of Agricultural Economics (1942); C. Wright Mills, "The Middle Classes in Middle Sized Cities," *American Sociological Review,* Vol. 11 (1946), pp. 520–529; James West, *Plainville, U.S.A.* (New York: Columbia University Press, 1945); D. Tomasic, "The Structure of Balkan Society," *American Journal of Sociology,* Vol. LII (1946), pp. 132–140; Hans Speier, "Social Stratification in the Urban Community," *American Sociological Review,* Vol. 1 (1936), pp. 193–202; W. Lloyd Warner, Marchia Meeker, and Kenneth Eells, *Social Class in America* (Chicago: Science Research Associates, 1949).

22. See footnote 11. Also Harold F. Kaufman, *Prestige Classes in a New York Rural Community,* Memoir 260, Cornell University Agricultural Experiment Station (Ithaca, N.Y.: March, 1944), p. 14; August B. Hollingshead, *Elmtown's Youth* (New York: John Wiley and Sons, 1949), Chap. 6; R. M. Williams, *Rural Youth in North Carolina,* Bulletin No. 324, North Carolina Agricultural Experiment Station (June, 1939); T. C. Hunt, "Occupational Status and Marriage Selection," *American Sociological Review,* Vol. 5 (August, 1940), pp. 495–504; August B. Hollingshead, "Selected Characteristics of Classes in a Middle Western Community," *American Sociological Review,* Vol. XII (1947), pp. 385–395.

23. Allison Davis and Robert J. Havighurst, "Social Class and Color Differences in Child-rearing," *American Sociological Review,* Vol. 11 (1946), pp. 698–710. Also

see pages 42–46 of this volume (*Social Dynamics*).

24. Frank Lorimer and Frederick Osborn, *Dynamics of Population* (New York: The Macmillan Company, 1934); National Resources Committee, *The Problems of a Changing Population* (Washington, D.C.; U.S. Government Printing Office, 1938), p. 140.

25. Richard Centers, "Occupational Mobility of Urban Occupational Strata," *American Sociological Review,* Vol. 13 (1948), pp. 197–203.

26. Kingsley Davis, Harry C. Bredemeier, and Marion J. Levy, Jr. (eds.), *Modern American Society* (Rinehart & Company, Inc., 1948), p. 611.

27. Allison Davis, "The Motivation of the Underprivileged Worker," Etc., *A Review of General Semantics,* Vol. III (1946), pp. 243–253.

28. See public-opinion poll in *Fortune* (February, 1940).

29. Harold W. Pfautz and Otis D. Duncan, "A Critical Evaluation of Warner's Work in Community Stratifications," *American Sociological Review,* Vol. 15 (1950), p. 212.

30. Allison Davis, Burleigh B. Gardner, Mary R. Gardner, *Deep South,* pp. 71–83.

31. Arthur Kornhauser, "Analysis of 'Class' Structure in Contemporary American Society—Psychological Bases of Class Divisions," in George W. Hartmann and Theodore Newcomb (eds.), *Industrial Conflict* (New York: The Cordon Company, 1939), p. 241; Richard Centers, *The Psychology of Social Classes* (Princeton, N.J.: Princeton University Press, 1949).

32. Condensed from Cleveland Amory, "The Proper Bostonians," *Harper's Magazine,* September, 1947, pp. 200–210; "Boston's Old Guard," *Harper's Magazine,* October, 1947, pp. 315–324.

33. W. Lloyd Warner and Paul S. Lunt, *The Social Life of a Modern Community* (New Haven, Conn.: Yale University Press, 1941), pp. 188–193.

PART FIVE

Social Processes and Forms of Social Interaction

A. INTRODUCTION: PRINCIPLES OF SOCIAL PROCESSES AND SOCIAL INTERACTION

In our discussion of the nature of sociology in Part One, we said that the field consists of the study of the elemental forms and processes of human association. In this section, our emphasis and focus will be on the processes. The social processes constitute the dynamic aspects of socio-cultural phenomena.

Specific social processes, such as competition, conflict, accommodation, and assimilation, are to be viewed as types of social interaction. Culture, group, and human personality are products of social interaction. A detailed analysis of the nature of human-social interaction per se, appeared in Part One. It was pointed out that human-social interaction consisted of the reciprocal influence among persons when they come into contact with one another. The contact, we said, is always on a symbolic-meaningful plane. This is what distinguishes human-social interaction from biological and physical interaction.

The social processes as forms of social interaction have been classified in many ways. Some classifications include only two categories, cooperation and opposition. Others, like that of Leopold von Wiese, divide the social processes into dozens of subtypes.[1] Ever since Robert E. Park's emphasis on what he considered the four major types of social processes—competition, conflict, accommodation, and assimilation [2]—sociologists have, by and large, limited themselves to the analysis of these social processes plus a fifth one—cooperation. *Competition* is usually conceived of as an impersonal, unconscious form of interaction, consisting of a continuous struggle for those values and objects considered desirable by a people. When competition becomes personal and conscious and the struggle for ends becomes a struggle against people, the process becomes one of *conflict*. *Cooperation* is defined as a social process, in which two or more persons aid each other and work together for like and common interests. *Accommodation* consists of the process by which persons or groups reconcile and adjust themselves to one another through a superordinate-subordinate pattern of relationship. (The child is subordinate to his parents; some Negroes have accommodated themselves to the whites' superior position in American society.) *Assimilation,* in sociology, means the process whereby persons come to share the same body of customs, traditions, and values although they were unlike in their initial ways. It is a fusion of unlike units of culture into a uniform pattern of culture.

Not much validated knowledge exists on the social processes. Some experimental tests and descriptive accounts are, however, sparsely interspersed in psychological, anthropological, and sociological literature. In addition one finds consensus on some theories governing the social processes. We shall list the major propositions and principles culled from the existent sources.[3]

1. Human beings strive for goals, and striving with others (cooperation) or against others (competition and conflict) are learned forms of behavior.

2. In the Western European–American culture, the rudiments of competition and cooperation appear among children during the first year of life, but these are not apparent until about the third year, after which they undergo rapid development until about the sixth year, when they are observable in all or nearly all children.

3. The social reform of the behavior and performance of an individual or individuals is affected when a given situation is changed from a competitive to a cooperative one, or vice versa.

4. Intergroup competition promotes intragroup cooperation.

5. The forms of competition and cooperation in a given culture are a function of the integration of a complex number of social, economic, and historical factors.

6. The primary goals for which socialized individuals compete, cooperate, or do neither are a function of their particular culture.

7. If the goals and values in any culture are scarce, the form of behavior is usually (but not always) competitive; if they are abundant, the form of behavior is usually (but not always) cooperative.

8. The life history of an individual reveals the unique and important role of his family group in transmitting the basic values of a culture, namely, competitive or cooperative predispositions.

9. People compete or cooperate both for material goods and for non-material ends such as privilege, prestige, or power.

10. No society reveals "perfect competition" or "perfect cooperation." Every society possesses a varying degree of both as well as of conflict, accommodation, and assimilation.

11. In contrast to competition, conflict is intermittent; competition is continuous.

12. Competition serves to make for division of labor in society.

13. Intergroup conflict promotes intragroup solidarity.

14. In intragroup and in intergroup conflict, when there are individuals who share the loyalties and values of the two factions, personality disturbances often occur.

15. In intergroup conflict, when the individual identifies himself with only one group, integration of the personality often occurs.

16. Coordinate accommodation results from conflict or competition when the participants are equal in power.

17. Superordinate-subordinate accommodation results from conflict or competition when the participants are unequal in power.

18. Accommodation prepares the way for assimilation.

19. Similarities in culture are conducive to assimilation.

20. A change from conflict to cooperation frequently depends on overcoming the stereotypes and false images that persons possess about others (see the case below, "From Conflict to Cooperation").

21. There is no correlation between culture areas and forms of social interaction. (The whole gamut of social processes are found within any one large area.)

These are but a few of the possible propositions governing the social processes. In the cases that follow, we have selected illustrations of a highly competitive society and a highly cooperative society. These are followed by a study of assimilation among Chinese immigrants in Hawaii and a study of the changes in the interaction, social-process pattern in an industrial plant as it went from conflict to cooperation.

B. THE KWAKIUTL INDIANS: A HIGHLY COMPETITIVE SOCIETY

Several experiments performed by J. B. Maller with school children showed that competition was a far more significant motivation in work performance than cooperation.[4] The question then arose whether competition as a primary human motivation and process was innate and universal or whether it was peculiar to American culture. Here anthropology again steps in to furnish us with some of the answers. The cases of the social life of the two primitive tribes—the Kwakiutl Indians and the Zuñi Indians—give us concrete evidence which denies any conclusion that the competitive drive is either innate or universal. Other anthropological studies have shown that some groups cannot even be characterized as cooperative or competitive. Some Eskimo tribes, for example, are more accurately described as "individualistic." [5] In any case, people will compete or cooperate with each other to the degree that the ethos of a society permits. The first two cases demonstrate that human beings raised in different cultures may differ markedly in the extent to which they display cooperative or competitive behavior. It follows, too, from a study of these tribes, that if differences in culture can produce significant differences in personal motivations and in the forms of personal interaction, neither competitive nor cooperative behavior can be instinctively rooted in human nature. Nor is it true that the competitive spirit is necessarily more conducive to human work, labor, and the general routine activities necessary for sustenance in the economic sphere of life. The ideal of cooperation may become the motivation for individuals if it is present in the value system of their particular culture.

There is not a total absence of cooperation among the Kwakiutl, but competition far outweighs cooperative behavior. The Kwakiutl are an extremely competitive tribe. In the opposite way, the Zuñi portray great degrees of cooperation while competition is held to a minimum.

Along *[6] the narrow strip of indented coast line stretching from Juan de Fuca Strait to Yakutat Bay live a number of Indian tribes differing among themselves in speech and physical characteristics but sharing a highly distinctive culture. Among these are the Kwakiutl. Hemmed in by rugged mountains and dense forest on the east the Kwakiutl have been crowded onto the beach, where they build their large plank houses. They wrest their living mainly from the sea, using salmon, candlefish, halibut, and mountain goat as the main items of diet. No land is cultivated, but the Indians pick wild berries and seeds from family-owned grounds and tend small clover gardens. Some animals are hunted in restricted and family-owned hunting areas. From the forest comes the red cedar used in the construction of houses, the large seagoing canoes, the richly carved boxes, and totem poles. On the whole, in comparison with the rest of the continent, the Kwakiutl are rich in material goods. Food is plentiful. In aboriginal days the Kwakiutl must have numbered from 10,000 to 20,000, but epidemics have twice decimated the population until in 1904 they numbered no more than 2,000.[7]

Upon an economic base of comparative plenty, the Kwakiutl have developed a system of economic exchanges that bears little relation to the problem of existence. Property is accumulated only to be redistributed or destroyed in a game in which prestige and self-glorification are raised to an egomaniacal pitch. More important even than material property as counters of prestige are the jealously guarded honorific names, titles, family traditions, and ceremonial prerogatives. Material property is valued only to the extent that it can procure or validate these prerogatives and names. The social structure reflects the great valuation of immaterial property in Kwakiutl life.

The Kwakiutl are composed of a great many tribes that are subdivided into bilateral family lines—the numaym [8]—the members of which claim descent from some mythical ancestor. The chief family within each numaym has its own history dating from a supernatural ancestor. The striking emphasis is upon rank. All tribes, numayms, and families are graded according to a strict pattern.[9] Within the tribe each individual is further classified as a nobleman, commoner, or slave, but the latter group, being for the most part made up of captives in war, are of no importance in the social structure. The nobility are the first-born of families of rank; the commoners are the younger sons and daughters. At the head of each numaym is a chief, one coming from a chiefly line. This chief possesses a certain limited political power.

Religion, too, is subordinated to the drive for rank and prestige, contact with the supernatural during the important winter religious ceremonials being based upon strictly owned, inherited, or otherwise validated prerogatives.

In a region renowned for the abundance of its sea life, the principal economic pursuit of the Kwakiutl is fishing.

The organization of fishing within the numaym is [10] essentially individualistic, though sometimes a group of brothers cooperate in fishing. Half the catch is given to the chief of the numaym to be distributed by him to all who need food during the winter, when economic life is suspended. It is always the responsibility of the chief to provide for his people when they are in need. The other half is used to feed the household of the men who caught the fish. The same distribution of the catch occurs even in those frequent cases when a number of canoes are needed to surround a school of porpoises to prevent their escape, but the usual method is individualistic—a man and his steersman hunt the porpoises alone. In salmon fishing, hunting, and berry picking also the members of a household pay a percentage of the food taken to their chief and use the rest for themselves. By paying this tax each member of the numaym is contributing to a communal food supply to be drawn upon by all.

Certain rivers belong entirely to a numaym, others to a tribe. Trespassing on such territory is forbidden, and the aggressor may be killed. These strictly maintained property rights are not related to any kind of food shortage. On the contrary the Kwakiutl are economically very well off and are not faced with the necessity for competing for a limited food supply.[11]

Only a relatively small proportion of the Kwakiutl's time is devoted to food getting. "The great occupation of the men, aside from hunting and fishing, was wood working." [12] The most time-consuming activity of the women is not the household routine or the gathering of berries but the making of baskets, mats, and cedar-bark blankets, property that is used in the formal distributions around which every significant aspect of Kwakiutl civilization is oriented. Woodworking is the great skilled craft on the Northwest Coast. The men can construct, out of a single cedar trunk, huge seagoing canoes holding sixty persons. With skillfully directed wedges, they split tar logs into planks to be used in house construction and in making beautifully carved boxes. Logs are carved into huge totem poles.

All the social relations among the Kwakiutl are keyed to the principle of rank, and each individual of any status in the community is motivated by an obsessive drive for prestige.

The people speaking the Kwakiutl dialect are divided into a number of tribes, each with a head chief and each arranged in a hierarchical order of rank and possessing certain crests and privileges obtained from the supernaturals. Each tribe is further subdivided into a number of family lines claiming descent from a mythical ancestor and cherishing a specific tradition. These family lines, the numayms, are also graded in rank. In addition, the individuals composing the numaym are divided into a nobility and common people. A slave class consisting of individuals taken captive in war or purchased does not form an integral part of the numaym, the slaves being regarded as property. The organization of the numaym is such that only a limited number of families are recognized.[13] Thus, the numaym possesses a fixed number of noble titles descending always in a strict line of primogeniture. The bearers of these names and the privileges that are attached to them form the nobility. All others are despised commoners. But the members of the nobility are not equal in rank. They are ranged in a hierarchy of nobility in the same way as their ancestors were supposed to have been ranked.[14] At festivals, at the great distributions of property, at the potlatches, whenever the nobility gather, this order of rank is strictly followed.

The possession of a title, however, does not in itself give the individual social prestige. Each claim to nobility must be validated by the distribution of property, blankets, boxes, and by the giving of feasts during which great quantities of valuable oil are conspicuously destroyed. Above all, an individual gains prestige by crushing a rival. It is this intense rivalry that is at the heart of Kwakiutl social relations. Property is given to a rival which he must repay with a 100 per cent interest. If he cannot meet this payment, he is crushed and loses in social status. Similarly, when a feast has been given to a rival, this rival must counter by giving a more elaborate and costly feast or lose in status. It is a war in which property is the weapon.[15]

As a result of the strong emphasis upon primogeniture the noblest names within the numaym tend to descend along the line of the firstborn, while the less noble names are held by the other family lines. The system, however, is complicated by the fact that another line of names descends through the maternal line, so that what might have developed into a rigid social stratification under a unilateral system of inheritance is much more diffuse. Nevertheless, within any given generation, all the names are ranged in a hierarchy of rank from the most noble name, which gives the individual rights to chieftainship, to the most unprivileged name. Further, when an individual takes on a name he assumes in his person all the greatness of his ancestors, whom he is thought to be impersonating. Therefore, when a man passes his name to his heir he necessarily relinquishes all rights to its use.[16]

Whatever rivalry exists between brothers is always indirectly expressed. In the socially recognized form of rivalry, in the potlatch, brothers do not compete against one another. Nor do members of the same numaym fight against one another with property. For if one is to gain the full prestige of having vanquished a rival that rival must be a worthy opponent. A nobleman does not compete with a commoner. He competes only with another nobleman of similar rank. This equation is carried to the point where the numayms are "perpetually pitted against each other according to their rank." In intertribal rivalry only certain tribes are traditionally paired off as worthy rivals.

Before proceeding with the discussion of rivalry for prestige it is necessary to familiarize the reader with the basic economic mechanism behind this competition. The Kwakiutl are a people of great wealth and they consider it honorable to amass a fortune. But it is not hoarding they are interested in. Wealth, such as blankets, boxes, and copper plates, is used in a game of rising in rank, of validating honorific titles and privileges.[17] Upon the occasion of taking on a name a man distributes a considerable quantity of blankets among the men of another numaym in the presence of the entire community. The recipients are obligated to accept the property and must be prepared to repay it at the end of the year with 100 per cent interest. Such men probably have property out at interest, which they call in at the end of the year to meet their payments. Should a man be unable to repay he is "flattened" and falls in social status. The victor, on the other hand, rises another rung in the social ladder. With each successful potlatch a man accumulates more renown as well as more property with which to conduct even greater potlatches. With prestige the driving motive in Kwakiutl society and with the basic intent of the potlatch the crushing of a rival, these property bouts take on a fiercely competitive tone.

The standard of value in the potlatch is the blanket, at present worth about fifty cents. The Kwakiutl also make use of bills of much higher denomination, called coppers. These are etched, shield like plates of copper with a T-ridge hammered on the lower half. Though they have little intrinsic value each copper represents thousands of blankets, its value being determined by the amount paid for it when it was last sold. Since each buyer makes it a point to pay more than the previous value of the copper, its denomination is increasingly higher. Thus one such copper was reported as worth 7,500 blankets.[18] Because of the high value of the copper its purchase brings the buyer distinction, but in addition, since he will have paid for it more than the last purchaser, it is a demonstration of his superiority.

Coppers are offered for sale to a chief of a rival numaym or to a rival tribe.[19] It is a challenge which the rival must accept or admit defeat. More than a challenge to an individual chief, it is a challenge to his numaym or tribe, who stand to gain or lose collectively depending upon whether the price for the copper can be met or not. All assist their chief with loans of blankets, the amount each contributes being in direct ratio to his nobility. Thus where the man next to the chief in rank gives one hundred blankets, a commoner may give only five. Nor do all the members of the numaym expect the chief to return the blankets that have been given for a potlatch, although generally these are returned with interest the day after the copper has been purchased.[20]

The purchase of a valuable copper adds prestige to the name of the individual, but it is an important economic investment as well, for at the next sale the copper will bring an even higher price. The economic motives are, however, only incidental in potlatching, as is indicated by the fact that one gains even greater prestige by destroying property.[21] As in the sale of a copper, the destruction of a copper is a challenge which the rival must meet with the destruction of one of an equal or greater value.

Even marriage among the Kwakiutl is phrased as a conflict for prestige.[22] When a chief desires to take a wife he calls his numaym together "to make war against all the daughters of the chiefs," to "make war against the tribes." Marriage is the most important means of obtaining honorific crests and dance privileges. It was pointed out previously that certain numaym names and crests descend through the son-in-law to the grandchild. The son-in-law may not display or make use of the prerogatives except at the time when he first received them but holds them in trust for his son when the latter comes of age. Thus, it is not the bride that a man pays for at marriage but the prerogatives that go with her. In this respect a marriage is conducted along precisely the same lines as the sale of a copper. Both for the father-in-law and for the son-in-law marriage represents a climactic point, an occasion for displaying their high rank by indulging in an elaborate potlatch. And like the purchase of a copper the marriage transaction evokes a display of hostility between the parties. The prospective son-in-law and his party of nobles armed with blankets and coppers descend upon the house of the bride's father to overwhelm him with property. Often a sham battle between the retainers of both sides takes place in which people may be killed. Or the father-in-law may make the party of the suitor run a gauntlet of flaming torches, or eat before a blazing and scorching fire. As for a copper, the price of a bride, that is for the prerogatives that go with her, is bid higher and higher as each of the nobles brings forward blankets "to lift the bride from the floor." [23]

The payment of the bride does not at all complete the marriage transaction.[24] When a child is born the father-in-law repays part of the bride price by bestowing some of the names and a quantity of property upon it. By doing this he is "dressing" his daughter and thus elevating her rank. Should he delay this property transaction it would be considered shameful. After two or more children have been born the father-in-law has repaid the entire amount with 300 per cent interest. Now he has returned the potlatch, and the marriage is considered annulled. The father has redeemed his daughter. She may or may not continue to stay with her husband. But rather than have his wife stay with him unpaid for, the husband makes another payment and the cycle of potlatching is resumed. With each payment the bride gains in rank until after four payments have been made, i.e., in four marriages, she attains real greatness. The payments are a symbol of her husband's wealth and of his regard for her. These property exchanges between son-in-law and father-in-law contribute to their prestige so that the relationship between them may be friendly. But it is not always so. In one case a man whose father-in-law was slow in ceding the promised dowry of numaym crests and property had an image made of his wife and in the presence of the assembled tribe fastened a weight around it and threw it into the sea. In this way he shamed his wife, and through her, her father. The marriage was broken off.[25]

Besides marriage the Kwakiutl recognize murder as an equally valid method of adding to one's privilege and rank.[26] A man claims as his own all the names and special privileges of his victim. Some of the most valued of these are the winter ceremonial dances. If a man met the owner of a dance and killed him, he could assume the right to give the dance himself. A commoner would hardly avail himself of this method of rising in status unless he had enough property to validate his assumption of the dance prerogatives. In the past, a number of wars were conducted primarily to increase the number of tribal names, crests, and dances.

Thus, every aspect of Kwakiutl life is oriented to the basic drive for prestige, which is maintained and augmented by the possession of two types of property, the nonmaterial—traditional histories, names, songs, special privileges such as the right to give a particular dance or the right to tie a dancer to a post—and the material—blankets, boxes, canoes, coppers. Neither property has much value without the other. A man might conceivably amass a fortune in blankets and coppers but, unless he had claims to nobility, material wealth would not carry him far. The situation is closely analogous to the one in our own culture, where in "society," wealthy families with "background" try to exclude the newly rich, while on the other hand pauperized families with background are handicapped by their lack of wealth. Among the Kwakiutl the latter condition is relatively rare, for the conditions of potlatching are such that once given a start—as the children of the nobility are—the accumulation of wealth becomes almost inevitable. In one essential respect Kwakiutl potlatching differs from economic exchange in many societies; the stakes are always above and beyond subsistence requirements. As has been mentioned previously food is held collectively by the numaym and the chief is responsible for feeding his people. Even such property as blankets may be used cooperatively in the competition between tribes or numayms. But while collective notions may have entered into the use of material property, the paraphernalia of nobility are strictly individualistic.

Congruent with the strongly individualistic tone of Kwakiutl society is the absence of any strongly centralized political authority or any legal structure.[27] The position of chief is mainly honorific and relatively devoid of political authority. A chief, as coming from a noble family in which the chieftainship is hereditary, is the spearhead of intertribal and inter-numaym rivalry because his are the highest names and the most honored prerogatives. At the head of all the numayms is the great chief of the tribe. His functions, too, are nonpolitical except that he may be instrumental in organizing a competitive potlatch with a rival tribe. In general the authority of a chief in legal matters is nonspecific.

The numaym, on the other hand, has a number of regulatory powers over its own members since it can refuse to support a projected marriage or a potlatch. In addition the members of the numaym can check a chief who becomes overbearing and too autocratic; they can kill him without incurring the vengeance of any united chiefly class. The murder of the chief falls in line with the attitudes of the culture, which though permitting the individual great leeway in expressing his personal glory nevertheless draw the line at overdoing. A chief may become so arrogant and no more.

For disputes within the group, action is taken only by the principles involved. Trespassers on numaym property may be killed by any member of the numaym, the action being individualistic and spontaneous. The Kwakiutl regard murder as an affront to their prestige, as a shameful happening that must be wiped out by the murder of some other individual not necessarily related to the murderer. In contrast to the situation in many other tribes a death puts the individual into a sullen mood, and calls for the death of another individual from another tribe or numaym so that another family may be made to feel the shame or grief. As in a potlatch, all the men of a numaym cooperate to avenge by blood the murder of one of their members, for the honor and prestige of the entire numaym is affected as well as that of the particular family of the victim.

As the secular organization of the Kwakiutl is built around rivalry for prestige and the display of honorific prerogatives, so is the religious. Among the Pueblo Indians of the Southwest religious performances are collectively performed for the collective good. Kwakiutl ceremonialism, on the other hand, though calling for collective participation is directed entirely toward individualistic ends. Ceremonial dances are owned like coppers, and may be given only by the rightful owner to demonstrate his nobility. Moreover, consistent with the emphasis upon rank, each of the dances is ranked in a hierarchical system. It is these dances, which confer the most valued Kwakiutl prerogatives, that are obtained through inheritance from the mother's line or through the murder of the previous owner.

In general, the religious organization of the Kwakiutl parallels the secular. As there are titles of nobility so are there recognized hierarchical distinctions in the use and ownership of religious prerogatives. The year is divided into two halves, the summer, when the secular social organization is in use, and the winter, when the entire social organization is dropped and a new organization based upon membership in religious societies is in force. With the ushering in of the winter ceremonial season new rank alignments are set up according to the greatness of the name a man holds as a member of a religious society. This does not imply, however, that there is any marked change in the status of the individual from the secular to the ceremonial season. Because of the method of inheriting the winter ceremonial religious prerogatives, these tend to become concentrated in the noble families. Religious prerogatives are but another aspect of the nobility and power of an individual of rank.

As over against the thoroughly collective and truly cooperative ceremonial organization of the Zuñi, Kwakiutl ceremonialism is fundamentally individualistic and almost always competitive. In a sense the members of a society cooperate to exercise their fellow initiate, but the motives are individualistic, for the concern of each member is to display his own special prerogatives whether it be that of carrying the corpse for the initiate or bringing in shredded cedar bark for him to wipe his face on.

As the relations between man and man among the Kwakiutl are marked by aggressiveness, so are the relations between men and the supernaturals. The Kwakiutl do not make themselves humble before their gods. In mythology, the hero boldly seeks out the god and demands his supernatural powers, or he kills the supernatural to gain his power, and when the gods inflict misfortune, the Kwakiutl insult and shame them, calling them slaves, the highest affront the Kwakiutl can pay.[28]

Public behavior on the Northwest Coast is dominated by the need of the individual to demonstrate his greatness over against his rivals. A man seeks great wealth not as an end in itself but as a weapon to crush a rival. By the humbling of his rival the individual builds up his own prestige. In that respect, Kwakiutl society is warlike, and the greatest rewards of society in terms of individual glorification go to the man who has conquered with property and by a display of privileges his most powerful rivals.

A man not only must establish his own individual prestige, but must extend his greatness to his children and grandchildren. To accomplish this a man assists his son in potlatching, he is careful to arrange an advantageous marriage for his children, he is punctual in making return payments after the birth of his daughter's first child so that she may not be shamed.

Consistent with the cultural demands placed upon it, the personality of the individual reacts in a manner that we would classify clinically as paranoid. The grandiloquent speeches made by the retainers of the chief at a potlatch may be characterized in our own cultural terms as megalomania. But for the Kwakiutl this unabashed boasting is culturally accepted and formalized. It is necessary to stress very strongly the fact that the Kwakiutl are not paranoid in terms of abnormal psychology. In reacting to their own environment they do not lack the sense of orientation that is so strikingly absent in the individual classified as abnormal. Kwakiutl society in contrast to many other cultures permits great latitude to the individual both in his attempts to secure individual aggrandizement and in his expression of self-importance—but always with the provision that he must not overdo it.

Public behavior in Kwakiutl society is integrated around a basic pattern of individualistic rivalry. Food for the most part is individually obtained and used, although the giving of presents of food to a chief for his acceptance of the responsibility of feeding the group in time of need is clearly a cooperative feature of food getting. The numaym functions cooperatively in the financing of a great potlatch. But the numaym as a unit functions over against outsiders as an individualistic and rivalrous group. The emphasis upon rank and prestige rivalry is consistently reflected in social relations, in marriage, in religion, and in law.

C. THE ZUÑI INDIANS: A HIGHLY COOPERATIVE SOCIETY [29]*

By the time the Spanish conquerors had come into the Southwest, the peak of pueblo civilization had already passed. At present the culture, in spite of "white" influences, is essentially the same as it was a number of centuries ago at the time of Coronado. The largest of the pueblos is that of the Zuñi. A population of 1,900 live in compactly clustered and terraced adobe houses, forming the familiar pueblo unit. Many of the Zuñi do not live in the main pueblo but live throughout the year scattered in a number of farming villages to return to Zuñi for the ceremonial dances and ritual observances that are held calendrically.

Government in Zuñi is centralized in a priestly hierarchy, which is concerned entirely with matters of religion. Civil law is given over to a secular body that, appointed by the priests, lacks all prestige. The mechanism of social control is not in the hands of a centralized authority but is vested in the sanctions of public censure. In practically all his activities, the individual must conform to the patterns established by a number of social groupings: the matriarchal household, which in the sharing of food is communally organized, the matrilineal clan, and religious societies and esoteric cults.

The Zuñi are primarily agriculturalists and have been so since early prehistoric times. Originally they planted their maize, beans, and squash by a system of hand irrigation from the springs. At present, with the development of a system of water control in connection with a government dam, the number and extent of their crops have increased. Famine, once prevalent, is practically eliminated. In fact, in material wealth Zuñi is rich. There are fruit orchards, corn and wheat fields, melon patches, peach orchards, and the greatly valued sheep herds introduced by

* By permission from *Cooperation and Competition among Primitive Peoples,* by Margaret Mead (ed.). Copyright, 1937, McGraw-Hill Book Company, Inc.

the Spaniards, so that for the most part food is fairly abundant. Still, differences in wealth do exist, but every principle of Zuñi social organization is opposed to an excessive concentration of a surplus in the hands of any one individual. Wealth is valued only for the immediate material comfort it can bring, and is highly fluid. Competition for the supply of goods is given no formal expression, and though individuals may quarrel over the ownership of sheep or peach orchards, such individuals are not the most respected in the community. It is rather the cooperative person ready to share his food with his relatives and needy friends, ready to assist his neighbor or religious or clan colleague in agricultural labor, who is most respected in the community. Ideally, wealth that has been accumulated is redistributed among the members of the village either during the winter-solstice ceremonies or in spontaneous gifts. In the economic as well as the ceremonial field the aggressive, competitive, noncooperative individual is regarded as the aberrant type.

Such culturally fostered noncompetitive and cooperative attitudes are all the more striking in view of the actual limitation of irrigable land suitable for cultivation.

In Zuñi, curiously, land shortage is not even recognized. "There is no feeling of land hunger." [30] What is felt most sharply is the lack of labor.

The Zuñi are not polygamists, but they have met the problem of land labor by organizing cooperative group labor wherever the physical conditions of the work allow it.

Fields used for cultivation belong either to an individual male or to a matriarchal household, but in either case they are worked by all the men in the household, who may be assisted by friends or relatives. All produce of the fields is pooled in one common storeroom to become the common property of all the women of the household. At hoeing and at harvesting time, when the amount of work to be done in the fields is considerable, a member of a religious fraternity asks the director for assistance and the latter then delegates a number of men to assist. The female head of the house or her daughter will also go to the men of the clan and ask them for help. The group thus assembled is of a miscellaneous composition, the men cooperating in the work for reasons of kinship, religious association, and friendship.

A wealthy family that has undertaken to entertain the masked god impersonators at the winter-solstice ceremonies works very busily for a year building up vast stores of food supplies. For the entire year members of the same ceremonial group as the man preparing for the feast are obligated to work with him in the fields and in the construction of the new house where the dancers will be entertained. All other people in the village make it a point to help at one time or another during that period in order to benefit by the supernatural blessings that go with such work, or, more practically, to get the material rewards of presents and food which are sent to all those who have helped. [31] Women, especially poor women, go about to these houses that are preparing for the festival in order to grind corn meal. They take back bowls of stew as gifts.

Always workers who have come to help must be rewarded with gifts or with food. Thus it is only the well-to-do who can call on their neighbors and clan kinsmen to help them in the fields. The poor families, those on the subsistence level, depend almost entirely upon the cooperative group effort of the men in the household.

Besides the fields of corn, wheat, and alfalfa that are scattered over the reservation, and the melon patches and peach orchards, the Zuñi cultivate small vegetable gardens just at the edge of the village by the river. These gardens, held in the matrilineal line, are worked exclusively by the women of the household. The crops of beans, onions, chilis, melons are stored in the household common storeroom as common property.

After the harvest, the wheat is threshed by horses. A common corral is constructed and the households in turn bring their wheat to be threshed.

Once food has been brought into the house it becomes the property of the women, to be used by them collectively as they see fit. The preparation of food, the grinding of the corn into flour, is women's work. Working in groups of three, the women crush, parch, and powder the corn grains on stone grinders.

The major source of wealth and in that sense the most valued property is the sheep herds. Sheep herding is a foreign complex introduced at an early time by the Spanish, and the attitudes surrounding sheep economy are at present alien to basic Zuñi economic concepts. Herded and, with some exceptions, owned by men, sheep represent a surplus and an important medium of exchange. They are the means with which foreign luxuries, furniture, kitchen utensils, guns, and automobiles can be bought. Sheep have been, in part at least, largely responsible for the rising standard of living of the Pueblo Indians. It is significant that the "mores of western civilization, precise ideas of property, individual ownership, acquisitiveness, prestige attached to material possessions all became focussed on this one form of property." [32] Yet prior to the establishment of trade on a firm basis, when flocks were still small and meant less in terms of Western luxuries, sheep herding was organized along lines similar to that of agriculture.

In distinction to land property, all sheep were owned by individual males, but kinsmen pooled their flocks and herded them on a cooperative basis. Though the capital was individually owned, the profits, the wool, and the newborn lambs were shared by all the group. The owner of the most sheep was the leader, and at shearing time, when the wool was gathered, he would settle all the debts of the group. What wool was left over was divided equally. Similarly with the lambs: partners took turns claiming the lambs born in successive years. All sheep were earmarked with the brand of the owner, but so long as he kept his sheep in the group his individual ownership was but a formal phrasing.

With the increasing size of the herds and the greater purchasing value of wool, skins, and mutton, the progressive tendency is toward greater individualism in respect both to the ownership of and to the use of the profits from the sheep. As far as the actual mechanics of herding are concerned, cooperation still holds. Herds are pooled together and herded cooperatively by groups of male kindred, each member taking turns in rotation at herding. At lambing time, however, each sheep owner is present to earmark each of his lambs as soon as it is born. If he is absent at this time, he will lose many lambs which will be earmarked with some other brand. Nor will he have just cause for complaint, since he should have been present to help. Lambing time begins about the end of April and lasts about three weeks, during which time the men and their wives live out on the ranch near the sheep. On the first day the men construct corrals for segregating the sheep; the women are busy grinding and preparing provisions. In the evening, after all have eaten, there is singing and dancing. "Everyone has a good time at lambing because they are living together in one big bunch." [38]

House building is likewise a collective undertaking, and, since a new house is almost always built upon the occasion of the winter-solstice ceremonies, all the men of the same ceremonial group work together in cutting and hauling the lumber that will form the heavy beamed roof and in laying the adobe walls. The women, especially the old women, are the plasterers. The dedication of the house by the priestly body will bring blessings to the entire village. Each individual worker will not only gain good luck for himself and his family, but will benefit materially. Thus the labor of house building is truly cooperative, the house builder providing meals and gifts for the workers and standing the entire expense of the construction, the other men working to fulfill the necessary ceremonial requirements of the winter-solstice. The end result will be gain for all. If the house building is not at the instance of the Shalako masked dance ceremony, it is constructed by the men of the household. In either event it becomes the property of the women. Though the men will have done all the heavy work of construction, once they leave the house they have no further share in it. Nor do men seem to feel that they have wasted their labor when they leave a house which they have helped to construct.

In no economic activity is competition formally sanctioned. In agricultural land there is an actual shortage of irrigable fields, as witnessed by the fact that practically no families produce enough wheat to last them to the next harvest, yet, as already mentioned, such shortage is not even phrased as a land problem; it is felt rather as a problem of labor. Of all activities, sheep herding would be expected to result in competitive relations, and to the extent that a good deal of litigation centers around the ownership of sheep this is true. Nevertheless, such litigations are more in the nature of family squabbles than the well-developed family rivalry that is found in Ifugao. In general the culture has removed all sting from a competition that might develop, by giving little weight to the possession of material goods per se. The Zuñi have no interest in accumulating more property than they can use, and when an individual does become wealthy he redistributes his wealth in the great winter festival of the Shalako. The major interest of the Zuñi is religious—the orderly ritual observance of the calendric ceremonies. It is in this sphere rather than in the economic that the individual gains full social recognition.

The individual in Zuñi is fitted into an intricate and closely knit social organization. A man is born with fixed kinship and clan affiliations. As a member of the matrilineal line of his mother, in his mother's clan he assumes a number of ceremonial obligations; as a child of his father's clan he assumes still other obligations. At marriage a man leaves the household of his mother to join the communal economic unit of his mother-in-law's household without in any way relinquishing his ceremonial obligations to his mother's house. At approximately puberty, the boy is initiated into one of the six dance groups comprising the male tribal society. At any time after this, or even before, he assumes membership in one or more of a great number of esoteric societies. Thus, at all times, a man is bound to a number of groups, and the greater part of his activity is in association with a number of these, especially the ceremonial groups. In practice, the situation of group alliance is less complicated for the woman. Primarily she is a member of a matriarchal household. Her duties are mainly economic, though, theoretically no woman is barred from full participation in ceremonial life. For one thing, it is not customary, and secondary, few women care to assume the heavy responsibilities that go with belonging to a religious group. Whether she belongs to a ceremonial society or not, the woman is still an active member of a collective household unit. In Zuñi one acts as an individual only in the sphere of sex, and "no action that is entirely personal and individual receives more than passing interest. Births, deaths, and initiations figure largely in local gossip, marriages do not." [34]

The household is the economic unit, and is, in all economic activities, cooperatively organized. It is a group of variable composition; a mother, her husband, her daughters with their husbands and children, to which may be added a fluctuating group of males, divorced, widowed, temporarily estranged, or unmarried sons. All occupy a single house with from two to six rooms, including a large general living room in which the entire household works, eats, and sleeps, and where guests are entertained. A number of rooms serve to store food and the sacred paraphernalia. In this crowded atmosphere, children playing underfoot, women working, people chatting, the individual lacks the privacy which we seek in our own civilization.

Within the household, relations are for the most part informal. Individual authority and responsibility are almost entirely lacking. "Ordinarily the female contingent of blood relatives presents a united front. A man finding himself out of harmony with the group will withdraw quietly whenever he chooses and ally himself with another group. With his departure obligations cease, and his successor fathers his children." [35]

In the things that count most in Zuñi life, in matters of ritual, the man is an outsider in the house of his wife. His most permanent ties are with the house of his sister, with whom he is united in the care of the sacred fetishes. On every occasion of moment he returns to her house. If she is in need or if her children are in need he will bring them food and gifts. If male labor is needed in the fields, a brother can be called on to assist. Similarly a woman is obligated to help her brother and her brother's children in a ceremonial and economic way. The woman, of course, as an owner of the house, is united with her own blood kin in the care of the sacred fetishes that are kept within it.

When a man marries, the ties of the blood group cut directly across the new set of obligations that are imposed on the man by marriage. He leaves his mother's house to live with his wife and mother-in-law. Here he cooperates in the economic labor of tilling fields that belong for the most part to his wife's household, with a group of males, his wife's sisters' husbands, who are more or less strangers to him. He lives with a group that cannot accept him completely, in which he is regarded as an outsider. Furthermore, the very stability of his marriage depends largely upon the whims of his wife, who may with little or no ado place his small bundle of belongings on the threshold of the home as a sign that he is no longer desired. It is not until a good many years have passed that he begins to achieve some sort of status in his wife's household, but for the most part he is regarded with suspicion as one who may, upon the dissolution of the marriage, spread slanderous bits of gossip about the household.

With regard to food, however, all in the house share equally or, rather, according to need. Yet here again it is the woman who controls the larder, who may if she sees fit trade foodstuff for some other necessities, even personal items. A man may not even enter the storeroom.

In view of the firmness of the blood tie crosscutting the economic obligations of the affinial group it is surprising that marriages show the degree of permanence which they do. Divorce, it is true, is common and simple, because the Zuñi do not like bickering and quarreling, and when a situation becomes too charged it is easily remedied by the man's moving out. Still, "a very large proportion of Zuñi marriages endure through the greater part of a life-time." [36] It is precisely because the Zuñi dislike quarreling that most marriages tend to remain peaceful.

Marriages are very simply arranged and attract little attention. In Hopi, where marriage involves a considerable gift exchange, it is the most frequent topic of conversation. In Zuñi, marriages are based largely upon sentiment and involve no property transactions beyond a formal ceremonial exchange. A young man announces his intentions to a young girl after a very brief courtship. If she is willing and her parents offer no objection, the marriage proceeds. On the fourth day the young man brings the girl a dress as a mark that he really intends to marry. The dress he gets from his mother or sister, and it is thought of as a gift from the mother-in-law. After this the girl takes corn from the boy's house to grind, in order to demonstrate her fitness as a housewife. In return for this corn she is given bowls of food. Then the girl grinds her own corn "to pay for the dress" and receives an equal amount of wheat in return so that her payment for the dress is but a formal phrasing. In fact, as a result of its scarcity, wheat is far more valuable than corn. The marriage is now completed. Beyond the formal ritual exchanges no property has been involved. Of course if a man has acquired, either by inheritance or through his own effort, a corn or wheat field he cultivates it for the benefit of his wife's household. Similarly, if he owns sheep he is in a position to contribute materially to the welfare of his family. And, as in our culture, many women prefer to marry wealthy men because of the greater luxuries the latter can give them. But this is a personal problem in Zuñi. The cultural emphasis is certainly not upon wealth as a necessary condition for marriage. Moreover, if a household owns its own fields, the man is primarily valuable as an economic asset because of the labor he can contribute.

Competition for a mate is given no formal expression. There are more men than women in Zuñi, and the woman is not dependent upon a husband for economic security. Girls might very well exercise personal choice in marriage. But girls who appear to be very particular and "choosy" about their marrying are admonished. And Zuñi mythology is full of stories about the girl who is punished by the supernatural because she shows no inclination to take the first man who offers her marriage.

We have seen that social relations in Zuñi are in great part structurally dictated. Men cooperate in agricultural work because they are members of the same household or clan group; they cooperate in sheep herding because they are united by kinship ties through the male line. In ceremonial activities the group that works together is also, though to a lesser extent, welded by clan affiliation.

In addition to obligations between kinsmen that are established at birth, the Zuñi have institutionalized a ceremonial friendship built around economic cooperation.[37] Such friends are under obligation to lend one another assistance in all large undertakings. But the fullest development of the relationship is in the giving of presents. One never trades with a ceremonial friend, as that would be even more undignified than trading with one's own blood kinsman, and indeed one's *kihe*—as such a ceremonial friend is called—is considered a member of the family.

The reasons for forming this relationship, which is formalized by the ritual washing of the hair to signify adoption into the family, are various. It may be desirable to enter into such a relationship with a man because he is rich or skillful at a particularly valued craft so that one may get fine gifts from him. Thus a number of men and women have kihe who are Navaho and Hopi because "they are such good weavers." Such material motives, however, are not the only ones involved in the formation of the friendship. The case is narrated of a man who ceremonially adopted a poor woman as his kihe because she was lonely and no one ever gave her anything. He felt sorry for her, and so at a religious dance he called her out and gave her a fine black dress.[38] Or again, children having become attached to one another have themselves adopted into each other's family. The relationship once entered upon is lifelong and may even be continued by the families after the death of one member. So close are the ties of the kihe to one another that a man not infrequently will give away part of his land to his ceremonial brother to the exclusion of the rightful heirs, and the gift will be socially sanctioned.

Strikingly characteristic of all social relations in Zuñi is the relative lack of emphasis upon wealth. Property does not figure in marriage. Individuals do not compete for a fixed supply, and in terms of the prestige an individual may achieve, property itself is not the determining factor. This does not at all imply that the Zuñi are unmindful of the blessings of material comfort or that they are completely disinterested in the accumulation of wealth. But they do frown upon any undue interest in material possession, upon acquisitiveness, covetousness, stinginess, or sharp practice in economic transactions. If a material object has value, it has that only as a means toward a specific utilitarian need. But hoarding—the piling up of goods far beyond that which is necessary for a comfortable existence—is practically unknown. Wealth circulates freely, and property rights are neither clearly defined nor strictly enforced. For one thing, material effects are never valued as a means to power and are only indirectly a source of prestige. The property that is really valued, as would be expected from the great emphasis upon ceremonial matters, is the non-material property such as songs, prayers, rituals. These are the principal prestige counters; their possession gives one authority, their abuse, power.

The principles of land tenure reveal further the basic non-competitive and non-individualistic property patterns in Zuñi. Most of the reservation consists of land unsuitable, at present, for cultivation. These uncultivated areas belong communally to the tribe and any man may stake out new fields wherever he wishes. Such fields, in contrast to those held by the female line of a household, belong to him individually and may be disposed of by him at his pleasure. But so long as he remains associated with a household either by blood or by marriage he cultivates the field for a communal end, the products that he raises becoming the collective property of the women of the household. It is even possible to appropriate land, the title of which is held by another family providing that it is not in use. For although distinctions are made between ownership and use of a field, these are by no means clear, and it is difficult to dispossess a family that has taken possession.

It is significant, too, that litigations over the ownership of land are rare and in most cases quickly settled. One might expect that disputes would arise frequently among a people whose concepts of ownership are so vaguely defined that boundaries between fields are marked only in one dimension, in width facing the road and not in depth.

Food is shared by all in the household and is based entirely on need, with no account taken of the field it has been grown in or of who has been responsible for producing it. If, for example, *A* should bring in some especially choice melon from his field, his wife does not feel that she has any more claim to it than her sister. A man may, however, take food from his own field to his female relatives, his mother, his sister, or a niece, providing he has not yet brought the food into the house. For then it falls entirely under the jurisdiction of the women in the house.

Personal property is by no means negligible in Zuñi. A good string of turquoise may be worth about $700, a woman's silver necklace from $50 to $75. A woman's ordinary dress is worth $35, and a pair of women's moccasins is valued at close to $100. Although these articles are freely loaned there is a strong sense of ownership attached to them. Each individual has absolute control over his personal property, and even the rights of a small child are recognized. A mother will not sell a doll or a string of beads belonging to a child without its consent, and she would insist on the money's being given to the child. Spouses have no control over one another's possessions.

Over against the individualistically phrased ownership of personal property is the important role played by gift giving in Zuñi economy. We have emphasized before that wealth in Zuñi is highly fluid, and there are any number of circumstances that make for this fluidity. Most important of these are the ceremonial exchanges that take place at marriage, at initiations, and at the great winter-solstice ceremonies. In none of these exchanges is any attempt made to secure an equivalent return. The emphasis is rather upon a one-way giving relationship.

Between members of the same family and in the ceremonial friendship, spontaneous giving of presents is of frequent occurrence. Here especially no attempt is made to maintain any kind of reciprocity. Between husband and wife it is almost always the husband who gives gifts, in addition to the necessary clothing for the household which he is required to buy. Parents are always giving presents to their children, and a man will rarely return from a trading expedition without bringing home something for his children,[39] his wife, or even a friend. If reciprocity does occur, it is quite informal and dependent entirely upon the inclination of the recipient of the first gift.

The cult which is the basis for all Zuñi ceremonialism is that of the *alacinawe,* the ancestors. They guide and protect and nourish human life and are beneficent beings in whose worship all participate regardless of age, sex, or affiliation with special cults. At all meals it is customary to offer some food to the ancestors, and at the special ceremony held in their honor great quantities of food are sacrificed in fire and in the river. They are asked to bestow rain, seeds, life, old age, wealth, power, fecundity, health, and general happiness. In a sense the ancestors are feared because they have too great a love for their dear ones on this earth and may wish to call them to the ancestor world. Therefore it becomes necessary to cut off by ritual the recent dead from the living.

Besides this basic ancestor cult there are six major cults in Zuñi.

Strikingly, too, all ceremonials are collective. On the western plains the Indians sought individual vision experiences; each young man attempted to obtain an individual relationship with a guardian spirit. But among the Zuñi only group ritual is effective. The masked katcina dances are group dances, and it is the collective rhythmic movement of a mass of men that will bring the rain. When the priests go into retreat into the ceremonial houses, the kivas, they go in groups. Even the planting of the prayer stick fetishes to the gods, the most individual of religious acts, must be done at a fixed time. A man who plants his prayer sticks without an official announcement would be suspected of witchcraft. In addition to the collective performance, all the blessings asked for are collective, it is rain for the group, fecundity for the group, long life for the group.

Out of the entire range of human behavior the Zuñi have selected the non-aggressive, sober, cooperative aspects to stress. It is to this norm that the child, if he is to fit into the cultural framework set for him by his parents, must conform. He is not broken or forcibly coerced into this pattern but is gradually fitted into it under the most subtle stress of social sanction.

But in Zuñi, as is common among the North American Indians, adult behavior is the norm that is held up to all children and to which they must grow up as quickly as possible. The little boy in Zuñi who can deliver the appropriate formal speech upon making a visit is held up to praise. "Just like a man," they say of him. Should he be sulky, uncooperative, greedy, impolite in talking out of his turn, or lazy, then he is reproved as being childish. This term of opprobrium, "childish," is even applied to old men who do not conform.

The age at which one is to graduate into adulthood is not fixed, but it is early. There is, however, an early period in the life of the child, especially of the small boy, that is marked by great freedom.

As we have seen, the great emphasis in Zuñi culture is upon the orderly, the sober processes of ritual life. In comparison with the amount of time the adult male gives to ceremonial participation and the great interest that religion has for him, economics plays a definitely minor role. The ideal man is not necessarily the wealthy man, but rather the ceremonially minded individual, the man willing to devote himself to the ritual routine of bringing supernatural blessing upon the group. In this, though his position in a priestly office necessarily sets him apart from the rest, he must avoid carrying his individuality too far; he must not be too officious. Zuñi stresses constantly the submergence of the individual in the group, and would frown upon the man who took advantage of his religious position to secure any undue prominence for himself. In his relations to his fellow men he must always cooperate in the work in the fields with the men of his household and with the men of his kiva in the religious performances. Toward all others within the community he may not display any competitiveness. The ideal man in Zuñi is a "person of dignity and affability who has never tried to lead and who has never called forth comment from his neighbors. Any conflict, even though all right is on his side, is held against him." [40] He must cooperate readily in both the economic and the ritual field.

D. THE PROCESSES OF ASSIMILATION AND ACCOMMODATION AMONG CHINESE IMMIGRANTS IN HAWAII [41]

Assimilation consists in the changes whereby persons who are "outsiders" come to share loyalties and interests with members of a given group. These outsiders may be the children born into the group, who although from the first physically a part of the group's population, must be socially incorporated into it. In the case of immigrants, however, the outsiders are commonly persons who are already integrated in a very different culture. For the latter, assimilation involves more than the rather unreflective adoption of the social definitions of the group such as is the case among children; it necessitates giving up old, customary ways of feeling, thinking, and acting, and embracing new cultural patterns—loyalties, sentiments, beliefs, and habits which may be those of the group with which the outsiders have come into contact, or which may represent new combinations growing out of the interaction between the group and the newcomers.

One approach, then, to the study of assimilation where immigrants are involved would be a consideration of the shifts in the group loyalties and group identifications which these persons gradually make. A good reason for focusing attention upon loyalties and identifications, of course, is that they tend to reflect the person's sharing of the group's purposes and objectives (consensus) and his willingness to participate collectively in the attainment of those ends. An index of the shifts in loyalties among immigrants is to be found in the different types of institutions of political and social control which they form or participate in at different periods of their immigrant experience. This is exemplified in a study of the trend toward assimilation among the first-generation Chinese in the Hawaiian Islands.

The existence of a Chinese group in Hawaii is accounted for primarily by the establishment of a plantation economy in Hawaii and the subsequent importation of laborers. On the sugar-cane plantations the Chinese, as has usually been true of plantation workers, constituted an isolated, dependent class.[42] If working as indentured labor, they were temporarily in a condition of servitude; in any case they were rather rigidly under the control of the politically dominant planters and their overseers. They had little opportunity to establish contacts with fellow-countrymen elsewhere in the Islands, or to develop institutions among themselves on the plantation. Only a small proportion of the Chinese, however, remained on the plantations more than a few years. Many returned to China; many drifted into other occupations in the rural and village sections of the Islands; others moved to the larger towns.[43]

Once off the plantations, the Chinese immigrants were freer to create a cultural life more in accordance with their own inclinations and needs. Among other things they established a great many institutions. Here we are concerned with only those institutions which reflect the shifts in the group loyalties and group identifications of the first-generation Chinese.

Students of immigration have often called attention to the fact that the immigrant usually comes from a local, narrow, immobile, peasant world, where kinship ties hold pre-eminence. It is difficult to overemphasize this fact in the case of the Chinese. The deepest sentiment which the Chinese immigrant brought with him was his loyalty to his clan or kinship group. This familial bond in the rural district of Kwangtung, from which most of the Chinese in Hawaii came, tended to be limited, moreover, either to the clansmen in his own native village or usually at most to the clansmen located in the same local district. It provided the basis for an immense amount of informal mutual assistance and cooperative activity at one time in the new habitat. But when formally organized, chartered family *tongs,* or societies, were formed in Hawaii to include all Chinese of the same surname, regardless of the locality in China from which they came or the dialect which they spoke, this represented an expansion of the familial identification and association much beyond that which existed in practice for the clansmen in his home village. Among the few family societies organized in Hawaii those for Chinese with surnames of Wong and Lum are notable.

Two other types of societies drew upon the local outlook and identifications of the foreign-born Chinese. One was the formally organized *tung heong hui,* or villagers' club; the other was the district *hui kuan,* or association. The villagers' club sought to bring together all the Chinese immigrants in Hawaii who had lived together in the same native village in China. The club, therefore, usually represented two or more clan groups, which in the Old World may have been bitter rivals or even feud enemies. It generally served to encourage intimate and personal relations among old-country neighbors; commonly it functioned to organize them in the interest of promoting developments in the home village, such as the reconstruction and enlarging of the village temples, the organization of methods of protection against bandits, the building and support of modern schools, the paving of streets within the village, or the construction of highways from the village to a near-by town or city. The district association represents the widest expansion of the local identifications upon the basis of which the Chinese immigrants in Hawaii formed societies.[44] These district associations correspond to the "company" of the so-called "Six Companies" which gained so much notoriety in California during the last half of the last century. Thirteen of these district associations were established in Hawaii. Their functions will be touched upon below.

It is significant that in each of these types of societies which drew upon the local identifications of the immigrant—the family society, the villagers' club, and the district association—the form of the immigrant institution called for an extension of local ties beyond that which the Chinese recognized in his native village before emigration. In co-operating with these societies he identified himself with institutions which had no exact counterpart in his homeland experiences.

The spread of nationalistic societies among the first-generation Chinese in Hawaii represents another significant expansion in their allegiances. In common with many other immigrant groups, the Chinese peasant immigrant possessed little or no national consciousness at the time he left his native village. In Hawaii the development of this national consciousness led to the formation of a number of nationalistic organizations and much active concern and participation in the reorganization of the government of China. In fact, some Chinese claim that Hawaii is the birthplace of the nationalistic movement which brought into being the republic of China.

The Chinese nationalistic societies established in Hawaii have been of three general forms. The first, and earliest in point of time, represents the transplanting of an old secret political and religious society from China. This organization has existed under a variety of names, but it is now generally called the Chee Kung Tong. While the accounts vary, the parent-organization seems to have been formed about two hundred and fifty years ago for the avowed purpose of overthrowing the Ching dynasty which had been set up in 1644 and of re-establishing the Ming dynasty. There were many branches of this society in China, outlawed by the Manchu rulers, of course, and with the migration of Chinese overseas branches were organized in nearly every area where there were large concentrations of Chinese immigrants. At least twenty-three branches, enrolling several thousand members, were established in the Hawaiian Islands in the towns and rural sections of each island where considerable numbers of Chinese congregated after leaving the plantations. These branches had local functions—benevolent, social, ritualistic, and otherwise—which ordinarily overshadowed the revolutionary purposes, but they co-operated with Dr. Sun and his revolutionary societies in finally overthrowing the Ching dynasty in 1911. Since the setting-up of the republic, however, the members of the Chee Kung Tong have been relatively indifferent, if not hostile, to the political parties in power in China.

The second form of nationalistic society which secured widespread allegiance among the first-generation Chinese in Hawaii during the first decade of this century proposed to replace the toppling absolute monarchy with a strong constitutional monarchy, retaining the Manchus, however, as the nominal rulers. The adherents of this society opposed Dr. Sun, and although greatly reduced in numbers, they still oppose the Kuomint'ang party and the nationalist government.

The third form of nationalistic society centered about Dr. Sun Yat-Sen, the first president of the provisional republic of China. Dr. Sun was himself a native of the small district from which the majority of the Chinese in Hawaii migrated. He received his early education in Hawaii and in later years visited the Islands several times in the interests of the revolution. Like the first nationalistic group, the societies which he and his associates instigated sought to overthrow the Ching dynasty, but differed from it in that their ultimate purpose was to set up a republic. Hundreds of first-generation Chinese in Hawaii joined these societies and contributed liberally toward the nationalist cause. Some of them returned to China to participate in the revolution, and, after the beginning of the republic, to hold offices in the nationalist government. The political events in China continue to be matters of concern among a considerable portion of the first-generation Chinese. The Kuomint'ang (National Peoples' party) has been active in Hawaii since its organization in 1912. Its territorial headquarters are in Honolulu, and three of the islands have sub-branches. A split in the party, reflecting similar divergent views held in China, has created what might be called a "left" and a "right" wing of the Kuomint'ang in Hawaii, and each has its own news-organ, which carries on editorial warfare with its opponents concerning political policies in China.

Still another phase of the shift in the group identifications of the first-generation Chinese appears in the willingness with which they organized and participated in societies designed to deal with problems confronting the Chinese community in Hawaii as a whole, located as they were under political authorities who had little or no sympathetic understanding of their cultural heritages. In such situations some peoples have demanded treaties and established what are now called extra-territorial rights; the Chinese set up institutions of political and social control which rather informally and non-publicly carried out a measure of the functions of extra-territoriality. The chief of these institutions, organized in Honolulu during the early eighties, was known in the English-speaking community as the United Chinese Society. While its functions were many, only a few of them will be considered here. From its beginning this organization assisted in the maintenance of order within the Chinese community through a system of arbitration. Civil and personal disputes which arose between Chinese could voluntarily be brought before the society for settlement, instead of taking them to the Hawaiian courts to be tried before white or Hawaiian judges. The district associations mentioned above also performed this function of arbitration for Chinese who had come from the same district, but in cases where the Chinese in dispute did not belong to the same societies organized on the basis of local, Old World loyalties, the United Chinese Society was usually resorted to. The society was also designed to facilitate concerted action by the Chinese community as a whole when the occasion demanded it. Thus, when a large part of the Honolulu Chinatown was twice destroyed by fire, and when a plague was spreading through the community, the society took the lead in dealing with these crises. Another important phase of this society's activities was concerned with acting as the chief medium between the Chinese community and the other racial communities in the Islands, or between the Chinese community and the Hawaiian government. This was especially the case during the eighties and nineties when anti-Chinese agitation was at its height.

The United Chinese Society was only one of many "accommodation groups," and one of the earliest at that, which were set up by the Chinese immigrants to deal with their common problems in the Hawaiian environment. Even in the character of these accommodation groups, formed from time to time, a gradual movement in the direction of assimilation can be discerned. Only a few examples can be suggested. The position of the United Chinese Society as the leading organization in the Chinese community has now been largely replaced by the

Honolulu Chinese Chamber of Commerce, which cooperates on many projects with the Honolulu Chamber of Commerce and other organizations of the interracial community. The arbitration functions of the Chinese immigrant societies have greatly declined as the Chinese have turned more and more to the Hawaiian courts. The maintenance of benevolent institutions among themselves is being replaced by participation of the Chinese community, solicited by Chinese teams, in the United Welfare campaigns and Red Cross drives. Another change, much more subtle but nonetheless real, has been the operation of social controls with the Chinese community, not merely for the sake of maintaining order within the community itself, but also in order to keep the behavior of some Chinese from reacting unfavorably upon the general status of the Chinese group in the larger, interracial community. This concern over status in the interracial community would seem to represent a still further expansion of the group identification of the Chinese immigrant.

Several of the first-generation Chinese extended their activities to the point of taking an actual part in the Hawaiian government. Some, of course, participated in the role of special functionaries by virtue of their knowledge of the Chinese language and culture, in such positions as those of Chinese agents for the Hawaiian Board of Immigration; interpreters for the courts, the immigration, inspection, customs, and other officials; detectives and policemen. Of more particular interest here, however, are those Chinese who became citizens of Hawaii. Under the Hawaiian government the naturalization laws did not follow the American pattern of declaring the Chinese alien ineligible to citizenship. Before the Hawaiian Islands were annexed to the United States in 1898, about seven hundred Chinese immigrants had become Hawaiian citizens; those still living in 1898 automatically became American citizens. Some of them exercised their voting privileges, although to the writer's knowledge none held an elective office. Citizenship represented, formally at least, a further degree of identification with the evolving Hawaiian society.

Intimate association with the first generation at different stages in their transition from familial attitudes to Chinese national consciousness and to any increasing willingness to participate in the interracial Hawaiian community has left unmistakable effects upon the Hawaiian-born Chinese. In fact, the whole assimilative process as it concerns the second generation needs to be analyzed in relation to this changing, shifting configuration of attitudes and interests of the immigrants. It is a process which has for its starting-point in any particular member of the second generation some none too simply defined position along the line of processual changes taking place among the first-generation immigrants themselves. A fuller consideration of this is beyond the scope of the present paper. If we focus our attention only upon the group identifications and political interests and activities of the Hawaiian-born Chinese, a few contrasting outcomes can be taken for illustration out of a continuum containing innumerable varieties of slightly differing configurations of attitudes and interests.

In the first place, a portion of the Hawaiian-born have exhibited interests, group identifications, and life-organizations little different from those of the first generation. Some of these were sent back to China in early childhood to be reared in the father's native village. Others who were born in Hawaii fifty or more years ago, especially those in the Chinese colonies in rural Hawaii, were reared in a cultural milieu which was preponderantly of the Old World pattern—a milieu in which the transitions mentioned in this paper were just beginning to be made among the first generation. A few of this group have settled permanently in their ancestral district in China. Some assisted in the Chinese revolutionary and nationalistic movements; some secured official positions or entered other occupations in various parts of China. Among those who remained in Hawaii, a number have taken an active part in the immigrant institutions and in bringing about the changes in them.

In the second place, there are those who waver back and forth between "things Chinese" and "things American." On the level of institutions of political and social control, they fluctuate between the Chinese immigrant societies and the American political institutions in the Islands, or try to participate simultaneously and whole heartedly in both. They are men of divided loyalties.

In the third place, by far the largest number of Hawaiian-born Chinese, especially those who have only recently reached adulthood and who are for the most part products of the towns and modern American educational institutions, have identified themselves completely with America, and the present tendency is more and more in this direction. They feel that their future as well as that of their children is tied up with Hawaii and the mainland United States. They tend to be indifferent to the Chinese nationalistic and other immigrant societies, and may be ardent members of the Democratic or Republican party organizations. Hawaii has made no attempt to draw racial lines in voting and in the right to seek election to office. In the 1934 election 5,447 citizens of Chinese ancestry, about 80 per cent of those eligible to vote, exercised their voting privileges; this comprised almost 9 percent of the total vote cast. A few institutions have been established whose purposes have been partly to stimulate these new citizens of Hawaii to participate in the political life of the Islands. Among these is one known as the "101 Republican Club"; two others are the Kau-Tom Post of the American Legion and its women's auxiliary. Chinese on one island have formed a "Native Sons of Hawaii," those on another island a civic association. But these citizens of oriental ancestry also take part in interracial political groups, such as the precinct and representative-district organizations and in the territorial-party organizations.

The growth in the number of those eligible to vote and their increased experience in practical party politics have begun to bring their rewards in the election, through the interracial-party organizations, of citizens of Chinese ancestry to city, county, and territorial offices, and the apportionment of an amount of political patronage to the Chinese group. Among the elective offices which have been or are now being held by Hawaiian-born Chinese are city supervisor, county surveyor, district magistrate, and representative and senator in the territorial legislature. Political patronage has secured positions for Chinese in practically every class of occupation connected with this system.

Back of this increased participation in the Hawaiian political life by descendants of Chinese immigrants is a new type of group loyalty—a loyalty to Hawaii not as a Chinese but as a native son or daughter, characterized by the appropriate patriotic attitudes and sentiments. It finds its expression in many ways, but among them are the desires to participate in the formulating of the country's laws and policies, to act as functionaries in the government, to defend it in times of crisis, and to co-operate with other citizens in Hawaii regardless of racial or national backgrounds in a common political life.

E. FROM CONFLICT TO COOPERATION: A STUDY IN UNION-MANAGEMENT RELATIONS [45]

The case to be presented tells the story of the development of harmonious relations between S. Buchsbaum and Company and the International Chemical Workers Union, Local 241, AFL (formerly the Novelty Workers Union, Local 241, AFL).

The Company was founded in 1888. Until the late 1930's, it was a small family business engaged in the manufacture of jewelry.

In 1935 the Company began experimenting with chemical processes and was able to convert during the war to the production of a number of plastic items for the armed forces. With reconversion the Company has shifted to production of plastic rainwear, belts, suspenders, and a number of other items. The Company still makes fine jewelry, but the jewelry department is now only a small part of total operations, in terms of number of workers employed.

The period of 1940–45 was one of tremendous growth for the Company. The number of workers rose from about 150 to a peak of 1600 at the time of reconversion. At this writing, the work force is close to the former peak figure and is expected to expand still further.

The Company has had a turbulent anti-union history. A union contract was signed in 1918, that union was broken in 1919. In 1935 another organizing attempt was broken up following a long and costly strike.

In 1940 the present union leaders were successful in organizing the Company and obtained a contract. Since that time, the union-management relationship has become extraordinarily harmonious. There have been no strikes or other work stoppages. While the contract provides for an impartial arbitrator, so far it has not been necessary to refer a single case to him.

The union-management relationship has these distinctive features:
1. The Union has assumed responsibility for shop discipline.
2. The Union has cooperated with the Company in building up production.
3. The Union has taken the initiative in introducing Negroes into the work

force and has worked with management to build up an unusually harmonious interracial work situation.

It is not our aim simply to present a pretty picture of cooperation. We want to know (1) how this relationship was developed, and (2) what general conclusions we can draw from it and apply to other cases.

We are therefore tracing the development of the relationship through accounts given us by Herbert J. Buchsbaum, President of the Company, Samuel Laderman, General Manager of the Union Local, and Sidney Garfield, Business Agent of the Union. The statements of these men are based upon several interviews with them.

Mr. Buchsbaum's Story

My first experience with unions was in 1918. Labor was scarce, the demand for merchandise strong. The union obtained a contract from the factories in our Association, gaining recognition, raises, and time-and-one-half for over 44 hours of work.

There was no check-off, no closed shop, no union security or genuine friendship from the employers. The union had to force collection of dues the best it knew how and either to refuse to work in the presence of a non-union employee or to make life so miserable for him that he joined up or quit.

The shop steward in our plant was quite belligerent, the employees suspicious, the foreman harassed, the employer frankly longing for the day when he could dispose of the union and its activities. Work slowed down, stealing was common, discipline bad. Other factories, at Association meetings, reported similar experiences. One factory not in the Association when interviewed by me, reported excellent working conditions and harmony. While at the time I could not appreciate the reason for this factory's success as a union shop, I now see that its operation did not contemplate destruction of the union but rather a class cooperation with it, whereas all Association shops were definitely set to hamper the Union at every turn.

All union demands were promptly refused but individual requests were granted. Active union members were discharged and were unable to get employment in an Association shop, but employees opposed to unions were advanced out of proportion to their skill or seniority. The unions retaliated by slow-downs, breakage, and stealing. The resulting friction proved costly but the end of the union was as certain as anything could be.

About a year later by agreement, one Association factory discharged its shop chairman for union activity, forcing a strike. The next day every Association factory including ours brought some fictitious orders into the plant under the name of the struck plant and ordered the workmen to do them. The workers promptly laid down their tools and walked out.

In our plant, my father and I, the foreman, and a few factory-trained office workers took over the jobs of the strikers. We hired helpers to whom we taught the trade as best we could. New York and St. Louis factories assisted where special skilled labor was required.

Some workers organized shops and tried for themselves. Most of them failed quickly. In a few months the employees came back, minus their union cards, and were re-hired one at a time with a sound anti-union lecture.

The ringleaders could secure employment only in non-Association shops.

Naturally, my father and I, having seen the union at its worst, took precautions against a recurrence by scanning carefully each employee for union tendencies and discharging them quickly if any were evidenced. When father passed away in 1926, I continued our policy.

In 1935 the union began organizing again. It came at a very critical time for the company when we had just finished construction of a new building.

I thought if I let the union in it would ruin my business. It seemed to me that I was fighting for my business life. My lawyer advised me that I could disregard the Wagner Act as it was in his opinion unconstitutional. So, I felt that I was really defending my constitutional rights. I was fighting the good fight for the American way of life.

Then the members of my Association were all backing me up with moral support and the Association gave me a check for $500 to help win the strike. I took that money and when I took it I became obligated to them. I couldn't sign a union contract without double-crossing them.

I felt the strike coming, so I signed a contract with a detective agency to keep me informed.

I just looked upon this as a battle. I was fighting and when you're in a battle you need to have scouts posted so you can know what the enemy is doing.

I received daily reports from the labor spy both before and during the strike. Those reports made me still more antagonistic toward the union. I got a lot of stories about what the workers were saying against me, and then, before the strike, there were reports on restriction of output. Take this one, for example:

B-1 *Reports for Friday, July* 26, 1935

Commenced work at 8:00 a.m. and quit for the day at 8:00 p.m.

After punching my time this morning I found the engravers sitting outside before 8:00 a.m. After exchanging greetings with them, the union steward came over to these men and said:

"You fellows want to take it easy today; I'm going in to tell those night fellows not to put out any more work—they're putting out too damned much work and I want to get in there before the boss gets here. But remember, you fellows take your time and I'll get that straightened out with the old man—about the hours."

When I got that report, I saw red. That seemed to me completely immoral. It made me more against the union than ever. I was determined to win this strike.

It went on for sixteen weeks and in the end the strikers were just left out. We dropped the detective and let the guard go because, while people were still picketing, we had our new crew all trained and we were producing the goods. The strike was over from our standpoint.

Now that I look back on it I can see that I could have accomplished the same thing in 1935 that I did in 1940. There were human beings there at that time, too. Instead I won the strike, but it was terribly costly. It meant training a whole new crew. If we had signed up in 1935 I'm sure that we would have got farther ahead in the succeeding five years. But maybe it's just as well that it went that way because I learned from the experience. I've done it both ways, and I can see that one way lies success and the other way there is constant friction and aggravation.

Nothing happened between 1935 and 1940 to change the way I felt about unions. I had a few friends who could see some good in unions, but I was arguing with them just as strongly in 1940 as I had in 1935. I thought they were crazy.

My mother has always been on the side of the workers. She used to say, "The poor people. They work so hard, and what do they get to show for it?" In the middle of the 1935 strike, she came into my office and pleaded with me to settle and take the people back. I certainly didn't want to listen to her then, because I knew that I was breaking the strike. I just said to her, "Mamma, you've got the wrong idea. This whole thing was stirred up by a few trouble makers—just a bunch of Reds. When we get rid of them, everything will be all right." That didn't satisfy her, but still she wasn't able to make me change—then or later.

But while I stayed the same, the world around me changed. By the time of the strike in January, 1941, the Wagner Act had been declared constitutional by the Supreme Court, and we were getting used to the idea. I didn't want to violate the law, and it wasn't just because of the penalty involved. Capital must believe in law and order because if you don't have law and order what protection is there for your capital?

The first break for the union came late in 1940 when they appealed to the government on some discrimination cases, and the National Labor Relations Board ruled that I had to post a notice in the plant announcing that the employees were free to join a union for collective bargaining purposes. Posting that notice was the last thing I wanted to do, but I had no choice.

When organization started in the plant, I did everything in my power to forestall it. I gave a nickel raise and promised more. I thought that would take care of everything. If the people became discontented, all I had to do was offer them a raise in wages, and that would take care of it. But it didn't in this case. Apparently that wasn't what they wanted at all. They just wanted to be organized.

With the union trying to organize, naturally I was worried, but still I didn't think they would be successful. I thought I had everything under control, that most of the people were loyal to me and to the Company.

I met with Sam Laderman before the strike, and he tried to convince me that he represented a majority of the workers, but I wouldn't believe him, and I challenged him to prove it to me. At the same time, I was on the watch for union tendencies in the plant. That was one thing I didn't hesitate about. If I found anyone who had any interest in the union or even if he was the son of a union member, I would have fired him as quick as look at him, no matter what he was doing in the plant.

When I came down to the plant that morning in January and saw that picket line, it was a great shock to me. I felt that those men had turned against me personally, that they were traitors and double-crossers. I was determined to get rid of them all, bring in a new bunch of people, and break the strike, just as I had in 1935.

I didn't see anything that could stop me. The strike could not have come at a better time, so far as we here were concerned. Before the war, January was always a slack time in our business. The Christmas rush was just finished up and the first of the year inventory was being held. Few orders were coming in, and the receipts from our Christmas sales were moving into the office. The Company was in a very strong financial position. In January we usually have to let out some of our people temporarily, so it wouldn't have hurt us at all to close down for a couple of weeks.

The union tried to block us from getting goods in and out of the plant, and they were pretty effective, but we were managing to move some things at night, and I was confident that in a couple of weeks the other unions cooperating with them would lose interest and we would be able to handle all our shipping and receiving.

While I made my plans to break the strike, I couldn't help noticing that it was different from our 1935 struggle. There were nearly all our own people on the picket line. I thought I knew them pretty well, even though they had turned against me. It was zero weather, and it was pretty cold out on that picket line. I stopped and talked to the boys, and I told them to come in the vestibule and picket. That's the kind of strike it was.

There was quite a bit of violence and sabotage in our 1935 strike. Expensive equipment was smashed, sand was thrown in bearings, materials were destroyed, and there were some bricks thrown through the windows.

The 1941 strike was quite different. A few people got beaten up, but the Company suffered no property damage. The union had good discipline on that point. There was one time when some of our people were trying to get through the picket line into the plant. They drove up in a car onto the sidewalk and right in front of the plant entrance to get the people in. That car endangered the lives of some of the picketers, and they rushed up and wanted to turn it over. Garfield stepped in then and wouldn't let them do anything to the car. That made an impression on me when I was told about it. I felt that these were responsible people. I didn't agree with them, but I could see that they were going out of their way not to harm the Company.

As soon as the strike started, Sam Laderman asked me to meet with him and a committee of the strikers. I didn't want to do it, and I called my lawyer three times to try to find some way out of it. Each time he told me I had to accept the invitation because it would have been a violation of the law not to meet with them.

On the second day of the strike I had lunch with Laderman and with a business acquaintance of mine who had a contract with his union. Up to that time I thought all union people were a bunch of racketeers. My friend reassured me on this point. He said that you could count on Sam Laderman keeping his word. He told me that Sam was a real human being. He liked opera. He disliked fights. There would be nothing he would like better than being friends with the employer if it were possible. He assured me that the union was always willing to discuss things from a reasonable point of view. And Laderman assured me that our contract would contain the standard clause that it would be no less advantageous to the employer than contracts the same union makes with any other firm.

That made an impression on me. I still had no idea of settling the strike but I agreed to meet with Laderman and a committee of the employees on the third day.

Well, we sat around the table and began talking. I knew all the men there. We were just a small firm at the time.

The first question one of the men asked me was this: "Mr. Buchsbaum, why are you against unions?" Now that was a good question and I welcomed it. I thought that gave me a chance to win them over to my line of reasoning. I stated: "I'm against unions because they limit production. They put production down to the level of the slowest employee and at the same time force impossible wage increases, driving the company out of business."

They started talking all at once. They didn't want to limit production, but increase it. They wanted to see the company go ahead.

I asked: "How can you increase production?"

I got answers fast. Each one had a sound suggestion for his department. First spoke one of the polishers. He told of the large door behind the polishing department used for in and out shipments—how in zero weather this door was opened many times daily, obliging the perspiring men to leave their wheels and go to the washroom to save themselves from catching cold. How a simple protecting partition would save about an hour and a half per man per day. Other suggestions equally good came from everyone in the circle. I took notes that I could see would save the Company thousands of dollars annually.

In that first meeting they really sold me a bill of goods. There was one thing that convinced me. When the workers began talking I saw that they had my interests at heart—as well as their own. I realized I had done them a great injustice in thinking that they had turned traitor to the Company.

I came to a decision—"All right boys; I have a different slant on this now. Go out and tell all the men to come back to work. We'll sign a union contract as soon as we can write it up. Only one condition—no hard feelings or discrimination against the workers who did not join the strike. Let's say they didn't understand your point-of-view. I didn't myself."

Right there we agreed in principle on the terms of the contract and signed a memorandum. That ended the strike. The men went right back to work.

Writing up the contract was relatively easy. Union recognition was their objective, and I gave them more than they wanted. I gave them the check-off system, virtually a union shop and job security. There were no strike and no lockout clauses, and no slowdowns; no limitation of output or wildcat strikes were to be permitted by the union. I granted an immediate raise of 5¢ an hour and wage scales were left open for further discussion in 60 days. I agreed to have an open accounting procedure so that all our figures would be laid on the table, and we chose an impartial arbitrator to decide any issues we could not settle ourselves.

A special labor management committee was formed to assist in promoting the welfare of the business and employees. The committee received authority to order work done by the maintenance department for the health, comfort, and convenience of the workers, to present suggestions for new things to manufacture and new methods of manufacturing.

Signing a contract did not solve our problems. We had some difficulties in the beginning, and it took about 90 days to get things smoothed out. We had a problem with our foremen. Of course, we explained management's new policy to them, but somehow or other they couldn't believe it. All they could see was that management had been brought to its knees by the union, and they assumed that management would be happy to have them sniping and undercutting the union in any way that they could.

In the past whenever they took a dislike to a worker they had been used to just telling him that he could go. They felt that their powers were being taken away from them. Another thing, they didn't understand the activities of the union chairman. They couldn't see why a worker should spend time doing anything but just his particular job when he was in the plant. Whenever they would see a group of people talking together they'd get mad and step right in and try to get them back to work. Sometimes the foreman might criticize a chairman who was really trying to straighten out a problem for the benefit of everybody concerned. That was a great injustice, and the people resented it.

I had to proceed very carefully those first three months. I didn't want anything to upset the situation. Finally, we even had to get rid of one of our foremen because he couldn't get along with the union. It was just impossible for the man to cooperate with the union. Now, Sid Garfield and I could have lunch together every day, but if the foremen have an anti-union attitude and are constantly having friction with the chairman, then you don't have union-management cooperation.

We couldn't have brought these foremen around if it hadn't been for the attitude the union leadership took. I didn't know what to expect of Garfield, but

I began hearing that when there were troubles in the plant he was stepping in and quieting things down. Naturally, when foremen have been in absolute control for a long time there are a lot of workers who think that as soon as the union comes in they can tell the foreman off. They go up to him with a chip on their shoulder and they feel that he shouldn't be able to tell them what to do at all. Fortunately, we had Garfield's full cooperation on that. He disciplined some of his people and there were one or two of them that he agreed to let go.

When I saw how Garfield was acting in the plant, I came to lean on him more and more. I found that when I tried to settle things on my own without calling him in I was worse off than I would have been if I had called him in. So I began calling him in, and he was very helpful in a lot of problems.

We had one problem in the beginning with the unorganized workers. Our contract required every new worker to join the union, but I had refused to push the old workers who were against it into the organization.

Some of these anti-union people would come in and tell me what had taken place at a union meeting. At first it would get me very annoyed, but then I began to ask questions. I'd ask them "Well, were you at the meeting?" "No," the person would say, "I wasn't there." "Well, then, who told you?" "Joe told me." "Was Joe there?" "No." "Who told him?" "Well, Tom told him." "Was Tom there?" It would go on like that and finally we'd find that there was no basis to the story at all. You see what that means. If you want to believe those things you can and you can let yourself get antagonized more and more. Now I don't listen to that sort of thing at all. If a person hasn't been in a situation himself I don't want to hear what he has to say.

In the first few months we had a lot of trouble with the non-union workers. It seems that these people wanted to themselves a higher status than the others. They felt they were being loyal to management, and they let it be known around that when better jobs opened up they expected to get the preference. That was the cause of a lot of dissension. Of course, they rode right along and got whatever benefits the union got, just like the unionized people.

The union kept after me on that issue. They wanted me to push the people into the union, and the more they talked about it the more stubborn I got. I thought I was defending democracy. But then, finally, I saw the light. I began to realize what dissension this was causing so I agreed to call them in one by one—there were only a few of them—and talk to them. I would call one of them in and tell him I wasn't going to force him to do anything but I thought it would be in his best interest and the best interest of the Company if he would join the union. The people would be very surprised and they would ask me if I really meant it. "Yes," I would say, "I do mean it." Sometimes a man would say, "Well, why should I pay my money to those crooks and racketeers?" Then I would have to give him a speech and tell him that those workers were really his own fellows, they had elected their own treasurer who accounted for the funds and that all that Sid Garfield and Sam Laderman got out of it was really peanuts in comparison with the services they performed. A lawyer would charge two or three times as much. But sometimes I'd only get on this speech when they would tell me that I had been the one who had told them that union men were crooks. They threw up my own words against me. Of course, before we were organized I had thought all union organizers had horns. It was hard to persuade the people that I had changed my mind, but finally we did get all of them into the union.

Our system of shop discipline just worked itself out. It all started when we had a problem with our washrooms. They are quite small, and there were a lot of people loitering in them. It got so bad that people who really needed to use the facilities had trouble getting in. The foremen didn't know what to do about it. They were very upset. Now I could have stuck a notice up there signed by the management but what good would that have done? It would just have antagonized people. Instead, I called in Sid Garfield and talked the situation over with him. He consulted his Committee and then he came back and said that they would be willing to assume responsibility for the problem. We agreed on a notice to be signed by him and by me, too, and we agreed that any worker who didn't obey the regulations could be sent to the union headquarters for a working card before he could come back on the job. The foremen would have that power. Just as soon as that notice was posted the problem cleared itself up. Nobody had to be sent to the union. Now that was a great discovery to me. I learned that a worker is more influenced by what his fellows think about him than he is by threats that he'll get fired if he doesn't do what management says. When these people were being disciplined by their own people it was much stronger than when management stepped in.

We've worked in that way ever since except that now when the foreman has some problem of discipline he doesn't act on it directly himself. He takes it to the chairman and the chairman handles the discipline. Being sent to the union is a club that is very seldom used. That's the beauty of it. For example, recently we had a big problem of tardiness. It was just a natural letdown after the end of the war. The people didn't have the same objective to work for. I know how they felt because I experienced a similar letdown. Still we had to get them back on the job. We worked it out with the union that people who were late could be sent to the union headquarters before they got a permit to work. Out of 1400 workers we only had to use that in 11 cases and now we have people coming in on time.

Our union-management relationship has greatly simplified the task of management in the shop. No longer responsible for discipline, foremen can function most effectively as teachers. We call them our "Know How and Show How" men.

When workers take pride in their performance, they work conscientiously without close supervision. In place of one foreman to 20 workers in 1940, we now have one to 100 workers.

We have found it advantageous to make union leaders supervisors or lead men. There is a tendency to pick the worker who produces the most. Now that man may not be the proper one at all. He may take a superior attitude and say: "Why can't you do as well as I did?", thus depressing the group.

When you pick a real leader who has the loyalty of the group, whether he is or is not the best producer, he is the best supervisor. The union is in a good position to spot leaders and we find it good policy to use these leaders.

In the first half of 1946 our dollar volume of sales per worker was three times what it was in 1940. I attribute much of this increase to the group spirit in the plant. In addition to the money workers get, they seek approval from their fellow-workers. When one fellow-worker says of another: "He's a good man on the job," it counts. When the group sets itself to do more and better work it approves of good workers and disapproves of slackers, and that spirit makes for top production.

We have several large dinner meetings a year, men and women, black and white. This helps to build good feeling. I've learned a lot listening to the men talk at these meetings. I got quite a shock once when one man had this to say: "Mr. Buchsbaum, it's all right for you to have a nice Cadillac car, a fine home and live in luxury. We like to see you go out in society. We like that—it makes us feel good—as long as you take care of us too, but if you can't see to it that we get a good living to take care of our families, we'd resent it. If you can't take care of us, you don't deserve that luxury."

Well, I thought that over. The man is absolutely right.

At another meeting, a Negro member gave us a little talk. He sketched the hardships of his race from slave days, the struggle to live clean and well, the fight for education. He said that through me and the union, the colored race in our plant had experienced a new birth of freedom. I was deeply touched by his words.

Before the union contract, we had very few Negroes in the plant. When we started taking war orders, I became aware of the law against discrimination, requiring a larger percentage of colored than we had. The union officials insisted on filling our quota and said they would be responsible for the peaceful assimilation. So, we proceeded to add them to our ranks with practically no trouble. Soon they requested equal opportunity for supervisory jobs, which we gave them.

First, it was Negro supervisors over Negro lines, then whites would get into the line, and now it's all mixed up and works fine. When they work side by side and know each other, race is forgotten.

Our office is unionized too, and there was a problem in bringing in Negroes. First, we started an office of colored on the floor above. Then when a white girl was sick, a colored girl would come down and cover her desk for her. They got to mixing together until it ceased to be important that colored girls worked in the office.

One of our plants with over 90 per cent colored people received an E award from the Quartermaster for excellence in war production of a critical item. Fine workmanship, speed, outstanding diligence—to quote General Barzinsky, who presented the flag—earned award. Colored people are excellent workers in a happy environment.

My whole attitude has been changed through this experience. I had to overcome all my early training. The trouble is that the businessman looks upon a union as an inanimate object, something that he grows up to hate. When he suddenly sees it before him as a group of human beings that he knows, he gets a different slant on things. Those fellows are the men he has been working with. Just because they belong to a union doesn't make them any different. He begins to realize that he can get along with them.

I used to think of myself as a distributor of largess, almost like the Medieval nobleman. I gave out favors, but I expected a great deal in return. I had a patronizing attitude, and I realize now that they resented it. Besides, I always kept them at arm's length. Now that's all changed. They want to do things for me; they do more for this Company than I can possibly pay them for. Now we get together and talk things out, and we understand each other.

The employees have security, and the Company has it too. We can expand our plants, add new items, plan sales campaigns, advertise, and seek foreign markets with never a fear of work stoppage or strife. We can work together to cut costs and increase production. Our union relationship has been a great asset in the development of the Company.

The Story of the International Chemical Workers' Union, #241, AFL

Mr. Laderman: To understand the cooperative relationship we have you must first consider certain background factors. In the first place, we were dealing with a very homogeneous group of workers at the start. The people who were later elected to our executive board all came into the Company at about the same time in 1935. They all started as unskilled help without other factory experience, so their future was all tied up with the Company. It would have been different if they had been workers who had had jobs in a number of different places. Then there would have been a number of different ideas about the union and about the Company, so it would have been harder to pull the group together. They were very loyal to the Company and expected to stay with it, so it was important for us to show them that we didn't mean to hurt the Company at all.

They didn't have any personal hatred for Mr. Buchsbaum. They knew he was struggling to build up the business, and they didn't want to do anything to hurt the business, but they did not have any say for themselves. They wanted to stand up for their rights. And then conditions in the country had changed between 1935 and 1941. Unions had become an accepted part of the thinking of most working people, and that naturally helped to make the Buchsbaum workers union-minded.

We started trying to organize the Company late in 1940. It was slow work at first. We knew that a majority of the people wanted a union, but they were afraid to sign up. It wasn't until January of 1941 that we were able to get anything done. When we got that National Labor Relations Board notice posted on the bulletin board, we were finally able to convince people that they were within their rights in organizing, and then we began signing them up.

We didn't want a strike. I've learned through my experience that you can get more in the long run through being reasonable and keeping your arguments before the employer than you can with a strike. Maybe you have to settle for a little less at first, but as you develop the relationship and win the confidence of the employer, you can do more for your members in the long run.

That's what I tried to do with Mr. Buchsbaum. I had a conversation with him before the strike. I told him that I represented the overwhelming majority of his employees, but he wouldn't believe it. He had had labor "racketeers" talk to him that way before, and it had been just a shakedown proposition. He had been paying money to keep some of those people out of the plant. He thought it was the same thing for us. That's why we had to show him we could take the people out.

Actually Mr. Buchsbaum forced the issue on us. At the time of the strike, we weren't very strong in the number of people we had actually signed up. We were concentrated in certain spots. For example, we had all of the polishing department, and those men were the core of our whole organization.

Now in spite of the attitude which the Company had shown, those people still had quite a bit of trust in it. They thought that if they could show Mr. Buchsbaum that a majority of the workers were in favor of the union, he would give them what they wanted. These men in the polishing department didn't want to do anything underhanded against Mr. Buchsbaum, so they decided to come right out in the open and wear their union buttons to work.

We knew they would be fired, and we warned them, but they wouldn't believe us. So we told them to go ahead, and that set it off. When they got fired, they came back to the union office pretty mad. "Now," they said, "we don't have any choice. We have to pull the whole plant."

Mr. Garfield: When you have a strike it's usually the result of a pretty aggravated situation and the people who stand out as the leaders are the aggressive type. It just has to be that way. A strike is a tough thing anyway and if you're going to have a successful strike you have to have leaders who are fighting men. The longer and more bitter the strike is, the stronger the position of these men is going to be and the less cooperative and rational they're going to be when you finally get down to negotiating.

Our strike was short. It only lasted about five days so that there wasn't a tremendous amount of time for bitterness to be built up during that period. Nevertheless the strike was the result of considerable antagonism on the part of the firm, and when the people were out, they felt pretty bitter about it. It was short but it wasn't easy. We were plenty tough. We had about twenty-five people out of one-hundred-fifty or so that we could really depend on and who were down every day for picket duty and so forth, and we just threw a picket line around the Company. Things have to be planned a little bit in a situation like that so I split the gang into two groups. One group was posted right in front of the Company door and the other group down at the street car where the people who were coming to work got off. When this second bunch met anybody coming to the plant they just caught them right then and there and asked them, "Are you with us or against us?" and there wasn't anything in between—it was either yes or no, and if the answer was no and they were against us, Wham! There was fighting then and there and a lot of people were hurt.

The group down in front of the door of the Company was the same way. They had one great big fellow there who was a wild character. He was really violent and I had to kind of keep control of him, but whenever things got going he was always in there with both fists flying. One of the supervisors tried to get five girls into the plant by hooking his arm into theirs and walking up to the door with them. This wild man cut in front of him and when the supervisor said, "You can't hit a man with glasses on," he just took the glasses off and handed them to him and then pasted him. The supervisor put his glasses on and just turned around and staggered away.

That just shows how things went. In spite of the fact that the strike was short, feelings were pretty high and we had the same things to contend with when we came back into the plant as any other outfit had.

The strike came so suddenly that we really didn't have time to organize co-operation with other unions, so that what we did get was more or less spontaneous. Just about the time the strike ended we had reached agreements with most of the people who would have been handling Buchsbaum materials, so that we were going to be able to close the plant up tight. And the longer the strike went, the tighter it was going to get, so, with that help, we had every expectation of winning out. (Editor's note: Mr. Buchsbaum expected to have less difficulty in moving materials as time went on. While he may have been mistaken, the important point is that he acted upon his estimate of the situation and did not feel he was going to be forced to make terms.)

On the second day of the strike, Sam Laderman met with Herb and a business friend of his with whom he had a contract. That made some impression, but the turning point came on the third day when Herb had to meet with the strike com-mittee. He didn't want to pay any attention to Sam or me. He just turned to the strikers who were on the committee and asked them what they wanted to get out of the union and why they had to have a bunch of outsiders come in and go between them and their own Company. He asked them if they were trying to ruin the Company; of course, the fellows told him that they weren't trying to ruin the Company at all and that actually they didn't want to do anything that would hurt it in the least bit. They said that, as a matter of fact, they felt that if they had a union there they could help the Company and they started to give Herb a num-ber of their different suggestions right then and there.

When these fellows began giving him their ideas, he sat down with his pencil and paper, added them all up, translated them into dollars and cents and announced that he realized how much these suggestions really meant to the Company, and from that point on he was on our side.

I guess he figured if there was some way that the people would give their cooperation as they had during that meeting in pointing out all those various things that meant increased profit, then he was for it.

I think something that made him trust me was rather interesting. During the strike, things were pretty rough for a while and we had a number of clashes when people tried to get into the plant. One time one of the men came flying down the street about sixty miles an hour in a car and ran right up on the sidewalk to the doors of the plant and tried to let people in that way. He might easily have run over some of our boys standing around, but they got between him and the door of the plant and had him trapped there. The strikers were all for taking care of him quickly right then and there and turning the car over in the street, but I knew enough to realize that that would be a bad move because of the great American tradition of respect for property so I made them leave the car alone. I don't mean that I was easy. There was one fellow who was trying to sneak in and I pulled him out of his car and just kicked him down the street.

When this incident came up, the chief Company detective was standing right inside the door with a gun in his hand but he was afraid to use it, and I found out later that he was impressed by what had happened and had gone up and told Herb Buchsbaum about my respect for property which apparently made some impression on Herb, too. It's the little things which make the difference.

Another thing which I feel really convinced Herb that we were on the level was when we had finally gotten around to reaching our agreement and he was holding out for only one thing. There were twenty people that he wouldn't let come back into the shop. Everybody else could come back under the agreement but these twenty, and he held out on that point until the very end. I told him that I couldn't quite see the way he was figuring and he just got real mad, but I kept talking to him and pointed out that everything was settled now but these twenty people. The way they'd always figured in the past was that people were pretty much like machines and they could shift them around any way they wanted. They would take them off when the work was scarce so that nobody felt any security in the job at all. When materials didn't come through or something like that they were just out of work for two or three weeks or until everything was set up again and then they were called back. I told him then that we didn't want a situation like that. We weren't trying to hurt the Company, and, in fact, had a proposal which was probably going to help it a great deal. We wanted an arrangement whereby, when work was scarce, it would be shared among all the people so that instead of a lot of people being laid off and a small group kept on at full time, everybody would be kept on at half time or as much time as the Company could give them on the amount of work on hand. I think when he saw that we weren't trying to put over some kind of an idea that would hurt him but were only thinking about the people, it convinced him. I asked him if he didn't want to take care of his people and he said, "Of course, I want to take care of my people. They're my people and I have some obligation toward them. They're my responsibility and I'm going to take care of them." When I pointed out how he could do it by sharing the work he finally agreed that it was a good idea and we got the whole thing settled. I think that was when he decided that he could deal with us and that we weren't out to cut the Company's throat.

This was very important but still only part of the picture. Cooperation demands mutual acceptance and it is also important that the union have confidence in the Company.

MR. LADERMAN: Here we had something to build on because the workers wanted to believe in the Company and were ready to believe in it if Mr. Buchsbaum acted in good faith. We were also very fortunate in having such a unified group to deal with on the executive board of the union, and Sid Garfield and I have worked together very closely with them from the beginning. It's not like some unions where there's a natural opposition between the local officers and the international representatives. Where you have that opposition or where you have factions in your local, the international representative has to be more aggressive and radical than anybody. If he tries a policy of cooperation, then there will be somebody from the local leadership that will stand up in a meeting and say that he demands so-and-so-and-so. Then the international representative has to get up and say, "What you're asking is way behind the starting line. That's nothing at all. Now I think we should go out and get such-and-such-and-such." You have to play politics that way, but here we've been able to work with a unified group, and we've always moved along together.

MR. GARFIELD: You have the situation frequently where companies are forced, by a strike or similar situation, into an acceptance of the union but there's nothing whole-hearted in it. After all, the agreement or the contract means nothing. It's the spirit in back of it. I've said that over and over again and I'll keep saying it. If you don't have the spirit of cooperation, it doesn't matter how many contracts or agreements you have signed. But as soon as we signed the agreement with Herb, he really started to back us up whole-heartedly. Actually, he started right off by giving some things we hadn't even asked for. We didn't ask for a check-off or anything like that but he granted it to us and after we got started he began calling the union in on things and backing us up completely when we needed backing.

The firm has taken advantage of every situation to enhance the prestige and power of the union in the eyes of the worker. Everything passes through the union office. All notices of raises, changes of time, changes of salary, or anything else, have to be initialed by me before they can be posted, so that everything that comes out must receive the union sanction. I think that demonstrates pretty well the kind of mutual confidence which exists.

Right after the contract was signed we had a period of transition, of course, when things had to settle down and people had to learn how to work under the new set-up. This was most difficult for the people who were in a supervisory capacity, particularly the foremen. They were suddenly changed from the all-powerful position to a position of more or less limited power. They didn't know quite how to take it and a few of them tried to carry on in the old way, running things with a high hand and trying to fire at the drop of a hat. Some we had to push into line. The foremen, like the union leaders, either had to change their type or get out, and some of them had to get out.

Even when the head of a company comes out and says that he accepts the union and signs an agreement there are always a lot of people in the company who don't believe that he's really sincere and who think the company is just accepting the union on the surface and is actually going to go along in its old manner and start counter-acting the union in every way possible.

We had some of those people here and actually before very long we had to get rid of two of the supervisors who couldn't seem to get straightened out at all. There was one foreman who kept sniping against us and who thought he was doing management a good turn. Some of the materials that came into his plant were distributed between that plant and another company, which got about 10% of the supply. This foreman, thinking that he could cripple the union activities, shifted an excessive proportion of this material to the other company, leaving this plant with a comparatively small supply. That meant that some of the work lines had to be shut down and some of the workers were laid off. It was quite a while before management caught up with him and let him know in no uncertain terms that he wasn't doing anything in their favor. That was the end of that.

We've had the same thing happen with superintendents, too. When this one superintendent first came into the Company he never had had any experience with unions and we heard from a number of different sources that he was going around saying to the people that he thought they were fools for paying their dues to the union and all that kind of stuff, so one day when he got in a jam and had raincoats piled up to the ceiling, the president told him to get that stuff straightened out in a hurry and asked me to come down and help him. It wasn't anything that you could straighten out by putting in a new process, it was just one of those things where the people had to give a little extra push. He called me up and asked me if I'd come down and help him. When I got there he told me what the situation was and I told him I wouldn't do a thing for him. He was a little surprised, of course, but I told him that I knew what he'd been up to and that he didn't have any right to go around telling our people that they shouldn't belong to the union, he should just keep his mouth shut. He said that he hadn't realized what he was doing or that we'd hear about it. I told him that we heard about everything that was going on, and then I helped him out of this jam. Well, you know, we've never had any trouble since then. Whenever anything comes up now he gets in touch with us immediately and we work it out before it's gone too far.

When a union enters a plant, it brings about a considerable number of changes, one of which is a decentralization of power. The foremen felt this very strongly, but they were not the only ones. A number of the people in the top ranks of management felt it as well because we had to keep them from mixing into shop discipline. They realize now that the union had to take the responsibility for discipline among the people. It's up to the plant superintendent and other people in top management to see that a flow of goods is maintained, to see that good floor arrangements are made so that materials can be processed quickly and efficiently, and people have the best conditions to work under. It is up to them to expedite work through the various departments. Beyond that the work with the people, particularly in matters of discipline, belongs to the union.

The new set-up meant that the chairman in the department was actually the foreman's partner and that the foreman didn't have to worry about anything except getting out the work. He was responsible for the technical aspects of the job and the chairman was responsible for the discipline of the people. He took care of all complaints and those things didn't have to be handled any more by the foreman. Some foremen didn't realize how good this was for them and insisted on carrying on the double responsibility. Those foremen who were willing to take advantage of the new situation were able to improve their efficiency considerably. Of course, this division of responsibility did not spring up overnight. It developed out of our experience.

In the beginning, we had a bunch of completely untrained, inexperienced people. There was only one person in the whole gang who had ever belonged to a union before and he wasn't very active at that time. The rest of the fellows were all very young and I attribute the success we had to one thing which may appear rather insignificant, but seems to me to be the most important thing in the whole situation. The thing I'm talking about is the unrestricted use of the telephone. We had that very definitely understood when we signed the contract. We had to have it because all these people had no experience or training at all, and furthermore, everything was very intimate and personal to them, so they had no way of making any kind of an unbiased decision in regard to any matter that might have come up. At the beginning there was a mutual understanding between the union office and the chairmen and executive board in the shop that at the beginning it would be much better, it would facilitate handling grievances, if the union knew immediately about grievances and was able to counsel with the chairman before any decisions were reached.

We agreed that any chairman or committeeman who had a grievance would make absolutely no effort to settle it on the spot, but would immediately get in touch with the business agent. That procedure had a number of rather important effects. One was that they didn't make any snap decisions which would have been colored by their closeness to the situation, and possibly by the lack of training and experience. Another was that they had the advice and critical assistance of someone who stood a little bit out of the immediate picture and wasn't so intimately and personally concerned with the issues at stake. The third thing was that by working with a trained and experienced agent on every grievance that came up, they gradually began to get some training along with their experience so that by the end of two years those people were thoroughly and intimately trained. They learned a great deal by experience, of course, but there was more than just trying to work things out for themselves as they went along. I can't over-emphasize how important I think that procedure is, even if a group can have that kind of situation for only six months or so I think they are going to profit very greatly from it. That early period after the union-management agreement is the most crucial one. It's the time when the whole situation has to settle down and you have to find the basis for future procedure, the time when feelings are the highest and the people are most on edge, and the time when the judgment of someone who is a little bit outside of the immediate picture is very badly needed.

If the people have to battle it out for a while before the agent appears on the scene there is a very great possibility that they may commit themselves to one line of action or another irrevocably, and when the agent arrives he finds them in so deep that he can't reverse the decision, without humiliating the union representative. That you just can't do, so you find that if the situation gets out of hand before the agent gets there, he may have to back up the mistakes that have been made.

Another thing, union leaders tend to change their opinions and lose their prejudices with experience. When a man is a worker on the line, the only grievances he knows about are those which directly concern him and in these he takes a personal interest so that he can't take a completely unbiased point of view. Now when a man becomes a committeeman, he has to think in terms of the group in his work section as a whole. When he becomes a shop chairman he can't think of himself or even of small work groups but he has to think of the whole plant; and whenever he wants to make a decision in favor of one group on one grievance he always has to keep in mind how it is going to affect everything else all the way up and down the line. For this reason it is important to give people an opportunity to get experience in their new situation and also to encourage them to bring their problems to the Business Agent who sits a little bit outside of the immediate situation and has an even broader point of view than the shop chairmen themselves, being concerned with not only one shop and the people in it, but with all the shops and the people throughout the Company.

We had to be very careful what we did in those early days because we wanted to establish precedents which would stand up later. In the years since 1941, we have succeeded in making labor relations experts out of most of our chairmen. They have had a good piece of experience and have taken their jobs seriously and really done a very excellent job. Management, in realizing this, has proceeded on the theory that the chairman should be about 50% overhead, that is, about 50% of his time has to be spent on the line and the rest of his time may be devoted to settling grievances and improving relations.

The shop chairmen or committeemen in some cases are also supervisors. These men work in a dual capacity simply because the firm has recognized the outstanding quality of some of the men we have elected. The supervisors are the only ones who are supposed to give orders to the people. They transmit the orders of the foremen directly to the individual and then check to see that they are carried out.

These supervisors are always from within the group with which they are working. They have close personal relationships with them and know the temper of the people from day to day. They usually work on the line or in very close proximity to it. The only difference between the supervisor and the other workers is the fact that he gets five cents per hour more for the responsibility which he shoulders.

When disciplinary measures must be taken, all punishments are meted out by the union, and by the union alone. Recently we had a fight down in the plant. The participants were called up before the executive board and given ten days off, plus a year's probation in the union. This kind of treatment has a very strong effect on a worker because it comes as a direct judgment from his fellow workers. It is in a way an expression of public opinion and everybody is very wary of having his fellow workers down on him. The workers themselves feel that this power belongs to them and they are able to express it through their elected representatives. They realize that and never forget they can get rid of their chairman simply by a ten per cent vote for a change, which will bring on a new election.

The union has also established other procedures and policies which are now accepted by the Company. We were the ones that insisted that people be given another chance at a different job if they didn't work out on the first one. That's worked out pretty well. Sometimes when a girl isn't satisfactory on a job I have the superintendent send her down and I talk to her and tell her that maybe she ought to try some other job. After we have a talk about it she goes back and the superintendent asks her if she would like to transfer to some other operation. She's usually quite pleased to do so and very frequently the results are better for everybody all the way around. One superintendent will have a girl that he wants to get rid of and another superintendent will have another girl who is unsatisfactory to him. Sometimes instead of having two people fired, I just have them switched and many times this has turned out to be a completely satisfactory operation. Both of them get rid of a girl who can't do her work and get a girl who works out very well.

In some respects we operate like a personnel department. We took over this transfer business little by little, or at least got into it because the superintendents who wanted to transfer people around very frequently ran into trouble with it. They would start transferring people simply to get rid of them because they didn't like them and, of course, that came to the attention of the union and we had to put our foot down. Little by little it got to the point where the superintendents checked with us before they made any transfers and it finally came under our jurisdiction. They recognized that we had some concern with the way people were transferred around so that now we check on transfers or make suggestions ourselves. We didn't have anything like that in the agreement. It just grew up little by little as we went along.

The superintendents who were used to firing their people any time they pleased soon realized that every time they fired someone they had to answer to the union and give some kind of reason for it. The same thing was true when they wanted to discipline someone. They couldn't lay someone off on a probation period, give them a cut in salary or even stand up and bawl them out without hearing something from us, so eventually the division of labor came about where the superintendents and foremen were very definitely concerned with the job of production and that was all, the union took over the job of discipline. People feel it much worse anyway when their own group or representatives of their own group bear down on them because if the superintendent or someone like that gets after them they just think, "Well, that's what he's supposed to do anyway," and write about half of it off because they feel they have their bunch in back of them anyway.

MR. LADERMAN: We were able to work out new ways of doing things because we weren't tied to any definite pattern from the beginning. This was kind of a miscellaneous shop, and we didn't have anything like it in our international, so we were free to work out rated and working conditions in a completely flexible manner. The same holds true with methods of production. A lot of unions have restrictions on methods of production, but everything was new here, so we left that up to management. I think that has been very important. You hear employers complaining all the time, "Why should I have to abide by somebody else's rates or standards when my conditions are different?" In a union where you have a number of shops making the same products, you have to have some uniform rules, but here we weren't tied down to anything.

MR. GARFIELD: We were always willing to try new ideas. Some of them were good and some of them were bad. Everything that we tried didn't work out but the good ideas we saved and the bad ones we discarded.

Since the union has come into the Company we have tried quite a number of systems for wages and work. At one time we tried an incentive system but this worked very badly and had to be given up in short order. The trouble was that all the emphasis was placed upon the individual. We had a terrific rush and everybody was competing with everybody else, they were fighting each other for materials and everyone was high strung and unhappy. Both morale and production fell off. After this experience we went back to our old ideas of group responsibility.

On that foundation, we have been working hard at all times to increase production. We've warned against restriction of output time and time again. The people are only cutting their own throats with that sort of thing, and if we find anybody even suggesting something like that, they hear from us in a hurry.

The emphasis of our union throughout has been upon this group responsibility. We have felt, always, that people were able to discipline themselves, were able to handle their work with a minimum of supervision and we have proceeded upon that basis. This has paid off because it has been possible to have a much larger proportion of workers in relation to supervisory personnel than we ever had before. The best example of this was in the plant where the superintendent took a three weeks vacation. During this time production was maintained or slightly increased and the plant of 350 people ran itself completely without any supervision except from the shop chairman. This was the plant which won the E Award for excellence in production. It should also be mentioned that all the people in this plant started as general help and that during the period when supervision was absent there were three shifts running, ninety per cent of the people being colored.

One of the most important events in which the company and the union had to cooperate was the introduction of colored employees. When we first conceived the idea of bringing Negroes into the plant it had to be sold to three different groups of people. We had to sell it to each single one of them on the basis of what they understood by themselves, and that was something different in each case. First, there was the case of management. Shortly after the outbreak of the war materials became extremely scarce, and the Buchsbaums realized that they would have to go into war work almost completely or fold up. If they were going into war work they would have to expand. They would have to take over a new plant. That seemed like a good idea so they went ahead with their plans. When they told us, we said that we thought it was a good idea, but we asked them if they had considered where they were going to get their labor to fill the plant. When we promised that the union would take the responsibility for introducing Negroes into the plants, they were willing to accept the idea.

The second case was that of the union itself. I found that we had a tremendous amount of opposition to the employment of Negro labor, people saying that they would under no consideration work with the Negroes and threatening to quit if Negroes were brought into the plant. In a case like that it does no good to try to talk to all the people at once. We took it up first with the executive board and put it to them something like this. We told them that any organization could not remain static. It had to do one of two things. It either grew and developed, or it withered and died, and at this point they had their choice in regard to our own union. We told them that they could stay as they were, in which case in very short order they would have no jobs to remain on at all, and they would find themselves out on the street. Or they could take the other choice and expand. The means of doing that was at hand: the incorporation of large numbers of Negro employees into the plant and into the union. Thus they had the choice of losing their jobs or of expanding and strengthening their union, retaining their jobs, and at the same time also making a democratic and patriotic gesture. That went over.

While a lot of the white people had threatened to quit before they would work with Negroes, we only lost about a dozen people this way. Nine quit by themselves, and two or three others had to be thrown out. We threw them out all right. We made it clear that this thing had to work and that we were not going to stand for any monkey business. Of course, there were some incidents. One day a Negro boy accidentally scratched a woman's hand with a nail when he was putting a box of supplies on her work table. She wasn't hurt badly, and it wasn't his fault, but her hand was bleeding pretty badly, and she was sent to the office to have it bound up. When she came back, she chased down the Negro boy and started calling him a black bastard and all that kind of thing, saying that he had done it on purpose and that he meant to kill her, and so on. Well, the union chairman stepped in right away. He gave her a card and told her to go down to union headquarters and cool off. It was clearly her fault.

Well, we let her wait around and lost about a day and a half work before we let her come back again. Before she came back, we said we weren't going to stand for any fighting or trouble.

ANALYSIS OF THE CASE

This is the story of a remarkably rapid and complete change from conflict to cooperation. Perhaps, if we sift out the factors which made the change possible and then go on to see how this approach may be applied in other cases, we will be able to enlarge our understanding of the problems of building cooperation in industry.

First, let us explain the change which took place in this particular company.

1. *Economic Factors*

Since wages were very low in the winter of 1940–41, we might think that economic factors were sufficient to explain unionization. Certainly the workers were seriously concerned over the level of their wages, but it must be remembered that most of them had never worked in factories before 1935 and that many of the workers had advanced in job skills and wages in the succeeding years, so that, relatively speaking, they were not so badly off. One of the workers explained his stand in this way:

> "At that time I was working steady and I was making about $100 a month. Prices were lower then, so I was doing pretty good. I was doing better than I had ever done before, but still there was this fear all through the plant. You were afraid to speak up and tell the foreman or the boss what you really thought. I think that's why I joined the union—for freedom of speech. I wanted to tell the boss when he was wrong just as well as when he was right."

The quotation is from James Whitfield, now vice-president of the union. He was the first to sign a pledge card, and he then went on to sign up forty other workers. Our evidence indicates that the motivation of other key workers in the organization drive was much the same as in this case.

On the company side, we find that Mr. Buchsbaum was not forced by economic considerations to make peace with the union. The strike occurred at a most favorable time for the company, and Mr. Buchsbaum was confident that he could break it, right up to the time that he made his decision to sign a contract.

Had the strike continued for a longer period, the company might have been under economic pressure and have been forced to sign a contract. However, there are many employers who sign contracts and yet do not establish harmonious relations with unions. Economic pressure is never a sufficient explanation for union-management cooperation.

To live with the union, Mr. Buchsbaum had to find an economic basis for the new relationship. The first step in this direction came through the meeting with the union committee.

While economic factors must receive careful attention in any union-management study, it is very clear that in this case, as in many others, these factors formed only a small part of the motivation of the people in both camps.

2. Role of the Government

But for the NLRB, Mr. Buchsbaum certainly would not have met with the union committee when he did, and, being confident that he could break the strike, he might never have agreed to such a meeting. However, the government did not create the new relationship. It simply set up certain conditions under which agreement became possible.

3. Establishment of Personal Contacts

The strike disrupted the old pattern of human relations. Mr. Buchsbaum had considered himself close to his workers, but now he could not meet with them except in the presence of "outsiders" whom he feared and distrusted. To reestablish relations with his workers, it was necessary to find some bridge to lead from the old to the new system of relationships. The mutual friend served to make such a transition possible. When Mr. Buchsbaum had lunch with Mr. Laderman and his business acquaintance, he was able to look upon the union leader as a human being with whom some agreement might be possible—although he remained determined to break the strike.

4. The Discovery of Common Values

Mr. Buchsbaum had always looked upon unions and union men as his enemies. Developments upon the national scene between 1931 and 1941 tended to weaken his anti-union position. At the time of the 1941 strike, he still felt that unions were bad for his business, but he was not so sure as he had been in 1935 that he was defending a righteous position. The law was against him, and this carried weight above and beyond the penalties that could be invoked for its violation.

This weakening of position might have led to capitulation, but that in itself is hardly the basis for a real working agreement. For cooperation to be possible, Mr. Buchsbaum had to change his sentiments so that he could think and feel: these union men are not my enemies; they are human beings that I can get along with.

Such a drastic change in his pattern of thoughts and sentiments could not be accomplished by logical processes alone, it involved a deep seated emotional readjustment. Nor could the new pattern be abruptly substituted for the old. New ideas and sentiments had to find a place in the old pattern and then, under the impact of further experience, further changes could be introduced until the new pattern could take shape.

In this critical initial period, Mr. Buchsbaum found three points of common values which enabled him to see the possibilities of agreement.

a. Mr. Buchsbaum felt his property rights menaced by the strike. Property rights, at the time, held a top place in his scheme of values. When Mr. Garfield stepped in to prevent the strikers from damaging the car, he appeared to show a similar respect for property. This was also a demonstration of order and discipline.

b. Mr. Buchsbaum was accustomed to thinking in terms of costs and volume of production. The suggestions made by the workers in the initial conference fitted perfectly into this pattern.

Furthermore, Mr. Buchsbaum had been accustomed to thinking of the workers as his people. He had a paternalistic attitude toward them and thought in terms of their personal loyalty to him. The union seemed to threaten this relationship. But the workers appeared to demonstrate their continuing concern for the welfare of Mr. Buchsbaum and his company. It therefore seemed possible for him to keep the loyalty of his workers although on a different basis.

c. Mr. Buchsbaum was a lover of fine music. He discovered that Mr. Laderman was a devotee of opera. As far as labor relations are concerned, this would seem to be an irrelevant consideration, but we are not dealing with logic. When new sets of human relations are to be developed, the interacting individuals need to find certain values in common. This is an important aid in providing the confidence, which enables the new relationship to develop.

5. *Agreement without Reservations*

Top management entered into the new relationship without reservations. There was no thought of getting rid of the union at some future date. On the contrary. Mr. Buchsbaum took pains to channel all benefits to the workers through the union structure. This served to strengthen the position of the union among the workers and it made possible the strong, positive program which the union leadership adopted.

6. *Supporting the Agreement in the Management Structure*

In the beginning, Mr. Buchsbaum made every effort to get foremen and even dissident workers to accept the new relationship. As Mr. Garfield's story indicates, new foremen and superintendents have not always been sufficiently informed and persuaded by top management, but whenever the question of management sabotage of the relationship is raised, Mr. Buchsbaum acts in unequivocal manner to support the agreement.

7. *Positive Contributions of Union Leadership*

The top union leadership led off with positive contributions to cooperation. Workers who could not accept the new relationship were disciplined. Fortunately, the strike had been so short and the victory so complete that the leaders were able to exercise such discipline without alienating the support of the rank and file.

Mr. Laderman and Mr. Garfield also began offering union help in production problems. That help took two forms. They encouraged the workers to produce more; they discouraged slowdowns and restriction of output. And, on the basis of their comparative background of factory experience, they were able to offer valuable suggestions in the field of industrial engineering.

The workings of the grievance procedure were not left to drift. It was probably important in the early stages of the relationship to have the advice or action of an experienced negotiator on every grievance. As Mr. Garfield points out, this prevented union representatives from committing themselves to untenable positions, and it served to build up a pattern for the handling of such problems. As the pattern took shape, it was possible to allow many problems to be handled at lower levels. This is, in fact, what has actually happened. While the union is still very strongly led by the two top officers, the executive board of workers in the plants is by no means composed of "stooges" for the top men. We have found instances in which the second level of leadership has overruled the two top men on the disposition of grievances or on the formulation of policy.

8. *The Building of Mutual Trust*

A large part of behavior in organizations is based upon personal commitments. Mr. Buchsbaum agrees to carry out a certain policy. Mr. Laderman and Mr. Garfield present the policy to their executive board and gain approval there. The members of the executive board undertake to sell the policy to the rank and file. But then, suppose Mr. Buchsbaum changed his mind and went back on his promise. In such a case, the top union officials would lose face with the executive board, and the executive board would lose face with the workers. The entire union organization would be threatened with disruption. The only way for the leadership to hold it together would be to adopt an aggressive anti-management policy.

The same conclusion holds true for the commitments made to management by the union leadership. Top management leads its subordinates to expect certain developments. If the commitments are then broken, the stability of the management organization is threatened.

It is therefore of crucial importance that on no occasion have Mr. Buchsbaum or the union leaders made commitments to each other that they have not undertaken to carry out in good faith. The relationship goes far beyond specific promises. The men have learned to know each other well enough so that they know what to expect from each other, in a wide variety of circumstances, even when no commitments are made. Without such mutual confidence and predictability, no stable system of human relations is possible.

9. *The Contract as a Living Document*

Neither party has treated the document as a complete definition and limitation of the relationship. Both have recognized that it is not the legal terminology but "the spirit behind it" which sustains the relationship.

They have further recognized that it is impossible to cover all possible cases in a contract and that therefore both parties must take a realistic view of the system of human relations they wish to maintain in settling problem cases.

The following case presents a good example of this approach. The contract provides that a new employee must be employed for three weeks before he acquires union protection. Up to that point, he may be discharged entirely according to management's discretion.

Recently a Negro woman was hired as a machine operator. Since she had only several days' previous experience on such a machine, the superintendent put her on the payroll in the "general help" classification at 10 cents an hour less than machine operators' pay. He explained that if she proved able to handle the machine, she would move up to the regular rate.

After several days on the job, the employee noted that all others working on this job, including some recently hired white girls, were receiving the regular rate. She complained to her union committeewoman. The union argued that the contract provided no learner's classification, that anyone operating a machine must therefore receive the regular rate. Management acknowledged its mistake and the employee received the increase. But several days later the superintendent discharged her, claiming that she was not capable of operating the machine efficiently.

The woman claimed that she was being discriminated against because of her color and being punished for taking her case to the union. The case was widely discussed in the work force, and the Negro employees were so agitated that production was seriously hampered. The superintendent argued that his decision was made simply in terms of the employee's lack of skill, with no thought of discrimination, and that, furthermore, since the woman had been on the payroll less than two weeks his action could not be challenged. Mr. Garfield argued that neither the superintendent's intentions nor the contract could alter the fact that the discharge was generally interpreted as discrimination for reasons of race and union activity. While only a few dollars was at stake for the company, this was a vital issue to the union.

The superintendent agreed to take the woman back for another week's trial period. At the end of this time, he was still convinced that she was unable to handle the machine efficiently, and he therefore wished to discharge her. The matter was then discussed with the union committeemen and the top union officials. On the basis of careful observations of her performance, they agreed that she was not able to do the job adequately. The superintendent thereupon discharged her. Feeling that the employee had now had a fair trial and that the position of the union had been protected, the representatives accepted the decision without protest. And there was no disturbance on the part of the rank and file.

In this case, the company had an unquestionable right, according to the contract, to discharge the employee. The stand on this right would have involved serious losses in production, perhaps culminating in a complete work stoppage. The morale of the work force would have been disrupted and union-management cooperation undermined—a high price to pay for the protection of management's prerogatives. Instead of applying the contract provisions in a literal and simple minded way, management recognized that maintenance of an effectively functioning social system was the chief consideration. The case was therefore settled in a way which would contribute to this goal.

10. *Flexibility on Both Sides*

No effort was made at the outset either by management or by the union to "draw a line" beyond which the other party must not be allowed to go. Each side has been scrupulous in its efforts to adhere to "the spirit of the contract," but legalistic interpretations were never allowed to block the development of the relationship. The leaders on both sides adopted a pragmatic approach. For management the goals have been to maintain a flexible plant organization, to lower costs, and to build up the volume of production. For the union, the goals have been to provide an ever-increasing measure of economic and emotional security for the workers. Both sides have recognized that the two sets of goals go together—that, in fact, neither one can be achieved without the other.

Therefore the problem has been one of joint exploration to find the means that will serve this common set of goals most effectively. It was in this way that the system of shop discipline evolved. And this approach had also resulted in the combination of supervisor or foreman with union chairman in some instances.

It should not be imagined that any of these adjustments represent final solutions to problems. New conditions demand new adjustments. The flexibility of the past may not be easy to maintain, but at least both sides are committed to the effort, so that there is more prospect of continuing successful adjustment than in cases where management or the union try to draw the line and reach final solutions in defiance of a changing world.

11. *Reinforcement of the New System of Relationship through Periodic Ceremonials*

Anthropologists, studying primitive tribes, have long recognized the importance of ceremonials for mobilizing the sentiments of groups of people. In our modern, industrial society, we tend not to utilize such tools because of their non-logical foundation. We like to think that all men are (or should be) dominated by reason. We are forced by experience to recognize that a large part of the behavior we observe is non-logical in character, and yet, because of our rationality bias, we are unable to deal skillfully with such behavior.

The effective industrial or union leader is the man who recognizes the sentiments of his followers and knows how to mobilize them to serve the goals of the organization. Such a leader recognizes the role ceremonials can play in union-management relations.[46]

In this case, management and the union representatives have eaten and drunk together regularly several times a year. They have talked together informally, and they have expressed their sentiments in formal speeches. The negotiation of the October, 1945, contract presents a good example of this approach.

When the negotiations were formally opened, management invited all the union shop chairmen and members of the executive board to a dinner. The first speech was made by Mr. Laderman. There he laid out both the long-run goals and those which the union would seek to gain in the current negotiations. Mr. Buchsbaum then replied. First endorsing the long-run goals of the union, he then discussed the position of the company and emphasized the problems of reconversion which would make it unwise for both parties to proceed too fast in this direction. There were a number of formal expressions of good will from members of management and the union during the evening.

The subsequent negotiations resulted in an agreement giving the workers a wage increase (in October and February installments) averaging about 13 per cent. While this proved to be below the figure won by some of the large industrial unions, it was considered satisfactory to the union for two reasons. First, the company had expanded tremendously and shifted the character of its operations during the war. In the uncertain reconversion period, it was considered more important for the company to be able to consolidate its newly won position and maintain its large-scale operations than for it to pay out larger benefits at the moment. And second, the union had the continued assurance that wages would rise with each improvement in the company's economic position.

To celebrate the signing of the contract, the union invited management, from president down to foreman, to the dinner which we have reported earlier.

The effects of such ceremonials are too diverse and widespread to permit precise measurement, but we are able to cite one concrete instance. Up to the time of the dinner, the union had been having trouble with one plant superintendent, who was new with the company. He refused to cooperate with his union chairman and seemed to be carrying on a harassing campaign, transferring her from job to job, placing her where she would not be so readily accessible to the workers, and so on. The union was preparing to act on this problem when the dinner made it unnecessary. The superintendent reported that the dinner gave him a better idea of his position in relation to the union, and the chairman reported that she was able, thereafter, to work with him in a cooperative manner.

12. *Development of a New Pattern of Thoughts and Sentiments*

Earlier we have pointed out that it was essential to find certain common values, which would make possible the development of new relationships. As a new system of human relations develops, it is inevitable that the people involved in it develop new patterns of thoughts and sentiments. And these new patterns in turn serve to support and reinforce the new system of human relations.

We can chart some of this development from the statements of the management and union leaders.

If the workers had originally appealed to Mr. Buchsbaum in terms of the need for job security, of the right of the worker to express himself on the conditions of his employment, and of similar democratic values, they would have elicited no positive response. These values had no place in the existing pattern, and therefore he could not respond to them. He responded instead to the values which had a place in that system.

Today Mr. Buchsbaum can think, feel, and act in terms that were completely foreign to him in 1940. Property, costs, and production are still important to his scheme of values, but human values have become integrated with them. His experiences since 1940 have shown that these original values are better served through acting also in terms of human values. Nor is this simply a question of means to ends. These values have become ends in themselves. Mr. Buchsbaum has found the new system of human relations rewarding in a direct, human way, quite apart from its contribution to efficient production. He gets satisfactions from feeling that he is contributing to the solution of race relations problems and that he has gained a position of leadership among the workers which was never his in the days of paternalistic control.

On the union side, there has also been a reorientation of thoughts and sentiments. When we talk to Mr. Laderman and Mr. Garfield today, we find them constantly and seriously concerned with problems of costs, efficiency, and volume of production. A similar outlook is found among the lower levels of union officers. The union recognizes that only through improving the performance of the company can it gain further improvements in the position of the employees.

FOOTNOTES TO PART FIVE

Asterisks indicate footnotes quoted from original source of case material.

1. Leopold von Wiese and Howard Becker, *Systematic Sociology* (New York: John Wiley & Sons, Inc., 1932). See also Part Four of this volume (*Social Dynamics*); Brewton Berry, *Race Relations* (Boston: Houghton Mifflin Company, 1951), pp. 158*ff*.

2. Robert E. Park and Ernest W. Burgess, *Introduction to the Science of Sociology* (Chicago: University of Chicago Press, 1921).

3. The first eight propositions come from Mark A. May and Leonard W. Doob, *Competition and Cooperation* (New York: Social Science Research Council, 1937), Bulletin No. 25. The other propositions were garnered from Émile Durkheim, *On the Division of Labor in Society,* translated by George Simpson (New York: The Macmillan Company, 1933), Book I; John Lewis Gillin and John Philip Gillin, *An Introduction to Sociology* (The Macmillan Company, 1944), Chaps. 24–27; Margaret Mead (ed.), *Cooperation and Competition among Primitive Peoples* (New York: McGraw-Hill Book Company, Inc., 1937).

4. J. B. Maller, *Cooperation and Competition, An Experimental Study of Motivation* (New York: Columbia University, Teachers College Contributions to Education, No. 384, 1929).

5. Mead, *op. cit.*

6. Condensed from Irving Goldman, "The Kwakiutl Indians of Vancouver Island," Chap. VI, in Mead, *op. cit.*

*7. A. L. Kroeber in *Encyclopaedia Britannica,* 13th ed.

*8. The numaym also includes individuals, not members of the bilateral family group, who have been given or purchased names belonging to the numaym.

*9. Originally all were equal.

*10. The present tense is used for narrative purposes only. The account refers to aboriginal conditions in the old days.

*11. The tribes living up the inlets and deeper in the interior were sometimes faced by famine.

*12. Ruth Benedict, *Patterns of Culture* (Boston: Houghton Mifflin Company, 1934), p. 174.

*13. Franz Boas, "Social Organizations and Secret Societies of the Kwakiutl Indians," *Report of the United States National Museum for 1895,* Washington, D.C. (1897), p. 338.

*14. *Ibid.,* p. 339.

*15. *Ibid.,* p. 343: "Formerly feats of bravery counted as well as distributions of property, but nowadays, as the Indians say, 'rivals fight with property only.'"

*16. *Ibid.,* p. 338.

*17. *Ibid.,* p. 343.

*18. Benedict, *op. cit.,* p. 344.

*19. *Ibid.,* p. 342.

*20. Franz Boas, "Ethnology of the Kwakiutl," in *35th Annual Report of the Bureau of American Ethnology,* 1913-1914, Part 2, p. 1341.

*21. "The rivalry between chiefs finds its strongest expression in the destruction of property." (Boas, "Social Organizations and Secret Societies of the Kwakiutl Indians," p. 353).

*22. *Ibid.,* p. 358: "Marriage among the Kwakiutl must be considered a purchase, which is conducted on the same principles as the purchase of a copper."

*23. *Ibid.,* pp. 359-366.

*24. *Ibid.,* p. 359.

*25. *Ibid.,* p. 366.

*26. *Ibid.,* p. 359.

*27. The material on law is from lecture notes by Franz Boas.

*28. Benedict, *op. cit.,* p. 221.

29. Condensed from Irving Goldman, "The Zuñi Indians of New Mexico," Chap. X in Mead, *op. cit.*

*30. Ruth L. Bunzel, unpublished manuscript.

*31. Gifts of food are given only to women, who control the food in the household. Men are fed only for their labors. Presents, often expensive items, go to members of the priestly body participating in the ceremonial housebuilding.

*32. Ruth L. Bunzel, unpublished field notes.

*33. *Ibid.*

*34. Ruth L. Bunzel, "Introduction to Zuñi Ceremonialism," in *47th Annual Report of the Bureau of American Ethnology,* 1929-1930, p. 476.

*35. *Ibid.,* p. 477.

*36. Benedict, *op. cit.,* p. 75.

*37. Most of the material on ceremonial friendship is from manuscript material of Dr. Ruth Bunzel.

*38. Elsie C. Parsons, "Ceremonial Friendship at Zuñi," *American Anthropologist,* Vol. 19, No. 1 (1917), p. 5.

*39. If a man has come back with many sheep he distributes a good portion of them among his children.

*40. Benedict, *op. cit.,* p. 70.

41. From Clarence Glick, "Transition from Familism to Nationalism among Chinese in Hawaii," *American Journal of Sociology,* Vol. XLIII (1937-1938), pp. 734-743.

*42. Edgar T. Thompson, "Plantation Expansion and the Plantation System," *American Journal of Sociology,* Vol. XLI (1935-1936), pp. 322-324.

*43. In 1910, a decade after the application of the American immigration law, the foreign-born Chinese male population was about 13,350, but only 2,761 Chinese still worked on the sugar plantations; 37 per cent of the foreign-born Chinese were concentrated in the city of Honolulu alone. By 1930, the foreign-born Chinese male population had declined to about 5,900; only 805 Chinese, including by this time some who were Hawaiian-born, were reported as employees on the sugar plantations; 55 per cent of the 7,500 foreign-born Chinese and over 77 per cent of the 19,700 Hawaiian-born Chinese were living in the single city of Honolulu, the two groups together comprising about 14 per cent of that city's total population.

*44. In some countries where large numbers of Chinese immigrants come from different provinces in China, provincial *hui kuans* or associations are often established. Almost all the Chinese in Hawaii are from the single province of Kwangtung, and, moreover, from only a few districts of Kwangtung. Cutting across this organization of the Chinese colony in Hawaii into district associations was one *hui kuan* which was based upon dialect, rather than upon locality, the group speaking this dia-lect being looked down upon by nearly all the old-world immigrants belonging to the district associations.

45. Condensed from *Applied Anthropology*, Vol. 5, No. 4 (Fall, 1946). Statements by Herbert J. Buchsbaum (president, S. Buchsbaum and Company) and Samuel Laderman (president and manager, International Chemical Workers Union #241, AFL); introduction and analysis by Andrew H. Whiteford, William F. Whyte, and Burleigh B. Gardner (from the Committee on Human Relations in Industry, University of Chicago, at the time of the study).

*46. See Benjamin Selekman, "When the Union Enters," *Harvard Business Review*, Winter, 1945.

PART SIX

Culture and Sociocultural Change

A. THE MEANING AND NATURE OF CULTURE: ANALYSIS OF THE MAJOR CULTURAL CONCEPTS

Like other animals, man employs his sense organs, his muscles, his nerves, and his glands in adjusting to the world around him. In addition, he creates his own environment by either symbolically reinterpreting what he sees or by actually modifying and reshaping what he finds. The animal's natural habitat is his only world; he reacts to it. Man's natural habitat is the clay of his prospective world; he recreates it. He builds houses out of the rock, establishes institutions out of houses, perpetuates the institutions with banner and ritual, transmits ritual to his progeny, who in turn add their own meanings, acts, and rhetoric to that which they find around them. In sociology and social anthropology, this man-made world is called his *culture*. Man alone possesses culture. It is his symbolic nature that enables him to develop a culture (see Part One). Through symbolization he determines his wants (non-biologic wants), reinterprets his sights, constructs means to his new ends, and is capable of passing both his values and their instruments on to others.

We do not know precisely the physiological and organic determinants of the symbolic-cultural faculty. Few natural scientists have even concerned themselves with the problem.[1] Whatever the organic explanations of symbolization may be, for the sociologist it is sufficient to accept as given that man alone is capable of it and that the collective products of symbolization are what is known as culture. Culture, therefore, consists of the mode of life created by man, and includes all the arts and artifacts resulting from symbolic interaction among men. A particular culture consists of the mode of life characteristic of a particular society. While culture is universal to man, each local manifestation is unique. Humans everywhere have created their own cultural environments; the creations of Americans are different from those of the Aztec Indians or the Chukchi Eskimos. Each society may be characterized, among other things, by a set of common cultural symbols, common understandings and meanings, resulting from the ongoing processes of interhuman communication and exchange. A society exists in so far as its constituent members possess a set of shared values, a set of common motives to achieve these ends, and a pattern of interaction conducive to the realization of these values. These shared values (material and nonmaterial), some of which are realized and others idealized, constitute the core of a people's culture. We frequently say that a society possesses culture, a group an ethos.[2]

This brings us to some important attributes of cultural phenomena. Obviously a culture is made up of items and traits—tools, ideas, habits, sentiments, and specific folkways. Culture traits have long been thought of, among social anthropologists, as the smallest identifiable units in a culture. As cells are to living matter, so traits are to cultural phenomena. In both instances, the terms refer to the parts that necessarily go to make up the larger whole.[3] However, only in so far as the parts fit together to make some larger structural form can we understand the significance of culture traits. An object in itself, as a substance, cannot be a cultural trait unless or until value and meaning are attached to it. Thus, coal buried in the mountains of Pennsylvania played no part in the economic cultural life of the Indians of that region. In the same way no use was made of metals in general by the Indians north of Mexico, except for a little copper.

It follows that an object becomes a cultural trait depending on the meaning that is attached to, and the use that is made of that object. It frequently happens, however, that the same substance is put to different uses by different societies or used in multiple ways within a given culture. Dogs, for example, are used primarily as pets by present-day Americans, but they were frequently used as food as well as draft animals by the Indians of the Great Plains. Vast differences also exist in the cultural meanings attached to other items. The Crow Indians, for example, believed in a host of spirits which inhabited animals, trees, stones, rivers, and stars. The coyote figures prominently in Indian folklore and mythology, and the creation of the earth and of man is attributed to him.

While similar items are given different meanings by different peoples, it also happens that the same item is put to different uses by the same people. Thus the yardstick is, for us, a measuring tool, a punishment rod, a lever to raise and lower windows, and so on. Glass is found in house windows, as watch covers, as an insulation substance, as well as in thousands of decorative pieces. The diversities in culture are the results of different interpretations of experience; different societies and various groups within a complex society frequently define the same situation in a different way and pattern their behavior accordingly.

If the cultural meaning of an item depends on the use to which it is put, it is difficult to understand the term *use* except in so far as some functional interrelationship is established among several of the items involved. Thus, for coal to be culturally meaningful, it would have to be related to the process of heating, perhaps to other items involved in the extraction of the coal from the earth, perhaps to a whole system of social organization which determines who should work—men, women, children of certain ages—in extracting the mineral. In addition, coal used for heating has, obviously, a different collective meaning from that of coal used for medical purposes or for machine-propelling power. Unused items or single culture traits in isolation mean little, therefore. Their significance emerges only when they are seen as fitting together into a pattern of traits. Culture pattern, then, consists of the configuration and combination of culture traits into a unified whole in which each of the parts is more or less adjusted to each other.[4] A particular culture pattern is, therefore, usually peculiar to a particular society or part of a society. Soviet communism, American capitalism, Chinese orientalism, Chicago urbanism, early New England puritanism —each conjures up a *system* of traits fitted together into a definite pattern, denoting at least a part of the mode of life of a people. Not only does culture pattern consist of a certain number of typical traits, but it also contains a unique and recurrent order in which these traits become related to one another. Certain customs and usages stand out; certain values predominate; certain beliefs are adhered to more than others. Each culture pattern reflects a hierarchy of overt routine acts as well as a rank order of beliefs and values, emphasizing some, minimizing others. In every culture pattern characteristic of a larger society or a smaller subsociety or group, one can expect to find some basic pivotal values that pervade almost every other phase of the cultural life of that society. These dominant values set the *theme* of the culture.[5] They are the dynamic forces in a culture. Rarely are the institutions in a culture free of these dominant themes. They are the forces that stimulate and control the behavior and activity of a group or a larger society.

Anthropologists have discovered themes among primitive folk. Ruth Benedict has been able to characterize types of American Indian cultures as Apollonian and Dionysian, with differences in dominant values and cultural imperatives that would mold and govern behavior and personality. In describing and analyzing the cultural system of the Yaqui Indians, E. H. Spicer applies the term *foci* to those values or attitudes around which interest is centered in Yaqui society and which operate to stimulate and guide activity. A third anthropologist, Erwin H. Acker-knecht—using data from an American Indian tribe, the Cheyenne; from a Melanesian people, the Dobu; and from the Thonga of South Africa—finds reflected in their medical patterns, in the meanings they attach to disease and illness, and in their curing practices the broader underlying beliefs and sanctions governing spirits and witchcraft. Thus, among the Cheyenne the cause of disease primarily consists of "invisible arrows shot by the spirits of wells, the mule-deer, and other spirits." Another anthropologist, Clyde Kluckhohn, observed that the "fear of the malevolent intentions of other persons" constitutes a basic theme that tends to order all sorts of behaviors among the Navaho. To mention another, M. E. Opler found that among the Chiricahua Apache society the thematic axiom that men are physically, mentally, and morally superior to women runs through almost every aspect of their culture—familial, political, ceremonial, economic, and recreational.

Themes and styles of culture are not, however, the exclusive properties of primitive, nonliterate societies. Literate-complex societies, and segments of complex societies, have their salient values and their culture keystones. To be sure, they are less obvious in complex social groupings where the personnel is heterogeneous and diverse. Evidence of cultural themes may be discerned without insuperable difficulties, nevertheless. Carl L. Becker, the late eminent historian and philosopher, repeatedly indicated that every age makes certain assumptions which express themselves in key words. In one of his lectures on history to a Yale University audience he stated that "in the thirteenth century the key words would no doubt be God, sin, grace, salvation, heaven and the like; in the nineteenth century, matter, fact, matter-of-fact, evolution, progress; in the twentieth century, relativity, process, adjustment, function, complex." [6] Key words reflect key values of a people of a given age.

In a similar fashion but based on more extensive empirical research, Geoffrey Gorer, the anthropologist, isolated four dominant themes characteristic of the Japanese people: physical modesty and personal cleanliness, dominance and superiority of the male, continuous subservience of the Japanese boy to his father and elder brothers, and correct social behavior. Given these four major themes, Gorer is able to trace their influences and potencies in almost every major institution of Japanese cultural life.

Similarly, other nations and other societies have had their culture themes suggested. The Greeks are said to have followed religious fatalism; Rome, an orderly government of men; France and the French have often been represented as an artistic, bohemian, fickle people;[7] the English, cold, reserved, and matter of fact.

It is not easy to pinpoint the theme or themes in American culture. Because of the rapidly changing nature of American life and because of its aggregation of heterogeneous parts, integration and cultural equilibrium are far from accomplished in American culture. Not all segments of the American population possess the same goals, profess identical beliefs, or live similar lives. The diversity, therefore, precludes the use of any simple term that can genuinely and accurately denote its pattern and theme. Such terms as democratic, capitalistic, materialistic, urban, mechanistic, idealistic, and secular are probably well-chosen labels and illustrations of this diversity. Nevertheless, evidence is emerging that some basically shared values and some underlying fundamental motivations toward given ends may be discerned as possible universals in the American pattern in its collective life. Robin Williams, Jr., in his latest book, *American Society*,[8] has outlined several major value orientations in America. They can easily stand for some of our dominant cultural themes:

1. An emphasis on personal achievement and personal success.
2. A tendency towards humanitarianism consisting of a readiness to aid others especially in the relief of material distress.
3. An emphasis upon efficiency and practicality.
4. Importance attached to material comfort and scientific-technological advancement.
5. Avowal of freedom and equality in political, economic, and social relations.
6. Importance attached to the intrinsic worth of the individual.

It is not to be construed from this listing that these value themes in American culture prevail Simon pure and unclouded. Hardly a society in complex Western civilizations can be found absolutely devoid of internal cultural contradictions and opposites. There exists a vast literature on this thesis. Some have even referred to American culture as "schizoid" in nature.[9] Robin Williams, Jr. has listed, along with his other dominant American values, what he has called "pervasive and powerful counter-currents of valuation." He says, "One of the chief conflicts, and in many ways the most important conflict, has centered around those diverse patterns which have as their common element *the ascription of value and privilege to individuals on the basis of race or particularistic group membership* according to birth in a particular ethnic group, social class, or related social category." [10] However, with all its impurities, the American character, though not hardened into a fixed pattern, is at least recognizable and familiar, like the outline of a form in a silhouette.[11]

It should be noted that the values of a culture frequently become embodied in the institutional framework of that culture. By *institution,* sociologists mean the organized system of rules, regulations, and social roles seeking to enforce the set of values of a group or a society. Major social institutions, such as the family, church, or government, consist of the organizations and structures that have developed to regulate and control behavior toward the values which a people hold essential to their survival and welfare. Institutions grow out of the mores—those standards and patterns of behavior considered essential to group welfare. However, unlike institutions, the mores are not organized; there is no formal execution of the mores.

In this section we shall present three significant items. The first includes excerpts from the Bill of Rights and the Preamble to the Constitution of the United States and illustrates the institutionalization of one of America's major value systems and culture themes—freedom. The second compares two polar types of basic value systems: the authoritarian-dictatorial with the laissez-faire–fatalistic. The first is referred to by the author as the ideology of the Commissar, the second as the mode of the Yogi. Between these two extremes is the value system of the democratic way of life. The last excerpt is from Ruth Benedict. It shows the variations in the values of two aspects of life and culture: adolescence and warfare. From her analysis one is forced to conclude that culture practices and culture patterns are not inborn or instinctive, that sometimes they even run contrary to maximum biological survival, and that the range of variation is indeed great.

1. *Preamble and Excerpts from the First Ten Amendments to the Constitution of the United States: Institutionalization of the Concept of Freedom*

We the People of the United States, in order to form a more perfect Union, establish justice, insure domestic tranquility, provide for the common defense, promote the general welfare, and secure the blessings of liberty to ourselves and our posterity, do ordain and establish this Constitution for the United States of America.

AMENDMENTS TO THE CONSTITUTION

Article I

Congress shall make no law respecting an establishment of religion, or prohibiting the free exercise thereof; or abridging the freedom of speech, or of the press; or the right of the people peaceably to assemble, and to petition the Government for a redress of grievances.

Article IV

The right of the people to be secure in their persons, houses, papers, and effects, against unreasonable searches and seizures, shall not be violated, and no warrants shall issue, but upon probable cause, supported by oath or affirmation, and particularly describing the place to be searched, and the persons or things to be seized.

Article V

No person shall be held to answer for a capital, or otherwise infamous crime, unless on a presentment or indictment of a grand jury, except in cases arising in the land or naval forces, or in the militia, when in actual service in time of war or public danger; nor shall any person be subject for the same offense to be twice put in jeopardy of life or limb; nor shall be compelled in any criminal case to be a witness against himself, nor be deprived of life, liberty, or property, without due process of law; nor shall private property be taken for public use, without just compensation.

Article IX

The enumeration in the Constitution, of certain rights, shall not be construed to deny or disparage others retained by the people.

2. Means and Ends in Extreme Cultural Types: The Yogi and the Commissar *[12]

THE STATIC SPECTRUM

I like to imagine an instrument which would enable us to break up patterns of social behaviour as the physicist breaks up a beam of rays. Looking through this sociological spectroscope we would see spread out under the diffraction grating the rainbow-coloured spectrum of all possible human attitudes to life. The whole distressing muddle would become neat, clear and comprehensive.

On one end of the spectrum, obviously on the infra-red end, we would see the

Commissar. The Commissar believes in Change from Without. He believes that all the pests of humanity, including constipation and the Oedipus complex, can and will be cured by Revolution, that is, by a radical reorganization of the system of production and distribution of goods; that this end justifies the use of all means, including violence, ruse, treachery, and poison; that logical reasoning is an unfailing compass and the Universe a kind of very large clockwork in which a very large number of electrons once set into motion will forever revolve in their predictable orbits; and that whosoever believes in anything else is an escapist. This end of the spectrum has the lowest frequency of vibrations and is, in a way, the coarsest component of the beam; but it conveys the maximum amount of heat.

On the other end of the spectrum, where the waves become so short and of such high frequency that the eye no longer sees them, colourless, warmthless but all-penetrating, crouches the Yogi, melting away in the ultra-violet. He has no objection to calling the universe a clockwork, but he thinks that it could be called with about the same amount of truth, a musical-box or a fishpond. He believes that the End is unpredictable and that the Means alone count. He rejects violence under any circumstances. He believes that logical reasoning gradually loses its compass value as the mind approaches the magnetic pole of Truth or the Absolute, which alone matters. He believes that nothing can be improved by exterior organization and everything by the individual effort from within; and that whosoever believes in anything else is an escapist. He believes that the debt-servitude imposed upon the peasants of India by the money lenders should be abolished not by financial legislation but by spiritual means. He believes that each individual is alone, but attached to the all-one by an invisible umbilical cord; that his creative force, his goodness, trueness and usefulness can alone be nourished by the sap which reaches him through this cord; and that his only task during his earthly life is to avoid any action, emotion or thought which might lead to a breaking of the cord. This avoidance has to be maintained by a difficult, elaborate technique, the only kind of technique which he accepts.

Between these two extremes are spread out in a continuous sequence the spectral lines of the more sedate human attitudes. The more we approach its centre, the more does the spectrum become blurred and woolly. On the other hand, this increase of wool on the naked spectral bodies makes them look more decent, and intercourse with them more civilized. You cannot argue with a naked Commissar—he starts at once to beat his chest and next he strangles you, whether you be friend or foe, in his deadly embrace. You cannot argue with the ultra-violet skeleton either, because words mean nothing to him. You can argue with post-war planners, Fabians, Quakers, liberals and philanthropists. But the argument will lead nowhere, for the real issue remains between the Yogi and the Commissar, between the fundamental conceptions of Change from Without and Change from Within.

It is easy to say that all that is wanted is a synthesis—the synthesis between saint and revolutionary; but so far this has never been achieved. What has been achieved are various motley forms of compromise—the blurred intermediary bands of the spectrum—compromise but not synthesis. Apparently the two elements do not mix, and this may be one of the reasons why we have made such a mess of our History. The Commissar's emotional energies are fixed on the relation between individual and society, the Yogi's on the relation between the individual and the universe. Again it is easy to say that all that is wanted is a little mutual effort. One might as well ask a homosexual to make a little effort towards the opposite sex and vice versa.

The Commissar's Dilemma

All attempts to change the nature of man by Commissar methods have so far failed, from Spartacus's Sun State through Inquisition and Reformation to Soviet Russia. This failure seems to be rooted in two disturbing phenomena which Kant could have called the Antinomies of Applied Reasoning. The first is the Antinomy of the Serpentine; the second the Antinomy of the Slopes.

The peak of Utopia is steep; the serpentine road which leads up to it has many tortuous curves. While you are moving up the road you never face the peak, your direction is the tangent, leading nowhere. If a great mass of people are pushing forward along the serpentine they will, according to the fatal laws of inertia, push their leader off the road and then follow him, the whole movement flying off at the tangent into the nowhere. This is what happens to most revolutionary movements, where the mass-impulse is strong and the inertia of the mass is converted into a violent centrifugal force. In the more cautious reformist movements, on the other hand, the momentum soon fades out and the ascending spiral first becomes a weary circling round and round the peak without gaining in height until it finally degenerates into a descending spiral; e.g., the Trade Unionist movement.

The second root of failure is the Antinomy of the Slopes, or of Ends and Means. Either the Means are subordinated to the End, or vice versa. Theoretically you may build up elaborate liberal or religious halfway houses; but if burdened with responsibility, and confronted with a practical decision to be taken, you have to choose one way or the other. Once you have chosen you are on the slope. If you have chosen to subordinate the Means to the End, the slope makes you slide down deeper and deeper on a moving carpet of common-sense propositions, for instance: the right of self-defense—the best defense is attack—increase of ruthlessness shortens the struggle, etc. Another well-known slope-pattern starts with the "Healer's Knife" and ends with the Moscow Purges. The fatal mechanism of this slope was already known to Pascal:

"Man is neither angel nor brute, and his misery is that he who would act the angel acts the brute."

The Yogi's Dilemma

The attempts to produce Change from Within on a mass-scale were equally unsuccessful. Whenever an attempt was made to organize saintliness by exterior means, the organizers were caught in the same dilemmas. The Inquisition flew off at a tangent; the Churches in the liberal era circle round and round the peak without gaining height. To subordinate the End to the Means leads to a slope as fatal as the inverse one. Gandhi's slope started with non-violence and made him gradually slide down to his present position of non-resistance to Japanese conquest: the Japanese might kill a few million Indians but some day they would get tired of it, and thus the moral integrity of India would be saved.

Obviously the prospects for the masses of common people are not brighter under this inverted Machiavellianism than under the leadership of the Commissars. One slope leads to the Inquisition and the Purges; the other to passive submission to bayoneting and raping; to villages without sewage, septic childbeds and trachoma.

B. THE DIVERSITY OF CULTURES [13]

A chief of the Digger Indians, as the Californians call them, talked to me a great deal about the ways of his people in the old days. He was a Christian and a leader among his people in the planting of peaches and apricots on irrigated land, but when he talked of the shamans who had transformed themselves into bears before his eyes in the bear dance, his hands trembled and his voice broke with excitement. It was an incomparable thing, the power his people had had in the old days. He liked best to talk of the desert foods they had eaten. He brought each uprooted plant lovingly and with an unfailing sense of its importance. In those days his people had eaten "the health of the desert," he said, and knew nothing of the insides of tin cans and the things for sale at butcher shops. It was such innovations that had degraded them in these latter days.

One day, without transition, Ramon broke in upon his descriptions of grinding mesquite and preparing acorn soup. "In the beginning," he said, "God gave to every people a cup, a cup of clay, and from this cup they drank their life." I do not know whether this occurred in some traditional ritual of his people that I never found, or whether it was his own imagery. It is hard to imagine that he had heard it from the whites he had known at Banning; they were not given to discussing the ethos of different peoples. At any rate, in the mind of this humble Indian the figure of speech was clear and full of meaning. "They all dipped in the water," he continued, "but their cups were different. Our cup is broken now. It has passed away."

Our cup is broken. These things that had given significance to the life of his people, the domestic rituals of eating, the obligations of the economic system, the succession of ceremonials in the villages, possession in the bear dance, their standards of right and wrong—these were gone, and with them the shape and meaning of their life. The old man was still vigorous and a leader in relationships with the whites. He did not mean that there was any question of the extinction of his people. But he had in mind the loss of something that had value equal to that of life itself, the whole fabric of his people's standards and beliefs. There were other cups of living left, and they held perhaps the same water, but the loss was irreparable. It was no matter of tinkering with an addition here, lopping off something there. The modelling had been fundamental, it was somehow all of a piece. It had been their own.

Ramon had had personal experience of the matter of which he spoke. He straddled two cultures whose values and ways of thought were incommensurable. It is a hard fate. In Western civilization our experiences have been different. We are bred to one cosmopolitan culture, and our social sciences, our psychology, and our theology persistently ignore the truth expressed in Ramon's figure.

The course of life and the pressure of environment, not to speak of the fertility of human imagination, provide an incredible number of possible leads, all of which, it appears, may serve a society to live by. There are the schemes of ownership, with the social hierarchy that may be associated with possessions; there are material things and their elaborate technology; there are all the facets of sex life, parenthood and post-parenthood; there are the guilds or cults which may give structure to the society, there is economic exchange; there are the gods and supernatural sanction. Each one of these and many more may be followed out with a cultural and ceremonial elaboration which monopolizes the cultural energy and leaves small surplus for the building of other traits. Aspects of life that seem to us most important have been passed over with small regard by peoples whose culture, oriented in another direction, has been far from poor. Or the same trait may be so greatly elaborated that we reckon it as fantastic.

It is in cultural life as it is in speech; selection is the prime necessity. The numbers of sounds that can be produced by our vocal cords and our oral and nasal cavities are practically unlimited. The three or four dozen of the English language are a selection which coincides not even with those of such closely related dialects as German and French. The total that are used in different languages of the world no one has ever dared to estimate. But each language must make its selection and abide by it on pain of not being intelligible at all. A language that used even a few hundreds of the possible—and actually recorded—phonetic elements could not be used for communication. On the other hand a great deal of our misunderstanding of languages unrelated to our own has arisen from our attempts to refer alien phonetic systems back to ours as a point of reference. We recognize only one k. If other people have five k sounds placed in different positions in the throat and mouth, distinctions of vocabulary and of syntax that depend on these differences are impossible to us until we master them. We have a d and an n. They may have an intermediate sound which, if we fail to identify it, we write now d and now n, introducing distinctions which do not exist. The elementary prerequisite of linguistic analysis is a consciousness of these incredibly numerous available sounds from which each language makes its own selections.

In culture too we must imagine a great arc on which are ranged the possible interests provided either by the human age-cycle or by the environment or by man's various activities. A culture that capitalized even a considerable proportion of these would be as unintelligible as a language that used all the clicks, all the glottal stops, all the labials, dentals, sibilants, and gutturals from voiceless to voiced and from oral to nasal. Its identity as a culture depends upon the selection of some segments of this arc. Every human society everywhere has made such selection in its cultural institutions. Each from the point of view of another ignores fundamentals and exploits irrelevancies. One culture hardly recognizes monetary values; another has made them fundamental in every field of behaviour. In one society technology is unbelievably slighted even in those aspects of life which seem necessary to ensure survival; in another, equally simple, technological achievements are complex and fitted with admirable nicety to the situation. One builds an enormous cultural superstructure upon adolescence, one upon death, one upon after-life.

The case of adolescence is particularly interesting, because it is in the limelight in our own civilization and because we have plentiful information from other cultures. In our own civilization a whole library of psychological studies has emphasized the inevitable unrest of the period of puberty. It is in our tradition a physiological state as definitely characterized by domestic explosions and rebellion as typhoid is marked by fever. There is no question of the facts. They are common in America. The question is rather of their inevitability.

The most casual survey of the ways in which different societies have handled adolescence makes one fact inescapable: even in those cultures which have made most of the trait, the age upon which they focus their attention varies over a great range of years. At the outset, therefore, it is clear that the so-called puberty institution is a misnomer if we continue to think of biological puberty. The puberty they recognize is social, and the ceremonies are a recognition in some fashion or other of the child's new status of adulthood. This investiture with new occupations and obligations is in consequence as various and as culturally conditioned as the occupations and obligations themselves. If the sole honourable duty of manhood is conceived to be deeds of war, the investiture of the warrior is later and of a different sort from that in a society where adulthood gives chiefly the privilege of dancing in a representation of masked gods. In order to understand puberty institutions, we do not most need analyses of the necessary nature of *rites de passage;* we need rather to know what is identified in different cultures with the beginning of adulthood and their methods of admitting to the new status. Not biological puberty, but what adulthood means in that culture conditions the puberty ceremony.

Adulthood in central North America means warfare. Honour in it is a great goal of all men. The constantly recurring theme of the youth's coming-of-age, as also of preparation for the warpath at any age, is a magic ritual for success in war. They torture not one another, but themselves: they cut strips of skin from their arms and legs, they strike off their fingers, they drag heavy weights pinned to their chest or leg muscles. Their reward is enhanced prowess in deeds of warfare.

In Australia, on the other hand, adulthood means participation in an exclusively male cult whose fundamental trait is the exclusion of women. Any woman is put to death if she so much as hears the sound of the bull-roarer at the ceremonies, and she must never know of the rites. Puberty ceremonies are elaborate and symbolic repudiations of the bonds with the female sex; the men are symbolically made self-sufficient and the wholly responsible element of the community. To attain this end they use drastic sexual rites and bestow supernatural guaranties.

The clear physiological facts of adolescence, therefore, are first socially interpreted even where they are stressed. But a survey of puberty institutions makes clear a further fact: puberty is physiologically a different matter in the life-cycle of the male and the female. If cultural emphasis followed the physiological emphasis, girls' ceremonies would be more marked than boys'; but it is not so. The ceremonies emphasize a social fact; the adult prerogatives of men are more far-reaching in every culture than women's, and consequently, as in the above instances, it is more common for societies to take note of this period in boys than in girls.

Girls' and boys' puberty, however, may be socially celebrated in the same tribe in identical ways. Where, as in the interior of British Columbia, adolescent rites are magical training for all occupations, girls are included on the same terms as boys. Boys roll stones down mountains and beat them to the bottom to be swift of foot, or throw gambling-sticks to be lucky in gambling; girls carry water from distant springs, or drop stones down inside their dresses that their children may be born as easily as the pebble drops to the ground.

In such a tribe as the Nandi of the lake region of East Africa, also, girls and boys share an even-handed puberty rite, though, because of the man's dominant role in the culture, his boyhood training period is more stressed than the woman's. Here adolescent rites are an ordeal inflicted by those already admitted to adult status upon those they are now forced to admit. They require of them the most complete stoicism in the face of ingenious tortures associated with circumcision. The rites for the two sexes are separate, but they follow the same pattern. In both the novices wear for the ceremony the clothing of their sweethearts. During the operation their faces are watched for any twinge of pain, and the reward of bravery is given with great rejoicing by the lover, who runs forward to receive back some of his adornments. For both the girl and the boy the rites mark their *entrée* into a new sex status: the boy is now a warrior and may take a sweetheart, the girl is marriageable. The adolescent tests are for both a premarital ordeal in which the palm is awarded by their lovers.

Puberty rites may also be built upon the facts of girls' puberty and admit of no extension to boys. One of the most naïve of these is the institution of the fatting-house for girls in Central Africa. In the region where feminine beauty is all but identified with obesity, the girl at puberty is segregated, sometimes for years, fed with sweet and fatty foods, allowed no activity, and her body rubbed assiduously with oils. She is taught during this time her future duties, and her seclusion ends with a parade of her corpulence that is followed by her marriage to her proud bridegroom. It is not regarded as necessary for the man to achieve pulchritude before marriage in a similar fashion.

The usual ideas around which girls' puberty institutions are centered, and which are not readily extended to boys', are those concerned with menstruation.

The uncleanness of the menstruating woman is a very widespread idea, and in a few regions first menstruation has been made the focus of all the associated attitudes. Puberty rites in these cases are of a thoroughly different character from any of which we have spoken. Among the Carrier Indians of British Columbia, the fear and horror of a girl's puberty was at its height. Her three or four years of seclusion was called "the burying alive," and she lived for all that time alone in the wilderness, in a hut of branches far from all beaten trails. She was a threat to any person who might so much as catch a glimpse of her, and her mere footstep defiled a path or a river. She was covered with a great headdress of tanned skin that shrouded her face and breasts and fell to the ground behind. Her arms and legs were loaded with sinew bands to protect her from the evil spirit with which she was filled. She was herself in danger and she was a source of danger to everybody else.

Girls' puberty ceremonies built upon ideas associated with the menses are readily convertible into what is, from the point of view of the individual concerned, exactly opposite behaviour. There are always two possible aspects to the sacred: it may be a source of peril or it may be a source of blessing. In some tribes the first menses of girls are a potent supernatural blessing. Among the Apaches I have seen the priests themselves pass on their knees before the row of solemn little girls to receive from them the blessing of their touch. All the babies and the old people come also of necessity to have illness removed from them. The adolescent girls are not segregated as sources of danger, but court is paid to them as to direct sources of supernatural blessing. Since the ideas that underlie puberty rites for girls, both among the Carrier and among the Apache, are founded on beliefs concerning menstruation, they are not extended to boys, and boys' puberty is marked instead, and lightly, with simple tests and proofs of manhood.

The adolescent behaviour, therefore, even of girls was not dictated by some physiological characteristic of the period itself, but rather by marital or magic requirements socially connected with it. These beliefs made adolescence in one tribe serenely religious and beneficent, and in another so dangerously unclean that the child had to cry out in warning that others might avoid her in the woods. The adolescence of girls may equally, as we have seen, be a theme which a culture does not institutionalize. Even where, as in most of Australia, boys' adolescence is given elaborate treatment, it may be that the rites are an induction into the status of manhood and the male participation in tribal matters, and female adolescence passes without any kind of formal recognition.

These facts, however, still leave the fundamental question unanswered. Do not all cultures have to cope with the natural turbulence of this period, even though it may not be given institutional expression? Dr. Mead has studied this question in Samoa. There the girl's life passes through well-marked periods. Her first years out of babyhood are passed in small neighborhood gangs of age mates from which the little boys are strictly excluded. The corner of the village to which she belongs is all-important, and the little boys are traditional enemies. She has one duty, that of baby-tending, but she takes the baby with her rather than stays home to mind it, and her play is not seriously hampered. A couple of years before puberty, when she grows strong enough to have more difficult tasks required of her and old enough to learn more skilled techniques, the little girls' play group in which she grew up ceases to exist. She assumes woman's dress and must contribute to the work of the household. It is an uninteresting period of life to her and quite without turmoil. Puberty brings no change at all.

A few years after she has come of age, she will begin the pleasant years of casual and irresponsible love affairs that she will prolong as far as possible into the period when marriage is already considered fitting. Puberty itself is marked by no social recognition, no change of attitude or of expectancy. Her pre-adolescent shyness is supposed to remain unchanged for a couple of years. The girl's life in Samoa is blocked out by other considerations than those of physiological sex maturity, and puberty falls in a particularly unstressed and peaceful period during which no adolescent conflicts manifest themselves. Adolescence, therefore, may not only be culturally passed over without ceremonial; it may also be without importance in the emotional life of the child and in the attitude of the village toward her.

Warfare is another social theme that may or may not be used in any culture. Where war is made much of, it may be with contrasting objectives, with contrasting organization in relation to the state, and with contrasting sanctions. War may be, as it was among the Aztecs, a way of getting captives for the religious sacrifices. Since the Spaniards fought to kill, according to the Aztec standards they broke the rules of the game. The Aztecs fell back in dismay and Cortez walked as a victor into the capital.

There are even quainter notions, from our standpoint, associated with warfare in different parts of the world. For our purposes it is sufficient to notice those regions where organized resort to mutual slaughter never occurs between social groups. Only our familiarity with war makes it intelligible that a state of warfare should alternate with a state of peace in one tribe's dealing with another. The idea is quite common over the world, of course. But on the one hand it is impossible for certain peoples to conceive a possibility of a state of peace, which in their notion would be equivalent to admitting enemy tribes to the category of human beings, which by definition they are not even though the excluded tribe may be of their own race and culture.

On the other hand, it may be just as impossible for a people to conceive of the possibility of a state of war. Rasmussen tells of the blankness with which the Eskimo met his exposition of our custom. Eskimos very well understand the act of killing a man. If he is in your way you cast up your estimate of your own strength, and if you are ready to take it upon yourself, you kill him. If you are strong, there is no social retribution. But the idea of an Eskimo village going out against another Eskimo village in battle array or a tribe against tribe . . . is aliento them. All killing comes under one head, and is not separated, as ours is, into categories, the one meritorious, the other a capital offence.

I myself tried to talk of warfare to the Mission Indians of California, but it was impossible. Their misunderstanding of warfare was abysmal. They did not have the basis in their own culture upon which the idea could exist, and their attempts to reason it out reduced the great war to which we are able to dedicate ourselves with moral fervour to the level of alley brawls. They did not happen to have a cultural pattern that distinguished between them.

C. SOCIAL AND CULTURAL CHANGE: AN INTRODUCTORY STATEMENT

It is fairly obvious that society, as a complex of social relationships, never stands still; it is in a perennial state of flux. The alterations in the nature, content, and structure of groups and institutions and in the relationships among men, groups, and institutions, during a sequence of time, constitute the field of social change.

Social change must be thought of as a continuous process. This does not imply that the rate of social change is always the same. There have been periods in history in which social change seemed quite slow. However, in contrast to geological or biological change, social transformation often occurs with amazing celerity.

Social change should not be confused with the concept of social progress. The former seeks to determine the principles governing societal variations. The concept of social change connotes an objective analysis of the causes and trends of these variations. On the other hand, social progress implies a normative, evaluative approach to social occurrences. Social progress is interested in a better society; social change is concerned with actual society. Social progress carries the implication of what ought to be; social change indicates what is or what is going to be.

The concept of progress goes back to the ancients. It was Lucretius (96–55 B.C.) who first used the word in the fifth book of *De rerum natura*. However, it was not until the seventeenth and eighteenth centuries that the theories of social progress became a real and absorbing subject of intellectual speculation. To Francis Bacon (1561–1626) and René Descartes (1596–1650) we owe the notion that man can make almost limitless progress by his own conscious efforts.

The first systematic attempt to formulate a theory of progress was made by Fontenelle (1657–1757), who set forth the doctrine of the indefinite cumulation of scientific knowledge which makes for the continual progress of man. Following Fontenelle, as might be expected once the concept of progress became one of the major problems of speculation, others sought to expand and promulgate additional theories. Abbé de Saint-Pierre (1658–1743), in his *Observations on the Continuous Progress of Reason,* held that civilization was but in its infancy and was constantly moving toward the maximum happiness for all the earth's inhabitants.

A. R. J. Turgot (1727–1781), who became one of the most distinguished statesmen in France, contended that the evolution of history and civilization is a cumulative matter, each cultural advancement accelerating the rate of progress. Historical progress, according to Turgot, is continuous and causally related. "All ages are linked together by a chain of causes and effects which unite the existing state of the world with all that has gone before."

Following Turgot's notion of progress in the past, Condorcet (1743–1794) viewed each historical epoch as a definite and unequivocal step toward an ultimate societal perfection and paradise.

In the nineteenth century, the idea of progress became the major motif of the early years of the newly born sociology. Thus Count Henri de Saint-Simon (1760–1825) attests to the coming of the golden age. "The golden age is not behind us, but in front of us. . . . Our children will arrive one day, and it is for us to clear the way for them."

Following Saint-Simon, Auguste Comte (1798–1857) developed in great detail the stages of intellectual and social progress.

For Herbert Spencer (1820–1903), the idea of progress was merged with the notion of evolution. He developed a theory of social progress in harmony with the theory of cosmic and biological evolution. Spencer believed that social evolution was part of a purely "natural" process, operating throughout the cosmic universe, and consisted of a movement from the simple to the complex and from the homogeneous to the heterogeneous brought about by the double process of integration and disintegration.

The most recent developments in the discussion of the theory of progress have led along two channels. One has consisted of a revival of the cyclical theory of history by Oswald Spengler, in his *The Decline of the West,* and by Pitirim Sorokin's work *Social and Cultural Dynamics,* emphasizing a movement of "ideational," "sensate," and "idealistic" social and cultural configurations. The other development has consisted of an outright abandonment of the term *social progress* and the substitution of the term *social change*.

William F. Ogburn, the major proponent of the theory of technological advances making for social change, is mainly responsible for the widespread use of the newer term since the publication of his book *Social Change*.

Ogburn is concerned with the relationship between inventions and social change. He doesn't deny that physico-environmental as well as biological factors play a role in bringing about changes in society, but he feels that neither exerts as much influence on social change as cultural innovations, or inventions.

By invention is meant the creation or the discovery of a new culture trait or element. Invention springs from a new combination and manipulation of already existing cultural elements. Social change takes place with the introduction into and adoption by society of this new element. An invention consists of a contrivance of that which did not before exist in the same form, although most of the constituent elements were present. Ogburn develops the thesis that four elements—need, cultural base, mental ability, tradition—are necessary for inventions to occur.

The origin, growth, and effects of inventions are all problems related to social change. Different types of inventions have differential social effects. Major inventions, when accepted by society, have major effects; minor inventions have less significant consequences. In our technological age, the impact of and the readiness to accept mechanical inventions appear to account for certain of the fundamental alterations in the associative life of man, even more so, perhaps, than man's social and ideological inventions.

Ogburn views his theory of social change as incompatible with the cyclical theories of social and cultural change. Inventions, because of their cumulative and crescive nature, make for progressive and unrecessive sociocultural growth rather than for the advance-and-decline point of view expressed by the cyclical theorists.

Spengler, Sorokin, and Toynbee are all advocates of large-scale cyclical theories to account for the movements and fluctuations of culture and society. Oswald Spengler, in *The Decline of the West,* formulated a cycle of events covering the birth, vigorous maturity, and senile decay of each of his great historical entities—Egyptian, Chinese, Classical, Magian, Mayan, Faustian, Russian, and several others. Each civilization has its own mathematics, science, religion, and art, and each develops in absolute independence of every other; there is no genuine inter-action whatsoever. Moreover, nothing can either accelerate or retard the ripening, flourishing, withering, and decay of any given culture.

A more recent theory of cyclical change springs from the writings of Pitirim Sorokin (*Social and Cultural Dynamics*). Sorokin studied Greco-Roman cultures from 600 B.C. to the present time, making briefer excursions into Egyptian, Arabic, Hindu, Chinese, and Babylonian cultures. Each of these cultures he found to be "logico-meaningfully" and "causal-functionally" related. He means that the parts of a given culture fit together meaningfully and congruently. Furthermore, each part of a culture tends to exert a causal influence on every other—such as philosophy upon art, art on law, and law on politics.

Sorokin builds his cultural and social categories on three major psychological types. The culture reflecting the *ideational* mentality has, for its essential characteristics, an attachment to the spiritual essence of existence and an indifference to the physical world; a belief in revela-tion and faith as the true sources of knowledge; a conviction that the realization of the good comes through self-discipline and through a changing personality rather than through the alterations in the outer world. The *sensate* mentality is found in the culture whose basic realities are found in empiricism, materialism, and a changing outer world. It has for its philosophy that of becoming rather than that of being. The third and final culture category is the *idealistic,* an ambivalent mixture of the two types described. Each of the major culture complexes passes from one of these main phases to another. During the last twenty-five centuries, several swings have occurred. Greek culture before the sixth century B.C., Sorokin holds, was predominantly ideational. With the end of the sixth century its ideationalism declined and its sensate forms appeared and grew. In the fifth and fourth centuries Greek culture be-came chiefly idealistic, giving way again to the sensate at the beginning of the third century. These shifts and swings have recurred until the present time. With the end of the nineteenth and in the twentieth cen-turies all the phases of our culture manifest unmistakable symptoms, according to Sorokin, of revolt against the sensate forms, from painting and science to economic and social relationships. After an idealistic period of transition, Sorokin predicts a rise of ideational forms in our Western culture.

Toynbee is the latest of the large-scale cyclical theorists. In *A Study of History* he analyzes twenty-one civilizations such as the Western, Hellenic, Egyptaic, Hittite, Indic, Sinic, Mexic, and Yucatec. The history of a particular nation such as England is understood, Toynbee holds, only as an integral part of the total history of the whole of Western civilization. Individual nations do not constitute his historical units; only civilizations do. A group of nations forms an entity of civilization. Each of these entities possesses an inner spiritual force, an *élan,* that drives it forward and ultimately spends itself, leading to the breakdown of the particular civilization.

The life and vitality in a civilization result from the response of this inner historical spiritual force to the multifarious challenges asserted first by nature and then by man. Once the initial obstacles of nature are overcome, the growth of a civilization depends on its great leaders. Religious leaders and creative minorities rank first in giving expression, direction, and form to the civilization. These leaders withdraw from and return to society to exert their constructive influences on the civilization. When the creative minority turns into a "dominant" minority, the civilization starts to crumble; external and internal proletariats (Toynbee defines proletariat as people *in* but not *of* the society) overwhelm the decadent civilization.

These ideas represent contemporary thinking on the problem of social change. The reader will note that many of these theories would be difficult to verify empirically. The cases which follow illustrate verifiable aspects of changes in our society.

D. SOCIOCULTURAL CHANGE IN THE
UNITED STATES

1. *Boston Three Hundred Years Ago; Boston Today* [14]

Few of us are aware of the momentous changes that have taken place in the daily living routines of people in the last half a century. If we were to project ourselves to Boston three hundred years ago, how radically different would our lives be not in the epochal historical events but in the simple every day modes of eating, sleeping, dressing, working and finding our pleasures.

Let us imagine first the physical aspects of this thriving little town of Boston which has a population of about two thousand people. The streets are narrow, deeply rutted and full of great holes. On either side of the road are drab, unpainted houses usually two stories in height, interspersed by shops and taverns each with a painted sign proclaiming their wares and adding a bright bit of color to the dun colored scene. Painted houses are a rarity and much stared at when they are to be found. Actually most houses are rather boxlike structures with little adornment of any kind. The interior of these homes have, of course, no central heating, but usually have several huge fireplaces which are poorly constructed so that rain and wind are an ever present reality. Sleeping rooms with few exceptions have no heat at all. It is customary to go to bed with a warming pan which is filled with hot coals, to take the chill and damp from the icy bedding.

Furniture is sparse and uncomfortably hard. Wooden chests are the repository for all things—clothes, bedding, papers, linen, and even food. Beds are made of a simple wooden frame with tall posts at each corner. Over this frame, cord is stretched back and forth to make a webbing and then a hay filled mattress is placed upon it. If you are a well-to-do member of the community you will have curtains about your bed to keep out the sweeping drafts while you sleep.

Stools and trestle tables are used for eating. Wooden dishes are customary although you may be the proud possessor of some pewter plates and cups. China is an extremely rare luxury. Food is quite plentiful and incredibly cheap, but water is seldom used for human consumption. Beer and cider will be your customary beverage and even the smallest child in your household will be sipping either of these liquids. Milk is used for cooking purposes but you will be considered a bit queer if you drink it. Turkey, venison, meat and fish pies, plum puddings, corn and fish dishes will appear on your table and you should have little difficulty in filling your stomach even on workman's wages. Your clothes will be made of rather coarse, homewoven materials—heavy, a bit itchy but practical and long wearing. Best clothes might be made from fine imported woolens, brocades and silks. Display in clothing is frowned on by the Puritan authorities and those low in the social stratum are forbidden by law to wear gaudy dress. Fashions change so slowly that a woman can and often does wear the same clothes from her wedding day until the day of her death.

If you are going to buy anything or sell anything you will have great difficulties in knowing whether you are making a good bargain, for the medium of exchange is uncertain. English money is forbidden for use in paying for colonial goods; material goods are paid in exchange. Some monies do trickle through however. Frequently musket balls are used in lieu of money and sometimes fur pelts are brought in as an exchange medium. Spanish silver money is also part of the currency because of the trade with the West Indies. Finally the colony of Massachusetts has decided to issue its own silver coinage and this bids fair to ease some of the difficulties.

You will learn what it is to live in a non-democratic form of government in Boston of three hundred years ago. There is a very sharp class distinction in the colony. Freemen are of the aristocracy and to qualify you must be a member of good standing of the Puritan Church; you must possess either in cash or property at least two hundred pounds and you must be industrious and law abiding. If you possess all three merits you are permitted to vote and help conduct the affairs of the colony. If you are not a member of this class, your daily life will be rigorously ordered for you by the ruling class and laws of all sorts from the spending of your leisure time to the amount of wages you shall be paid will control all your waking hours. When the colony in Massachusetts had a population of 25,000 in 1670, only 1100 people had the right to vote.

Church going is imperative if you are to participate in community life at all. Weddings, funerals, barn raisings and births will be the great occasions for celebrations and feasting. If you are a man you will spend some time in the conviviality of the tavern.

And what of life in Boston today—it is in most respects like many of the other large American cities. Its 2,500,000 metropolitan population is highly diversified in nationality and religious background. The majority religion is now Roman Catholic although the small Unitarian minority, stemming from Puritan ancestry, still consider themselves the elect. Boston teems with industry, with a great money market, with the shipping trade and with mills in its environs. Culture is still a precious commodity and the Boston Symphony Orchestra, the Fogg Museum, and lecture series of all sorts are well supported and well attended. Her educational institutions are known the world over and her better restaurants serve food which is a delight to the gourmet.

Boston politics are said to be largely in the hands of the Irish Catholics with a goodly portion of the population getting out to vote. Physically, it is a city offering the great contrasts of the new and old for Boston is proud of her history and has preserved a great many of her old buildings and historical sights. Boston is a metropolitan United States city and as such is familiar to all of us but it also contains something of the Boston of three hundred years ago and conveys a sense of great change with a sense of great continuity.

2. *Social Trends in the United States* [15]

Social trends constitute the particular directions and predominant tendencies in the associative life of man. It purports to signalize the basic pathways of change in the social life of man including his demographic, institutional, communal, and group processes and activities. The study of social trends differs from specific occurrences at any particular time or place in that it seeks to determine the general tendency of events over a period of time in one or more places.

In this treatment any allusions to specific trends will be limited to the United States. While the United States does not reflect the trends of other countries or of the world at large in all instances, in many phases, such as urbanism, centralization of governmental functions, the growth and expansion of these governmental functions, changes in the size and function of families, the spread of mass education, there are striking similarities.

Social changes are often dependent on the demographic aspects of a people. Population trends frequently determine socioeconomic trends; social trends influence the rate at which a population grows, its geographic distribution within a country and among nations, its marital status, its rate of birth and death, and its health.

The United States, which contains between six and seven per cent of the world's population, shows some interesting growth trends. While the population is increasing, the rate of growth is falling. Since 1790, the year of the first decennial census, the number of persons in the United States has increased numerically. In that year the population total was approximately four million; in 1940, the figure was nearly 132 million. However, since 1860, every decade has shown a smaller increase than the preceding one. The cessation of European immigration to the United States after World War I contributed to a sharp decline since then.

In addition to immigration, population grows by the factor of natural increase. This consists of excess of births over deaths during a given period. American birth rates still exceed death rates so that the American population continues to grow. But for the last several decades births have not exceeded deaths in the same degree. For example, in 1915 the excess of births over deaths was 10.9 per 1,000 total population; in 1940 it dropped to 7.1. Since World War II the ratio has tended to climb again, due to the large increase in births. But whether this will remain a permanent phenomenon is highly questionable.

In addition to a declining trend in the rate of population growth, the bulk of Americans are, on the average, getting to be an older people. The proportion of older persons is greater than it was years ago. One measure of our aging population is the increase in median age. In 1800 it was sixteen years; in 1940 it was approximately twenty-nine years. In 1850, 5 per cent of the population in the United States were over sixty years of age; in 1940, the figure reached 10 per cent. One estimate places the proportion over sixty by 1980 at 20 per cent, or four times the 1850 figure.

This change in the age picture of our population has largely been due to two factors. First, through the curtailment of immigration to the United States, fewer persons are added to our younger age groups, since the bulk of immigrants were in this age category. Second, the average expectancy of life has increased. Whereas the expectancy of life at birth for males was only thirty-five years at the close of the Revolution, it was fifty-five years in 1920, fifty-nine years in 1930, and sixty-three years in 1941. The life expectancy of females follows the same course, except that females live two or three years longer.

The implications of an aging population are several. It will have an effect on our economic institutions, for one. On the whole there is likely to be a decline in business investments, especially in those areas that serve the younger population. A larger proportion of our population will be in need of financial support. Recreation and leisure-time activities will probably adjust themselves to an older age pattern. Adult education will probably take on new life.

Trends in population not only alter the age-distribution picture, but also affect the nature of America's communities. The United States has indeed become a country of urban people. In 1790, the country was predominantly rural. One hundred years later, over one-third of the population was urban. By 1940, the cities accounted for 56.5 per cent of the people in the United States. However, between 1930 and the last decennial census the urban rate of growth has shown a marked decline. The urban population during these ten years has shown an increase of 7.9 per cent, the smallest percentage increase in our entire national history. Compared to the first decade of this century, which showed a 39.3 per cent increase, and to the 1920–1930 decade of 27.3 per cent, the next lowest in our history, the years of 1930–1940 stand out as a significant decline.

This decline in the urban growth rate was most probably due to the decline in the net internal migration from rural areas (especially during the depression years), the virtual disappearance of net foreign migration, and the drop in the rate of natural increase. The war has altered this trend toward greater urbanization, but whether it has made for a permanent change remains to be seen.

One other aspect of this urban trend must be mentioned. In the last fifteen years a significant shift in the distribution of urban residents has taken place. A large number of cities proper have either failed to show an increase or have actually lost population. Indeed, nearly one-third of the cities of 100,000 or more inhabitants and about one-fourth of the cities in the 25,000–100,000 size group have shown a decrease in numbers between 1930 and 1940. However, outside of the limits of these central cities but in areas close and peripheral to these cities, there has been during this same period a marked increase in population. The rise and expansion of these suburban areas has given rise to a new urban complex, the metropolitan districts. Thus, in 1940, the 140 metropolitan districts in the United States as defined by the Bureau of the Census had a total population of 62,-966,000 persons, or almost half the population of the country. Of the population resident in the metropolitan districts, 20,170,000, or 32 per cent of the total, lived in the outlying areas, that is, outside the central cities. This was 16.9 per cent greater than the figure for the previous decade.

This trend of suburbanism has serious social implications for local government, real-estate values, and ways of living. Some central cities, especially their central business districts, have been threatened by depopulation and blight. The problem of maintaining urban public services such as policing, fire protection, sanitation, education, and recreation at increasing costs in the face of declining income from taxation because of the movement to the fringes of the city has already been faced by some major cities. Traffic problems to and from the center of the city have also added to the difficult functioning of city life.

Nor does the trend of suburbanization spell the end of urbanization. It is actually a significant aspect of the total urban way of life. And the general urban trend has led to interesting speculation as to its responsibility in the formation of a unique type of person resulting from the faster tempo, the greater density of population, the anonymity of its social relations, the heterogeneity of its people, the greater mobility, its specialization, and—in general—its commercialized living. One thing is certain; the city spells a new way of life—a way of life different from the rural way of life.

Rural life, too, has shown several interesting trends in the past decades. Some of the demographic changes have already been mentioned. One might note, chiefly, the rapid decline in the birth rate, a trend that always reflects the city's ways. Farm areas, while declining in birth rates, have considerably higher rates than urban areas. Within the rural region, the 1930–1940 decade has shown a marked increase (14.5 per cent) in nonfarm population while the farm population has remained about the same.

The number and the percentage of tenant farmers in the United States increased steadily from decade to decade until 1930. In 1880, 25.6 per cent of the farmers were tenants; in 1930, 42.4 per cent. By 1940, the rate declined to 38.7 per cent. In these fluctuating trends the increases are chiefly accounted for by mortgage foreclosures and increased corporate ownership and the decreases by the shift from share-cropper status to that of wage worker.

American farming has always, on the whole, been relatively highly mechanized. This mechanization has gone forward steadily. More automobiles, tractors, trucks, and motor-driven farm implements have characterized the farm in recent decades. The percentage of all farms receiving electricity moved from 11.6 in 1935 to 27.1 in 1940. In 1941 it reached approximately 35 per cent.

The increase in the use of the machine on the farm, as well as the general advent of new technologies such as the radio and the moving picture, has broken down the isolation of rural life at greater pace during the last decades. Consolidated schools have replaced the one-room schoolhouse; the town church has grown at the expense of the open-country church; farmers' organizations have made inroads into the heretofore almost complete individualism of the farmer.

With the rise of the city and the alterations in rural life have also come changes in the nature and functions of family life in the United States. The marriage rate, except for variations due to fluctuations of the business cycle, has remained relatively stable during the last five decades. As for divorce, however, the last seventy-five years have shown a marked increase in the proportion of broken marriages in the United States. A steady decrease in the size of the family has also been characteristic in this country. In 1790 the average number of persons per household was 5.7; by 1940 it had dropped to 3.8.

Family functions have also changed. Processing of food at home has decreased during the last century. During the same years, the family responsibility for the education of its children has diminished. In fact, the school, in the form of the nursery school, has made great inroads even among preschool-age children.

Commercialized recreation in the form of theaters and ball games has also taken the family members away from home. However, radio and television have helped to retain recreation in the home. By and large, however, the family has become an instrument for personality development of children and for affectional functions.

Education has also shown significant trends in the last decades. For many years there has been a trend in education in the direction of the practical and the vocational. Technical, vocational, and trade schools have been established in our cities. The extreme vocationalism between the two world wars brought a reaction on the part of some educational leaders; a significant cry has gone out for general educational curricula.

The effect of new and better means of transportation, in general, has been in the direction of centralization of power and educational administration in state and national centers. In education, the American tradition is one of local administration. However, the educational functions of state bureaus have increased considerably over the years. Even the federal government has become more concerned with educational policy if not administration. The intrusion of state and federal centers into local education has often begun with grants-in-aid, to which later has been added some prescription as to policy.

The shift from local to centralized control in education has also characterized the trend in government. When the federal constitution was written, it provided for a federal system of government based on the principle of a division of power between the federal government and the states. There were many reasons for the selection of this type of government. The two major reasons for this were, perhaps, the fact that there was strong feeling on the part of the framers of the Constitution against powerful centralized control and the wide divergence of problems in the individual states. Consequently, the only powers of the federal government were those assigned to it in the Constitution, while all other powers remained in the hands of the individual states.

The years have shown a marked tendency to break down this system; there has been an increasing trend toward the shift of power and responsibility from local governments to state governments, and from the states to the federal government. This trend became noticeably strong during the middle of the last quarter of the nineteenth century. This expansion of the federal government can be illustrated by the greatly increased number of annual federal grants-in-aid to the states. Even prior to the last depression, between 1915 and 1930, the funds provided by the national government to the states increased more than tenfold. During the subsequent years, federal aid to states increased at an even greater rate. These federal grants have been accompanied by federal regulations concerning their use. With the complexity of problems, which often overlap state boundaries, this trend is likely to continue.

In recreation, over the past decades, the United States manifested a strong trend toward formalization and commercialization. This is consistent with the increase in urbanization; shorter working hours, making for a greater amount of leisure time; and the rise and development of new instruments of entertainment, the radio and motion pictures.

The first radio-broadcasting station in the United States began sending out programs in 1920; in 1941, 912 stations were in operation. Nearly one-half of these were associated with some major network; out of these sources poured forth, to over 50 million listeners daily, music, drama, news, lectures, debates, comments on current events, and a vast mass of advertising. In 1922 only about 60,000 American homes were equipped with radios; twenty years later there were approximately 30 million homes with radios, and the total number of sets in the country was above 56 million.

The estimated weekly attendance at the movies is over 85 million people. In 1940 the number of motion-picture theaters in this country was over 19,000 with paid admissions amounting to more than a billion dollars.

Another major recreation is athletics, with baseball, football, prize fighting, and the like drawing huge crowds. Attendance at the major professional-league baseball games for 1940 was over 10 million people, while the football "bowl" games had a total of more than 278,000.

This spectator type of recreation is seemingly the most popular form of entertainment in the country, although in recent years there has been a growing interest in active participation in different types of recreation. Municipalities and states have, in recent years, developed large numbers of parks and recreational areas for this purpose. In 1926, 43 of 48 states had state parks and areas used for recreational purposes, with a total of 2,613,271 acres. By 1939, every state had within its borders some such area, with a total expanse for the 48 states of more than six million acres. In cities, more and more park planning is being directed toward the areas where adults and children can walk in natural surroundings, engage in games or picnic with friends, row, swim, play tennis, baseball, horseshoes, and skate. Public interest in municipal recreation has definitely developed during the past quarter of the century. In 1917, six and one-half millions were spent for municipal recreation; ten years later it reached over 30 million. During the depression, with the help of federal grants the high rate of expenditures was kept up.

In addition to forms of recreation found in spectator and participant sports and in the new American interest in motorized outdoor life, organizations of every type and for every purpose have become a fundamental aspect of American life. With the increasing demand for opportunities for profitable and pleasurable use of leisure time, and with the ever growing desires of people for forms of entertainment which entail large expenditure of funds, there has grown up a vast and intricate system of clubs to take care of the many and varied interests of the citizens. Individual initiative in the use of leisure time seems to have given way somewhat to group initiative along the lines in which persons, having mutual interests, form clubs, societies, or associations. Indeed, government, philanthropic organizations, and cooperative associations are fundamental units in establishing the present-day pattern of leisure-time activities. This is due largely to the fact that there has been a growing demand for a large variety of amusements adapted to the changing seasons and to different class interests. As might be expected, the network of clubs, organizations, and associations, with a wide variety of programs, includes overlapping memberships. Many groups combine entertainment for the members with more serious social and economic interests.

The great number of these organizations is due not only to increasing free time but also to the wide and ever growing world of activity, with more freedom of movement and greater opportunities of contact with all forms of modern life. Not only are these associations interested in sports and amusements per se, but also in various social problems. Thus, much time is spent in the promotion of solutions to social and civic problems as well as in the stimulation of hobbies and special interests. It is difficult to classify in a precise way the organizations interested solely in recreation as against those which have a more serious purpose. Fraternal organizations, as leisure-time groups, have had a rather important place in the social life of American people. They seem to have reached their peak in 1925, when they had a total membership of around 35 million. Since 1925, membership has declined, interest has dwindled, and attendance at meetings has lessened.

Of more recent growth are the luncheon clubs. This movement was launched in 1910 with the organization of 16 Rotary clubs into a federation known as Rotary International. In 1916, the Kiwanis International was established. In 1917, the Lions International, the Civitan International, and the International Association of Gyro clubs was formed. In 1940, there were 25 luncheon-club federations with a total membership of about 500,000. Along with the rise of membership in men's clubs there has risen a parallel movement among women's organizations, with huge memberships and an emphasis on either pure recreation or some form of self-education and community service.

The trends in population, community, family, education, and recreation constitute the major areas of social pathways in the United States. In religion, church membership showed a decline between the wars, a tendency toward church mergers, and general inclination toward greater liberalism. In the field of labor, a marked growth of unionism; governmental participation and regulation of worker activities in the form of wages, hours, and collective bargaining; the cleavage in the organized-labor movement; the increased importance of industrial as against craft unionism; and the increase of the frequency of industrial disputes characterized the last three decades in the United States. Finally, man has begun to think in terms of "one world"—a necessity springing from the combined trends in technology, economics, and philosophy.

E. TECHNOLOGY AND SOCIOCULTURAL CHANGE

1. Manchester: The First Industrial City [16]

The rapid emergence of Manchester from a thriving manorial market town into a great industrial city follows a pattern of change that was duplicated in rapid succession in many parts of England with the introduction of new machinery and an almost complete reorganization of production which had its revolutionizing effect not alone in production and marketing but in the way in which people lived.

Manchester as early as 1641 was importing linen yarn from the Irish, weaving it, and returning it in its finished state. It was a flourishing trading center for its locality where the lord of the manor taxed articles brought for sale into the market. It was governed by a court which possessed nearly all the powers of present municipal corporations. Before 1780 when Richard Arkwright introduced its first factory, there was a gradual emergence of a powerful class of commercial men together with local gentry, clergymen, lawyers and physicians who had begun to dominate the scene in the changeover from an agrarian economy to a commercial one. The bulk of the population were weavers, spinners, dyers, small shopkeepers. The work of spinning and weaving was done either in the workers' homes or in the homes of small masters. One of the notable changes that technology brought was not only the substitution of the factory for the home but a change of the work done by men and women. Prior to the advent of the factory spinning was women's work and weaving men's work. In the mill, spinning became the work of the men, weaving the work of women and both were dependent on the help of children.

In the space of seventy-nine years, 1772–1851, the population of Manchester and environs rose from 25,000 to 367,232. This expansion was due of course to the ever increasing demand for labor brought about by the geometrical increase of new factories and new industries. Up to 1780 most of the people lived within a radius of a quarter of a mile from the city's center, but the population pressure together with the need for new factory sites brought about an ecological pattern very similar to that which is found in present day industrial centers. The old homes became the location of new factories and the city's residential areas moved outward. Around the factories grew the slum housing so frequently found around industrial sites in all parts of the world. Between 1830 and 1850 there grew up in Manchester the concentric patterns frequently found in all major cities in modern times but which was an entirely new pattern at that time.

Although the growth was chaotic and in a sense planless, it followed a cultural development which foreshadowed industrialization and urbanization. Political power and social leadership changed over to the new factory owners, bankers, and wealthy merchants and became centered in propagating the interests of this new class. The laboring class was also sharply different from the old artisan group in the background, interests and a way of life. They were made up of landless rural laborers, many coming from Ireland, remnants of the old artisan class and ambitious and enterprising men from all walks of life, few having been born in Manchester.

A significant change in the manner of working due to the factory system had a real influence on the every day patterns of familial behavior. During the pre-factory days it was the family who determined working hours, amount of production, division of labor and the marketing of the product. With the advent of the factory, the factory overseer of necessity set the working times, the amount of work and the kinds of work to be done. This change was basic and brought with it a tremendous adjustment for the men particularly. Many of the factory owners of that period declared that they used women and children not because they were to be had at a cheaper wage but primarily because they accepted the discipline of the factory system with a docility which the men could not bring themselves to do. How great a problem this was can be seen by the extensive use of the blacklist among owners of those who would not or could not adjust to the loss of individual working ways.

More than a third of the employees employed in the 16 major industries in Manchester in 1851 were women. The use of women's labor was of course not revolutionary itself because women did a great share of this type of work prior to the advent of the factory. But the work was done at home under the supervision of the father of the family, and the family worked as a unit. Under the new system various members of the family worked either in various factories, or if they worked in the same one had no direct contact with one another. The dominance of the home as an economic center was completely shifted and had as a consequence a great loosening of familial ties with a real breakdown of much of the social control extended by the family.

The free labor market and the constant necessity to sell one's labor for the best price one could get brought with it much economic insecurity and social distress. The new industrialists found themselves with the problems of channelizing their new labor force and developing new institutions for the purpose of social control. Politically this meant creating a municipal administration which could cope with the necessity for new sanitary installations, health measures and law enforcement. A struggle between the shopkeeping class and the industrialists ensued and ultimately a municipal charter was granted which enables the municipal government to extend and expand much needed services.

New institutions were formed both of philanthropic and educational nature as well as recreational centers supported largely by the industrial class. Parks, concerts and botanical parks and libraries were developed for the amusement of working groups. Newspapers began to play an influential role in the city. The workers themselves found new interests largely due to the close association of peoples. Lodges, cooperative and socialist societies and mass meetings formed a new bond and a new means of communication.

It has been said that the most dominant characteristic of this changeover for the mass of people in Manchester was from individualism to regimentation, a regimentation largely due to the urban milieu rather than superimposed by government. Standards and values were regimented by what people saw and desired—new products becoming available to the mass, new forms of entertainment, new opportunities all extended their powerful influence to bring people into an adjustment with the new milieu. What was lost was lamented by some, but the new exerted a powerful force.

2. *The Role of the Machine in American Culture* [15]

Modern man has often been characterized as a creature of machines. Almost every aspect of man's life is related to mechanics in some form or other. Can we imagine how sharply our mode of life would be changed if some force were to destroy at the same time the electric-light bulb, the electric motor, the automobile, the telephone, the radio, the airplane, the tractor, and the diesel engine? Numerous consequences would result which might seem only remotely connected with these machines. For example, we could not get around nearly so much as we now do, and it would take us three or even four times as long as it does now. Our cities would be considerably smaller and fewer in number. Many more people would have to devote themselves to the growing of food. News of what was happening outside of our own community could not reach us so easily, so completely, or so rapidly as it does today. Wars would be far less destructive to human life and property. Families would probably be larger than they are at present. In short, although these illustrations could be multiplied endlessly, we can see that just these few major inventions that we have listed are enough to influence our lives very strongly.

Man had indeed become so dependent on technology, and his social institutions have been so modified by the use of machines, that the period in time in which we live is often referred to as the Machine Age.

We seldom think about the machines that surround us and that are ever present in doing a multitude of tasks for us. We readily accept new technological inventions without much conscious thought, because we are machine minded. We have come to expect machines to replace all sorts of chores that were customarily done by hand.

The Machine Influences Business. The machine, along with various sources of power, gave rise to the factory system. Under this new mode of manufacture, men who had previously plied their crafts of hand spinning, weaving, and looming at home had to go to the mills and factories to do their work. The factory system can be said to be the cornerstone of our modern capitalistic economy.

The amount of goods which a man could produce in one day increased tremendously with the aid of power-driven machinery. A worker in a modern textile mill can produce as much cloth in eight hours as many hundreds, perhaps thousands, of men could produce 150 years ago when most of the work was done by hand or with the aid of crude and simple machines. Technological inventions have led, therefore, to an increase in the production of goods as well as in the creation of many new goods.

Not only was the new machinery responsible for the rise of the factory system and for a vast increase in the type and amount of goods produced, but the unit of production and operation became ever larger.

As machines grew in size and number, the method of doing business was altered to meet the new technology. Thus the corporation was created to take care of the problems brought by the complex machinery that was introduced. Many businesses became so large that no single person could finance the cost and installation of the new machinery and operate successfully. A new means of arranging for the financing of this type of business was introduced whereby a corporation was formed which sold shares of stock to anyone interested in investing money in the venture. The stockholder then became a part owner of the company and the money raised by this method was used for the purpose of building factories and obtaining machinery. When the company made a profit, stockholders participated in the sharing of the profit.

In 1909, two hundred of our largest corporations owned and controlled 26,063 millions of our capital. Ten years later, their assets rose to 43,719 millions, and in 1929, they increased to 81,074 millions. It is quite easy to observe that new machines have permitted greater concentration of wealth and have also brought about larger business and production units.

With the greater complexity of large-scale industries, there arose a need for a different kind of supervision and management than that which had been performed in the small shop, usually by the owner himself. In large plants it became necessary to place increased emphasis upon the supervisory and managerial aspects of the work. This new need also increased the importance of the personnel man and the efficiency expert. Both are concerned with increasing and promoting plant productivity. The personnel man seeks to obtain the best possible adjustment of the employee to his work, while the efficiency expert tries to develop methods whereby the best use of available machinery and equipment will be made.

Does the Machine Make for Unemployment? The question very frequently raised is whether the machine is responsible for unemployment. This is indeed a difficult question to answer. It is certainly true that workers are idle because there is no buying market for their products. But the lack of such a market can scarcely be attributed to any one factor in our economic system. Rather it may be said that it is the general functioning of the whole economic system that might be held responsible for depressions and unemployment.

However, it is obvious that the machine will cause temporary unemployment. With greater efficiency of machines, fewer and fewer men are required to operate them. In some cases, machines are entirely automatic and require no human manipulation. Thus the automatic elevators in apartment houses frequently oil themselves, turn the power on and off, and operate with so simple a mechanism that any passenger can run them.

We can see that in the case of the automatic elevator a permanent operator is no longer needed and thus he becomes unemployed. Similarly, at the beginning of the twentieth century the horse-and-carriage industry employed about a million men whose work became, for the most part, unnecessary when the automobile came into general use. It is important to remember, however, that while men lost their jobs when the elevator became automatic, the demand for automatic elevators steadily increased. Thus the elevator industry expanded, and many more persons were needed to manufacture and install them than were originally employed in operating them.

The same process occurred with the workers in the horse-and-carriage industry. While approximately one million men lost their means of livelihood with the emergence of the automobile, the automobile industry developed to a point where many millions were being employed in the production of this invention. The new industry not only gave work to those directly connected with the manufacture of cars but to many additional millions in garages, filling stations, bus driving, steel and rubber industries, trailer camps, road building, and so on.

Thus, while the machine does cause unemployment temporarily, new inventions give impetus to the expansion of old industries and the creation of new ones, so that there is a much greater demand for labor, and those who are initially displaced by the new machine can be reabsorbed in other types of work. In times of depression, the worker displaced by a machine has a more difficult time in becoming reabsorbed, but it cannot truly be said that the machine alone is responsible for unemployment in depression periods. It is rather the dislocation and malfunctioning of our whole business and economic structure that causes joblessness.

The Machine Has Made People More Interdependent. The fact that machines are making people more dependent upon one another is clearly seen on farms and in rural areas. Here again, the most immediate consequence of technology has been in economic production. The constant increase in mechanization on the farm has resulted in a dramatic increase of produce raised annually by an individual farm worker. In 1787, the surplus food produced by 19 farmers in this country was sufficient to feed only one city person. But in recent years, 19 people on farms have been able to produce enough food to supply 56 nonfarm people in this country and have enough left over for 10 people living in other countries.

It is easy to see, then, what part the machine has played in the development of cities. Only when the farm could produce enough to support more people than those found on the farms themselves could cities with large populations rise, because city people have, after all, to depend on farmers for their food. And more and more people were needed in the cities because the factories were located there. Quite naturally, therefore, country people started to migrate to urban centers. Besides there being a greater need for workers in factories, there was less need for them on the farms, where machines were able to perform the tasks of many hand laborers. Technology also made it possible to concentrate a large number of persons in a comparatively small area by providing rapid transportation between work and home; huge apartment dwellings; electricity and gas for lighting, heating, and cooking; a constant water supply; and sanitation facilities.

Some people are inclined to attribute the very existence of the modern city to the machine. The communication and transportation inventions greatly facilitated the exchange of goods between the city and the farm and from one remote area to another. Raw goods and produce could get to the city person; he, in turn, could send his manufactured product back to the rural dweller. The machine thus permitted a greater specialization and a greater division of labor among people in different areas. It made one region within a country dependent on another, and one country dependent on other countries. The United States, for instance, buys rubber, coffee, cane sugar, and tin from foreign countries. They, in turn, buy machinery, automobiles, beef, cotton, and so on from us. Never before were we in such close contact with the rest of the world. Through the radio, people in San Francisco know what is happening in Russia almost as soon as the events occur. Technology has surely caused the world to shrink, thus making for interdependence.

The Machine Has Also Changed the Family. We are all familiar with the old adage, "Woman's place is in the home." In bygone centuries, women had many home responsibilities, such as cooking the meals, supervising the training of children (particularly daughters), sewing, spinning yarn, weaving cloth, candle and soap making, and a multitude of other tasks. Homemaking, however, is considerably changed today, largely due to the advance of technology. Meals are readily available in restaurants, or much of them come already prepared in cans. Small children are sent to nursery schools, and older ones spend much of their time in school or engaged in supervised recreation. Clothes are easily bought ready made. Even mending is done by many laundries and cleaning establishments. As a result, women have found themselves with leisure time on their hands. Many of them have gone to work for wages outside of the home.

The functions of the family have changed. Social activities and recreation outside the home have increased. The school has supplanted the home as an educational institution. In short, the family has become primarily the unit of affection, procreation, and personality development of children. Because of the curtailment of many functions of the family by the machine, some people even attribute the increase in divorce to the machine.

Government Has Been Gradually Changed by the Indirect Influence of Technology. Just as technology affected the organization and integration of industry and business, so it pervaded government. The changing structure of our economic life created problems which became the concern of all. Unemployment, agricultural distress, exploitation of the laborer, exploitation of the consumer, competition of foreign markets, the rise of monopoly, and widespread crime and disease called for governmental participation and control of business. These are the reasons we have a Securities Exchange Commission that looks after financial trading in Wall Street. We also have laws which state the number of hours one may work. Many other laws, too, are now governing people's businesses.

Consolidation and centralization of government have also risen with technological development. The airplane, bus, truck, diesel engine, radio, and telephone operate in the spread of industries across state and even regional lines. Thus the state line tends to lose its significance, creating problems which must be handled by a highly centralized government.

Technology has also left its imprint on the schools. Consolidation and centralization on the elementary and secondary levels; the rise of visual educational techniques; specialization in institutions of higher learning; and the growth of technical, vocational, and trade schools are all instances of the impact of technology.

From this brief summation, it would appear reasonable to conclude that few, if any, areas of our social life have been untouched by technological influences. Notable changes in our customs and ways of doing things have been closely bound up with major machine innovations. There is every reason to believe that this close tie between men and machines will persist and that man-made technology will continue to change man's society.

3. *The Social Effects of a Single Material Invention: The Radio*

In general, the relation of social change to technological inventions may be thought of from the standpoint of primary and derivative influences. By primary influences are meant those immediate results brought about by the first contacts that an invention makes with an individual, a number of individuals, or a group. By derivative influences are meant the changes that occur in a series of events following each other as links in a chain.

The influence of an invention on society is a function of the degree of its adoption. The extent of adoption determines the degree of social change, because to the extent that society adopts an invention—to the extent that an invention spreads through and is used by the members of a group—it has changed the mode and content of the life of the group from its previously existent, preadoptive state. The adoption of an invention adds to, replaces part of, or supplements the culture of a society.

Social adoption of an invention does not inevitably follow the invention; the advent of inventions do not lead to immediate adoption. Adoption follows only after a favorable social response, reception, and acceptance of the invention. But there are also resistances to the adoption of inventions. In fact, resistance may be found present, in one form or another, to almost every invention. The automobile was spurned (frequently with the dictum "get a horse"); the adoption of the telephone was slow; the skyscraper was attacked; and numerous other innovations have been resisted. Adoption, acceptance, and spread of an invention follows after these resistances are overcome. The following is a listing of the multiple derivative social effects of the invention and adoption of the radio.*[17]

* By permission from *Recent Social Trends,* by President's Research Committee on Recent Social Trends. Copyright, 1933, McGraw-Hill Book Company, Inc.

I. On Uniformity and Diffusion

1. Homogeneity of peoples increased because of like stimuli.
2. Regional differences in culture become less pronounced.
3. The penetration of the musical and artistic city culture into villages and country.
4. Ethical standards of the city made more familiar to the country.
5. Distinctions between social classes and economic groups lessened.
6. Isolated regions are brought in contact with world events.
7. Illiterates find a new world opened to them.
8. Restrictions of variation through censorship resulting in less experiment and more uniformity.
9. Favoring the widely spread languages.
10. Standardization of diction and discouragement of dialects.
11. Aids in correct pronunciation, especially foreign words.
12. Cultural diffusion among nations, as of United States into Canada and vice versa.

II. On Recreation and Entertainment

13. Another agency for recreation and entertainment.
14. The enjoyment of music popularized greatly.
15. Much more frequent opportunity for good music in rural areas.
16. The manufacture of better phonograph music records encouraged.
17. The contralto favored over sopranos through better transmission.
18. Radio amplification lessens need for loud concert voices.
19. Establishment of the melodramatic playlet with few characters and contrasted voices.
20. Revival of old songs, at least for a time.
21. Greater appreciation of the international nature of music.
22. Entertainment of invalids, blind, partly deaf, frontiersmen, etc.
23. With growth of the reformative idea, more prison installations.
24. Interests in sports increased, it is generally admitted.
25. Slight stimulation to dancing at small gatherings.
26. Entertainment on trains, ships, and automobile.

III. On Transportation

27. Radio beams, enabling aviators to remain on course.
28. Directional receivers guide to port with speed and safety.
29. Aid furnished to ships in distress at sea.
30. Greater safety to airplanes in landing. Radio system also devised now for blind landing.
31. Chronometers are checked by time signals.
32. Broadcast of special weather reports aid the aviator.

33. Brokerage offices on ships made possible.
34. Receipt of communications en route by air passengers.
35. Communication between airplanes and ships.
36. Ships directed for better handling of cargoes.

IV. On Education

37. Colleges broadcast classroom lectures.
38. Broadcasting has aided adult education.
39. Used effectively in giving language instruction.
40. Purchasing of textbooks increased slightly, it is reported.
41. Grammar school instruction aided by broadcasting.
42. Health movement encouraged through broadcast of health talks.
43. Current events discussions broadcast.
44. International relations another important topic discussed, with some social effects, no doubt.
45. Broadcasting has been used to further some reform movements.
46. The government broadcasts frequently on work of departments.
47. Many talks to mothers on domestic science, child care, etc.
48. Discussion of books aids selection and stimulates readers.
49. The relationship of university and community made closer.
50. Provision of discussion topics for women's clubs.
51. Lessens gap schooling may make between parents and children.
52. New pedagogical methods, i.e., as to lectures and personality.
53. Greater knowledge of electricity spread.
54. The creation of a class of radio amateurs.

V. On the Dissemination of Information

55. Wider education of farmers on agricultural methods.
56. Prevention of loss in crops by broadcasting weather reports.
57. Education of farmers on the treatment of parasites.
58. Market reports of produce permitting better sales.
59. Important telephone messages between continents.
60. Small newspapers by radio broadcasting.
61. News dissemination in lieu of newspapers, as in British strike.
62. News to newspapers by radio broadcasting.
63. Transmission of photographic likenesses, letters, etc., especially overseas where wire is not yet applicable.
64. Quicker detection of crime and criminals, through police automobile patrols equipped with radio.

VI. On Religion

65. Discouragement, it is said, of preachers of lesser abilities.
66. The urban type of sermon disseminated to rural regions.

67. Services possible where minister cannot be supported.
68. Invalids and others unable to attend church enabled to hear religious services.
69. Churches that broadcast are said to have increased attendance.
70. Letter writing to radio religious speakers gives new opportunities for confession and confidence.

VII. On Industry and Business
71. In industry, radio sales led to decline in phonograph business.
72. Better phonograph recording and reproducing now used.
73. Lowering of cable rates followed radio telegraph movement.
74. Point to point communication in areas without wires.
75. The business of the lyceum bureau, etc., suffered greatly.
76. Some artists who broadcast demanded for personal appearance in concerts.
77. The market for the piano declined. Radio may be a factor.
78. Equipment cost of hotel and restaurant increased.
79. A new form of advertising has been created.
80. New problems of advertising ethics, as to comments on competing products.
81. An important factor in creating a market for new commodities.
82. Newspaper advertising affected.
83. Led to creation of new magazine.
84. An increase in the consumption of electricity.
85. Provision of employment for 200,000 persons.
86. Some decreased employment in phonograph and other industries.
87. Aid to power and traction companies in discovering leaks, through the assistance of radio listeners.
88. Business of contributing industries increased.

VIII. On Occupations
89. Music sales and possibly song writing have declined. Studies indicate that broadcasting is a factor.
90. A new provision for dancing instruction.
91. A new employment for singers, vaudeville artists, etc.
92. New occupations: announcer, engineer, advertising salesmen.
93. Dance orchestras perhaps not increased but given prominence.

IX. On Government and Politics
94. In government, a new regulatory function necessitated.
95. Censorship problem raised because of charges of swearing, etc.
96. Legal questions raised beginning with the right to the air.
97. New specialization in law; four air law journals existing.
98. New problems of copyright have arisen.
99. New associations created, some active in lobbying.
100. Executive pressure on legislatures, through radio appeals.

101. A democratizing agency, since political programs and speeches are designed to reach wide varieties of persons at one time.

102. Public sentiment aroused in cases of emergencies like drought.

103. International affairs affected because of multiplication of national contracts.

104. Rumors and propaganda on nationalism have been spread.

105. Limits in broadcasting bands foster international arrangements.

106. Communication facilitated among belligerents in warfare.

107. Procedures of the nominating conventions altered somewhat.

108. Constituencies are kept in touch with nomination conventions.

109. Political campaigners reach larger audiences.

110. The importance of the political mass meeting diminished.

111. Presidential "barnstorming" and front porch campaign changed.

112. Nature of campaign costs affected.

113. Campaign speeches tend to be more logical and cogent.

114. Appeal to prejudice of local groups lessened.

115. An aid in raising campaign funds.

116. Campaign speaking by a number of party leaders lessened.

117. Campaign promises over radio said to be more binding.

118. High government officers who broadcast are said to appear to public less distant and more familiar.

X. On Other Inventions

119. Development stimulated in other fields, as in military aviation.

120. The vacuum tube, a radio invention, is used in many fields, as for lowering elevators, automobile train controls, converting electric currents, applying the photo-electric cell, as hereinafter noted, a new science is being developed by the vacuum tube.

121. Television was stimulated by the radio.

122. Developments in use of phonograph stimulated by the radio.

123. The teletype is reported to have been adapted to radio.

124. Amplifiers for radio and talking pictures improved.

125. Geophysical prospecting aided by the radio.

126. Sterilization of milk by short waves, milk keeping fresh for a week.

127. Extermination of insects by short waves, on small scale, reported.

128. Body temperature raised to destroy local or general infections.

129. The condenser with radio tubes used variously in industry, for controlling thickness of sheet material, warning of dangerous gas, etc.

130. Watches and clocks set automatically by radio.

XI. Miscellaneous

131. Morning exercises encouraged a bit.

132. The noise problem of loud speakers has caused some regulation.

133. A new type of public appearance for amateurs.
134. Some women's clubs are said to find the radio a competitor.
135. Late hours have been ruled against in dormitories and homes.
136. Humor as a mode of expression perhaps hampered in broadcasting.
137. Growth of suburbs perhaps encouraged a little bit.
138. Letter writing to celebrities a widespread practice.
139. Irritation against possible excesses of advertising.
140. Development of fads of numerology and astrology encouraged.
141. Automobiles with sets have been prohibited for safety, in some places.
142. Additions to language as "A baby broadcasting all night."
143. Aids in locating persons wanted.
144. Used in submarine detection.
145. Wider celebration of anniversaries aids nationalism.
146. Weather broadcasts used in planning family recreation.
147. Fuller enjoyment of gala events.
148. Home duties and isolation more pleasant.
149. Widens gap between famous and near famous.
150. Creative outlet for youth in building sets.

F. RESISTANCE TO INVENTIONS

We mentioned in the introduction to the last section that frequently an invention finds resistance to its adoption. Several writers have attempted to isolate the reasons for resistance to the adoption of inventions. W. F. Ogburn has accounted for ten general reasons for resistance to technological innovations.[18] Bernhard J. Stern discovered fourteen factors involved in society's resistance to medical innovations.[19] The major factors acting as impediments to the spread of technological innovations may be listed as follows:

1. Failure of inventions themselves due to their own mechanical inefficiencies and inadequacies.

2. Tendency of people to adhere to well-established habits and ways of life, old ways tending to become sacred ways.

3. The difficulty in the acceptance of the new with increase in age. Early ways and habits tend to dominate.

4. The greater the group homogeneity and group solidarity the greater the opposition to innovation.

5. Economic profits as a factor in technological innovation in industrial capitalism.

6. Opposition to inventions causing extensive societal dislocations.

7. Vested interests. Groups and segments in society tend to oppose innovations that threaten their preferred *status quo.*

In the following case study we have an account of the opposition to the spread of anesthesia.[20]

The commonplace use of various agents for the relief of pain in surgical operations is taken for granted at the present time, and the most important discovery of American medicine in the last century is in danger of being forgotten. Surgery without anesthetics is too horrible to contemplate, yet not until 1846 was there a practical means of controlling pain. But at the time there were four principal claimants of the title of discovery, all of them Americans and all responsible for so much bickering and blustering that the true magnitude of the discovery was clouded and is today forgotten, while all the mechanical products of American ingenuity are still praised as the greatest contribution to humanity.

The slightest operation in pre-anesthetic times was deservedly viewed with horror and repugnance. John Hunter, the famous English surgeon, spoke of operations as "humiliating examples of the inexpertness of science," and of surgeons as "no better than armed savages."

The surgeons themselves looked upon operative surgery as the lowest and poorest branch of the profession, and care and finesse were forgotten in the attempt to minimize the patient's suffering.

Still there were some who became hardened to the profession, and in 1784 one James Moore, a member of the Surgeons Company of London, published a pamphlet descriptive of a "Method of Preventing or Diminishing Pain in Several Operations of Surgery." There was no remarkable advance described in his paper, but the introductory paragraphs are so accurate a comment on early medicine that they are well worth repeating.

He says:

"If any of the professions were in a particular manner to be distinguished by the name of humane, we might naturally expect—it would be that whose particular object it is to relieve the sufferings of humanity. And, if a greater degree of compassion and sympathy were looked for among any one class than any other, we should expect to find it in the breasts of those who pass their lives in the duties of so benevolent a profession as physicians. Physicians have been accused of a want of feeling for the distresses of human nature and surgeons of actual cruelty."

The lack of consideration for those in pain was not, however, due to lack of interest but to a lack of agents to control pain. From the earliest period of medical history there are stories of various schemes to control pain. Opium, laudanum, alcohol and such drugs were tried and found wanting. After Mesmer spread his mysterious doctrines, hypnotism was used with considerable success. But there was nothing that was easily and universally applicable to all cases, and the general public had good reason for avoiding the early hospitals.

It remained for a young American citizen to perfect a process that is still in use with very little change. The natural expectation would be that he would be rewarded for his work, but, to the contrary, never was a man more abused and never were more absurd attempts made to discredit a product of patient and careful experimentation. Even today there are some groups that wish to deny any honor to him, although for the great part this is due to local sectional jealousy and not from the violent personal hatred that was so evident at the time.

There were several individuals, all of whom were possessed of sufficient experimental information to obtain credit for the discovery, but either through fear, carelessness or lack of proper appreciation of its value they all withheld their knowledge till after Dr. W. T. G. Morton had braved the unknown and demonstrated the possibilities of ether. A careful study of the evidence can not help but convince the unprejudiced observer that Morton was alone responsible for the introduction of ether into use as an anesthetic, although Dr. Horace Wells, of Hartford, Connecticut, and Dr. Charles Jackson, of Boston, were working along the same lines and Morton very probably worked with them to some extent. Dr. Crawford Long, of Atlanta, Georgia, had used ether prior to Morton, but as I shall show later did not fully appreciate the importance of the material.

Morton was born in Charlton, Worcester County, Massachusetts, on August 19, 1819. His education was slightly better than the ordinary and from earliest childhood he tried to fit himself to become a physician. For various reasons, principally lack of funds, he was unable to achieve his ambition and we find him in early manhood shifting back and forth from one job to another. A disastrous business venture caused him to become dissatisfied with a commercial career, and he decided to take up some profession, even though it could not be the very one he wanted. The dental profession had just broken away from medicine and founded its own schools, and as this had some resemblance to his earlier desire, young Morton decided to take up dentistry.

At this period, dentistry left much to be desired. Dr. Chapin A. Harris, a founder of the first dental school, said in 1840: "The profession is crowded with individuals, ignorant alike of its theory and practice, and hence its character has suffered in public estimation—the calling of the dentist has been resorted to by the ignorant and illiterate and, I am sorry to say, in too many instances by the unprincipled. . . ." This was none too severe an indictment, and it was only through the efforts of such men as Harris and Morton that dentistry was to survive as a separate profession and eventually become recognized as one of public necessity.

The Baltimore College of Dental Surgery was founded in 1840, and Morton was one of the early students. While there he met Horace Wells and later they set up in partnership in Boston. As usual with such affairs there was not enough business for both and they separated, Wells going to Hartford and Morton staying in Boston.

At this time there were many lecturers touring the country who gave entertainments at the clubs and lyceums, where the natives of the smaller communities whiled away the winter hours. Among these was a Mr. G. Q. Colton, who came to Hartford and gave a demonstration and lecture on nitrous oxide, or "laughing gas," as it was popularly known. When the gas is administered in an impure state the characteristic symptoms of exhilaration are quite amusing to an audience and his lecture was very generally successful. Dr. Wells was very much interested and induced Colton to give a private demonstration on December 11, 1844. At this time Wells noticed that the subject was immune to physical pain. This fact made him wonder whether or not he could use it for his purposes, so he voluntarily took the nitrous oxide. Wells experimented during the winter and used his own patients as subjects. Early in 1845 he went to Boston to give a demonstration before Dr. John Warren's class of medical students. Owing to poor equipment or haphazard administration he was totally unsuccessful, for the patient cried out, the students jeered and Wells returned to Hartford discouraged and discredited. His lack of experience alone prevented him from being successful, but the entire matter so weighed on his high-strung mind that he retired from practice, and after a short stay abroad he committed suicide. This tragic ending, together with Wells' pleasing personality, did much to bring trouble on Morton's head at a later date. Wells should have all the credit that is justly due him, but if the world had been compelled to wait for some development to come from his work, there would have been a much longer period of time before the process was entirely perfected. As a matter of fact nitrous oxide was practically abandoned until G. Q. Colton resurrected the method in 1862.

Morton had assisted Wells at this fiasco and they must have discussed the subject thoroughly, but outside of the fact that Wells tried and failed at a public demonstration, while Morton tried and succeeded, there is no reason to believe that one helped the other to any great extent. The inhalation of fumes in medical practice was no new feature; in fact, ether was used in extreme cases of consumption and had been used as a local refrigerant at various times. Wells and Morton were working along the same lines and it is no wonder that it is difficult to assign credit definitely to one or the other, for they were associates and students together during the entire period, up until Wells's public demonstration. Morton had begun to work along different lines, and he drew as much inspiration from other sources as he did from Wells.

After the break in partnership, Morton had prospered, in fact, work came in so rapidly that he was compelled to hire several assistants. He had made several improvements in dental techniques, and he was one of the best known practitioners in the city. His craving for a medical education still remained unsatisfied, so that in 1844 he entered Harvard Medical School. Morton was required to select one man from among the medical men of the city as preceptor or guide, and he chose Dr. Charles T. Jackson, then acknowledged the foremost chemist of the city and the one man most likely to help Morton in his work. The latter had not completely hidden the fact that he hoped to find some agent capable of deadening pain and Jackson had suggested sulphuric ether as a local application over sensitive tissue and they had discussed the properties of several other drugs at various times. Jackson claimed later that he knew that sulphuric ether would produce stupefaction when inhaled, but he did not make any such assertion publicly prior to Morton's demonstration.

The few known facts concerning ether impressed Morton and he set himself to determine all the properties of the substance. He read what little he could find and experimented with ether on small animals and on himself. It was customary for those who knew a little about ether to inhale the fumes up to the point where dizziness and a slight degree of intoxication was produced. This "ether jag" was well known among medical students and chemists and was practiced more or less openly. Morton tried to carry the state beyond the intoxication stage and at one time made himself deathly ill by inhaling the fumes of ether and opium together. His attendance at the medical school must have been rather sketchy, for he was carrying on these experiments together with his dental practice at the same time.

On September 30, 1846, he administered the ether to one Eben Frost for the extraction of a tooth. The next day the Boston *Evening Journal* published a news item concerning this event. Morton then felt that he must give a public demonstration, so he went to Dr. John Warren, Professor of surgery at the medical school, and asked permission to appear before the surgical clinic at the Massachusetts General Hospital. Warren had known Morton for some time and had a good opinion of the latter's professional attainments, so he readily gave consent. In this matter Morton showed that he was willing to jeopardize his reputation by appearing before the same group that had condemned Wells.

At that time the Massachusetts General Hospital was the largest and best in the city of Boston, and in addition to its size and convenience had a surgical staff that was second to none in the country. The building was an impressive structure, standing as it did near the Charles River, where that stately Bulfinch dome and granite columns at the entrance gave an air of dignity and eminence that was well upheld by the standards of medical practice in the institution. It was especially noted for the neatness and cleanness of the interior, a matter that was as generally emphasized in the hospitals of that time as it is today.

The operating amphitheater was directly under the dome and presented a much different appearance than the tiled and aseptic rooms now in use. Around about the old room were large cases containing surgical instruments, while chairs and tables of curious and unusual construction were scattered here and there about the pit. The many hooks, rings, pulleys and other restraining devices that were to be found on the walls all testified to the necessary brutality of surgery of the period. The profound learning of Boston medical society was shown by the presence of an Egyptian mummy whose lugubrious countenance must have been an ever-inspiring spectacle in this den of horrors. The surgeons themselves were accustomed to come directly from their offices in all the glory of whiskers, stovepipe hats and frock coats, with their spare instruments in their pockets, for sterilization was as yet unknown and patients still died of "bilious fevers" and "humours." There was generally a crowd of medical students on the benches that sloped up in tiers from the pit, and their appearance could not have been very inspiring, for the students of that age were notoriously unkempt.

Warren had set the date for October 16, 1846, and there was to be a representative gathering of the surgeons of the city. There had already been much angry discussion as to the possibility of Morton doing what he claimed, and there was a considerable group that did not like him personally, for his rather shy nature and the fact that he was only a dentist or at best merely a medical student was not entirely in his favor.

There was great difficulty in getting an inhaler suitable for the occasion. As there was no precedent for this work, Morton was accustomed to administer the ether from a bottle with a long snout that was inserted in the patient's mouth and on which he sucked rather than by the administration of the ether with a mask over the mouth and nostrils as is done today. The instrument maker was not able to devise an appliance that entirely satisfied Morton and at last he took a hand and made something up to his own specifications. Warren was kept waiting beyond the time agreed upon, and he had about decided that Morton had failed him, so that he turned to his colleagues and said, "As Dr. Morton has not arrived, I presume he is otherwise engaged." Just then Morton came. The patient was willing to have anything done to alleviate the pain and with few preliminaries the administration began. The spectators rather expected a repetition of the Wells fiasco, but nothing unusual happened and the patient soon lapsed into a deep slumber. Morton turned to Warren and said, "Your patient is ready, sir"; and the operation was begun while an astounded silence fell on the room. Accustomed as the surgeons were to the struggles and torture of their patients, this seemed like black magic. Warren finished and broke the silence with, "Gentlemen, this is no humbug." Dr. Bigelow chimed in with, "I have seen something today that will go round the world." There should have been a prayer of thanksgiving offered up in the old Puritan town on that occasion if ever.

The news spread rapidly and Morton was called upon to administer the ether for many cases. There were many references to the discovery in the Boston and New York papers, at first quite complimentary, but soon there was criticism and doubt as to the merit of the preparation. Morton had added some aromatic oils to the sulphuric ether to disguise the odor, but he had told the surgeons at the hospital that the active agent was none other than the ether. There was nothing essentially wrong in Morton's conduct in this regard, for he had assumed an immense amount of risk in his experimental and practical use of the agent, and the unpleasant results that followed when the application was in unskilled hands only emphasized this point.

Unexpected opposition came from some of the clergy, based on the assumption that pain was the direct consequence of original sin and therefore must be endured. Morton was threatened with prosecution and there was general condemnation of this terrible drug that set aside the laws of God and man. Dire pictures were painted of the use of this drug by criminals and all the hysterical fire of misguided religious zeal was brought to bear upon the matter.

One clergy man wrote of ether as "a decoy in the hands of Satan, apparently offering itself to bless Woman, but in the end it will harden society and rob God of the deep earnest cries that rise in time of trouble and help." Such stupidity seems incredible, but there were to be even more serious attempts to discredit Morton. No scurrility was too harsh to be applied to him, and the half truths and slighting comment often came from his neighbors and professional associates, the ones who were the first to be freed from the intolerable agony of pain that had so long burdened the human race.

Following the custom of time, Morton patented his discovery. There is no doubt but that he hoped to profit by his effort, and in any other branch of endeavor there would have been no objection. However, there has always been considerable feeling among the medical and dental practitioners that humanity has need of every process for the alleviation of suffering without let or hindrance, so that rights and patents held by any one practitioner are foreign to the spirit of medical justice. Be that as it may; Morton gave his formula freely to the Massachusetts General Hospital without charge and only intended to profit by the sale of the preparation, called "Letheon." But everyone knew that he was using ether and there was no particular need of buying a patented preparation when the pure ether could be obtained from a chemist.

It is interesting to note that the physician-author, Oliver Wendell Holmes, in a personal letter to Morton suggested the use of a new term "anesthesia" to describe the state produced by the application of the drug. Dr. Holmes continued as a friend and supporter, and it was only through the help of such men as Holmes, Warren and Bigelow that Morton was able to weather the storm that was about to break.

The opposition grew stronger within the first few months of the new year (1847) and the storm of protest and recrimination aimed at Morton fouled his fame and even today is responsible for the lack of appreciation of his work. The most abominable blow came from the members of his own profession in the form of a manifesto, published in the Boston *Daily Advertiser* and signed by Dr. J. J. Flagg and most of the leading dentists of Boston, making a formal protest against the use of ether and predicting all sorts of dire calamities from its use. This was to confront Morton at every turn and be used to discredit him when he went to other communities.

Cheap cynicism and irony were lavished upon the discovery by jealous medical men from less enlightened areas as follows:

Professor A. Westcott, of Baltimore, remarked that if Morton's sucking bottle would perform all the marvels accredited to it, the proper place for its use would be for squalling infants in the nursery; R. M. Huston, M.D., Philadelphia, "Quackery"; William C. Roberts, M.D., New York City, "Humbug and a patented nostrum."

The editors of a New Orleans medical journal could not understand why the surgeons of Boston were captivated by such an invention, when mesmerism had accomplished a thousand times greater wonders.

It seemed as if the entire medical profession, outside of a few men in Boston, felt personally insulted that they had not been taken into confidence regarding this invention.

The efforts to discredit Morton are too loathsome to repeat. He was persecuted unmercifully, his dental practice broken up, his personal morals viciously attacked and every possible effort made to alienate any affection that his friends might have for him. The attacks were carried into his own home and he and his wife suffered endless humiliation. There was not any limit to which his enemies would not go, and at times it was actually dangerous for him to appear in public. When he went to a small town near Boston to escape his persecutors, he was burned in effigy on the streets. Such humiliation is seldom the lot of him who has benefited mankind with one of the truly great gifts.

Dr. Jackson, his old preceptor, had been included with Morton when the patent was taken out. The attorney advised that this be done, for Jackson had prior knowledge of the work and that might have been sufficient to bring the originality of the discovery into question. Jackson had refused to be included at first, saying that he might lose his professional standing by taking out a patent on a secret preparation. This objection he finally withdrew, and when the patent was issued Jackson was a co-patentee. Later Jackson was to claim the entire credit for the discovery in a letter to the French Academy of Sciences, and the final result was an extremely virulent quarrel between Morton and Jackson. The most that can be said of Jackson's claim is that more credence could be given to it if there were any record of his making a public statement concerning the properties of ether, prior to Morton's demonstration. If Jackson did know all about the material and its uses, as he very probably did, he was perfectly willing that Morton assume all the risk and responsibility of manslaughter that attached to the administration of the drug.

An application was made to Congress for recognition of Morton's discovery and to obtain an appropriation worthy of the work. The lawmakers were so hectored and flustered by the claims and counterclaims of the partisans of Jackson and Wells that they were unable to come to a definite agreement; no credit was given to anyone and Morton retired, poorer and more discouraged than ever.

There was an additional claimant at this time, One Dr. Crawford Long, of Georgia. He had seen ether used for jags and sprees, had experimented with it on some patients and, it is said, used ether for anesthetic purposes four years prior to Morton's public demonstration. The evidence is quite obscure on this, but Long himself admitted in the *Southern Medical and Surgical Journal* of December, 1849, that he had not progressed far enough to be sure of his ground. Such action as he took after the public interest in Morton's work would seem to be simply an effort to steal Morton's glory. Long abandoned his experimentation and certainly had no appreciation of the possibilities of the drug. He was simply one of the many others who had the chance to bring the hidden facts to light but was incapable of doing so. Sir Humphrey Davy had written of nitrous oxide in 1800, that it was capable of producing stupefaction and insensibility to pain. The materials for all the discoveries that have blessed mankind have stood ready at hand since the beginning of time, but only those who are able to recognize and put the unknown to use should have credit as discoverers.

Wells and Long both deserved better fortune. Jackson has not a glimmer of justification in his claim. Morton succeeded where the others failed but reaped a whirlwind of abuse that was the most humiliating ever visited on a great pioneer.

The shoddy methods used to discredit Morton were entirely unjustified. The only considerable honor that he received in his lifetime was a gold medal from the French Academy of Sciences and an honorary medical degree from an American University. There is every reason his name should rank with those of the great Americans, for to him must go the entire credit of risking his life and happiness in order that mankind be freed from pain.

The epitaph on his tombstone in Mount Auburn Cemetery at Cambridge best describes his lasting claim to fame:

DR. W. T. G. MORTON

BORN AUGUST 19, 1819

DIED JULY 15, 1868

INVENTOR AND REVEALOR OF ANAESTHETIC INHALATION.

BEFORE WHOM IN ALL TIMES SURGERY WAS AGONY.

BY WHOM PAIN IN SURGERY WAS AVERTED AND ANNULED.

SINCE WHOM SCIENCE HAS CONTROL OF PAIN.

G. PERSONAL CONFLICTS AND SOCIOCULTURAL CHANGE [21]

Culture contact situations bristle with problems which are of interest to all students of human behavior. The meeting of two diverse ways of life is an ever-present phenomenon, but few techniques have been developed for adequately controlling the data relative to it and in consequence little beyond speculation has been achieved in attempting to deal with the problems connected with it. During the summer 1938 the writer had the opportunity to investigate a situation of this kind and a preliminary report has been made of the results.[22] The contacting elements in this case were three closely related groups of native Indian cultures of northwestern California on the one hand, and the encroaching pioneer white civilization of the 1850's on the other. Their meeting, dating in all important respects from the mid-century onward, was therefore recent enough that it was possible to get some first hand native and white accounts of events giving specific details of time, place, and participating characters. This was in fact the reason for selecting this particular instance of contact. It offered the opportunity for recording a large number of concrete responses to well-defined situations. Although it is an irksome procedure it is felt that this approach provides the only valid foundation for inference and generalization. The method is not new since it conforms to the case history, biographical or autobiographical techniques for collecting social data; but it is not consistently employed in anthropological field work and frequently informants' generalizations regarding what "the people" did are taken instead.

In the most general terms the problem was to analyze the factors and processes involved in the acceptance of new objects, institutions, and behaviors introduced by the whites. Since cultural responses are in the last (or first?) analysis personal ones, the case history method had the special merit in giving the problems sharper definition. For one thing, its intimate and concrete character pointed up personal dilemmas of acceptance or rejection; and by ramifying and intensifying the inquiry into inter-individual and situation responses it soon developed that it was quite feasible to deal with personalities, even though some of them were temporally remote. The suggestion came from the Indians themselves. The older, more conservative members of the communities repeatedly attributed the evils accompanying the present social disintegration of their community life to the shameless and wilful ways of the half-breed. At first this sounded like mere rationalization, an off-hand judgment prompted by a well ingrained respect for an irreproachable parentage in terms of the old order. For aboriginally there was a strong feeling of high birth, manifested among the well-born by a reserved, prideful, and dignified demeanor. The half-breed with his dubious hybrid background therefore seemed a natural scapegoat. But this in itself was significant, and once the clue was given it soon became apparent and there was something more than emotion back of the conservative's denunciation. By the dual procedure of checking genealogies when significant breaches with the old customs occurred, and by taking note of the careers of the descendants of early marriages, there emerged a rather consistent pattern of mixed bloods disavowing old customs, defying native taboos, and taking up the new way of life.

This naturally is not to say that mixed bloods were the only accepters of the new, but as compared with the alternate category of fullbloods, there could be no doubt that the factor of mixed parentage was a critical one in determining cultural bias. For this the reasons are not far to seek. It is not enough to say that the half-breed, more than any other, reached out eagerly, to embrace the white man's way of life. At best that only begs the question, even where such things as iron and automobiles are concerned, and at its worst it amounts simply to an expression of complacent ethnocentrism, a tacit presumption that ours is the best of all cultural adaptations.

More to the point is the fact that the half-breed child had a white father who, in accordance with our traditions, dominated his household; and even though more often than not he lived on a material pioneer level with the Indian he did have an ideological background stimulated by sufficient contacts with his kind to keep it alive and a potent element in the child's conditioning. Added to this is the fact that the mother must necessarily have had some inclination toward participating in the new culture even to have consorted with a white man. In just what terms we can characterize her predisposition, whether as curiosity, frivolity, dissatisfaction, escape, frustration, or otherwise, still awaits a further but not impossible analysis. So, too, does the attitude of her father or brothers who, in some cases at least, wholeheartedly subscribed to the marriage. To concern ourselves for the present only with the consequences of the union, there is the further important consideration of a mixed heritage, cultural as well as racial, converged in the child; and for the effects of this we need go no further than our everyday observations. For such a person there is no recognized place in either sphere. He is miscast for both fittings. This cannot fail to produce unease and dissatisfaction, and this, quite apart from the foregoing considerations, would make him a likely subscriber to the new order. Certainly the old one offered him nothing and with its renouncement there was at least the chance to break its bonds. This is what the Yurok half-breed did, and for reasons too intricate to attempt to unravel in this place, the majority of his kind still seek the releases but evade the checks and balances of the white man's living pattern. Whether he is to blame or not, he is still malcontented, still de-socialized.

The possibility of thus defining an element in native society predisposed toward accepting innovations introduced by the whites suggested the likelihood that there were yet others. Proceeding upon the thesis that a social displacement was the key factor in the preceding cases a watch was kept for comparable situations. It appeared as critical again in the cases of widows and the abandoned children of white men, perhaps of fatherless children generally. Under the aboriginal system whereby a widow could expect to marry the brother of her deceased husband there was considerably less economic insecurity, if not anxiety, than under our own. By marrying across the cultural boundary a woman forfeited this insurance and if she were bereft of her white husband's support she could count only on her family blood ties, and these were not geared for such strains—or she could marry an Indian. There are no complete records and this, like the case of half-breeds, cannot be treated on a statistical basis; but of the instances upon which there is information it can be said that the widow has with remarkable consistency refused to accept either of these alternatives. Instead she has more actively embraced white culture by undertaking her own support under the new economy: by her own gardening (a new trait), by either laundering, cooking, or house cleaning for the few white families or the soldiers at the fort. This may be thought of as a further manifestation of her initial predisposition to associate with whites as indicated by her marriage, but it has doubtless been precipitated and stimulated by her widowhood. The cases of fatherless children, other than those abandoned by white men, are not so clear cut but they create a suspicion that the early loss of either parent is likely to promote a more receptive attitude toward a newly introduced pattern.

In not quite the same category were instances of an apparently chronic inability to adjust to the demands of the old system: men or women several times married and separated, fractious or rebellious individuals who never attained much support or status, repeated disturbers of the peace, those who resorted to force and aggression in preference to the traditional modes of compromise. Distinct, but related to them, were the physically afflicted. Actually instances of this sort were hard to ferret out, but the number included a blind man, one with a speech defect, a cripple, and several who were chronically ill. These were especially prominent in accepting the various sectarian versions of Christianity that had been offered to the Yurok, Karok, and Hupa, as well as the hybrid Catholic-Indian-Shaker Cult. Along with the doctrine came all of the mores of Western civilization with which Christianity has come to identify itself.

Finally, there were the young people; in numbers, and perhaps otherwise, this was by all odds the most important category of accepters of the white man's way. Infiltration of new ideas, things and behaviors through this channel was more gradual, more insidious, and more certainly subversive of conservatism. This is expectable. It is no more than a recognition of what happens in the gradual evolutionary change of culture which daily takes place around us. On all sides, if we conceptualize it, we can see the slow, gradually accelerating development and acceptance of change by youth, and the sloughing off of the old with the death of the head-shaking, tongue-clucking, or passively resigned elders. The process becomes as clear as could be wished for in a detailed study like the present one. The way for change along this channel is prepared by the malleability and suggestibility of children, whose motor, ideological, and affective patterns are not yet irrevocably set. Unbiased by familiar and unconsciously compelling behavior sets and cultural standards, to them one way of doing a thing seems as good as any other. This susceptibility was enhanced by two circumstances in the contact situation being discussed. The first was the curiosity of children (and others), sharpened as it was by the marvels of the new culture. Childhood recollections of informants give a picture of them as curious hangers-on about the houses, stores, mining camps and barracks of the white man—very often in defiance of the admonitions of their elders. Secondly, there was the amused or sentimental paternalistic attitude of the whites toward native children which manifested itself in the impulse to give them bits of food, clothing, or cast-off knickknacks. These subtle processes etched away at the foundations of the native culture and bit by bit, continuously and surreptitiously, substituted the elements of a new structure.

The conceptualization of the young as a category of susceptibles to innovation is not likely to provoke a challenge, but it is not to be expected that the other categories will be accepted as such without more supporting evidence. It is not a generally accepted proposition that the misfits, the maladjusted, and the underdogs are in the vanguard of cultural innovation. At least no such formulation has been offered and it is likely to evoke a negative reaction. In fact it at first appears to controvert the view, for which there is certainly some evidence, that a new trait or behavior must have the sponsorship of some eminent member of the society of receivers before its general acceptance can be assured.[23] In native terms this would mean that the equivalent of a chief or an esteemed leader of the group would have to sponsor the new trait; and presumably such an individual, if he had not been set in his high place by a rather rigid system of hereditary succession, would have had to achieve a rather harmonious and satisfying adjustment with his culture to have attained his esteemed position. This obviously would take him out of the category of a misfit. Indeed he would be the more firmly attached to his culture's standards because of his position, and the less likely to propose a break with them. This is what the data upon the Yurok, Hupa, and Karok indicated. The ranking members in the social hierarchy were the conservatives, and they condemned the breaches of custom instigated by their inferiors as defined above. Furthermore, although it was found that exceptionally an esteemed elder might lead the way and set a new fashion it was evident from informants' responses that such a one was more likely to be condemned as a renegade than to be admired and imitated.

Here, however, was a problem. The occasional eminent renegade could not be ignored; he was, so to speak, at the heart of the problem. The fact that he appeared only sporadically was significant; so the reaction was to him. It was therefore suggested that he really did not constitute an exception to the rule, that appearances were deceiving, that the explanation of his renegade behavior lay in the fact that he was not so well adjusted to his culture as his high position would seem to indicate. Admittedly more evidence was needed and accordingly another group (the Tsimpshian Indians of British Columbia) was chosen for what light its contact with the whites could throw on this and related problems. By no means all the relevant data can be presented here, but the writer would like to offer briefly a few cases which have significance for an understanding of the relationship between personal conflicts and cultural change.

An appreciation of the contact situation is a prerequisite for an understanding of the Indian's attitude toward the things the white man brought; hence a brief review of this is necessary. The first continuous pressure of Western civilization on Tsimpshian life began in 1834 with the establishment of a Hudson's Bay Company trading post at Fort Simpson. But for about twenty years the effects of the contact were remarkably limited. An armed truce existed between the representatives of the two cultures. The fort was in a constant state of siege, and mutual suspicion, hostility, and avoidance marked the interrelations of whites and Indians. The stockaded company grounds and everything within were diligently guarded; none of the approximately twenty employees was allowed to associate with the natives or even to go about the village. No more than one heavily guarded Indian was allowed within the fort at one time, and then only if he had a considerable number of furs for which he was doled out the white man's price almost exclusively in rice, molasses, biscuits, and potatoes from an undisplayed stock. Under the circumstances the Indian saw extremely little and knew practically nothing of the white man's culture. This state of affairs prevailed until 1855–1860 at which time a compromise was reached. By its terms the gate to the fort was thrown open and

Indians were allowed to look over the inside. There they could shop over the stock, observe and talk with the employees. The latter for their part began to circulate among the natives in the village and soon most of them had married Indian women.

Concomitantly came what was probably the most potent of all influences upon the lives of these natives. This was a brand of militant, all embracing Christianity, brought by one of the most talented and forceful missionaries of whom we have record. His name was William Duncan. His story is a long one and the effects of his work over sixty years have been of the most far reaching character. Here it need only be said that in 1862 he founded the model, completely self-sustaining, Christian village Metlakatla thirty miles from Fort Simpson. His idea was to make a complete and uncompromising break with the old system by outlawing it and replacing it throughout, from economy through religion, with European patterns and ideals. It cannot be denied that he was successful. Removal to Metlakatla with him, which was voluntary, meant an unqualified renunciation of Indian customs; and a great many natives made this move. Their reasons for doing so are the answers to our inquiry into motivations. Here we can treat with only a few of the most illuminating cases.

The most striking instance was that of Legex, the recognized ranking chief of all the heads of the nine tribes congregated at Fort Simpson. This was a major feat of conversion and it would seem to contradict the conclusions regarding maladjustment suggested on the basis of the Yurok, Karok, and Hupa data. Duncan himself, in a published account of his work, lays stress on the removal of Legex to Metlakatla in 1863, and while counting it a great victory for Christianity, pays tribute to the man's courage and strength of character, fully recognizing as he did what inward torment and sacrifice the decision must have cost a man of this chief's standing.[24] But Duncan did not know the whole of the story, or if he did he gave no intimation of it.

The truth is that Legex was in an intolerable situation in 1862 and Duncan's new life offered him an escape from it. At the death of his predecessor sometime before Duncan's arrival at Fort Simpson there was a tribal split over the question of a successor. Just prior to the death of this incumbent the Haidas, a predatory neighboring group, had attacked and killed a number of important individuals of Legex's tribe. The sentiment for a bloody revenge was strong. It was played up by a militant group of younger men of whom Legex was the leader. He was a "brave man" as they say, which means that he was haughty, sensitive to insult, and cruelly vindictive. The issue of succession was between himself, a nephew of the deceased chief, and a younger brother of the latter. Legex had the most aggressive backing and was installed in the head chief's place, with the promise and express purpose of taking revenge on the Haidas. Disgruntled, the other contender, who was his uncle, renounced his tribe and accepted a lesser chief's place in another of the nine tribes to which he also had a legitimate title.

Legex and his followers immediately began preparation for the revenge. These involved an elaborate deception designed to get the whole of the Haida group in an especially constructed house where they could be completely wiped out. This death trap was built, but it was never used. Counter machinations were afoot. They involved the interplay of several contrary purposes and personalities and finally culminated in a ceremonial act which completely forestalled Legex and his supporters. Another chief, acting as a representative of popular opinion, sprinkled eagle down on the head of Legex, an act which in itself compelled a renunciation of blood revenge and forced a negotiated compromise. This opened the way for Legex's defeated uncle and his other ill wishers to destroy his prestige. They did this with a vengeance, setting to work on an underhanded campaign of sneering at his announced intentions, of questioning his bravery, of attributing false pretext to the stand upon which he took title.

This was too much for Legex. He stood the undercurrent for several years, growing more vicious, ill tempered and defeated all the while. He tried to kill Duncan in 1858, but his ostentatious bluster and pot-valiance crumbled at the crucial moment. He was a frustrated man; and finally at his own instigation, the inner council of elders of his tribe met secretly to consider his plight. They agreed that he should clear out entirely, but that his chief's name and place would not be filled as long as he lived. It was understood that he was to go to Metlakatla and attempt to reconcile himself with the new order established there, but at the same time he was to retain his rank and the privileges which went with it in accordance with the continuing native pattern at Fort Simpson. That in itself tells much of the story. To those who never knew of the secret meeting, even those of his tribe, this capitulation had but the appearance of an incomprehensible traitorous act. They could not understand a chief abandoning his people and joining up with a man who had sought to destroy the tradition-sanctioned order of things. They referred to Legex contemptuously and bitterly as a white man. He had a difficult struggle, as Duncan testifies; but withal he seems to have made a rapid adjustment to the regime at Metlakatla. In all outward respects at least he was a devout Christian when he died in 1869.

A pertinent sidelight on this story is offered by the behavior of the uncle whom Legex displaced. He never forgave Legex. He "hated to see his face" and did everything he could to undermine his nephew's influence. And so it came about that it was out of this man's chagrin and hate that Duncan got his first welcome outside the protection of the fort where he had labored for almost a year in preparation for his first sermon to the Indians. For this and for subsequent sermons and lessons to the Indian children the embittered uncle offered his house to Duncan, not out of love for what Duncan represented but in order to affiliate himself with a new power or influence which seemed likely to enhance his own prestige and simultaneously to detract from that of his rival. He continued this scheming play, and so identified himself with Duncan, until he was again thwarted by Legex's conversion. He then reversed his policy, declared against Metlakatla, and at any mention of going there put the alternative of his own or the detested Legex's leadership before his followers.

A second major phenomenon which for long was puzzling was the removal of practically the entire Gitlan tribe to Metlakatla, their head chief instigating and leading the movement. This was another occasion, the first in fact, for rejoicing and praise of motives by Duncan. But there was more to this story, too. Doubtless many of the Gitlan embraced the new life with mixed motives; but some of them, and they were numerically not inconsiderable, can be credited with no more Christian or pro-white sentiments than those which motivated their chief. His were characterized by an impotent and unsatisfied yearning for revenge. Again the cause of this internal conflict predated Duncan's arrival, and goes back to a series of murders.

The trouble began many years before when several of the Gitlan, including their head chief's brother and nephew, were killed by members of the Gitlutsau, another of the nine affiliated tribes congregated at Fort Simpson. Only two unimportant men of the latter tribe were killed in the fray, so that the score was far from even, the Gitlan feeling that it could not be so until, at the least, two Gitlutsau chiefs had been killed. Nevertheless, to keep the feud from spreading through the network of kinship bonds connecting the two warring groups with members of the other tribes, an attempt was made by representatives of these interested outsiders to bring about a peaceful settlement. The Gitlutsau were ready to pay off and quit but would submit to no loss of face in doing so. The Gitlan, likewise out of pride, were even more opposed to a compromise, and the feud therefore dragged on for years, exacerbated by brushes, insults, and occasional injuries or murders by one side or the other. The Gitlan, unable to agree on concerted action, worked at cross purposes and let their chances slip by. Their shame and sense of defeatism increased as they felt their prestige slipping from them. Relatives of their murdered ones "would not look the Gitlutsau in the face." Their situation was the more intolerable since their summer camping grounds adjoined those of their enemies.

Matters stood thus when Duncan set out to found Metlakatla; and the upshot was that in a surprise move a body of approximately three hundred Gitlan followed him there within a few days. Collectively their reasons closely paralleled those of Legex.[25] But for their head chief, whose clan brother and uncle had been killed years before, and who instigated the move, this was not the end. It was only an expedient. He assumed office with great native pomp and ceremony just before leaving for Metlakatla, and went there dedicating himself to revenge. His preoccupation with the idea caused his wife, who wanted to become a Christian, to leave him and return to Fort Simpson. He then designed a marriage connection with a family of an alien group which also had a grudge to settle with the Gitlutsau. Conspiring with them, a marriage feast was planned and several of the most important men of the Gitlutsau were invited with the intention of killing them. Whiskey was generously ladled out to the visitors during the feast and the evening culminated with the killing of the two ranking chiefs and others of the Gitlutsau. The score was thus finally evened and the Gitlan chief was vindicated. But in the fight he was badly wounded and almost lost his life. Complications developed in his wounded leg and he became bed-ridden. Caring nothing for the life at Metlakatla and afraid to go to Fort Simpson, he stayed with his wife's people and allowed them to take him, an invalid, to Metlakatla. There he was converted and ultimately asked for a reconciliation with the Gitlutsau.

The assumption, founded upon the limited evidence of the Yurok, Karok, and Hupa investigation, that there is a positive correlation between eminence (not notoriety) and cultural conservatism made it highly desirable to determine what motivations were behind the seemingly exceptional behavior of these two most prominent additions to the community of Metlakatla. From the foregoing it can hardly be doubted that it was the embroilment resulting from a personal conflict with the old system of values which stirred these men to abandon the system and to seek an escape from its intolerable complications. And this despite their high positions, a circumstance which it now appears is more likely to confuse the real issue than to clarify it if we accept it on its face value. An esteemed social status, while a good index, is no certain criterion of a completely successful cultural adjustment. Personal difficulties and incompatibilities foment in the high places as well as in the low; and if this case material proves anything it indicates that this is one stimulus, if not the stimulus, to cultural change, the acceptance of new patterns and standards being the means of relieving personal strain or dissatisfaction.

The second inference to be tested by this information was that eminent individuals, provided that they do make radical departures from the accustomed modes and standards, are more likely to be repudiated than followed by members of their society. It is impossible at this date to make any statistical estimate of the character of the responses to the renegade behavior of Legex and the Gitlan chief. The statements of informants testify to the fact that they were condemned for it. Doubtless they had their supporters as well; but the impression persists that they were condemned more frequently and vigorously than they were defended. The very fact of their high position made their apostasy more flagrant and incomprehensible. True, practically all of the Gitlan in following their chief, overtly at any rate, endorsed his decision to embrace the Metlakatla version of Western civilization. At the same time it should be recognized that the group as a whole was subjected to the same embarrassments and indignities as was the chief, and an unknown number of its members had reason to feel the sting of contempt as acutely as he did. Legex's difficulty, however, was an individual one and was treated as such. Only six people went with him to Metlakatla, and none of these was a prominent individual in his tribe.

One other instance must suffice for this necessarily incomplete demonstration. The individual concerned was one of the sub-chiefs in one of the nine tribes at Fort Simpson. As a member of the inner council he acted as an advisor to the chief and was consequently one of the determiners of group policy. In this capacity he was certainly a man of influence. Yet he was one of the first, even before

Legex or the Gitlan, to accept Christianity and by his own precept and example to encourage the adoption of the new life associated with it. He was the father of an 85 year old informant who had vivid recollections of some of these attempts to inaugurate a new order. At the bottom of all of them lay two sources of discord and dissatisfaction with native life. The first was his pacific nature. He was temperamentally a moderator and a conciliator as could be shown by enlarging upon some of the circumstances which reveal this attitude and by the direct testimony of the man who knew him best. From this it is clear that the aggressive and bellicose spirit of Tsimpshian life was not congenial to him. Moreover, by 1865 the situation at Fort Simpson had become appalling to even more calloused souls. The second element in his disaffection was his bitterness toward, and his fear of, witchcraft. He was convinced that two of his children had succumbed to sorcery, the victims, as he believed, of envy, hate, and intrigue. In fact one of the local sorcerers freely rumored it around that he was responsible for the death of both children, and furthermore that he intended to kill the only remaining child, the above mentioned informant.[26]

This anxiety alone was enough to prompt the espousal of a system of law and order which condemned and sought to suppress such evil practices. It produced one of the most quietly insistent "progressives" at Fort Simpson, a man who probably did more new things first than anyone else there. And for this he had to take the unpleasant consequences. He was ridiculed and called a white man; his behavior, it was said, was unbecoming to a chief; he was likened to Legex who wore white men's clothes and put "ice" (spectacles) in his eyes. But in one respect he differed from Legex, and for this he doubtless got credit. He did not abandon his people. He had a strong conviction of his responsibility for their guidance and support, and this was explicitly the reason why he never moved to Metlakatla, though he often visited there. He early became a Christian himself and put his son under the care and training of the first missionary to establish himself at Fort Simpson after Duncan left.

Probings into other personal histories proved equally enlightening. The results substantially alter the bald and superficial picture of a man of importance shedding his old and well-fitting cultural garment and eagerly accepting one of a new cut. This was the crux of the problem; but no less convincing and corroborative were the person by person analyses of the house memberships of these leaders which split up under the inducements of Western civilization. This process of household disintegration is the very epitome of the Tsimpshian cultural breakdown. It was at the core of the acceptance movement, and an analysis of it in terms of personal relationships reveals the internal stresses and inadequacies which by comparison gave attractiveness to the new order and opened the way for its piece-meal acceptance. Tsimpshian culture, like many another, crumbled through the resignation of interest in it by individuals and, to be repetitious, we can never know why until we know these individuals.

Tsimpshian houses were large and often contained from twenty to forty people, practically all of whom were related to the house chief on their maternal side. Although the bonds of kinship and mutual support rested upon a matrilineal system and by it a man's brother or his sister's son (not his own) was heir to his status and property, there was an emphatic insistence, verbal and institutional, upon paternal interest in off-spring. The distinction between theory and practice is nowhere more pronounced. Theoretically it was the duty of the mother's brother to sponsor and assist his heir. Actually it was the child's father who groomed him, pushed him, and contributed the bulk of the great financial expenditure necessary to the child's rise in status. Without a father to take the initiative and work for his advancement a boy had no more chance than an orphan in our culture. This lack has made freelancers, pioneers, liberals, or convention flouters of many men among us, and so it did among the Tsimpshian. A case in point is offered by the kinship cluster headed by the sub-chief, whom we may call X, last discussed.

Around 1855 the house headed by this man accommodated over forty individuals, seventeen of whom were theoretically potential heirs to his name and the property and status symbolized by it: three half brothers by two men other than his father, one blood brother, one clan "brother," one mother's sister, one clan "sister," four nieces, and six nephews. On the face of it this array of heirs appears propitious for the perpetuation of X's family line and its tradition. Actually by 1870, and even before, this kinship unit which, with others like it, was fundamental to the whole social structure was completely dissolved and there was no heir in sight. This in fact was clear from the beginning for none of these individuals had any more than a nominal claim on the high place for which birth had put him in line. All were dependent upon the house head economically and socially. Their fathers had done nothing to establish them and they could do nothing themselves. The house head X was himself too engrossed in forwarding the interests of his own son to give the necessary aid to his own heirs. He helped his several nephews and brothers incidentally but his main responsibility was to his son.

Under these circumstances the doom of this family could almost have been foretold. Its structure crumbled early, the members scattered, and the house itself was abandoned by 1870. By this date the oldest half-brother had died; the second had joined his wife's people who lived in a distant village near his only inherited portion, some hunting grounds; and the youngest, who had no legal interest in the family property at all, had departed for Victoria to live and work like a white man. The blood brother, though third in line, had no more chance than the others as long as X lived. When the latter around 1865 moved as regent into the house and place inherited by his young son, the brother stayed on as his surrogate and caretaker in the old and otherwise abandoned house for a time, and then moved about living with other relatives. He really had no home and he was, in consequence we may take it, one of the first to build and move into one of the new style family individual houses so strongly insisted upon by the missionary in 1874. The clan "brother" likewise found an appeal in this new ideal and for precisely the same reason. Years before he had voluntarily resigned what subsidiary interests and claims he had in a certain house when the headship fell to a sorcerer whom he dreaded for the same reason that his clan brother X did. Ever after he was a transient, living with X or others of his clan relatives. In 1874 he was also without a home and predisposed we may assume to a fundamental change in the living pattern.

Three of the the nephews and one niece had neither father nor mother. All of them early followed Duncan to Metlakatla where at least one of the nephews figured prominently as a militant defender of the missionary and was jailed for it. One other nephew and two nieces were without a mother. Their father could do no more for them than to put them first under the protection and support of his father-in-law who died before 1860, then upon his death under the care of X. By 1870 one of the nieces was dead, the other had gone away to work in a cannery. The nephew, so rebellious and uncooperative that X ordered him out of the house, left Fort Simpson for an island spot from which place he became the shingle supplier for the new houses built after 1876. The father of the remaining niece was, with his wife, likewise a dependent on X. They all went to Metlakatla with the others. By 1870 the three remaining dependent nephews were dead; but by this time there were two others, and a sister of one, all half-breeds. None of them had a chance in the old culture, if indeed it was ever considered that their native connections were anything to boast about. The widowed mother of the half-breed brother and sister took them to Metlakatla where they received some education and training from Duncan. The boy worked for the Hudson's Bay Company and his sister married the manager of the post. The other half-breed nephew by 1874 was in Victoria, and he never returned.

This situation is a typical one in only one respect, that all the potential heirs to X's place were in 1870 without hope in or responsibility for the old system and therefore were not interested in its perpetuation. The responses are typical; the process of disintegration throughout is the same, as could be shown by a similar analysis of some 20 house memberships. Aboriginally some solution would have been found, some legitimate heir would have been groomed for the place; but by 1870 and progressively thereafter the game did not seem worth the price to the majority of those theoretically concerned. A characteristic of the whole process is the early and relatively easy disaffection of the less secure, and the forestalled, and the unbonded members of the relationship clusters. They melted away from the system which held nothing, or little, for them anyway.

The individual thwartings and harassments so far considered are apart from and in addition to those which rocked and seethed through Tsimpshian complacency and brought it to a state of near panic by 1870. Smallpox struck in 1862 with mystifying and terrifying severity. Hundreds died and those who could fled in all directions. The event was cataclysmic, depleting the population and introducing disorder, consternation, and uncertainty. At about the same date whiskey and firearms began to be more readily available to the Indians and the two in conjunction contributed to the pandemonium and created a reign of terror. Brawls and shootings were common; force, pot-valiance, and treacherous feuding destroyed confidence and promoted a sense of insecurity, futility, and anxiety. Repeatedly this was given by informants as the reason for the acceptance of the strong arm rule of Her Majesty's gun boats or Duncan's dictatorial regime at Metlakatla. They were the lesser of two evils in the eyes of many and were accepted by them with mental reservations. Unfortunately for them, they were soon to discover when it was too late to retract that this was not a question of half-measures. With its law in control Western civilization had a stranglehold on Tsimpshian culture. It was only a question of time until it could make itself felt directly or indirectly in every aspect of native life.

If it seems too much to admit the conclusion that the disgruntled, the maladjusted, the frustrated, and the incompetent are preeminently the accepters of cultural innovations and change, it might be relevant to point out that the inward conflicts which these imply lie at the root of the factional splits which are familiar aspects of change within our own cultural milieu. Personal dissatisfactions of this sort give rise to reform parties and clubs, to orthodox and unorthodox sects and cults, to utopian communities and even political states. They foment in other quarters as well; and here we may take note of the disappointments, the resentments, and the frustrations which characterize the psychology of minorities. It is not sufficiently appreciated that the members of the submerged elements of a population are rendered susceptible to subversive promises and ideologies of all sorts by their discontents. That they collectively put their faith in a messiah to lead them out of their oppression is but the final and most obvious manifestation of their incompatibility. Finally, to put a finger on the ultimate source of all cultural change, it may be bold but it is not unreasonable to suggest some kind of personal conflict as the primary motivation for invention. In other words, there are good reasons for believing that the inventor is such because he feels, rather acutely and personally, a dissatisfaction with the customary and accepted ways of doing things. This is demonstrably true of the social inventor, the "liberal," and it is no less reasonable to posit some motor or affective thwartings at the source of technological inventions. We should have to exempt, though only in part, the admittedly special case of the professional inventor of our 19th and 20th century civilization. He does not really alter the picture but only adds to it.

For the present these suggestions must stand on their merits as impressions only. It is not impossible to test their worth, as the foregoing material is intended to demonstrate. To prove anything in the sphere of social science we must hold ourselves to the task of a systematic investigation of concrete case material. In the present instance more of such material is needed, but from the evidence of the data at hand it seems that we are justified in concluding that personal conflicts play a critical if not a determinative role in cultural change.

H. SOCIAL CHANGE RESULTING THROUGH COLLECTIVE ACTION: COLLECTIVE ACTION IS STIRRED BY ATTACK ON SACRED MORES [27]

Six years ago, the town of Perry, Georgia—population 1,500—was a sleepy, complacent spot surrounded by gently rolling farm country. Located a few miles south of Macon, it seemed settled forever as just another forgotten corner of Georgia. Its main street comprised one block of business establishments. A look of weather-worn shabbiness hung about the town. The people went slothfully along, conducting whatever business came to hand.

Running past their door and forming the town's business block, U. S. Highway 41 sped carloads of tourists from the north on their way to Florida. But few of them ever noticed shabby little Perry.

Then, in 1944, something happened. A simple but amazing plan of action upset the little community. Within a year, Perry was almost a boom spot. Population jumped to 2,500. The town was brought to an invigorating peak of efficiency and prosperity. Yet nothing new had been discovered. The story of how this Southern town pulled itself up by its bootstraps offers a program which can work in any community, anywhere.

Perry's idyllic idleness was shattered in June, 1944, when an unassuming, obscure man arrived in town. Few people outside Georgia had ever heard his name. He is Charles A. Collier, vice-president of the Georgia Power Company, and a fourth-generation Georgian. For 50 years Collier had been a devoted but critical native of his state. For as many years he had watched its deterioration. And having studied the state and its people he devised a plan for its salvation—a simple plan called "Georgia's Better Home Towns Program."

Convincing the power company that if it would contribute $250,000 to promote the plan he could put Georgia on its feet, he came to Perry one day and invited himself to speak at a meeting of the Kiwanis Club. To the amazement of that town's 35 leading citizens, he read them a frightful indictment of their state and town. With a prophet's fervor he hurled these disturbing facts at them:

Some 60 per cent of Georgia's rural young people left their homes every 10 years; more than 1,000,000 native-born Georgians—mainly the college educated—had moved to other states; 92 per cent of Georgia's farm buildings had no water service; 82 per cent were without sanitary facilities; 77 per cent needed rebuilding. He told them that their sons coming home from the war with government loans totaling $45,000,000 would be forced to go elsewhere to invest their money.

Then bluntly he turned to telling them about Perry. "Your town," he said, "is dirty, shabby, unsightly, slothful. Your buildings are unpainted. Your people are indifferent. You could increase your business tenfold in one year, if you wanted to—but you're just plain lazy!"

Having tossed this bombshell at his listeners, Collier threw a stack of pictures on the table and said: "Just take a good look at your town!"

For a few moments there was frozen silence at the lunch table. Then the men began to study the pictures. "This isn't Perry," was the first typical outburst as they looked at shabby buildings, unkempt streets, uncollected garbage and unsightly alleyways.

"Look at them closely!" challenged Collier. Names on stores were clearly visible. People walking on the streets were easily recognizable. When Collier got up to leave, the citizens of Perry remained at the table. They began to talk among themselves.

Fighting mad that anyone should speak of their town in such a manner, they began to protest. But all protests added up to one grim fact—the truth of Collier's statements. They had a nice town—but a neglected one. They were fine citizens—but careless. Said one councilman: "This is not time for talk. Perry people have always worked together in an emergency. This is an emergency. Let's get the people together."

Young George Nunn, mayor of the town and president of Kiwanis, put the matter to a vote. To a man, they decided to join the Better Home Towns Program. The mayor promptly designated C. E. Andrew, President of the Perry Loan and Savings Bank, to head a committee to launch the industrial end of the program. Frank Hood, local field representative of the Collier plan, was asked to act as adviser.

Perry began to move. The following day the local *Houston Home Journal* carried a front-page story, told what was wrong with Perry and what must be done, and announced a meeting next day. Everybody came to the New Perry Hotel lobby for that meeting. The Garden Club and the Sorosis Club were on hand to discuss the beautifying end. Boy Scouts and Girl Scouts came to ask about "the dirty work" to be done. The bank president, mayor and councilmen were on hand. The old folks came, many a gray head nodding approval of the program. Half a dozen farmers plodded in to take instructions back to the "home folks." Every crossroad, school, church and business had a representative present.

The meeting was brisk. Said Andrew: "The first thing all of us will do is clean-up paint-up, light-up—and then build up."

The people went home and went to work, as if they had heard a battle trumpet. An added motive for the clean-up drive was the return of Perry's top war hero, Gen. Courtney H. Hodges. When all the town's painters were exhausted, an amazing group of amateurs appeared on the streets. Store owners wielded paint brushes, bank clerks learned to handle mops, housewives pushed lawn mowers. With tireless constancy the whole town went after one thing—dirt. Boy Scouts, Girl Scouts and Sunday School classes turned their spare time into work time.

The women's clubs turned to landscaping. Shrubs were planted, new trees were hauled in. With grim tenacity the whole town cooperated, and yet a jovial good-fellowship flowed along with the driving current. "Have you swatted your last fly?" or "Did you remove that pebble?" might be the greeting of a housewife at the grocery store, or the banker might salute the mayor with "How's your back-alley coming along?"

Within a few weeks every store sported a new coat of paint. Every house reflected the back-breaking efforts of the housewives. Alleys became bright little passageways. White picket fences, bright blooming shrubs, houses shining inside and out showed the results of a furious drive that lasted six weeks. Yet these first results only served to stimulate an aroused citizenry for more important tasks.

They came to a new meeting, eager to vote money for much-needed town improvements. In a series of thundering resolutions this little band of people voted (1) an allotment of $90,000 for new sewers; (2) an extension of the water works system to cost $50,000; (3) a street and sidewalk paving program; (4) purchase of a motor grader to keep dirt streets in better condition; (5) a new $150,000 courthouse; and (6) a new recreation park with swimming pool.

There was serious intent, now, behind the program they launched to make their town one they could be proud of.

"We could have had this ten years ago," said the amazed mayor.

I. THE ROLE OF DIFFUSION IN CULTURAL CHANGE *

Our solid American citizen awakens in a bed built on a pattern which originated in the Near East but which was modified in Northern Europe before it was transmitted to America. He throws back covers made from cotton, domesticated in India, or linen, domesticated in the Near East, or silk, the use of which was discovered in China. All of these materials have been spun and woven by processes invented in the Near East. He slips into his moccasins, invented by the Indians of the Eastern woodlands, and goes to the bathroom, whose fixtures are a mixture of European and American inventions, both of recent date. He takes off his pajamas, a garment invented in India, and washes with soap invented by the ancient Gauls. He then shaves, a masochistic rite which seems to have been derived from either Sumer or ancient Egypt.

Returning to the bedroom, he removes his clothes from a chair of southern European type and proceeds to dress. He puts on garments whose form originally derived from the skin clothing of the nomads of the Asiatic steppes, puts on shoes made from skins tanned by a process invented in ancient Egypt and cut to a pattern derived from the classical civilizations of the Mediterranean, and ties around his neck a strip of bright-colored cloth which is a vestigial survival of the shoulder shawls worn by the seventeenth-century Croatians. Before going out for breakfast he glances through the window, made of glass invented in Egypt, and

* From *The Study of Man* by Ralph Linton. Copyright 1936, D. Appleton–Century Co., Inc. Reprinted by permission of publishers, Appleton-Century-Crofts, Inc., pp. 326–327.

if it is raining puts on overshoes made of rubber discovered by the Central American Indians and takes an umbrella, invented in southeastern Asia. Upon his head he puts a hat made of felt, a material invented in the Asiatic steppes.

On his way to breakfast he stops to buy a paper, paying for it with coins, an ancient Lydian invention. At the restaurant a whole new series of borrowed elements confronts him. His plate is made from a form of pottery invented in China. His knife is of steel, an alloy first made in southern India, his fork a medieval Italian invention, and his spoon a derivative of a Roman original. He begins breakfast with an orange, from the eastern Mediterranean, a canteloupe from Persia, or perhaps a piece of African watermelon. With this he has coffee, an Abyssinian plant, with cream and sugar. Both the domestications of cows and the idea of milking them originated in the Near East, while sugar was first made in India. After his fruit and first coffee he goes on to waffles, cakes made by a Scandinavian technique from wheat domesticated in Asia Minor. Over these he pours maple syrup, invented by the Indians of the Eastern woodlands. As a side dish he may have the egg of a species of bird domesticated in Indo-China, or thin strips of the flesh of an animal domesticated in Eastern Asia which have been salted and smoked by a process developed in northern Europe.

When our friend has finished eating he settles back to smoke, an American Indian habit, consuming a plant domesticated in Brazil in either a pipe, derived from the Indians of Virginia, or a cigarette, derived from Mexico. If he is hardy enough he may even attempt a cigar, transmitted to us from the Antilles by way of Spain. While smoking he reads the news of the day, imprinted in characters invented by the ancient Semites upon a material invented in China by a process invented in Germany. As he absorbs the accounts of foreign troubles he will, if he is a good conservative citizen, thank a Hebrew deity in an Indo-European language that he is 100 per cent American.

FOOTNOTES TO PART SIX

Asterisks indicate footnotes quoted from original source of case material.

1. Leslie A. White, "The Symbol: The Origin and Basis of Human Behavior," *Philosophy of Science,* Vol. 7 (1940), p. 458; C. Judson Herrick, "A Neurologist Makes Up His Mind," *Scientific Monthly,* August, 1939.

2. The term *society* is frequently used in two different ways in sociology. Sometimes it is employed as synonymous with social relationship, with human interaction, thus being denuded of any organismic essence. At other times, society is used to signify a discrete social unit, a social group. When it is used in this way, a society refers usually to an inclusive group encompassing other social groups. Society thus used usually means a local, territorial group (community), in which are found the major institutions that link and define the relationships among the groups that are contained in the society. A society, therefore, may be a small village, a nation, an urban community, or a large territorial region such as the Orient. We shall use the term *society* as synonymous with social relations, and *a society* as synonymous with a social group.

3. A word of caution must be mentioned

about the efficacy of the concept *culture trait*. It should be borne in mind that that which constitutes a culture trait depends to a considerable degree on the arbitrary selection of any item as a trait. However, it appears that almost every cultural trait is made up of other traits, and those, in turn, of still others, and so on perhaps ad infinitum.

Suppose we consider a classroom as a unit or trait of a larger complex, any American university. It is not difficult to see that every classroom is made up of other units, such as desks, blackboards, windows, students, and so on. Even each of these units can be subdivided into still smaller units. The blackboard may be said to be composed of slate, wooden paneling, screws, and the particular position it occupies in space such as perpendicularity to a horizontal floor base. Need we stop here? One might even desire to separate these last units into atoms, protons, electrons, and what not.

It should, therefore, be understood that the term *culture trait* is a relative term. It makes sense only in so far as it designates that all reality, physical or cultural, is made up of parts. But just what these parts are is another question. Science frequently has to make arbitrary assumptions about the exact nature of these parts; which assumption is valid depends on the pragmatic test and on empirical verification. If the Einstein assumption of the mass-energy unit of physical reality holds up better than the Newtonian units in the empirical test, then the former is said to be more scientifically valid. When an item is considered a trait of a culture, it is considered a trait only on a relativistic basis, that is, in relation to the purpose one has in mind. One can assume the classroom as a trait if it helps to explain the larger unit, the American university. The blackboard also becomes a trait if it is deemed as essential in the understanding of the component parts of the university. If it is not so, but is essential to the unit, the classroom, then it becomes a trait to this latter. "The form a trait assumes at a given point in time will thus be determined by its context

rather than by any quality inherent in it" (Melville J. Herskovits, *Man and His Works: The Science of Cultural Anthropology*, New York: Alfred A. Knopf, Inc., 1948, p. 172).

4. The late Ruth Benedict, an eminent American anthropologist, made a pioneering contribution to the idea of culture pattern in her *Patterns of Culture* (Boston: Houghton Mifflin Company, 1934). The idea of culture pattern received some of its initial impetus in the writings of another anthropologist, Bronislaw Malinowski. His school of anthropology, usually referred to as *functional anthropology*, "holds that the . . . laws [of cultural processes] are to be found in the function of the real elements of culture. The atomizing or isolating treatment of cultural traits is regarded as sterile, because the significance of culture consists in the relation between its elements . . ." (Bronislaw Malinowski, "Culture," *Encyclopedia of the Social Sciences* [1931], Vol. IV, p. 625). For further refinement of the concept of culture pattern and for suggestions for the empirical detection of patterns, see Clyde Kluckhohn, "Patterning as Exemplified in Navaho Culture," in Leslie Spier, A. Irving Hallowell, and Stanley S. Newman (eds.), *Language, Culture and Personality: Essays in Memory of Edward Sapir* (Menasha, Wis.: Sapir Memorial Publication Fund, 1941), pp. 109–130.

5. M. E. Opler suggested the term *theme*. He states "that a limited number of dynamic affirmations . . . , themes, can be identified in every culture and that the key to the character, structure, and direction of the specific culture is to be sought in the nature, expression, and relationship of these themes. . . . The term 'theme' is used here in a technical sense to denote a postulate or position, declared or implied, and usually controlling behavior or stimulating activity, which is tacitly approved or openly promoted in a society" ("Themes as Dynamic Forces in Culture," *American Journal of Sociology*, Vol. LI [1945], pp. 198–206). See also Herskovits, *op. cit.*, pp. 214–226; Albert K. Cohen, "An Evaluation of Themes and Kindred Concepts," *Ameri-*

can *Journal of Sociology,* Vol. LII (1946), pp. 41–42; Morris E. Opler, "An Application of the Theory of Themes in Culture," *Journal of the Washington Academy of Sciences,* Vol. 36 (May 15, 1946), pp. 137–166.

6. Carl L. Becker, *The Heavenly City of the Eighteenth-century Philosophers* (New Haven, Conn.: Yale University Press, 1933).

7. An anonymous aphorism is frequently quoted: "France is an absolute monarchy, tempered by songs."

8. (New York: Alfred A. Knopf, 1951), pp. 388*ff.* See also Kingsley Davis, Harry C. Bredemeier, and Marion J. Levy, Jr., *Modern American Society* (New York: Rinehart & Company, Inc., 1948), Chap. II.

9. Read Bain, "Our Schizoid Culture," *Sociology and Social Research,* Vol. XIX (1934–1935), pp. 266–276. See also Jean Paul Sartre, "Americans and Their Myths," *The Nation,* Oct. 18, 1948, pp. 402–403.

10. Robin Williams, Jr., *American Society* (New York: Alfred A. Knopf, Inc., 1951), p. 439.

11. See Henry Steele Commager, *The American Mind* (New Haven, Conn.: Yale University Press, 1950).

12. From Arthur Koestler, *The Yogi and the Commissar* (New York: The Macmillan Company, 1945), pp. 3–6.

13. From Ruth Benedict, *Patterns of Culture* (Boston: Houghton Mifflin Company, 1934), pp. 19–29. Used by permission of the publisher.

14. Portions of the material for this section adapted from W. E. Woodward, *The Way Our People Live* (New York: E. P. Dutton & Co., Inc., 1944), pp. 11–37.

15. From unpublished manuscript by Joseph B. Gittler.

16. Material for this section adapted from Leon S. Marshall, "The Emergence of the First Industrial City: Manchester, 1780–1850," in Carolina F. Ware (ed.), *The Cultural Approach to History* (New York: Columbia University Press, 1940), pp. 140–161.

17. President's Research Committee on Recent Social Trends, *Recent Social Trends* (New York: McGraw-Hill Book Company, Inc., 1933), pp. 153–156.

18. William F. Ogburn, "Technology and Society," mimeograph, pp. 15*ff.* See also National Resources Committee, *Technological Trends and National Policy* (Washington: Government Printing Office, 1937), pp. 61–64.

19. Bernhard J. Stern, *Social Factors in Medical Progress* (New York: Columbia University Press, 1927).

20. C. A. H. Smith, "The Discovery of Anesthesia," *Scientific Monthly,* Vol. 24 (1927), pp. 64–70.

21. From H. G. Barnett, "Personal Conflicts and Cultural Change," *Social Forces,* Vol. 20 (December, 1941), pp. 160–171.

*22. "Culture Processes," *American Anthropologist,* Vol. 42 (1940), pp. 21–48.

*23. Ralph Linton, *The Study of Man* (New York: Appleton-Century-Crofts, 1936), pp. 344–345.

*24. John W. Arctander, *The Apostle of Alaska* (New York: Fleming H. Revell Company, 1909), pp. 157–164.

*25. It should be stated that these reasons are not my deductions or constructions. They were offered, as given, by informants.

*26. Around 1870 one entire house membership moved to Metlakatla as a result of their head having killed this sorcerer. The murderer was arrested and faced imprisonment or death in Victoria. At his insistence his relatives appealed to Duncan who agreed to have him released on probation if he and his family would move to Metlakatla—another instance of an escape through accepting the new order.

27. Carol Hughes, "Perry, Georgia, Leads the Way," *Coronet,* Vol. 21, No. 6 (April, 1947), pp. 130–132. Coronet Copyright, 1947, by Esquire Inc.

PART SEVEN

Some Problems of Personal and Social Disorganization

A. THE LIFE HISTORY OF A DELINQUENT

It is almost an axiom that some condition of order and system pervades all forms of existence—physical, biological, and social. The solar system of the planetary orbits, the unity of the biological organism, the political state, the familial group, the industrial plant, the baseball game, all seem to testify to some tendency toward order and organization. Emerson in his *Monadnock* went so far as to say that "the world was built in order and the atoms march in tune."

Whether the world displays an intrinsic order or whether its orders are the creative systems of man has been a subject of philosophical discussion for centuries; it is certainly a metaphysical point, unlikely to lead to any concrete solution. The scientists, including the sociologist, have at least accepted as a starting point that some organization and order do exist. The very essence of the group, culture pattern, and social personality implies an arrangement of parts into an integrated whole. It is true that the operating system does not always perform smoothly, perfectly, and effectively. Some semblance of organization, however, is actually discernible. In addition, thinking man seems to compare that which exists with his imaginative images of ideal orders. In both instances, social order and social organization have their concomitants in social disorder and social disorganization. When affairs deviate either from the existent order or from the desired order, the inference is that there is social disorder. It is this deviation that is referred to as social disorganization. It consists of the relative decline and breakdown of those factors that have made and do make for the effective patterning of collective living.

Strikes and absenteeism in an industrial plant, revolt against the state, vice and crime or acts against the mores and legal systems—all these events create disorder or a malfunctioning of an organized pattern of men and their values. It should be noted that disorder may function for a period, out of which may arise another form of organization which will create a new order. Thus political revolution may cause a state of political disintegration out of which may come a stable pattern for a new type of state. Social problems in any given period in a culture are the concrete manifestations of some form of social disorganization.

It should also be noted that the person is the individual concomitant of social disorganization. It is the individual who deviates from the existent order which is reflected ultimately in the social forms of that order. The individual deviate and the social problem are two sides of the same coin of societal dissension. One way to understand the dynamics of social disorganization is to comprehend the nature of the individual deviate. Sociologists have long been interested in a number of social problems in our society. Chief among these have been the problems of criminals, divorce, juvenile delinquency, race and minority-group relations, and wars.

The following case history of a delinquent is the detailed narrative of a career of one of five brothers, all of whom had long records of delinquency and crime starting in early childhood and continuing through adulthood. At the time of this study these brothers ranged from twenty-five to thirty-five years of age. Together they had served a total of approximately fifty-five years in correctional and penal institutions. Clifford R. Shaw, from whose book *Brothers in Crime* this case is taken, says: "They had been picked up and arrested by the police at least eighty-six times, brought into court seventy times, confined in institutions for forty-two separate periods, and placed under supervision of probation and parole officers approximately forty-five times."

The case that follows is the story of Edward Martin (the name is of course fictitious), next to the oldest. In 1938 he was thirty-three years of age. His earliest experience in stealing occurred when he was six years old. During the eighteen years in which he was actively delinquent he was arrested twenty-three times, appeared in courts on delinquent and criminal charges eighteen times, served ten periods of confinement in correctional and penal institutions, and placed under the supervision of probation and parole officers thirteen different times.

The case of Edward shows the dynamics of the factors working to make him a delinquent and the fashion in which they operated to prolong his delinquency. His case suggests that delinquency is quite closely related to the cultural and economic conflicts which confront the immigrant family in the physically deteriorated and socially disorganized communities in larger American cities.

The reader should note that under the stress of basic deprivations and failure to find personal identity in the home, school, and other socially acceptable institutions, the boy joins and identifies with, from an early age, childhood street-corner gangs. Through identification with these gangs, he takes over their values. These in turn deviate from the normally accepted values of our society, thus defining the boy as a delinquent when identification with these groups leads to overt acts consistent with his identification. Thus the lack of membership in and identification with delinquent groups holds the key to the understanding of why some children, reared in the same blighted areas as their delinquent peers, pursue socially acceptable avenues of behavior.

I

My mother and dad were born in Europe.[1] Both of them were born in a little village on the outskirts of a large city. The folks on father's side were farmers. Mother's folks have had schooling and occupied positions of importance in the village. About five years after their marriage, they wanted to come to America. Mother had a step-brother who came here some years back, and wrote nice letters about this country. In the exchange of letters, my dad was given the necessary instructions in applying for passage to America.

After mother received the necessary money from her step-brother and friends in this country, they bade their old friends good-bye. They booked steerage passage on an old tramp steamer, and arrived in New York some twelve days later. Completing their quarantine period at Ellis Island, they took a train to Chicago. There they were met by my mother's step-brother at the depot and escorted to a flat which he had rented for them.

During the next four years of adjustment two of us kids were born. Father worked in a tannery at this time and things seemed to be going along fine. The money borrowed by them to make the trip was paid back. But, with the beginning of the following year things began to change. Pa had liked his drinks even in the old country, but he had been moderate. During the first four years he very seldom took a drink of liquor until his debt was paid. Paying his last debt, Pa celebrated the occasion by getting drunk. And from that time on he continued to celebrate. As the saying goes: Pa went to the dogs. He lost all sense of responsibility. His drinking brought us trouble and misery.

The responsibility of caring for the family fell on Ma's shoulders, but it became a little too great for her to carry. Pa lost his tannery job several times, but because of his skillfulness he had been called back time and again; the foreman, however, got tired of doing this, and fired him for good. We had to move for lack of rent. Moving to a flat a few doors east of the place of my birth, we lived here about ten months, when we were forced to move again. While living here, I recollect my first impression of a drunken man. How he would weave from side to side, fall down heavily, and snore like a buzz-saw hitting a knot. When we moved from here I was a very sick baby and I recall Ma holding me in her arms and pleading with the landlady not to throw us out. With the help of my generous godfather, from whom we received a horse and wagon for moving, we moved to an old ramshackle frame building where the rent was $4.50 per month. We lived alongside the main line of a railroad and the house trembled and the windows rattled every time a train roared by. During the beginning of our stay here, I would get frightened when the trains passed by, as it seemed that the house was falling down on us. We lived in a rear building, facing an alley to one side, and the railroad on the other.

As I was too young for school I used to pass the time away by watching the trains go by. In the winter time, after a big snow, I would pass the day by jumping into the snow pile in our yard, or whatever took my fancy. During the first winter here, another baby came, making it a little harder for us all. The winter James (a brother) was born, I recall the house was cold at least half of the time, for lack of fuel. During these cold spells when Pa came home drunk, we often saw Ma crying, and seeing her cry, we kids also cried. Pa had luck in always finding a job, and would work until he received his pay, and then, getting drunk for several days, he would lose the job. While drunk he had fights with the neighbors and all who came his way.

Being five years old, Ma took me to a parochial school, where she wanted me to attend, but being a little young, the teachers told her to wait another year. Shortly after this we moved again, a half block south, into a basement flat alongside the railroad. Michael was born here. It was here that I first saw the neighbors steal coal from a car standing near the house. To me it seemed that the men and women must have emptied a half car, throwing coal into the yard; then all the neighbors helped each other fill their coal sheds. I recall the railroad bull asking the people about the half-empty car, and everyone denying their guilt. When I was a little over six years old, we moved to a place near the river, another basement flat in a rear building. Here my youngest brother, Carl, was born.

It was while living here that I got lost while trying to follow my older brother to a strange part of the city. John and some older boys were going somewhere and because I was too young, they refused to take me along. After chasing me home several times, I followed them at a distance. They spotted an empty wagon going in their direction, and jumped and sat on the tailgate. When I saw them get on, I tried to catch up and get on, too. Being too small, I couldn't run fast enough to catch up with the horse. After I chased the wagon for several blocks, I lost track of them.

After what seemed like miles of walking and after numerous stops for rests, I realized I was lost. Not knowing my street address, I tried to find my way home. I walked and walked for hours.

I finally reached a park I had visited with an older boy. Darkness having settled sometime before, and to make matters worse it now began to rain, I went into a nearby hallway to wait until the rain ceased. I sat down to rest, and then knew nothing more because I fell asleep. How long I slept I do not know. I woke up when I felt a weight on my leg. Looking up, I saw a man standing over me. He asked me something in a language I didn't understand. I told him in English that I had become lost, but that I could find my way home now. After telling him this, he refused to let me go home alone, because it was very late. He took me first to his wife, next door, which happened to be a saloon, then with a few directions from me, he carried me home. For this, Pa gave me a licking with a cat-o'-nine-tails.

Pa appeared to be drunk more often, and Ma began going to work at truck-farming in the suburbs. So we were left alone from early morning until late at night. Ma would give John a dime to buy a nickel loaf of bread, and a nickel's worth of sausage, which had to last until she came home.

I lived here only a short time when I got acquainted with the other roughnecks, picked up most of their bad habits, and learned how to do all the things they did. When Ma started working and there was no one to care for us I learned how to go junking; that's picking up bottles, rags, copper, lead, brass, zinc, or anything that was of value to a junker. Whenever we saw anything of value while walking around aimlessly, we would save it until we had enough to take to the junk-yard ourselves, because we would get a better price here than from the junkman who went up and down the alleys and streets. It was while living here that I learned to fight for everything I got. From stealing coal, wood and junking, I learned to protect the pennies for which I had worked hard. Many of the children here turned out to be bad eggs. Most of them wound up in the Big House. Many still live in this vicinity.

When I heard tales about the way schools punished children, I was afraid to go to them. Ma had taken me there two years previous but being too young, I didn't start. Now, being about seven years old, Ma took me there again. On my second day I received a few blows over my hand, and then began playing hookey with the other boys. While playing hookey, we would walk over to the railroad tracks with coal bags and wait for the coal cars to pull in. We would board them and throw off as much coal as possible, fill our bags, and either carry the coal home and put it in the coal shed or sell it for ten cents a bag.

When the shows would open at noon we truants were in the front line, waiting to buy a nickel ticket, which would allow three of us kids to see the movie. We always had candy which one of us would buy at the five-and-ten-cent store, for an amount equal to the price of the show, split it in equal shares, and enjoy the thrillers that the nickel shows held. During the winter time, when Ma would be at home, going to the shows was a good place, and the best place to keep out of the truant officer's hands. About the time that school ended for the day, we would leave the show, first cleaning ourselves in the washroom and then return to the places where we had hid our books, get them and go home.

The following days of truancy varied. Sometimes, if it was warm, we would go over to the river and swim or learn to swim in the old swimming hole that was formed by the caving in of the river bank. Taking chances of drowning, we would play many games of follow-the-leader, trying to outdo each other in this swimming hole. On other hookey days, if we weren't stealing coal, we would go junking. Other days saw us playing over on the railroad tracks, jumping on lumber piles, chasing each other, playing "it," throwing stones into the river, trying to outdo each other in everything we played.

During this period, I learned to fight and shift around for myself, found how to make show money, and pick up articles from rear porches, which had a value in the junk-yard. By this I mean if us kids would see a washboiler on someone's porch, we would sneak up and take it. We would rip off the bottom, and being copper, we would get from five to ten cents for it from the junkyard and then we would divide the money up which was usually spent for candy. Everything was split equally. When junking, we would try to get either copper, brass, or lead, as this metal paid a good price, and wasn't too heavy for us, as was iron. Iron was cheap, and you had to get a lot in order to get show money, and it was very heavy to carry. Not having anyone to look after us while Ma was working, it was no wonder that I came to do and learn these things.

Getting to know the truant officer, from the older boys, it was no trouble to keep out of his hands, because the older boys usually saw him first. In the chase through yards and alleys, the older boys would take hold of my hands, and I just seemed to be flying instead of running. He would chase us smaller boys, but we wouldn't try to outrun him. Making sure he wasn't too close, we would run in someone's yard, and secrete ourselves on someone's porch or shed until he ran past.

When I was about eight years old and still playing truant while Ma worked, the truant officer came to our home one evening. After telling Ma of my truancy from school, he stated that the juvenile authorities had sent him with an order from the court for my appearance on such-and-such a day. Arriving at the court, I was impressed by the sternness here, and when Ma led me to the bar, my knees were knocking. Standing before the bar, I heard my name called. The judge called my name again because he did not see me. He began to ask questions, when a policeman standing to my left stated I was here. Being undersized and undernourished, I recall the judge leaning over his bench and looking at me where I stood without shoes, a torn pair of pants, and a bald head. I don't know what his thoughts were.

All I recall was that a policeman led me to a sideroom, where they had about ten kids bigger than myself. In here I found out that they were going to take me away from home, and put me in the Parental School. Thinking that they were only scaring me, I sat in the room with the other boys, who were talking with their mothers and fathers. When two more boys were brought into this room, and hearing that they were going to the Parental School, it finally penetrated my head that they weren't joking as the kids in the neighborhood did.

Whatever you did, whether it was truancy or stealing coal, it was all right as long as you didn't get caught. Having no one to take me in hand, I followed the flock.

Every time I thought of being away from Ma and the rest, I cried all the harder. Finally a policeman ushered us into a horse-drawn carriage, where some of the kids told me to shut up. Passing through the Loop, I stopped crying, as my curiosity got the best of me. The big buildings awed me, and I couldn't believe they could build them that high. I recall the City Hall, especially, as it was one of the biggest then. During the ride, the kids' happy spirit got me, and when we reached the school, I laughed and joked with the rest.

On reaching the school, we were led to the main office, where the officers drew lots in picking out the boys they wanted. A man from Cottage E drew me, and led me away to the shower room, where he gave me another bald head and forced me to take a bath. A bath was something new to me. Never having one at home I thought it was something useless, which I plainly stated, adding a few cuss words to emphasize my point. But a few pokes and blows across my ribs and seat forced me to take one anyway. I was then given school clothes. Later, I was led to my cottage where I saw my brother, John.

Not being used to this kind of life of rules and regulations, I got myself into plenty of trouble. When being taught to drill, I got mutinous with one of the kid officers. When first taking up this drill exercise, I took it as a joke; after a spell, when it began to get tiresome, I refused to obey the officer. Getting tough with me did no good, as I got tough myself and told him to put up his dukes. After his refusal, I called him a few bad names. Being an officer, he called my brother, John, and told him to tell me that I couldn't use bad language, and had to obey orders. Leaving John and I together, John told me what they would do to me if I didn't do what I was told.

That evening I had to chew a piece of soap for swearing. I soon found out I had to live quite differently from the life I led at home. Although I felt homesick once in awhile, I really liked this place. I liked the clean clothes, clean bed sheets, and baths, and all the many other things which up to this time I had never known. The meals to me were very delicious, and the atmosphere agreed with me. I liked a lot of things about the place. There was a swimming pool, which I fell in love with. The schooling, and the teachers were more than considerate. I was taught my ABC's and multiplication tables here. I was taught how to plant seeds, how to pick flowers, and do a little truck-gardening.

A few days after I came out of the Parental School I was walking down the street with my brother John. We met a friend of his who had just been in a fight with a kid. Hearing this kid swear, I told him it's wrong to swear, and that he would get punished for it. He, in turn, wanted to know since when did I become a sissy and a teacher's pet. I soon found out that I was getting into fights for sticking to the new ideals I had been taught. When some of us kids would get in groups and talk about something, the kids would use a cussword here and there. When it was said in my presence I would resent it by telling the kids that it was a sin and not to swear. As a rule, the kids were a little bigger than myself and would resent my butting in. After a verbal fight, it usually would end up with, "You want a punch in the nose?" After declaring himself, the kids would take sides, for or against him, which usually ended in a fight between the two of us. I found out I would have to fight every kid I knew, because everyone that I knew swore like a trooper.

Eventually this ideal wore away, as I began to mix with the kids. Before long the Parental School was a thing in the past, and I was doing the same things I had done before. While fighting for my new ideals I received a name for being tough. And, because the kids found out I had been in the "band house" as they called it, the tough character stuck.

While playing hookey from school one winter, a kid brought a note home asking mother why I haven't been in school for the last several months. I had spent that day with the other kids on the railroad tracks. We built a fire, stole some spuds from a box car, and had barbeque spuds. We then spent the day flipping rides on and off the different freights that pulled in. Between this we had a bunch of snowballs, and from our hiding place we would throw and try to knock off someone's derby. If the man happened to see us, we would run like hell. If the man caught us he would kick us in the pants. Derbies used to be our weakness during snowtime. After I had cleaned up, and getting my books together, where I had hid them, I started home with a cheery whistle on my lips.

Not suspecting I had been found out as a truant, the cheery whistle soon became a squawk of pain. After getting a good licking from Ma, I was promised a better one from Pa. Knowing the weight of Pa's hand, I made myself scarce before he came home. Afraid to go home that night, I found a warm entrance, a back hallway, where I lay down and fell asleep. The hallway got a little chilly and I woke up. Looking for a warmer spot, I walked to the top of the stairs. Finding an open door, I walked into what seemed to be an empty, warm room. I started to lay down when I bumped into an obstacle. Lighting a match to see what I had bumped, I nearly jumped out of my skin, in getting out of this place. Of all hallways to pick from, I picked an undertaking parlor, and the room I was about to lay down in was full of caskets. Leaving in a big hurry I walked around for about a half-hour until I spotted an empty milk wagon setting in a vacant lot. Climbing into the back of it, I lay down, and shivered through the rest of the night. That morning with my teeth chattering and froze stiff, I wended my way to a friend's house, where I sat before the fire, thawing out. Afraid to go home, I passed the day around the river and railroad tracks sitting before a fire, cooking spuds.

That night I found a warm hallway, and slept contentedly until a night watchman saw me, and turned me over to a cop. After being questioned as to why I was sleeping in a hallway, I was given a ride in the paddy-wagon and turned over to Pa. Knowing what to expect, I wasn't disappointed. Ten minutes after the wagon left, my yells woke up most of our neighbors. With my hand on my sore seat, I nevertheless was glad to crawl into bed with the rest of my brothers and fall asleep.

Because I played hookey so long, I received another request to see the Judge again. After stating I would not attend school, I received another Parental School term. This time I spent eleven months there. I always recall them as pleasant ones. I had no trouble with the kids. The food was swell, except the codfish we got on Fridays. I didn't like this so well, but the orders were you had to eat everything or be punished. So, with a hand over my nose, I would manage to eat it.

II

Yes, sir, I will always recall my stay at the Parental School as pleasant. Although I had overstayed the time set by the Court, the authorities couldn't get any answer from my folks in regard to coming there and taking me home. Finally, one chilly autumn day I was dressed up and, in care of an officer, I was brought home.

My folks had moved a half-mile west while I was in the school and I was rather surprised when I was taken to this new address, as I still thought we hadn't moved. The place they had moved into was a basement flat next to an alley. This place was cold as an icebox. Being next to the alleyway, the windows when open, would bring in the garbage smells. Now and then I would see a rat chewing a hole in the sill trying to get in. To me they looked as big as a cat. When I went to bed I would hear them nibbling on the sill, and us kids were always afraid of them getting through and jumping on us, as the windows were near the ceiling, and above our bed.

I returned to school the following day after my return from Parental. Having no friends in this neighborhood, I stuck to my older brother, John. I got along fine at school and liked it. At least until the time I began going astray. I attended school pretty regular, excepting a period when a light cut over my eye got infected, and nearly blinded me.

I attended school that winter and the following spring and I made fair headway, up to the time I made friends with a fellow named Stock. Late in the spring, while on my way home for dinner, I found a penny laying in the school yard. Eating a sandwich, which usually consisted of two slices of homemade bread, a little lard and a slice of onion, I wended my way to the nearest candy store. As most of us know, a candy store is like a magnet when you have money in your pocket. I had a penny in mine. Arriving at the store I saw my brother Johnny and Stock standing in the doorway. Speaking to my brother for a moment or two, he introduced me to Stock.

A few weeks later having an infected eye, I was permitted to stay home. Strolling towards the candy store I saw Stock standing out in front, with a basket on his arm. After greeting him, he said he was waiting for my brother. Telling him that

John went to school, he asked if I wanted to come along to the city. I recall one thing that he pictured for me in answering my questions of "why" and "for what." That was a sort of glowing picture of a ride on the "L" and the big buildings I would see, and all at his expense. This was like giving me a dish of ice cream for nothing.

I accepted the invitation and all others after that. Going along for about two weeks I began getting curious as to why he received money and things to eat from the different places he would go to. Although I was told these places he went to were people who knew him and his family and were helping them out, I began thinking different, as every time I went along he went to different homes. I went along for the ride. But when he came to the place he wanted, I was asked by him to wait on the corner while he went from house to house in that block. After going to most of the homes, he would come back with money and a basket of food. One day I heard him ask for food at a strange place, and then I knew what he was doing was begging.

Seeing him get food and money this way, I decided to take a basket the next time I went along. Having only the barest necessities at home a basket of food would really be appreciated by us kids. Seeing me with a basket at our next meeting, he didn't like the idea of me cutting in. During my former trips I acted as his stooge. By this I mean I had to carry his basket when it became full, to repay him for the carfare or "L" fare he spent on me. Although this fellow never cared for school, he was very shrewd and a schemer. In me he had a helper and a companion for almost nothing. As I said before, although he didn't like the idea of me taking a basket, he didn't refuse to pay my fare. John, in the meantime, had been sent to St. Charles.

Later on, we seldom paid an "L" fare, as we had learned how to find holes or openings that we crawled through that gave us an inlet to the train. Being small boys we would manage to squeeze through the most impossible places, and take the craziest and some of the most dangerous chances, just to sneak a ride on the "L." Going with Stock I was taught the technique of begging, and getting the hang of it, I helped my family and myself with a bigger and better larder.

During this start of my begging, I began to play truant during the afternoons. Later, it became so I was truant all day. Stage by stage, I quit school altogether in order to devote all my time to begging, having learned the ropes through Stock.

I would go from house to house, as Stock did, and give the folks a long, hard-luck story that would make them sympathetic; for this we would get some eatables, or a little change. Although I gave a hard-luck story, the funny part of it was that, as far as we were concerned, it was a true one. Most of the homes we told our tales of woe were very sympathetic, and usually gave us a helping hand.

After begging for about a year, I had more truancy trouble. Taken to court I was described as a habitual truant. The Judge, not knowing how to dispose of my case at the present time, my case was continued for two months, and I was sent to the Juvenile Detention Home at G—— and F—— streets. This was my second time here in the past year, as I was picked up for begging about six months before this, and had spent about seven weeks here before I was sent home.

In this place we had very little to do. Scrubbing floors was the main item of work. After being awakened in the morning, we had to make our beds. After the beds were made, the guards would pick out the biggest boys, order them to scrub the bedroom, and the smaller boys would push the beds to one side. After scrubbing the open section, the beds would be moved into it and the rest of the whole dormitory was scrubbed. After this was done, we would wash up and march upstairs to the dining room for our breakfast. Before eating, one of the guards would call the roll. We answered our names as being present. After a short morning devotion of thanking the Lord for our daily bread, we ate our breakfast. After breakfast, we would go to the playroom and pass the rest of the day the best way possible (usually fighting).

In the summer time, the kids would spend most of the time in the walled-in yard, walking around, or playing a game of playground ball occasionally. However, we small kids were too small to play ball with the other kids. We spent most of our time fighting. Most of my fights were with the dagoes or shines. When I first came here the shines were the ones I had to fight most of the time. I always had to be on guard because there were two nigger partners with whom I was always fighting. If they caught me unaware they would both gang up on me, and I had my hands full fighting them until the guard, hearing the commotion, would come and break us up. Being on my guard, this didn't happen very often. When I caught them apart, I had a swell time giving them a trimming. After spending most of my seven weeks in this manner, I was turned over to my parents. On my second trip, my time was spent in the same manner, only more fighting. In most of the eighteen months I had spent in the Detention Home, at various times, I recall them mostly as months of fighting.

After a two months' wait, I saw the Judge again, and was sent to the Chicago and Cook County School. A very able and understanding man was in charge, and it is a pleasure for me to say this, as he was like a father to the boys in his care. Although the Parental School wasn't bad, the Cook County School was the best of any school I have ever been in. I really was sorry when I was released. I hated to leave this place. The work was pleasant, not hard at all. The country air, and the fresh food was of the best.

When I was told I was going home in the morning, I felt rather bad as I would have liked to stay here. Being home a short time, and living at another new address, which, by the way, happened to be another basement flat in another frame shack (which since that time has been demolished) I began begging again. Conditions at home were as bad as ever. Our meals were of the very cheapest and not enough to supply our needs. Not having the necessary food, and no way of getting it, begging was the only way I could receive the necessary food and clothes. Begging was a necessity, because it raised our standard of living to a slightly higher degree;

and it became a means of paying our rent. Although it went against my boyish pride when I got an inkling of the type of people who did this, nevertheless, I knew it was necessary in my case.

While begging on the North Side I was stopped by a lady who asked me what I was doing with such a basket under my arm, and why I wasn't in school. She was dressed in a gray, two-piece suit, and in the way she asked the questions I thought she was a truant officer and was ready to run. Reading my thoughts, she assured me I had nothing to be afraid of. Telling her of conditions at home, she told me to come over to her home the coming Saturday as she had some clothes and things she wanted to give me. Reading my doubts as to my coming, she made me solemnly promise I would be there Saturday.

My word was my bond. Although being suspicious of her good intentions and thinking that I would walk into a trap, I, nevertheless, though with great misgivings, went there that Saturday. After giving her my word of honor, I had to go. To my great surprise it was no trap, and after spending several hours at her home, in which she asked about everything at home, she gave me some clothes, a basket full of eatables, and a dollar. With another promise that I was to return the following Saturday, I bade her good-bye. The many following Saturdays proved to be days of friendship for me and the rest of the family. She drove over to our home; found conditions as I had told her. She proved a good friend and a helping one. All of us kids received presents from her and help in many forms.

After making her friendship, I got into trouble over my truancy. Out of a wintry sky I was arrested at home by a policeman, taken to the Juvenile Home, and brought to court a few days later. Having no idea as to the reason or suddenness, I heard some woman employed by the court tell the Judge that I was a beggar and wouldn't go to school; that I was a little blackguard and should be sent to St. Charles for eighteen months. Upon her recommendations, the Judge sent me there. Turning me over to some parole officer, I was taken aboard a train for St. Charles. Arriving at the depot we were met by an officer of the school. Getting into his model T Ford touring car, he drove the three miles to the school, and I nearly froze to death getting there.

At the school I was taken to the Administration Building, asked several questions, the answers to which were duly recorded. I was then taken to the receiving cottage where I went through a breaking-in and quarantine stage for two weeks. After two weeks I was questioned by the supervisor as to where I came from and the type of work I had done and liked. The supervisor would assign you to a cottage where the boys were about the same height. If you were a little boy you were assigned to the little boy's cottage; if you were a big boy you went to the big boy's cottage. I don't know why he asked about the work I liked, because you never got what you would like to learn.

Each cottage had a certain type of trade, and if you were transferred to it, you did that line of work unless you were assigned to something special. There were also eight farm cottages and if you came from the country you would be assigned to one of these. In my case, although I was rather small, I escaped the smallest cottage, and was assigned to Cottage R.

The house father of this cottage had charge of a fruit garden, which was called the south garden. This is where I worked with the other boys of my cottage. We worked in split shifts. In the afternoon, the morning detail went to school, and the morning schoolboys worked in the afternoon detail. I was assigned to the morning detail and afternoon school.

After working here about two months I was assigned to work in the main kitchen. The main kitchen is where all the food is cooked for the boys of all cottages, excepting the farms. At certain periods of each day, morning, noon and night, two boys from each cottage would come to the main kitchen pulling a little covered carriage containing several pans about a foot square. We would take and fill these pans with whatever food we cooked for the rest of the boys. Their food was cooked in big steam kettles, and our's over a range.

Working in the kitchen made me exempt from any of the duties in the cottage. While the other boys were drilling and the new boys learning how, I would sit on the lawn and watch them.

We quit work around 6:00 to 6:30 o'clock in the evening. If I knew the boys were to drill that night, I would prolong my stay at the kitchen until I felt certain the boys were nearly through before I came to my cottage. On evenings of playdays I would manage to be at the cottage a little earlier. I had no intention of running away. The work wasn't hard, the food was excellent. I was getting fat, and was content.

Some eighteen months after my arrival, I was given a blue slip, which meant on the morrow I was going home. After getting the slip, I walked over to the receiving cottage where I received some of my old clothes, sent from home. I took them to my cottage where I put them in the dressing room locker.

The following morning I donned my own clothes, bade the boys goodbye, walked over to the Administration Building where I reclaimed what few possessions I had and got on board the school bus with the other ten boys who were leaving.

Arriving at a downtown terminal, I walked about the downtown section, looking at some of the improvements that had been made during my absence. This country was at war with the Germans at this time. Spotting a recruiting station, I tried to join the army. I was told to wait a little longer, as this country wanted some of the grownups sent to France before they would start sending kids. Completing my sight-seeing, I decided to walk the four miles home, and save the car fare. When I arrived at my new address, I found the flat that my folks lived in. No one being home I found an open window, crawled in and looked the place over. The apartment was another basement flat, but this one in a two-story brick building. Four rooms, toilet in the hallway, and gas for lighting purposes. Although a nice, cool place in the summer, it was hard to heat in the winter. . . .

I quit the shoe job, and took up Stock's and Stanley's company. What were the number of places we entered I don't recall; they were too numerous to mention. In the beginning when entering a home, I was mostly interested in getting money, and took nothing but that. Later however, until my arrest, I began taking watches and jewelry, as did Stock, who always took everything of value in the jewelry line. Jewelry, such as watches, I sold for whatever I could get. Not knowing its value, I didn't get much. The other things, if we couldn't sell them, we gave to someone we liked, or threw them away. We entered the homes in many ways. On some, we used a skeleton key, in others the windows were open. Still others, we forced our way in by either breaking a window, or breaking down the door as quietly as possible. In some, we would crawl through an open transom. In others, as in flats, the icebox was an easy means of entrance. In several of these burglaries we nearly were caught.

When no one answered the doorbell after a moment of ringing, we would take it for granted that no one was home. Gaining an entrance in a quiet way, we would be surprised in the act of burglary by the owner who had been sleeping. After a hurried exit by way of a window or door, we eluded the man or woman by running through yards and alleys. In one place, the first floor, which I entered through an open transom, I couldn't open the rear door. Telling Stock to go to the front, I began walking towards the front door. While passing a bedroom I was seized by the owner, who awoke when I began speaking instructions to Stock. Being seized so suddenly, my reactions were those of a frightened animal. Feeling my arm pinioned, I involuntarily stepped back, jerking loose the hold. Seeing a giant of a man (well, he looked like a giant, anyway) I whirled around and ran the way I came. Knowing that I would never get out the way I had come, I leaped through a closed window. Shielding my face with my arms, my only bruise was a bump on my elbow which I received when I landed in a heap on the rear porch. Yelling for Stock to run, I leaped to the ground, jumped over the rear fence, and ran hell-bent for election. After chasing me for three blocks I lost the man through the maze of yards and alleys which I ran through.

After these narrow escapes, we really made sure no one was home by ringing the front and rear doors. Sometimes the bells were out of order, and we would make enough noise to wake up the dead by pounding on the door just to be sure the people had gone.

Prowling houses too numerous to mention or recall, I was finally picked up at the house in late October. What happened was Stanley Runcer and Stock had been picked up while roaming on the North Side. The policemen, finding a bunch of jewelry on their persons, knew they had a couple of burglars. During the grilling process, Stanley gave in and implicated Stock and myself in numerous jobs. All three of us were taken in a car, driven to most of these places we had burglarized, and told to confess that we had been there. If Stanley stated we were there, we admitted our guilt; in others which Stock and I committed without Stanley when also pointed out, I denied I had been there. I had found two rings in a wall-safe, and thinking them of no value, I gave them to one of my friends.

Knowing if I admitted my guilt I would get others into trouble, I denied all knowledge of being there. Thinking the rings had no value, I failed to tell Stanley and Stock about them. After Stanley admitted being there, Stock did also. I tried my best to convince them we weren't there, or that if they were, I wasn't. My statement of not being there was said in such a manner that I implied a meaning of "No," but the thing went over their heads. They even went to the trouble of recalling how Stock and I had given Stanley a boost to an open window, and how he had broken an egg in the purse when he found no money in it. The police then began to question me about the whereabouts of the two rings I had taken from there. I denied knowing anything about them. After being transferred to the Juvenile Home, the police would come and question us every few days. They came to the conclusion that I had taken them without letting Stock and Stanley know about it. Failing to get the address of my friend, they asked Stock. Having taken Stock to this friend several times, they received the address from him and found the rings there.

Held at the Juvenile Home, pending trial, scheming on how to escape from here, I finally found a way out. Being separated from Stock, I couldn't let him in on it, so with the help of another boy we forced two screen locks and escaped by way of the fire-escape on Armistice Day, 19—; two days before I was to appear in court. Reaching my home unmolested I snuck into the house, put on some other clothes, and slept in a hayloft above a stable nearby. The next day I went to the friend, who got in trouble on my account. Hearing that they had to go to court with me, I was told that I would get them into more trouble if I wasn't there. Hating to cause them trouble, I let them turn me over to the police, and saved a lot of trouble. At court the following day, I found the rings I had taken were valued at $3400.00. For this I was sentenced to St. Charles again, but managed to escape a few days before my transfer.

In this escape, seven of us boys got away, Stock, myself, and five others. Whether Stanley was in this I don't recall. Using the hayloft for a bedroom we stayed away from home about a week. We sent the different kids we knew to find out if the cops were looking for us. Finding the coast was clear, we used the utmost caution in approaching the house. Not wanting to take any chances, I would send some kid to see if the cops were at the house waiting for me. Being told no one was there, I would come in through the alleyway because the entrance to the house was the nearest from there. Knowing if the police came it was usually at night, I was always ready to flee at the first knock on the door; half of the time I slept with my clothes on.

Picking up the string where the police broke in, we continued our burglaries, and began breaking into stores as well as houses. A fellow named Shorty and myself broke into a tavern about two o'clock in the morning. Getting what cash was left in the till, we made ourselves a collection of the best wines, liquors and cigars. Having come into possession of several skeleton keys, we found one of the keys opened the side door of this tavern. Locking the door again, we waited until the place closed before we made our entrance. On the way out we spotted the telephone box where the nickels, dimes, and quarters were held. Not wanting to leave that, we jerked it off the wall. In doing so the owner heard the noise in the adjoining room. Working in the dark, we wrapped the stuff, including the telephone box, into a bunch of newspapers. With the bundles under our arms, we got as far as the door, when the lights were snapped on, and the owner pointed a gun at us. Making us sit down in one of the booths, he called the police. Late that afternoon, we were taken before a judge in a sideroom; because the fellow got his things back, we were let go with a promise to be good boys. It was a lucky thing they didn't know I had run away from the Juvenile Home.

Meeting Stock, I told him about my experience. Having had some experience with the police, I began to look at them as enemies of my freedom, and when in their vicinity I was always ready to run at their slightest movement in my direction. A few days after Christmas, we went out to a wealthy section of Chicago. Entering a first-floor flat, we found clothes, cigars, whiskey, and another telephone coin box. On the way out we ran into a bunch of boys standing in front of the house. While on their way to see the boy who lived in this flat, they watched us enter through the rear. Getting more boys they surrounded the front and rear entrances. Coming out the front way, we ran into the boys in front. Stopping us at the front of the building, they asked what we were doing there. Not wanting to answer them, we told them to mind their own business. Since keeping steady company with Stock I had many fights while with him, because he would get tough with anyone who got fresh, and I would have to back him up. Though outnumbered by more than two to one, we fought against odds before. Telling them where they could go, we started walking when one of the older boys said to grab us and hold us while he got the rest of the boys. The three of us having had many such fights, fought free of these boys. Knowing that more help was coming, we knew to stay was to get caught. This place being on H—— Avenue we ran south on H—— Avenue to W—— Avenue. Here we ran in different directions as there were a dozen boys chasing us. Running at top speed, we gained a little lead in the three-block run before separating.

On separating, I ran west to the first alley. Running south here, I began to lose the boys chasing me. Running through alleyways and yards, I shook off all but one tall fellow of nineteen, who stuck on like glue. Tiring out from the hard run, I sought a hiding place. The neighborhood wasn't as dense as it is today. Buildings were in small clusters of mostly two-story apartments, and the clusters a block or so apart. Because it had snowed recently, my tracks were easy to follow. Losing the big boy, and being winded, the only place of concealment I could find was the rear porch of one of the apartments. Finding a place on the second floor, I caught my second wind. If I happened to be seen now, I would have the advantage over my pursuer.

The cards must have been stacked against me. No sooner had I found this spot then the lady of the house saw me on her porch. She opened the door, and inquired as to my business. Watching the alley for signs of approaching pursuers, I tried to tell the lady that I was playing "it," and was trying to avoid being seen. While speaking to the lady the fellow I had lost followed my footprints in the snow to the house where I was hiding.

He told the lady he had been chasing me all over town, and that I had robbed a flat. Being a conscientious lady she called the cops, while I tried to talk my way out of this. But, I was held by this fellow until the police came. This fellow holding me was too big and powerful to fight, weighing about 200 pounds and standing six feet four. The police drove me to their district station and locked me up.

I was grilled and questioned all day, but I admitted nothing. While being questioned, some cop recognized me as being over at his station before his transfer here. What he did was tell the officers who I was and who I worked with. Of course I didn't know this. Knowing that I would never disclose the others' identity, they laid a nice trap and used me for bait. Knowing I would join Stanley Runcer and Stock at first opportunity, they released me that evening, December 30th. Trailing me, they came in contact with a person who knew the three of us and most of our habits. However, figuring I had another lucky break, I slept at home that night. While looking for Stock the next day, I heard that he had gone to the I—— Theatre, a small show and swimming pool combined. Paying the show's admission charge, I stood in the long waiting line. Getting halfway to the ticket collector, I saw the same policeman standing near the collector, looking the people over. Unseen by them I managed to reach the outer door and make myself scarce.

Meeting Stanley and Stock, I was told how they had been pointed out in the show by someone, but with the help of a kid who was with them, they made good their escape. Reciting our experiences during the past two days, we stayed away from most of our usual places, excepting a little restaurant in which we always ate. We never ate at home.

After keeping out of sight most of the day, we decided to go to the restaurant and eat. Entering the restaurant we sat down to eat. Stock ordered a hamburger sandwich, Stanley an egg, and myself a dish of homemade rice pudding. Although hungry for food, upon entering the restaurant, I got a depressed feeling as though something was wrong. Looking around, I saw nothing to cause this feeling. About half-way through with the eating, the door opened. In came a fellow I knew, but never spoke to, with the two policemen that had arrested me, and chased Stanley and Stock out of the show. Whispering "cops," I made believe I didn't know Stanley and Stock. Walking up to me they greeted me by name. I said, "Hello." Having lost what little appetite I had, I stood up, dropped a dime on the counter and started to walk out. Taking a short step or two I was asked to sit down, and not to be in such a hurry. The cops told me I had lots of time. Sitting down, one of the cops asked me who my friends were, sitting alongside of me. I disclaimed all knowledge, and stated I had seen them for the first time. Having been pointed out as to their identity, the cops had to have their fun also, by listening to the tall lies and stories about the great mistakes they were making. After listening to our lies they cut short the comedy and took us to their district station, where they found out about our Juvenile escape and St. Charles sentence.

My first stay at St. Charles wasn't bad, as I avoided the drilling most of the time. This time I haven't any compliments to write about the place, as I received the full power of the system that was in vogue at this time. I also started my second term by putting out the wrong foot.

Here after less than two weeks, I tried to make an escape with two other boys. Some stool pigeon was let in on the attempt, and reported me to the housefather. Our plan being only in the first stage, I was given an hour squats. I had said a fellow could squeeze through one of the windows. This I mentioned to one of the boys who I figured would make the attempt with me. He mentioned this to his friend, and some other kid overheard it, and reported to the housefather. A few days later I was transferred back to the cottage I had been in my first time. With my transfer went the report about my attempt to escape.

After given assignment to his cottage, I was given a lecture by the housefather on my attempted escape, and told what he would do to me if I tried it on him. I didn't mind the lecture because we were all given one, but the way he spoke of my attempted escape and the punishment I would get gave me the impression that I was supposed to be too yellow to run away while in his cottage. After hearing this speech, I made up my mind to run away the first time I was given a chance. A week later I made friends with a boy who had run away several times before my first release. His name was Lester Thomas and he was from down state. Asking him if he wanted to go again, he said he did. I also asked if he had any ideas of how to escape. Stating he had, he mentioned that the officer's bathroom was the easiest place to get out of in the cottage. There was a drainpipe running to the ground, and being on the second floor, we could slide down it to the ground. The windows of all cottages were fixed to a certain extent. The basement windows were either screened or barred. The first floor windows were fixed to open about four inches from the top or bottom. The windows on the top floor, being about 20 to 25 feet above the ground, opened all the way, as the height was a little too great for a boy to take a chance of jumping out. The doors were locked at all times.

I studied the place the next time I was outside and saw it was a safe means of exit. We planned our departure to leave the following evening shortly after eating our supper. After supper the following night, we left the dining room, where we were swabbing the waxed floor, walked upstairs to the officers' bathroom, bolted the door from the inside, and quietly opened the window. Then, getting a good hold on the drainpipe, Harry and I slid to the ground. . . .

III

After our capture and return to St. Charles we were put in the punishment line for the day.

About six months later I again escaped and I caught an early morning cattle train bound for Chicago, and got home in time to watch the people rush to work, and also early enough to have a bite of breakfast at home. I managed to stay away for a month in which time I pulled a couple of burglaries and some jail breaks. Stock being in the can, I worked mostly alone. After arriving home I had heard that two younger brothers were placed in another orphan home. I resolved to get them out and went there the following visiting day, and did. I did not wish to let them run loose and get picked up, so I took them along on a few burglaries the next day.

On leaving St. Charles I lost the rosy outlook about life. I had a subconscious feeling that I was going to make somebody pay for the treatment I had received there. I had no intentions of behaving myself, and I didn't have any intention of quitting my burglaries. Having exchanged stories with boys about their causes for being here, I learned to be more careful in the future. Being seventeen years of age I knew I would be taken to the County Jail if I were caught again, as I had passed the age of sixteen, which was the limit of the Juvenile Home.

Making friends with the older boys I knew, I made no attempt to commit any burglaries until I had a market for some article which would make me some money.

(After committing one burglary, Edward went to California. While there he was arrested and turned over to a representative of the Chicago Police Department.)

Finding the cop a sound sleeper, I knew I could get away when I chose. Seeing the western towns were so many miles apart, the country sparsely settled, and the risk of capture too great, I bided my time. On the third night of the ride, we began hitting towns closer together. Having followed our course by watching the towns on a railroad map, I saw we were entering the state of Kansas. Knowing the time was ripe to leave, I waited until the wee hours of the morning, when folks sleep the soundest. When the train made periodical stops for lunch, I looked over the cars for a means of escape. At the end of each car, opposite the lavatory, I noticed a small window with a bar mounted on the outside above the window. Studying the distance to the top of the car, I knew I could swing myself on top, as I was pretty active, and had done things much more difficult. Hearing the next stop would be K——, some hundred and fifty odd miles away, I knew my time had come, as the train was due in Chicago that night, and by the time the train hit K—— the cop would be wide awake, and my last chance gone. On getting up I had to step over his outstretched legs to reach the aisle. Successful in this, I made believe I wished to use the lavatory. Watching the cop out of the corner of my eye, I saw him sleeping. Holding a hand across my stomach as if I had cramps, I walked to the lavatory. Getting out of sight of the few people watching me, I quickly opened the small window opposite the lavatory. Reaching up, I grabbed hold of the bar above the window, climbed out and stood on the sill. I managed to force the window down to a few inches of closing, to cover my means of exit. Getting a good grip on the bar, I swung myself to the top of the car. Being four cars back of the engine, I ran the car tops to the engine tender. Occasionally I glanced over the car tops to see if I had been followed, although I knew I was pretty safe here. I was taking no chances, because what I did others could also do.

While riding the freights west, I had learned to balance myself on the tops of moving and swaying freight cars; so running the tops of this train was no trouble. A short time later I noticed the train was slowing down. Looking about in the dark, I saw coal and water chutes. Knowing that this was the reason for the reduced speed, I got off when the train stopped. Spotting a bunch of coal cars about a hundred feet away I ran towards them. Climbing on one, I took a position overlooking the train. Watching the passenger cars carefully, I saw someone get off, using a flashlight. The flashlight gave indications of the owner looking for someone and being in a hurry about it. Who it was I wasn't sure, but from all indications, I figured it to be the policeman I had left.

The area in which the train made the stop was rather desolate, and I had no intention of missing this train, cop or no cop. Keeping my eye on the flashlight and the train I soon lost sight of the flashlight going in the opposite direction. I heard the engineer give the highball but I still sat quiet and waited for the first chug of the engine. Being quite close I knew I could catch it even though these passenger trains pick up speed mighty fast. Hearing the chug, I ran for the tender, jumped on, and stayed there till the train slowed down when it came to the Kansas City yards. I jumped off and laid down close to the tracks which prevented me from being seen by the people in the cars passing above me. After the train passed, I stood up and looked at it. I saw the conductor get off his seat on the rear platform and hurriedly enter the car. Leaving there in a hurry, I made my way to the other end of town, where I bought myself something to eat and caught another freight to Chicago. Having caught a hot shot, I got into Chicago early the next morning.

Knowing I was hot, I stayed at a friend's place. Occasionally I would send a boy to my home to inquire if the police had been there. Although I knew I wasn't guilty of the charge I had been brought back on, I expected to be framed into jail on my past record with Stock. After staying away for a week, I figured I was pretty safe. Going home one morning, I found the coast clear. On entering the house, however, I had a very strong feeling that the policeman I had escaped from would be over that night. My feeling was as strong as if the policeman had told me himself. Just how I knew this, I don't know. Preparing myself a hide-out for this occasion, I felt pretty secure. When bedtime came, I took off my shoes and layed across the bed, with my clothes on. About one o'clock the knock came and I knew who it was. Picking up my shoes, I crawled into my hide-out, just in time as the door opened a little too soon. While hiding, I heard the tread of heavy feet walking about from room to room looking for me. My hide-out was a sub-basement underneath my bed, where a cover of linoleum concealed the opening. Coming into the bedroom I had just left, I heard him questioning my younger brothers as to where I had gone. I heard him say he knew I was here because the lady in front had seen me here and told him. Having expected him, as I have stated, I told the members of my family to say that they had not seen me for three months and to stick to it. Questioning and threatening got him nowhere, so with an angry attitude he finally left the house. Even after he left I stuck to my hide-out, as I didn't wish to take any chances of him spying through the window and seeing me.

After feeling sure that he had left for the night, I came out of hiding, undressed and went to sleep. Though staying at home, I was very cautious in approaching or leaving the house. I would send someone out to make sure no cops were around before I left my home, and I also had someone go to my home to make sure no cops were waiting for me when I came back.

After I had escaped from the policeman and came back to Chicago, I made the rounds of my friends' homes, and told them I had escaped from the cops. I inquired if the cop I had run away from had been around inquiring about me. Hearing he hadn't as yet, I said to tell him, if he came, that they had not seen me for several months. Expecting the cop to come around inquiring about me, and not wishing to be caught, I made up a signal with my friends, which was to let me know if I had a clear coast. If I got no answer to my signal, they were out, or the cop was there.

About a week after this I went out on my first burglary since coming back.

After being placed on adult probation at the age of seventeen, I went home. Having nothing to fear, I tried to find a job. I had no luck, but kept looking for a month. One day when I was answering an ad in the paper, I ran into William Sloan and Earl Wooms at the place where I went for the interview. Since we didn't get a job, we walked out together. Since we had met in St. Charles, being in the same cottage, we exchanged tales as to what happened since we last saw each other. Telling each other where we lived, we made dates to meet the following day to look for work.

Having no success in getting jobs, we began discussing ways and means of getting some money as we were all broke. All of us having burglary experience, we decided to break into a place the next day. Over-sleeping that night I missed my appointment with them. Hoping they had waited I dressed hurriedly, and went to where I was to have met them. I found they had gone. Walking about the neighborhood, I met Joseph Wyman, who I also knew from St. Charles. Telling him I had missed my date with Sloan and Wooms, he said he wanted to come in with us. Meeting them that evening, I told them about Wyman and what he had said. We all agreed to let Wyman in with us, and went to his house to tell him.

Going up north in a bunch, we were chased by someone in plain clothes. Four of us were too noticeable, so we worked in pairs. Going north with William Sloan we entered an apartment by breaking a small hole in a window. Having a better idea of values and a greater means of disposing of stolen articles, I took a fur coat which I knew could be sold for a nice sum. When we split up our spoils, I took the fur coat as a share of my end. Finding a market through Joseph Wyman I sold it for a hundred dollars, and gave Wyman twenty for getting the sale. Having enough to last awhile, I quit going out, and began running around with Wyman. Running around with Wyman I was taken to my first brothel house, where I sowed my first wild oats at eighteen.

About ten days after selling the coat, Earl and William Sloan were arrested prowling a policeman's home. The officer, coming home, saw them through the window. Dashing in suddenly, he seized Earl while William made a getaway. They beat Earl up and he confessed the name of his partner, his address and all he knew about Wyman and I. Laying a trap, they caught William coming home, and recovered about eight hundred dollars of stolen merchandise. Although they had nothing on me, they nevertheless were looking for me. William Sloan refused to implicate me. Working through a stool pigeon in the neighborhood, the police lay a trap for Wyman and myself. Having been with Wyman until late, I slept at Wyman's house. While sleeping there, I had a dream of the police, and on waking up, I had the funniest premonition of danger if I went to my neighborhood. Wyman wanted to go to his girl's house who lived near my home. When I told him about my dream, he ridiculed me for telling him such stories. I let him talk me into going along but I kept a lookout for the police. Getting to his girl's house safely, I sat in a chair while he talked to his girl. We sat there for about ten minutes and heard a Model T horn in the alleyway. Seeing who it was, I didn't answer it, as I had no use for the owner of it.

Although he did me no harm, I didn't like this fellow. He was a sneaky looking person whom I knew as a stool pigeon. Though I knew him, and he knew me, I never spoke to him, unless necessary. He blew the horn some more and called my name. Hearing him call, I told Wyman to answer, as I didn't care for his company. Wyman walked out to his car, spoke to him a few minutes, and came back, stating that the fellow had something important to tell me. I told Wyman to tell him I wasn't interested. Wyman returned with another statement that it was important for me to see him. Still refusing to go, Wyman said he would go with me to hear what could be so important. I walked to the car in the alley and asked what was so important. The first thing he asked was, "Have you a gun?" I asked him why he said that and he told me of a grocery store where there was only an old man about seventy years old running it. As I listened to him, I thought to myself, "A guy like him is just the type to take advantage of an old man at the point of a gun, and at that I doubted if he had enough courage to even do that alone." Hearing his story, which I figured was phony, I stated I had no gun and didn't hold people up, and wouldn't even try holding up an old man who was trying to get along. I refused his offer of letting me in on his tip and I started to leave, when he pleaded with me to look the place over for him and let him know what I thought of it.

Although I didn't want anything to do with him, I let Wyman talk me into going for the ride anyway. Getting into the back seat with Wyman, I said there was something phony about this. I knew him as the sneaking, ratting type, not to be trusted. The reason soon became apparent. It was a frame-up. He had been watching my movements and, being a cops' stool pigeon, he had reported the coat incident. Having planned a trap, intending to catch or sheet me holding up a store, the police were waiting in their car at the head of the alley, ready to follow his car. After getting me into the car and hearing me say something was phony, he drove in the direction opposite the one he was told to take by the police. The police noting the change of direction, overtook his car, and at the point of pistols Wyman and I were taken to their car and driven to the detective bureau.

Upon being questioned about the fur coat, I denied all knowledge of ever having had one. Going to work on Wyman they got all the dope they needed. One poke at Wyman's jaw and he told everything. He even took them to the party who bought the coat. When they showed me the coat, I denied ever having seen it. After eleven days of seeing the coat, and then their Gold Fish (Third Degree), I still denied seeing the coat. The Gold Fish was their term for taking me into a fairly large room, where I was questioned and beaten—mostly beaten. Using systems of being kind one time then beating me the next, I still denied having seen the coat. The police gave up beating me, and booked me. I was booked for burglary, indicted by the grand jury, and held at the county jail pending trial. At trial, Sloan who was sentenced with Wooms on other burglaries said he had stolen the coat and given it to me to sell for him. On his statement, my charge was changed, and I was sentenced from one to ten years at the reformatory for receiving stolen property. I stayed at the county jail two weeks after being sentenced until they had a bunch of fifteen boys before transferring us. The police hand-cuffed us three to four in a bunch and we were piled into a paddy wagon, driven to the Chicago and Alton station, and under the care of armed guards placed aboard a train. . . .

IV

On being paroled, I was promised a job with a cab company as a clerk. Arriving home, I visited my sponsor who promised me the job. I was instructed where and when to go to work. I reported for work on the day set and worked here for five months, until my brother James who had been committed to St. Charles, escaped and came home. While taking him to a place in the suburbs of Chicago we were stopped and locked up on suspicion. Finding me a parolee, the cops tried to frame a larceny of an automobile charge on me. Failing to make it stick, they got in touch with the parole officer, who sent me back to the reformatory as a violator of my parole, because I had left the city limits. I had understood when I left the reformatory that I could go anywhere in the county.

On my return to the reformatory, I was given my same number back, followed the same routine the other new boys do, and did the same work at the tailor shop as I did before my parole. For this violation, I stayed here twenty-two months before I received another parole. Being released this time, the sponsor said I would have to find my own job. Being unable to account for all of the past five years, or supply satisfactory references, I didn't land any job, excepting one that was temporary. Getting discouraged by not being able to land a job, I began hanging around with petty stick-up men who held up anyone or anything that was easy. Never having any liking for holding up people, I turned down several offers of being in on a heist. These fellows were what is known as the dancehall type. Most of their evenings were spent at a cheap dancehall in the neighborhood. Keeping their company, I began passing my time here, too. Though I knew nothing about dancing, I liked to listen to the orchestra. I always did like music. By keeping their company, I got into several fights in the dancehalls.

Some three months after my release, there was a big free-for-all in which we ran out a half dozen dagoes, because of their boasting and familiarity with some of the dancing teachers. A half hour later, one of the boys saw these fellows coming back with reenforcements. Seeing we were outnumbered a good two to one, we made a quiet exit. After this some of the fellows came here carrying guns. A few days later one of the boys carrying a gun was challenged to a fight. Thinking he had put the gun in his overcoat in the cloakroom, he placed it in mine instead. Our coats were of the same color and hanging close to each other. On leaving here, I placed the overcoat on my arm and walked home. The day had been mild. When I hung the coat up at home, I heard a heavy sound where the gun hit the wall. Investigating, I found the gun. Knowing whose gun it was, I tried to return it the following day. I was unable to see the owner and I brought the gun home. Then having several days of mild weather, I forgot about the gun. Some days later I got into a conversation with a friend about theatres and decided to see one with him. After picking a new theatre on the north side, I took a street car with him that evening. The weather still fairly mild I carried the coat over my arm, forgetting that the gun was in the pocket. On my way home because I got tired of carrying the overcoat on my arm, I slipped it on. Fishing for cigarettes, I felt the gun.

Not wishing to get caught carrying a gun, we took a side street to the carline. When we got to within a block of the carline we were stopped by two plain clothes men. While talking to us they patted me around the pockets, and overlooked the gun. After shaking us down, we tried to talk them into letting us go. This they refused, and said we would have to go to the station; having the gun was no consolation. Although I knew how to use a gun, I didn't care to kill anyone and not being a killer, I was in a quandary. Having been ordered to walk to their call box, I was tempted to use the butt end on the cop's head closest to me. Night having fallen, I made up my mind to throw the gun to the ground at the first opportunity. But I made up my mind too late, as we passed the only open space of ground. Thus, missing the only opportunity of disposing of the gun, I was on the verge of using it at the call box. One policeman went to the phone to call the patrol wagon; the other took up a position to the left of us, my partner being in the center.

As I knew I would be sent back to the reformatory if I were caught with a gun, I figured my chance of getting away was now or never. Having watched for my chance, I slid my hand into my pocket. Pulling the gun out slowly I had just started saying, "Stick 'em up," I cut short the words when I saw my chance fail. The policeman didn't know how close he was to a peaceful surrender or gun battle. On entering the paddy wagon, I had no chance of hiding the gun here. Hoping to get locked up in a cell without another search was my last chance of disposing of the gun. I had no such luck. My partner did. He was locked in the cell and I was held out for questioning, and another shakedown. The funny part of the search was that they left the pocket in which I had the gun till the last. Being the only pocket that wasn't searched, when the cop put his hand on the gun he was looking me in the face. As he felt the gun I could see his eyes bulge out a little. He was the cop that stepped back while at the call box. Pulling the gun out, the three other cops who were watching me saw it. Saying, "Why, it's a gun," they came close and took several swings at me, and knocked my hat from my head. On finding the gun, they rushed me into the captain's office for grilling. When asked about the gun I gave them a tall story and stuck to it.

I have never been a stool pigeon and I have never tried to get anyone in trouble when arrested. I had no intention of telling them who the owner of the gun was. I knew I would be sent back to the reformatory anyway. I tried my best to clear the fellow with me, but being in the company of a criminal like me went against him. Brought to the police court, I was given a year in the House of Correction, or, in other words, the Bridewell, as it is called. The parole officer had stated at my trial they didn't want me as a violator, and gave me the impression, and also the judge, that whatever sentence he gave me, I wouldn't be returned to the reformatory. This was the second time I had trouble with the parole office. On the last parole violation I heard a bad report read to me at the parole board meeting. Why the parole officer lied about me I don't know. In his report he stated I never worked or never tried. On hearing that statement I proved it erroneous. At the police court they lied again as I soon found out on entering the Bridewell.

The Bridewell! What a dump this is! I never knew a place as filthy as this existed.

I was given another paddy wagon ride, and transferred to the county jail where I waited two weeks for a transfer back to the reformatory. Having a little over eight months left to serve of my maximum sentence, I didn't mind. During the eight months at the reformatory I began thinking over my past life, wondering if I would end up like the derelicts at the Bridewell. The human wrecks I saw and spoke to had a great deal in making me change my ways, when I received my final discharge from the reformatory some eight months later.

On receiving a discharge I felt a free man. While on parole I was free also, but always under a strain. The parole is a bigger handicap than one can imagine. Although I hadn't stolen or burglarized since my first conviction to the reformatory, I seemed to fall into the hands of the police and having a record and being a parolee, I was given the extreme penalties. Should I have been lucky enough to have received a discharge instead of a parole, I firmly believe I would never have gone to jail again as a criminal offender. Parole was a handicap to me as they are to most fellows. I don't say this about everybody. Some, a parole helps to keep them out of trouble; some need parole supervision. The parole officers are always under the impression that you are still stealing, and never try to understand their wards, by either a cheery word or a pat on the back. To me, they seemed to carry a chip on their shoulders. Some may say I don't know what I am talking about. I'm only telling what it meant to me. If the parole system is here to stay, the officers appointed will find they will have less trouble with their boys by cooperating in a friendly manner instead of the methods they used with me.

Since leaving the reformatory with a discharge, I have never been in trouble. I have had many chances of making easy money. I still know a lot of fellows I did time with, and with whom I still speak. But, I've come to my senses. I knew crime never paid, but it took a long time before waking up to the fact. Being unable to find a job on my release, I managed to get a few odd jobs in the first two months. Looking about for opportunities, I found I could go to work for myself if I could borrow enough money. I was able to do this and have been working since that time.

B. THE PROBLEM OF RACE AND RACE PREJUDICE

1. *Ethnocentrism and the Idea of Racial Superiority in World History: The Rise of the Nordic Myth* [2]

By ethnocentrism is meant the tendency on the part of members of one group, race, or society to hold the members of other groups, races, or societies as inferior. The tendency is not inborn, but results from the application of the shared attitudes and values of one's in-group associates toward outsiders. Ethnocentrism—the term coined by Graham Sumner —seems to be rather widespread, if not universal.

The Caribs believe that they "alone are people." The Lapps call themselves "human beings," implying that non-Lapps are not. Literally translated, Kiowa is "real or principal people." The Greenland Eskimos believe that Europeans have been sent to Greenland to learn virtue and good manners from them. The highest form of praise an Eskimo can extend to a European is that he is or soon will be as good as a Greenlander.

The feeling of superiority that people feel toward their own way of life and their own group is not limited to the "primitives." The ancient Greeks referred to non-Greeks as barbarians. It is, of course, true that the Greek word *barbaros* did not have the identical meaning that our own word *barbarian* has, but it definitely attributed strangeness, rudeness, and inferiority to non-Greeks.

Nor is this feeling of superiority limited to ancient peoples.

This strongly rooted attachment to one's own way of life and one's own people has been observed through the ages by poet and scientist, widely traveled diplomat and secluded scholar. As Oliver Wendell Holmes so aptly remarked, "the people in every town feel that the axis of the earth passes through its Main Street." Paul Radin, in the following passage from his book *The Racial Myth,* traces the history of ethnocentrism from ancient times.*

The records of all people, primitive and civilized, begin with this dream of a Golden Age where people never grow up or where they rest after the strain of their earthly experience. Originally, certainly, this was a democratic realm in which no distinctions, racial or national, existed. Manifestly its main purpose was to forget reality, to forget the conflict of the animal human being with the human animal as he slowly and inconsistently sloughed off his pristine heritage. But life was too much upon him. It seemed to confirm his most pessimistic forebodings about the apparent wickedness of the human heart, about the unchangeability of human nature, and to pollute his thought at the very fountainhead. Realities obtruded themselves upon him everywhere and reached unpleasantly even in that one dream which he had sought to keep free from life's enveloping egotism. The Golden Age thus became tarnished and in an apparent effort to save it man confusedly pushed it ever farther away from him, into the past. But he never forgot it, never ceased speculating upon why it had disappeared and when it would return again. Romanticists like the ancient Egyptians put it to comparatively little use. But those stubborn realists the Semites, more particularly the Hebrews, found in its symbolism a much desired refuge. By that time however, this glamorous dream had become completely saturated with the smell of the world, had become simply an aureoled mirror of a specific order, the Semitic world of 800 B.C.

Doubtless this had happened before, among countless peoples, but the peculiar enmeshment of the realities of life with an old compensation dream received its first significant expression among these early Hebrews maintaining a militant and precarious existence in a country open and exposed to attack on all sides. That they should have survived at all was an achievement of which they could well be proud; that they should have succeeded in welding the disparate elements of their civilization into a new and specific unity, with a quality all its own, was almost a miracle. As such they regarded it. For them it became a proof that God had intervened in their behalf, that they were the elect of the Deity, a chosen nation. The peoples around them, alien in blood and speech, were not merely different, but the rejected of the Lord. If, however, they were superior to the rest of mankind, it was not by virtue of any inherent racial trait, nor because of their outstanding gifts, but because they possessed the one prime virtue—that of obeying the Lord's commandments.

The Jews were thus well launched on a program that must inevitably have led to a belief in their national and racial superiority when the thunders of the Prophets and the vicissitudes of war frustrated them. Defeat, captivity, and insecurity forced upon them a revision of the old dream. It was no longer the yearning for the re-

* By permission from *The Racial Myth,* by Paul Radin. Copyright, 1934, McGraw-Hill Book Company, Inc.

turn of a Golden Age but the yearning for a haven of rest, for the coming of a Messiah who would usher in a new order of values. They could still glory in their title of the Chosen People and cling to the memory of their transitory victories and national independence but, fortunately, there could be no further strengthening of that illusion, born of a dream and of human egotism, that they were inherently a superior race or a superior nation. After the destruction of the Temple by Titus in A.D. 70 and their final dispersion, the Jews developed a strong racial pride which possessed many of the characteristics of a belief in racial superiority. But here again the economic and cultural function fate bestowed upon them came to their rescue.

For the Jewish formula, the elect of God as opposed to the rejected of God, the Greeks substituted the children of light as opposed to the barbarians. In this they were at one with the vast majority of peoples. For most tribes and nations the contrast has always been between those who are in and those who are not, those who speak your language and those who speak a different one, those who possess your virtues and vices and those who have alien virtues and vices. From the beginning of time the members of one group have always regarded it as something of an impertinence not unmixed with the ridiculous that other groups should converse in accents that had no meaning for them or sin in a fashion unknown among themselves. The Greeks were the first to formulate this opposition, so dear to the human heart, and they have left us in the word "barbarian," i.e., the strange, the uncouth, the whole epitome of racial contrasts and racial evaluations.

If the Greeks developed no marked feeling of racial superiority, the reason is to be sought in the simple fact that for them other people did not exist, so that there was no need for despising them and manifestly little need for emphasizing their own importance. It remained for that part of Greece that had but recently identified itself with the true Greek tradition and culture, Macedonia, to produce the man who prided himself upon being a Greek and who sought to demonstrate Greek superiority by conquering the world. He conquered the world and proved Greek superiority, but at the fortunate price of including under the designation Greece all those who adopted the Greek language as their mother tongue and Greek culture as the frame in which to work out their individual destinies. Obviously there was no room here for any theory of inherent racial traits or for a doctrine of Greek superiority, since the world that mattered was Greek.

While Alexander the Great was spreading Greek culture over the Orient and creating a pannationalist if not an internationalist civilization, a small and stubborn people were slowly emerging from obscurity on the Italic peninsula who were, for a time, at least, to preach the doctrine that racial purity was a merit in itself and that national superiority was a fact that the conquered and the inferior peoples of the earth should duly recognize and pay homage to. The civilization of Latium and its capital Rome was the ideal soil for such a theory. A farming people of homely virtues, surrounded by an opulent Greek civilization on the south and a virile and integrated Etruscan culture on the north, who within a period of two centuries succeeded in conquering and dominating Italy from Etruria to Apulia and from the Tyrrnenian Sea to the Adriatic, and who yet remained fundamentally untouched, might well interpret their victory as due to having remained untouched and justifiably extol those traits in their character in which they differed from their luxurious neighbors.

These traits, the Romans insisted, were a racial stock with little if any foreign admixture, frugality, simplicity, courage, and the power of enduring hardships. Clearly these were the virtues of husbandmen and warriors, of realists close to the soil and none too quick in their mental reactions. Like true peasants, they hated the refinements of civilization as long as they knew nothing about them and succumbed to them with voracious alacrity as soon as they were introduced. The conquest of Greece (146 B.C.) and the close contact with the Hellenistic Orient brought these refinements to Rome, and after the purists and the jingo politicians could preach and rant to their hearts' content about the simple virtues that had supposedly led to the Roman victory over their rich and supercultured neighbors; the Romans themselves preferred to forget them. The insistence upon racial purity had been abandoned long before. Significantly enough, it had developed not so much from the dislike of Romans to intermarry with foreigners as from the unwillingness of the Roman patricians to intermarry with the Roman freedmen. When that conflict ceased, the doctrine of caste and racial purity lost much of its meaning and became merged in the much larger thesis of the superiority of being a Roman citizen.

Yet, as so often happens whenever the semblance of democracy and rusticity has gone, the poets and intellectuals looked back with sentimental enlargement upon their rural past and combined it with the Latin version of the myth of the Golden Age. For the greatest poet of them all—Virgil—there was to be no return to pristine hardship and frugality. Even if, as he says, "some stains of the oldtime sin live on, to bid man tempt the sea in ships, girdle his towns with walls, cleave his furrows in the soil," still the new age was upon them. A better race is to displace our own and in the new realm all that will be required of man is that he know virtue and, recognizing it, watch, hour by hour, the fields grow more yellow with ripening corn, the grapes hang on the uncouth bramble, the oak drip with honey-dew, and mankind be as one.

Thus confusedly and inconsistently did the Romans pass from racial to national arrogance and end in a poet's dream of universal brotherhood. Like the Greeks, the lure for domination and empire had at least this saving grace: it destroyed the essential basis for the illusion of one particular race or one particular people who were superlatively and inherently endowed.

Roman nationalism as such ceased to have any significant ethnical meaning after Caracalla declared all people living within the Roman Empire, Roman citizens, and received its final death thrust when, in the fourth century, A.D., it was overwhelmed by early Christian universalism and the doctrine, derived from the Jewish prophets, that all peoples were as one within the loving kindness of God, if they but accepted Him.

By the seventh century Christianity reigned supreme over most parts of the old Roman Empire, and racial and national designations were rendered secondary in importance to religious ones. Faith thus cut across biological and cultural barriers. An Italian, Spanish, or French Catholic, heir of the Roman tradition and culture, was as one with the unmannered British or the mead-drinking German Catholic, still bewildered and befuddled from the intoxicating contact with the mature and complex culture. Any theory of racial purity had, of course, no place here.

But if the doctrine of national superiority was, to all intents, excluded, that did not imply that peoples had suddenly lost their ineradicable urge for designating the beliefs they held as inherently true, proper, and altogether superior and contrary faiths as viciously and ludicrously false, improper and inferior. . . .

In the struggle for supremacy that began in the sixteenth century in Europe, each country was, in characteristic fashion, led to interpret the traits that presumably gave it a temporary victory as the earmarks of superiority. Aided and abetted by poets and professors, a formidable list of specific national virtues was drawn up which were supposed to have held true from the beginning of their history and to have found expression in every phase of their life.

The sanguinary cruelty of Castile and Aragon, easily enough explicable when we remember the ceaseless battle they waged against the Arab invaders of Spain for seven hundred years, was reinterpreted as the stern, uncompromising valor and faith of a disinherited people struggling to regain its patrimony. The natural and possibly inevitable tendency for a people, after a hard-won victory stretching over centuries, to exclude from all participation in their government those against whom they had fought so long, and to pride themselves that no blood of their hated enemies, Arabs and Jews, flowed in their veins, was interpreted as a proud consciousness of their racial purity.

Similarly, the set of manners connected with those highly formalized games the tournaments and the courts of love of the thirteenth and fourteenth centuries, which bore no relation to the general level of manners even of the small minority who participated in them, was accepted as evidence of the innate French feeling for courtesy, of their ineradicable sense of honor, of their love of form. With this was coupled the theory that the French have instinctively always expressed themselves with crystal clarity and that they represented the epitome of rationality.

The English, on the other hand, because their soldiers and traders conducted themselves with a stubborn courage and a reckless fear of consequences, born of the fact that they had no set and accepted standard of behavior to which to conform, were accredited with an inborn resistance to formalized patterns and a rugged individualism that brooked no control. They were sung and extolled as a people who were ready to sacrifice their all in the defense of personal liberty.

The Italians were to attain no unification largely because of these northern harassers. And although her poets might lament Italia's possession of that unhappy gift of beauty which made her the lure for the lustful ill-mannered foreigner and brought unmerited destruction upon her, yet this apparent tragedy has also meant that she remained civilized and free from the dangerous sentimentalism of the newly unified nations. When the Italians finally attained their unity, in our own time, the period had passed for Italy, at least, where a poet's slogans were to have great validity.

Unhappy Germany, always on the periphery of the great movements that swept over Europe, was to wait till far into the nineteenth century to attain unity, even of a kind. But fortunately the type of unity she achieved was then definitely on the wane and making place for a newer and true integration, on economic foundations. Thus her interpretation of why she had won and what characteristics in her people had made her victory possible, which in no wise differed from the assessments Spain, France, and England had made before her, sounded strange in the ears of the business civilization of Europe. They then went on to specify precisely what were the earmarks, biologically and psychologically, of the Germanic people. In a manner, of course, this was simply the old dream of a Golden Age refurbished in a smart Prussian uniform.

In Europe the people on the periphery of ancient Mediterranean civilization were the Celts, the Germans, and the Slavs. The contact of the Slavs with this major civilization was indirect and late and was further complicated by the Tartar invasions from Asia. The Celts, being closest to the Romans, came to grips with it first, proved apt pupils, and were eventually completely overwhelmed. The Germanic tribes, who had probably come originally from South Russia and the upper Danube, found themselves squeezed between the Celts who were on the point of being Romanized and the Slavs with whom they were deadly enemies. That part of their country directly exposed to Roman influence was small but large enough, nevertheless, for Roman influences and Roman legions to make considerable progress. It is not too much to say that the prospects for a Roman conquest of the Germanic tribes were, at first, as bright as those for the Celtic tribes had been a century before. Then unfortunately came the defeat and annihilation for the Roman cohorts under Varus in the pesky Teutoburger forest, where a monument to the German leader Arminius now stands.

All the German ills seem to go back to their victory in the Teutoburger forest. As we view German history in retrospect, that victory meant that Roman civilization was to reach her piecemeal, that she was never to know when it could come and to what extent it would influence her at a particular time.

Christianity, the heir to the Roman civilization, came to the various Germanic tribes at different periods. The Visigoths and the Ostrogoths received its full force only in consequence of their invasions of Spain and Italy, although they had been nominally converted a few generations before; the other German tribes had to wait till the beginning of the eighth century and then it was relayed to them by a Romanized Briton St. Boniface. Throughout all this period (A.D. 400–700) the various Germanic tribes pushed from place to place, waged a most relentless war upon one another. Not even the most exaggerated accounts of the atrocities attributed to the so-called uncivilized tribes of aboriginal America, Africa, or Oceania can vie with the cruelties perpetrated by the Germans upon one another. Then, before their western branch, the Salic Franks, had been completely saturated with Roman Christian culture, and shortly after those beyond the Elbe had been initiated into it, the genius of one of their leaders, Charlemagne, added to their ultimate confusion by his triumphal invasion of Italy. This led to the complete Romanization of France and to another premature and disastrous victory for the peoples of Germany proper—premature because they had but recently come into intimate contact with Christianity and could only be rendered more confused by Germanic triumph; disastrous because it inevitably led to a false evaluation of their importance and because it was so short-lived.

What these Germans were like we know from a number of epic poems they have left us, the famous Nibelungenlied and Gudrun. If the Nibelungenlied is a picture of the German character, we can best sum it up in one phrase—the glorification of intemperance, intemperance in hate and in love, in action and in thought. The element of gentleness and of normal human sympathy is, in this famous poem, associated not with the German hero but with the Romanized Hun Attila (Etzel) and the Romanized Goth Theodoric The Great (Dietrich von Bern). For anything comparable with these orgies of blood and frenzied murder lust, we have to go to the ritualized cruelty of the Iroquois Indians in the treatment of their enemies, as described in the Jesuit Relations in America. Nor was this gratification of an undisciplined murder instinct confined merely to the Germans proper. We find it among the Franks and among the Scandinavian groups. The Eddas are full of it.

Like all peoples whose ideal is military prestige, personal courage and tribal loyalty loom large. So it does among the Ashanti of West Africa, among Kipling's Fuzzy-Wuzzy, among the Dakota and the Iroquois Indians. *Deutsche Treue* and *deutscher Muth,* this old German loyalty and courage, with their *furor teutonicus* and the berserker rage, have their counterpart in the Crazy-Dog madness of the Crow Indians and the running amuck of the Malays. In other words, these characteristics are not German; they are not local but simply inevitable aspects of a certain economic order, of certain political and social crises.

The great intellectual and artistic awakening which began with the birth of Goethe ended with the advent of the Third Empire in the spring of 1933. It looked, for a time, as if in one supreme effort they wished to make up for all that they had lost; as if finally they were to come into their own and find their rightful place in the sun. The number of their great men was legion and embraced the whole realm of human endeavor, except the fine arts. They attained to a great literature at last, and even though it was small in compass it contained one of the greatest figures in world literature and developed specific forms and qualities which were not only duly recognized by other nations but which influenced foreign thought for the first time in German history. In music they produced something absolutely new. For more than two centuries, one supreme composer was to follow upon another and their music was to sweep everything before it. Only Italy could even remotely threaten their supremacy here. In philosophy and science, although the fundamental concepts and the methodological principles had been established in the seventeenth and eighteenth centuries by Italians, Frenchmen, and Englishmen, they could critically evaluate these achievements and complete the edifice. Even an economic system like capitalism, depending upon specific social developments and technological advances which had been subsidiary in Germany, was incorporated into their own social structure, rationalized, and integrated in a fashion which, for practical effectiveness, was unique. To cap this colossal accomplishment, they perfected a powerful military machine, overwhelmed their hereditary enemy France—taking an almost infantile pride in humiliating her—and achieved a long-postponed unity.

Is it surprising, then, that they were crazed by the contemplation of their greatness and that a wondering world acquiesced to their own assessment?

Yet victory hath its stings and its vanities. A conquering people, when it settles down, is apt to look back upon its past with a certain degree of inquietude. Had it always been so great; and if not, how was this to be explained? Even though it may regard the rest of the world as degenerate and awaiting its quickening touch, the thought that this achievement had come so late is intolerable. An attempt is consequently made to erect a pedigree of greatness.

Now what is common to the Germanic peoples? Certain physical traits. Nothing could very well be more concrete. These were a robust constitution, tall stature, light complexion, blond hair, blue eyes, and a long head. But where are Germans to be found who possess all these traits? Not even the most enthusiastic defenders of Nordic and Teutonic superiority claim that all of them can be found frequently united in one individual. Blond hair, blue eyes, and long heads are enough. At a pinch, the combinations of any of these traits or, indeed, one of them alone will suffice.

With the typical modern propensity to discuss everything from the viewpoint of so-called metaphysical principles, the German then proceeded to describe the Germanic genius in terms of the principles of continuity, superiority, and performance.

The extent to which they pushed their theory of the continuity of physical type and the necessity of having only one of the Germanic criteria is best exemplified by L. Woltmann. Italians like Dante, Michelangelo, and Raphael; Spaniards like Velásquez and Murillo, Frenchmen like Voltaire, Diderot, and Gounod, although having an admixture of the brunet race, "were geniuses not because of, but in spite of, their mixed blood." [3] But more, these Italians, Spaniards, and Frenchmen were all descended from real Germans on their father's side. Giotto, Alighiere (Dante), Bruno, Ghiberti, Vinci, Santi (Raphael), Vecellio (Titian), Tasso, Buonarotti (Michelangelo), Velásquez, Murillo, Vaz, Arouet (Voltaire), Diderot, Gounod were respectively, Jothe, Aigler, Braun, Wilbert, Wincke, Sandt, Wetzell, Dasse, Bohurodt, Velahise, Moerl, Watz, Arwid, Tietroh, and Gundiwald! Woltmann even forgot that Vinci and Vecellio, for instance, were simply the names of towns. Of such stuff, manifestly, are visions made, but for externally mature men to present them in a flimsy scientific guise, and for equally mature men to accept them, indicates only too clearly that specific emotional factors were at work. . . .

If it was difficult to obtain either any general unanimity or general acceptance for the theory of a specific Germanic race, it was comparatively easy to do so for the existence of specific Germanic qualities. The world—more particularly Europe —has for many centuries now been accustomed to describing peoples in terms of national characteristics. These have always differed, depending upon the nation with which one started. The Frenchman has different national traits for a German than he has for an Englishman or Italian, and the German genius looks different when viewed by a Frenchman than when viewed by an Englishman or Spaniard. There seem to be two very simple rules followed in such characterizations: first, the more a nation differs from your own the more ridiculous it is and the more definitely inferior; second, the specific differences are those which innately belong to a nation. According to this interpretation, of course, the specific differences are desirable if they are your specific differences and undesirable and essentially reprehensible if they are the other person's.

All the theorists, in assuming a specific German genius, kept before them particularly the marked contrast between German lyricism and mysticism, on the one hand, and the rigorous and utterly unemotional philosophic system of Kant as well as the equally rigorous and majestic forms of the Bachian music, on the other. This contrast gave them the *Leitmotifs* of the romantic and manifestly adolescent opera they composed. There are two such motifs, *Minne* and *Treue* (love and fidelity), and both have, so to speak, their external and their internal side. Their external aspect is sexual desire and the *furor teutonicus,* their internal aspect, "the quiet yearning thought for the elect of one's heart," and the courageous all-sufficing and steadfast loyalty and fidelity to kinsmen, friends, and one's promise. Together, *Minne* and *Treue* gave rise to a third trait, which the German theorists regarded as basic, *Innigkeit* (inwardness). This it is that transforms what among other nations would merely be clear, cold, brilliant thinking, into a fundamental, warm, and profound penetration of essences. The abstruse and forbidding terminology introduced into philosophy by the successors of the great philosopher and scientist Leibnitz, and subsequently adopted and rendered even more complicated by Kant and Hegel, had much to do with the success with which the rest of Europe accepted the German evaluation of themselves and this, in turn, naturally reenforced the belief in the correctness of their analysis.

No matter what work on German culture one picks up, if it is written in the nineteenth or twentieth centuries, the themes of German fidelity and inwardness will be developed from the very beginning. In that horror-inspiring blood bath which is the theme of the *Nibelungenlied,* German scholars actually claimed to see the highest poetical expression of German fidelity and loyalty (*das hohe Lied der deutschen Treue*). Professor Kluge even insists that what to us seems the inexpressible lust and weakness of the hero Siegfried is but an expression "of that pure deep love which must end tragically because of its fullness." [4] And it is this same divine love that transforms Siegfried's wife from a simple-minded Gretchen to a bestial and treacherous murderess. In similar fashion did the poet Hoelderlin sing at the end of the eighteenth century:

> Sacred heart of my people, my Fatherland
> All-suffering, like mother-earth you sit
> Silent, reviled, though from your depths
> Their very best have they suckled
> From you came the essence of thought, its fruition,
> Gladly they plucked your fruit, though they scorned you . . .
> O Land of deep serious genius,
> Land of Love! . . .

Thus poets have always sung whether their names were Hoelderlin or Euripides, Shakespeare, Wordsworth, or Rupert Brooke, and they have sung so enchantingly and convincingly because they have always dealt with a time that never was on land or sea, and with the consecration that comes from dreams. Even the mocker Heine felt this. And do not the people from whom he has sprung still say with the Psalmist,

> If I forget thee, O Jerusalem,
> Let my right hand forget her skill,
> Let my tongue cleave to the roof of my mouth!

But to have taken it seriously, to have thrust it violently into the arena of real life, into the realm where egotism, self-seeking and unkindness are the dominant mainsprings of our actions, and then to have wept, whined, murdered, and dealt death and injustice in every direction, that has been reserved for the Germany of the twentieth century. Unmindful of the advice of the greatest man she ever produced, that they guard themselves against hating life and fleeing to the desert simply because all their springtime dreams did not mature, the Germans became embittered. Instead of hating life, however, and fleeing to the desert, they did something infinitely more stultifying and infinitely more dangerous for themselves: They stayed in the very midst of life and enclosed themselves in a tight-fitting armor of steel—in an adolescent dream, clothed in the verbal panoply of a scientific approach. That their tortuous history needed the sanctuary of dreams no one would possibly deny. Indeed no one will deny that theirs has been a tragic fate and that they are not to be held responsible for that initial victory against the Romans in the Teutoburger Forest. But, surely, they might have recognized by this time that the great periods of their history correspond to the periods in which they have been greatly influenced by foreign thought and culture, that it is then they have come into their own and made unique and significant contributions to culture, and that they fall into senescence and crudity as soon as they retire to their tight-fitting armor. This happens, of course, to all peoples.

It is for this reason, therefore, that it behooves them to recognize the fact that a carefully constructed theory of a German or Nordic race is but the compensation myth of confused late comers, of people whose historical rhythm has not synchronized with that of the rest of the world and who have, in consequence, always come to the table too late and with a poor appetite.

2. The Subtle Aspects of Covert Prejudice in an Individual: A Narrative Case of Intergroup Opposition through Toleration

Social opposition and intergroup prejudice take many forms. There is *toleration,* which implies a sufferance of the existence of the undesirable; a tendency to endure and permit the existence of different opinions, beliefs, and racial types without according full equality and standing to these differences. Then there is *predilection,* which signifies a preference for A without necessarily an aversion for B. Other forms of social opposition are discrimination, scapegoating, persecution, and so on. Now, each of these types of opposition may express itself in overt, external form, or prejudices may be carried around covertly, in the form of personal attitudes and predispositions. Often the predisposition is different from the action, the attitude from the opinion. People frequently "don't mean what they say." In the following case we see the dynamics of the disparity between latent prejudicial attitudes and verbal pronouncements of tolerance.[5]

The woman with the pink velvet poppies wreathed round the assisted gold of her hair traversed the crowded room at an interesting gait combining a skip with a sidle, and clutched the lean arm of her host.

"Now I got you!" she said. "Now you can't get away!"

"Why, hello," said her host. "Well, how are you?"

"Oh, I'm finely," she said. "Just simply finely. Listen, I want you to do me the most terrible favor. Will you? Will you please? Pretty please?"

"What is it?" said the host.

"Listen," she said. "I want to meet Walter Williams. Honestly, I'm just simply crazy about the man. Oh, when he sings! When he sings those spirituals! Well, I said to Burton, 'It's a good thing for you Walter Williams is colored,' I said, 'or you'd have lots of reason to be jealous.' I'd really love to meet him. I'd like to tell him I've heard him sing. Will you be an angel and introduce me to him?"

"Why, certainly," said her host. "I thought you'd met him. The party's for him. Where is he, anyway?"

"He's over there by the bookcase," she said. "Let's wait till those people get through talking to him. Well, I think you're simply marvelous, giving this perfectly marvelous party for him, and having him meet all these white people, and all. Isn't he terribly grateful?"

"I hope not," said her host.

"I think it's really terribly nice," she said. "I do. I don't see why on earth it isn't perfectly all right to meet colored people. I haven't any feeling at all about it—not one single bit. Burton—oh, he's just the other way. Well, you know, he comes from Virginia, and you know how they are."

"Did he come tonight?" said her host.

"No, he couldn't," she said. "I'm a regular grass widow tonight, I told him when I left, 'There's no telling what I'll do,' I said. He was just so tired, he couldn't move. Isn't it a shame?"

"Ah," said her host.

"Wait till I tell him I met Walter Williams!" she said. "He'll just about die. Oh, we have more arguments about colored people. I talk to him like I don't know what, I get so excited. 'Oh, don't be so silly,' I say. But I must say for Burton, he's heaps broaderminded than lots of these Southerners. He's really awfully fond of colored people. Well, he says himself, he wouldn't have white servants. And you know, he had this old colored nurse, this regular old nigger mammy, and he just simply loves her. Why, every time he goes home, he goes out in the kitchen to see her. He does, really, to this day. All he says is, he says he hasn't got a word to say against colored people as long as they keep their place. He's always doing things for them—giving them clothes and I don't know what all. The only thing he says, he says he wouldn't sit down at the table with one for a million dollars. 'Oh,' I say to him, 'you make me sick, talking like that.' I'm just terrible to him. Aren't I terrible?"

"Oh, no, no, no," said her host. "No, no."

"I am," she said. "I know I am. Poor Burton! Now, me, I don't feel that way at all. I haven't the slightest feeling about colored people. Why, I'm just crazy about some of them. They're just like children—just as easy going, and always singing and laughing and everything. Aren't they the happiest things you ever saw in your life? Honestly, it makes me laugh just to hear them. Oh, I like them. I really do. Well, now, listen, I have this colored laundress. I've had her for years, and I'm devoted to her. She's a real character. And I want to tell you, I think of her as my friend. That's the way I think of her. As I say to Burton, 'Well for Heaven's sakes we're all human beings!' Aren't we?"

"Yes," said her host. "Yes, indeed."

"Now this Walter Williams," she said. "I think a man like that's a real artist. I do. I think he deserves an awful lot of credit. Goodness, I'm so crazy about music or anything, I don't care what color he is. I honestly think if a person's an artist, nobody ought to have any feeling at all about meeting them. That's absolutely what I say to Burton. Don't you think I'm right?"

"Yes," said her host. "Oh, yes."

"That's the way I felt," she said. "I just can't understand people being narrowminded. Why, I absolutely think it's a privilege to meet a man like Walter Williams. Now, I do. I haven't any feeling at all. Well, my goodness, the good Lord made him, just the same as He did any of us. Didn't he?"

"Surely," said her host. "Yes, indeed."

"That's what I say," she said. "Oh, I get so furious when people are narrowminded about colored people. It's just all I can do not to say something. Of course, I do admit when you get a bad colored man, they're simply terrible. But as I say to Burton, there are some bad white people, too, in this world. Aren't there?"

"I guess there are," said her host.

"Why, I'd really be glad to have a man like Walter Williams come to my house and sing for us, some time," she said. "Of course, I couldn't ask him on account of Burton, but I wouldn't have any feeling about it at all. Oh, can't he sing! Isn't it marvelous, the way they all have music in them? It just seems to be right in them! Come on, let's us go over and talk to him. Listen, what shall I do when I'm introduced? Ought I to shake hands? Or what?"

"Why, do whatever you want," said her host.

"I guess maybe I'd better," she said. "I wouldn't for the world have him think I had any feeling about it at all. Oh, can't he sing! I think I'd better shake hands, just the way I would with anybody else. That's exactly what I'll do."

They reached the tall young Negro, standing by the bookcase. The host performed introductions; the Negro bowed.

"How do you do?" he said. "Isn't it a nice party?"

The woman with the pink velvet poppies extended her hand at the length of her arm and held it so, in fine determination, for all the world to see, until the Negro took it, shook it, and gave it back to her.

"Oh, how do you do, Mr. Williams," she said. "Well, how do you do. I've just been saying, I've enjoyed your singing so awfully much. I've been to your concerts, and we have you on the phonograph and everything. Oh, I just enjoy it!"

She spoke with great distinctness, moving her lips meticulously, as if in parlance with the deaf.

"I'm so glad," he said.

"I'm just simply crazy about that 'Water Boy' thing you sing," she said. "Honestly, I can't get it out of my head. I have my husband nearly crazy, the way I go around humming it all the time. Oh, he looks just as black as the ace of—er—. Well, tell me, where on earth do you ever get hold of them?"

"Why," he said, "there are so many different—"

"I should think you'd love singing them," she said. "It must be more fun. All those darling old spirituals—oh, I just love them! Well, what are you doing now? Are you still keeping up your singing? Why don't you have another concert, some time?"

"I'm having one the sixteenth of this month," he said.

"Well, I'll be there," she said. "I'll be there if I possibly can. You can count on me. Goodness, here comes a whole raft of people to talk to you. You're just a regular guest of honor! Oh, who's that girl in white? I've seen her some place."

"That's Katherine Burke," said her host.

"Good Heavens," she said, "is that Katherine Burke? Why she looks entirely different off the stage. I thought she was much better-looking. I had no idea she was so terribly dark. Why, she looks almost like— Oh, I think she's a wonderful actress! Don't you think she's a wonderful actress, Mr. Williams? Oh, I think she's marvelous. Don't you?"

"Yes, I do," he said.

"Oh, I do, too," she said. "Just wonderful. Well, goodness, we must give someone else a chance to talk to the guest of honor. Now don't forget, Mr. Williams, I'm going to be at that concert if I possibly can. I'll be there applauding like everything. And if I can't come, I'm going to tell everybody I know to go, anyway. Don't you forget!"

"I won't," he said. "Thank you so much."

The host took her arm and piloted her firmly into the next room.

"Oh, my dear," she said. "I nearly died! Honestly! I give you my word, I nearly passed away. Did you hear that terrible break I made? I was just going to say Katherine Burke almost looked like a nigger. I just caught myself in time. Oh, do you think he noticed?"

"I don't believe so," said her host.

"Well, thank goodness," she said, "because I wouldn't have embarrassed him for anything. Why he's awfully nice. Just as nice as he can be. Nice manners, and everything. You know, so many colored people, you give them an inch, and they walk all over you. But he doesn't try any of that. Well, he's got more sense, I suppose. He's really nice. Don't you think so?"

"Yes," said her host.

"I liked him," she said. "I haven't any feeling at all because he's a colored man. I felt just as natural as I would with anybody. Talked to him just as naturally, and everything. But honestly, I could hardly keep a straight face. I kept thinking of Burton. Oh, wait till I tell Burton I called him 'Mister'!"

3. *Major Facts about Race* [*][6]

Man incessantly seeks to compromise with his conscience or with his innate humanitarianism, by rationalizing his predatory behavior. He must convince himself that the act of grabbing is somehow noble and beautiful, that he can rape in righteousness and murder in magnanimity. He insists upon playing the game, not only with an ace up his sleeve, but with the smug conviction that God has put it there.

We need not speculate upon the arguments with which primitive man presumably convinced himself that he was glorifying God by getting dominion over

[*] By permission from *Apes, Men and Morons*, by E. A. Hooton. Copyright, 1937, G. P. Putnam's Sons.

"the fish of the sea, and the fowl of the air, and over every living thing that moveth upon earth." Possibly the necessity of self-justification arose only when civilization had advanced to the status of cannibalism and slavery, and man had begun to make a real business of battening upon his own kind.

Certainly the specious excuse of racial difference has served ever since Ham saw the nakedness of his drunken father and Noah, awakening from wine with a bad hang-over, exclaimed, "Cursed by Canaan, a servant of servants shall he be to his brethren!" From immemorial antiquity hereditary variations of bodily form had been made the basis of charges of racial inferiority in mentality and in capacity for civilization. With this contemptible subterfuge our European ancestors justified their enslavement of the Negro and their virtual extermination of the Indian and of many other primitive peoples. The "white man's burden" has been perpetrated in the name of liberty.

Under these circumstances, a physical anthropologist, who has devoted most of his research activity to the study of race, desires emphatically to dissociate the findings of his science from the acts of human injustice which masquerade as "racial measures" or "racial movements," or even "racial hygiene."

I therefore intend to assert bluntly and simply what I believe to be the best consensus of scientific anthropological opinion upon what races are and what they connote.

1. A "race" is a physical division of mankind, the members of which are distinguished by the possession of similar combinations of anatomical features due to their common heredity.

2. There exists no single physical criterion for distinguishing race; races are delimited by the association in human groups of multiple variations of bodily form and structure—such as amount of pigment in hair, skin, and eyes; form of the hair, shape of the nose, range of stature, relation of head length to head breadth, et cetera. These criteria are of mainly hereditary origin, but none of them is wholly impervious to environmental influences, such as the effects of climate, diet, exercise, and altitude. It follows that race is essentially a zoological device whereby indefinitely large groups of similar physical appearance and hereditary background are classified together for the sake of convenience.

3. Anthropologists have found as yet no relationship between any physical criterion of race and mental capacity, whether in individuals or in groups.

4. While it is conceivable that physical races may differ in psychological characteristics, in tastes, temperament, and even in intellectual qualities, a precise scientific determination of such differences has not yet been achieved. Such discrimination, if it is possible, must await the development of better anthropological and psychological techniques.

5. Race is not synonymous with language, culture, or nationality. Race is hereditary; language is a culture acquisition. A Negro may speak English as his native tongue. There is no Aryan race. Aryan is a term applicable only to a family of languages spoken by populations heterogeneous in race, nationality, religion, and

other aspects of culture. There is no "German race," properly so-called. Such terms imply nationality, use of a common language, and some degree of conformity to a pattern of culture, but nothing more.

6. Physical anthropologists, as yet, are unable precisely to grade existing human races upon an evolutionary scale, upon the basis of the sum total of their anatomical deviations from apes and lower animals. Each race displays a mixture of advanced and primitive characteristics. A definitive rating of the evolutionary rank of each human race presupposes the completion of many anthropological and physiological researches which have not even begun.

7. A "pure" race is little more than an anthropological abstraction; no pure race can be found in any civilized country. Racial purity is restricted, at best, to remnants of savage groups in isolated wildernesses. The present races of man have intermingled and interbred for many thousands of years so that their genealogical lines have become inextricably confused. Physical classifications of race merely attempt to delimit groups of approximate physical uniformity, with a restricted assumption of similar heredity.

8. The composite origin of most of the existing races of man is demonstrable. Thus the Polynesian represents a stabilized blend of White, Negroid, and Mongoloid elements. The so-called Nordic race is probably a hybrid derivative of several strains present in Europe during the glacial period, to which have been added in Historic times Alpine, Mongoloid, and other racial elements (carried by Lapps, Finns, Slavs, and other peoples who have mixed with the inhabitants of the "Nordic" area).

9. The study of the results of hybridization between the most physically diverse of modern races—such as the Negro and the Nordic, or the Mongoloid and the brunet Mediterranean White—has not demonstrated that fertility is decreased, or vitality diminished, by such crossings. The hybrids exhibit a wide range of combinations of features inherited from both parental races, but no degeneracy, provided that both parental stocks are normal. It is probable that racial susceptibilities and immunities to certain diseases are different in hybrids from those obtaining in the parental races, but this subject has been insufficiently studied.

10. Within each and every race there is great individual variation in physical features and in mental capacity, but no close correlation between physique and mentality has been scientifically demonstrated. Knowledge of human heredity is still far from perfect and altogether inadequate as a basis for attempts to secure specific combinations of physical and mental features by selective breeding. A scientifically valid program of eugenics, at the present, must be limited to the restriction of breeding among the insane, diseased, and criminal, and to the encouragement of reproduction in individual families with sound physiques, good mental endowments, and demonstrable social and economic capability.

Each racial type runs the gamut from idiots and criminals to geniuses and statesmen. No type produces a majority of individuals from either end of the scale.

While there may be specific racial abilities and disabilities, these have not yet been demonstrated. There are no racial monopolies either of human virtues or of vices.

4. *Resolutions and Manifestoes of Scientists on Racial Prejudice*

a. RESOLUTION OF THE AMERICAN ANTHROPOLOGICAL ASSOCIATION
(December, 1938) [7]

WHEREAS, The prime requisites of science are the honest and unbiased search for truth and the freedom to proclaim such truth when discovered and known; and,

WHEREAS, Anthropology in many countries is being conscripted and its data distorted and misinterpreted to serve the cause of an unscientific racialism rather than the cause of truth;

Be it *resolved,* That the American Anthropological Association repudiates such racialism and adheres to the following statement of facts:

(1) Race involves the inheritance of similar physical variations by large groups of mankind, but its psychological and cultural connotations, if they exist, have not been ascertained by science.

(2) The terms "Aryan" and "Semitic" have no racial significance whatsoever. They simply denote linguistic families.

(3) Anthropology provides no scientific basis for discrimination against any people on the ground of racial inferiority, religious affiliation or linguistic heritage.

b. PSYCHOLOGISTS' STATEMENT (EXCERPTS) AT THE ANNUAL MEETING OF THE AMERICAN PSYCHOLOGICAL ASSOCIATION
(December, 1938) [8]

The current emphasis upon "racial differences" in Germany and Italy, and the indications that such an emphasis may be on the increase in the United States and elsewhere, make it important to know what psychologists and other social scientists have to say in this connection.

In the experiments which psychologists have made upon different peoples, no characteristic, inherent psychological differences which fundamentally distinguish so-called "races," have been disclosed. This statement is supported by the careful surveys of these experiments in such books as *Race Psychology* by Professor T. R. Garth of the University of Denver, *Individual Differences* by Professor Frank S. Freeman of Cornell University, *Race Differences* by Professor Otto Klineberg of Columbia University, and *Differential Psychology* by Dr. Anne Anastasi of Barnard College. There is no evidence for the existence of an inborn Jewish or German or Italian mentality. Furthermore, there is no indication that the members of any group are rendered incapable by their biological heredity of completely acquiring the culture of the community in which they live. This is true not only of the Jews in Germany, but also of groups that actually are physically different from one another. The Nazi theory that people must be related by blood in order to participate in the same cultural or intellectual heritage has absolutely no support from scientific findings.

Psychologists look elsewhere for the explanation of current racial hatred and persecution. It is certain that the Nazi race theories have been developed not on the basis of objective fact, but under the domination of powerful emotional attitudes. A well-known psychological tendency leads people to blame others for their own misfortune, and the Nazis have found in the Jew a convenient psychological scapegoat for their own economic and political disabilities. In certain Czechoslovakian localities as well, Jews are now being blamed for the dismemberment of the country. There can be no doubt that economic factors are also directly involved, as the recent enormous levy on Jewish capital in Germany has amply demonstrated. Theories of Jewish plots and machinations are an excuse, a rationalization, for the expropriation of badly needed property. This attitude is not new nor is it restricted to Central Europe.

Racial and national attitudes are psychologically complex, and cannot be understood except in terms of their economic, political and historical backgrounds. Psychologists find no basis for the explanation of such attitudes in terms of innate mental differences between racial and national groups. The many attempts to establish such differences have so far met failure. Even if successful they would offer no justification for repressive treatment of the type now current in Germany. In the scientific investigations of human groups by psychologists no conclusive evidence has been found for racial or national differences in native intelligence and inherited personality characteristics. Certainly no individual should be treated as an inferior merely because of his membership in one human group rather than another. Here in America, we have clear indications of the manner in which members of different racial and national groups have combined to create a common culture.

Council Members:

> F. H. ALLPORT, Syracuse University
> GORDON ALLPORT, Harvard University
> J. F. BROWN, Kansas University
> HADLEY CANTRIL, Princeton University
> L. W. DOOB, Yale University
> H. B. ENGLISH, Ohio State University
> FRANKLIN FEARING, University of California,
>   Los Angeles
> GEORGE W. HARTMANN, Columbia University
> I. KRECHEVSKY, University of Colorado
> GARDNER MURPHY, Columbia University
> T. C. SCHNEIRLA, New York University
> E. C. TOLMAN, University of California

c. Biologists' Manifesto (Excerpts) at the Seventh International Genetics Congress, Edinburgh (*August 28, 1939*) [9]

The question "how could the world's population be improved most effectively genetically" raises far broader problems than the purely biological ones, problems which the biologist unavoidably encounters as soon as he tries to get the principles of his own special field put into practice. For the effective genetic improvement of mankind is dependent upon major changes in social conditions, and correlative changes in human attitudes. In the first place there can be no valid basis for estimating and comparing the intrinsic worth of different individuals without economic and social conditions which provide approximately equal opportunities for all members of society instead of stratifying them from birth into classes with widely different privileges.

The second major hindrance to genetic improvement lies in the economic and political conditions which foster antagonism between different peoples, nations, and "races." The removal of race prejudices and of the unscientific doctrine that good or bad genes are the monopoly of particular peoples or of persons with features of a given kind will not be possible, however, before the conditions which make for war and economic exploitation have been eliminated. This required some effective sort of federation of the whole world, based on the common interests of all its peoples. . . .

The day when economic reconstruction will reach the stage where such human forces will be released is not yet, but it is the task of this generation to prepare for it, and all steps along the way will represent a gain, not only for the possibilities of the ultimate genetic improvement of man, to a degree seldom dreamed of hitherto, but at the same time, more directly, for human mastery over those more immediate evils which are so threatening our modern civilization.

(original signers)

F. A. E. Crew, F.R.S.	J. S. Huxley, F.R.S.
J. B. S. Haldane, F.R.S.	H. L. Miller
S. C. Hardland	J. Needham
L. T. Hogben, F.R.S.	

d. Statement Drafted at Unesco House, Paris, by Group of Scientists on Race [10]

1. Scientists have reached general agreement in recognizing that mankind is one: that all men belong to the same species, Homo sapiens. It is further generally agreed among scientists that all men are probably derived from the same common stock; and that such differences as exist between different groups of mankind are due to the operation of evolutionary factors of differentiation such as isolation,

the drift and random fixation of the material particles which control heredity (the genes), changes in the structure of these particles, hybridization, and natural selection. In these ways groups have arisen of varying stability and degree of differentiation which have been classified in different ways for different purposes.

2. From the biological standpoint, the species Homo sapiens is made up of a number of populations, each one of which differs from the others in the frequency of one or more genes. Such genes, responsible for the hereditary differences between men, are always few when compared to the whole genetic constitution of man and to the vast number of genes common to all human beings regardless of the population to which they belong. This means that the likenesses among men are far greater than their differences.

3. A race from the biological standpoint may therefore be defined as one of the group of populations constituting the species Homo sapiens. These populations are capable of interbreeding with one another but, by virtue of the isolating barriers which in the past kept them more or less separated, exhibit certain physical differences as a result of their somewhat different biological histories. These represent variations, as it were, on a common theme.

4. In short, the term "race" designates a group or population characterized by some concentrations, relative as to frequency and distribution, of hereditary particles (genes) or physical characters, which appear, fluctuate, and often disappear in the course of time by reason of geographic and/or cultural isolation. The varying manifestations of these traits in different populations are perceived in different ways by each group. What is perceived is largely preconceived, so that each group arbitrarily tends to misinterpret the variability which occurs as a fundamental difference which separates that group from all others.

5. These are scientific facts. Unfortunately, however, when most people use the term "race" they do not do so in the sense above defined. To most people, a race is any group of people whom they choose to describe as a race. Thus, many national, religious, geographic, linguistic, or cultural groups have, in such loose usage, been called "race," when obviously Americans are not a race, nor are Englishmen, nor Frenchmen, nor any other national group. Catholics, Protestants, Moslems, and Jews are not races, nor are groups who speak English or any other language thereby definable as a race; people who live in Iceland or England or India are not races; nor are people who are culturally Turkish or Chinese or the like thereby describable as races.

6. National, religious, geographic, linguistic, and cultural groups do not necessarily coincide with racial groups; and the cultural traits of such groups have no demonstrated genetic connection with racial traits. Because serious errors of this kind are habitually committed when the term "race" is used in popular parlance, it would be better when speaking of human races to drop the term "race" altogether and speak of ethnic groups.

7. Now what has the scientist to say about the groups of mankind which may be recognized at the present time? Human races can be and have been differently

classified by different anthropologists, but at the present time most anthropologists agree in classifying the greater part of the present-day mankind into three major divisions, as follows: the Mongoloid division, the Negroid division, the Caucasoid division. The biological processes which the classifier has here embalmed, as it were, are dynamic, not static. These divisions were not the same in the past as they are at present, and there is every reason to believe that they will change in the future.

8. Many subgroups or ethnic groups within these divisions have been described. There is no general agreement upon their number, and in any event most ethnic groups have not yet been either studied or described by the physical anthropologists.

9. Whatever classification the anthropologist makes of man, he never includes mental characteristics as part of those classifications. It is now generally recognized that intelligence tests do not in themselves enable us to differentiate safely between what is due to innate capacity and what is the result of environmental influences, training, and education. Wherever it has been possible to make allowances for differences in environmental opportunities, the tests have shown essential similarity in mental characters among all human groups. In short, given similar degrees of cultural opportunity to realize their potentialities, the average achievement of the members of each ethnic group is about the same. The scientific investigations of recent years fully support the dictum of Confucius (551–478 B.C.): "Men's natures are alike; it is their habits that carry them far apart."

10. The scientific material available to us at present does not justify the conclusion that inherited genetic differences are a major factor in producing the differences between the cultures and cultural achievements of different peoples or groups. It does indicate, however, that the history of the cultural experience which each group has undergone is the major factor in explaining such differences. The one trait which above all others has been at a premium in the evolution of men's natural characters has been educability, plasticity. This is a trait which all human beings possess. It is, indeed, a species character of Homo sapiens.

11. So far as temperament is concerned, there is no definite evidence that there exist inborn differences between human groups. There is evidence that whatever group differences of the kind there might be are greatly overridden by the individual differences, and by the differences springing from environmental factors.

12. As for personality and character, these may be considered raceless. In every human group a rich variety of personality and character types will be found, and there is no reason for believing that any human group is richer than any other in these respects.

13. With respect to race mixture, the evidence points unequivocally to the fact that this has been going on from the earliest times. Indeed, one of the chief processes of race formation and race extinction or absorption is by means of hybridization between races or ethnic groups. Furthermore, no convincing evidence has been adduced that race mixture of itself produces biological bad effects. Statements that human hybrids frequently show undesirable traits, both physically and men-

tally, physical disharmonies and mental degeneracies, are not supported by the facts. There is, therefore, no biological justification for prohibiting intermarriage between persons of different ethnic groups.

14. The biological fact of race and the myth of race should be distinguished. For all practical social purposes race is not so much a biological phenomenon as a social myth. The myth of race has created an enormous amount of human and social damage. In recent years it has taken a heavy toll in human lives and caused untold suffering. It still prevents the normal development of millions of human beings and deprives civilization of the effective cooperation of productive minds. The biological differences between ethnic groups should be disregarded from the standpoint of social acceptance and social action. The unity of mankind from both the biological and social view points is the main thing. To recognize this and to act accordingly is the first requirement of modern man. It is but to recognize what a great biologist wrote in 1875: "As man advances in civilization, and small tribes are united into larger communities, the simplest reason would tell each individual that he ought to extend his social instinct and sympathies to all the members of the same nation, though personally unknown to him. This point being once reached, there is only an artificial barrier to prevent his sympathies extending to the men of all nations and races." These are the words of Charles Darwin in the *Descent of Man* (2d ed., 1875, 187–188). And, indeed, the whole of human history shows that a cooperative spirit is not only natural to men, but more deeply rooted than any self-seeking tendencies. If this were not so we should not see the growth of integration and organization of his communities which the centuries and the millennia plainly exhibit.

15. We now have to consider the bearing of these statements on the problem of human equality. It must be asserted with the utmost emphasis that equality as an ethical principle in no way depends upon the assertion that human beings are in fact equal in endowment. Obviously, individuals in all ethnic groups vary greatly among themselves in endowment. Nevertheless, the characteristics in which human groups differ from one another are often exaggerated and used as a basis for questioning the validity of equality in the ethical sense. For this purpose we have thought it worthwhile to set out in a formal manner what is at present scientifically established concerning individual and group differences.

(1) In matters of race, the only characteristics which anthropologists can effectively use as a basis for classifications are physical and physiological.

(2) According to present knowledge there is no proof that the groups of mankind differ in their innate mental characteristics, whether in respect to intelligence or temperament. The scientific evidence indicates that the range of mental capacities in all ethnic groups is much the same.

(3) Historical and sociological studies support the view that genetic differences are not of importance in determining the social and cultural differences between different groups of Homo sapiens, and that the social and cultural changes in different groups have, in the main, been independent of changes in inborn con-

stitution. Vast social changes have occurred which were not in any way connected with changes in racial type.

(4) There is no evidence that race mixture as such produces bad results from the biological point of view. The social results of race mixture whether for good or ill are to be traced to social factors.

(5) All normal human beings are capable of learning to share in a common life, to understand the nature of mutual service and reciprocity, and to respect social obligations and contracts. Such biological differences as exist between members of different ethnic groups have no relevance to problems of social and political organization, moral life and communication between human beings.

Lastly, biological studies lend support to the ethnic of universal brotherhood; for man is born with drives toward cooperation, and unless these drives are satisfied, men and nations alike fall ill. Man is born a social being who can reach his fullest development only through interaction with his fellows. The denial at any point of this social bond between man and man brings with it disintegration. In this sense, every man is his brother's keeper. For every man is a piece of the continent, a part of the main, because he is involved in mankind.

FOOTNOTES TO PART SEVEN

Asterisks indicate footnotes quoted from original source of case material.

1. Clifford R. Shaw (ed.), *Brothers in Crime* (Chicago: University of Chicago Press, 1938), pp. 168–219.

2. From Joseph B. Gittler, "Man and His Prejudices," *Scientific Monthly,* July, 1949, pp. 43–48; and case condensation from Paul Radin, *The Racial Myth* (New York: McGraw-Hill Book Company, Inc., 1934), pp. 6–17, 21–22, 29–31, 33–34, 35, 37, 37–41, 42, 44–46, 47–51. Courtesy of McGraw-Hill Book Company, Inc.

*3. F. H. Hankins, *The Racial Basis of Civilization,* 1926, p. 91.

*4. *Geschichte der deutschen Nazionalliteratur,* p. 39, 1931.

5. From *The Portable Dorothy Parker.* Copyright 1927, 1944, by Dorothy Parker. Reprinted by permission of The Viking Press, Inc., New York.

6. From E. A. Hooton, *Apes, Men and Morons* (New York: G. P. Putnam's Sons, 1937), pp. 151, 152–154. Dr. Hooton is a prominent anthropologist at Harvard University, and curator of somatology, Peabody Museum of Harvard University.

7. *Science,* Vol. 89 (Jan. 13, 1939).

8. A statement prepared by the Executive Council of the Society for the Psychological Study of Social Issues, representing an organization of more than 400 professional psychologists. See Ruth Benedict, *Race: Science and Politics* (New York: Modern Age, Inc., 1940), pp. 261–264.

9. *Journal of Heredity,* Vol. 30 (1939), pp. 371–373.

10. Unesco stands for United Nations Educational, Social and Cultural Organization. The statement was drafted by Prof. Ernest Beaglehole, New Zealand; Prof. Juan Comas, Mexico; Prof. L. A. Costa Pinto, Brazil; Prof. Franklin Frazier, United States; Prof. Morris Ginsberg, United Kingdom; Dr. Humayun Kabir, India; Prof. Claude Levi-Strauss, France; Prof. Ashley Montagu, United States. Text revised by Prof. Ashley Montagu, after criticisms submitted by Prof. Hadley Cantril, E. O. Conklin, Gunnar Dahlberg, Theodosius Dobzhansky, L. C. Dunn, Donald Hager, Julian S. Huxley, Otto Klineberg, Wilbert Moore, H. J. Muller, Gunnar Myrdal, Joseph Needham. See *Congressional Record—Senate,* 1950, pp. 14562–14563.

Index

A

Accommodation, 169, 189–195
Ackerknecht, E. H., 229
Allport, F. H., 334
Allport, Gordon, 334
Alorese, 35
American Anthropological Association on race, 333
American Psychological Association on race, 333
Amish community, 104, 110–129
Amory, Cleveland, 167n.
Anastasi, Anne, 333
Andaman Islanders, 104, 105–110
Anderson, E. L., 166n.
Anesthesia, opposition to spread of, 266–273
Angell, Robert Cooley, 99n.
Anna, case of, 22–28
Anthropology, functional, 290n.
Apollonian culture pattern, 228
Around the World in New York, 135–137
Assimilation, 169, 189–195
Aztec Indians, 226

B

Bacon, Francis, 241
Bain, Read, 47, 55n., 291n.
Barnett, H. G., 291n.
Beaglehole, Ernest, 339n.
Becker, Carl L., 291, 299
Becker, Howard, 165n., 223n.
Beegle, J. Allen, 165n.
Beggar family, case of, 31–34
Benedict, Ruth, 29n., 34, 224n., 228, 291n.
Bercovici, Konrad, 166n.
Berry, Brewton, 223n.
Bill of Rights, 231–233
Biologists' Manifesto on race, 335
Boas, Franz, 224n.
Bredemeier, Harry C., 167n., 291n.

Brothers in Crime, 293
Brown, J. F., 334
Bunzel, Ruth L., 224n.
Burgess, E. W., 165n., 223n.

C

Cantril, Hadley, 100n., 334, 339n.
Cassirer, Ernst, 6
Centers, Richard, 167n.
Change, sociocultural (*see* Social change)
Chase, Stuart, 129, 165n.
Cheyenne, 229
Child rearing, influence on, of class, 42–46, 55n.
   of race, 42–46, 55n.
Chinese immigrants in Hawaii, 189–195
Chiricahua Apache, 229
Chukchi Eskimos, 226
Civilizations, types of, 243–245
Class, social, 148–164
   case, of upper-upper, 151–160
      of lower and middle, 160–164, 166n.
   personality and, 42–46
   principles governing, 149–150
Cohen, Albert K., 290n.
Cohen, Morris R., 165n.
Collective behavior, 85–99
Comanche, 34
Comas, Juan, 339n.
Commager, Henry Steele, 291n.
Common-sense knowledge, 14–15
Community, 101–148
   classification of types, 102–104
   meaning of, 101
   polar types, 103–104
   primitive-folk and modern urban, 104
   sacred-secular, 104
   urban, 134–148
Competition among Kwakiutl Indians, 170–179
Comte, Auguste, 242
Condorcet, 242
Conflict, union-management, 195–223